BARRON'S

PRAXIS I
PPST

4TH EDITION

Robert D. Postman, Ed.D.
Professor and Education Dean
Mercy College

BARRON'S

To my wife Liz
A joy to behold
This book is dedicated to you.

All inquiries should be addressed to:
Barron's Educational Series, Inc.
250 Wireless Boulevard
Hauppauge, NY 11788
www.barronseduc.com

ISBN-13: 978-0-7641-4312-0
ISBN-10: 0-7641-4312-3

Library of Congress Catalog Card No. 2010920205

PRINTED IN THE UNITED STATES OF AMERICA

9 8 7 6 5 4 3

10%
POST-CONSUMER
WASTE
Paper contains a minimum
of 10% post-consumer
waste (PCW). Paper used
in this book was derived
from certified, sustainable
forestlands.

Contents

Preface

This book shows you how to do your absolute best on the Paper-Based PPST and Computer-Based PPST and helps you get started in a teaching career. Hundreds of prospective teachers field-tested preliminary versions of this book and dozens of experienced teachers and subject-matter specialists reviewed the book to ensure that it provides you with the subject-matter preparation and practice tests you need.

The practice tests in this book have the same question types and the same question-and-answer formats as the real tests. The practice tests also have the look and feel of the real thing—complete with uneven margins, open space, and the single and double columns found on the actual tests.

My wife, Liz, a teacher, was a constant source of support and she made significant contributions to this book. My children, Chad, Blaire, and Ryan, have also been a source of support as I worked on this and other books over the years.

Special thanks to the undergraduate and graduate students and those changing careers who field-tested sections of this book. I am particularly grateful for the contributions of Ryan Postman. I am also grateful to experts at state education departments and colleges throughout the country for talking to me about teacher certification requirements.

You are entering teaching during a time of tremendous opportunity, and I wish you well in your pursuit of a rewarding and fulfilling career. The next generation awaits. You will help them prepare for a vastly different, technological world.

Robert D. Postman

PPST Test Dates

For details on test dates, late registration dates, or additional test information, check the Praxis web site *www.ets.org/praxis/*, or call the Praxis center at 609-771-7395; TTY 609-771-7714.

Computer-Based PPST

The Computer-Based PPST is administered by individual appointment at computer-based test centers. Call 800-953-6673 (TTY: 800-529-3590) for an appointment.

PART I

TESTS AND STRATEGIES

CHAPTER 1
Pre-Professional Skills Test (PPST);
Computer-Based PPST

CHAPTER 2
Test Preparation and
Test-Taking Strategies

Pre-Professional Skills Test (PPST); Computer-Based PPST

TEST INFO BOX

Most chapters begin with a Test Info Box. Read it for information about these tests.

The Educational Testing Service (ETS) offers the PPST tests. Contact ETS for registration forms, admission tickets, testing accommodations, or test scores.

You can register online and you can receive your scores online.

Educational Testing Service
Box 6501
Princeton, NJ 08541-6051
Website: *www.ets.org/praxis*
609-771-7395
TTY 609-771-7714
FAX (609) 530-0581 (24 hours)
E-mail: *praxis@ets.org*

The PPST Tests

Pre-Professional Skills Test (PPST), paper-based
Computer-Based Pre-Professional Skills Test (PPST), a computer version of the test

Reading
Writing
Mathematics

Read Me First!

This section explains the steps you should take in beginning your test preparation. Read it before going on.

What's Going on with the PPST?

Teacher certification examinations have been around for years. Until recently, most states relied on the National Teacher Examinations (NTE). The NTE is no longer given. Recently, states have focused on the reading, writing, and mathematics skills tested by the Paper-Based PPST and the Computer-Based PPST.

The Good News

The good news is that the PPSTs focus on a central core of reading, writing, and mathematics skills. In this book, you learn how to prepare successfully for each test.

PPST—The Inside Story

The PPSTs were developed by the Educational Testing Service, an educational testing organization that administers over 6,000,000 tests yearly all over the world. The PPSTs consist of three separate tests: (1) Reading, (2) Mathematics, and (3) Writing—multiple choice and essay. The test is available in two forms: the Paper-Based PPST and the Computer-Based PPST.

PPST Summary

	Paper-Based PPST	Computer-Based PPST
Reading	40 multiple-choice questions 60 minutes	46 multiple-choice questions 75 minutes
Writing Multiple choice	38 multiple-choice questions 30 minutes	44 multiple-choice questions 38 minutes
Essay	1 handwritten essay 30 minutes	1 typed essay 30 minutes
Mathematics	40 multiple-choice questions 60 minutes	46 multiple-choice questions 75 minutes

WHAT ARE THE TESTS LIKE?

The Paper-Based PPST and the Computer-Based PPST each assess reading, English, writing, and mathematics skills. The Paper-Based PPST is a pencil-and-paper multiple-choice test with one handwritten essay. The Computer-Based PPST is a computer-based multiple-choice test with one typed essay.

The Paper-Based PPST and the Computer-Based PPST are described below.

Paper-Based PPST

You take the Paper-Based PPST on scheduled test dates along with many other people. You may also take the test on a special date because of religious beliefs or a disability. The multiple-choice items are all prepared in advance. You mark your answers on a standard answer sheet and handwrite your essay. You can skip items and come back to them and you can change your answers to items you have already answered.

READING

The 60-minute reading test has 40 multiple-choice items. Each item has five answer choices. There are some long passages of about 200 words, some shorter passages with about 100 words, and some statements of a few sentences. According to ETS, test items are partitioned as follows: literal comprehension 55%, critical and inferential comprehension 45%.

WRITING

The 60-minute writing test is partitioned into a 30-minute multiple-choice section and a 30-minute essay section. There are 38 multiple-choice items with four answer choices. There are 21 usage items and 17 sentence correction items. You are given an essay topic on which to write your essay. Each section contributes 50% to the final score.

MATHEMATICS

The 60-minute mathematics test has 40 multiple-choice items. Each item has five answer choices. The test measures a wide range of mathematics topics primarily from the pre-college curriculum. According to ETS, test items are partitioned as follows: conceptual knowledge 15%, procedural knowledge 30%, data representation 30%, geometry and measurement 15%, and reasoning 10%. You may NOT use a calculator.

Computer-Based PPST

You take the Computer-Based PPST just about any day of the week and almost on demand. You sit in a cubicle in front of a computer screen while a video camera mounted overhead records your actions. The computer selects all the items before you take the test. You use a mouse and a keyboard to enter your answers directly on the test screen. You type your essay.

A special "mark tool" lets you mark a question so that you may return later to answer the question or change your answer. A review screen shows the questions you have answered, those marked for return, and those not seen at all.

READING

The 75-minute reading test has 46 multiple-choice items. Each item has five answer choices. There are 200-word passages, 100-word passages, and some statements of a few sentences. You indicate your answer by clicking an oval. According to ETS, test items are partitioned as follows: literal comprehension 56%, critical and inferential comprehension 44%.

WRITING

The 68-minute writing test has a 38-minute section with 24 error recognition and 20 sentence correction items and a 30-minute essay. For error correction, you indicate your answer by highlighting the part of a sentence that contains an error, or by highlighting "No error." For sentence correction, you click an oval to indicate your choice. You type your essay on the topic presented. According to ETS, test scoring is partitioned as follows: error correction 27%, sentence correction 23%, and essay 50%.

MATHEMATICS

> **Tip**
>
> Recently, the mathematics section of the PPST has been modified to include different types of mathematics questions of varying difficulty. This book is reflective of those types of questions.

The 75-minute mathematics test has 46 items. You indicate your answer by clicking on an oval. According to ETS, test items are partitioned as follows: conceptual knowledge 15%, procedural knowledge 30%, data representation 30%, geometry and measurement 15%, reasoning 10%. You may NOT use a calculator.

Should I Take the Paper-Based PPST or the Computer-Based PPST?

You will probably want to take the Computer-Based PPST, if for no reason other than the Computer-Based PPST is offered more frequently, and usually on shorter notice. You may even be able to get an appointment for the computer-based test in a day. A primary reason for taking the Paper-Based PPST is because there is not a Computer-Based PPST test center near you. There are about 300 centers for the computer-based test, but there are many more sites for the paper-based test. Another main advantage of the computer-based test is that you will not have to mark a separate answer sheet. Answer sheet marking errors are a main cause of problems on any paper-based test. It's a potential problem worth avoiding.

TIP

All states accept scores from either the Paper-Based PPST or the Computer-Based PPST. The version you choose to take should be the one you feel most comfortable with.

But there are other reasons for taking the Paper-Based PPST. Some people have difficulty navigating the computer-based test. If you are uncomfortable with computers, then paper may be the way to go. You may just like to work with a pencil and an eraser. It will usually be more familiar. You may want to mark the test booklet. You may prefer to read passages in that booklet. You may enjoy the "social" atmosphere you'll find with a paper-based test. The cubicles for the computer-based test are not very friendly. And if you want to avoid any possibility that you will be video recorded, then paper is for you.

PPST Registration and Scoring

Paper-Based PPST Registration

Visit the Praxis website at *www.ets.org/praxis*.

Computer-Based PPST Registration

The Computer-Based PPST is offered at more than 300 centers and colleges. To register call

(800) 853-6773
(800) 529-3590 (TTY)

Test Scores

Paper-Based PPST scores are available through the Praxis website. Computer-Based PPST Reading and Mathematics scores are available immediately at the test center. Computer-Based PPST Writing scores are available later through the Praxis website.

PPST Test Locations

Where you take the Paper-Based PPST is very important. Check for locations near you. Register as soon as possible. Early registrants are more likely to get the choice location.

You must take the Computer-Based PPST at one of the 300 centers. Go to the Praxis website for an up-to-date list. You may be able to register for a test and take the test that same day.

Where to Send Your Scores

The Praxis Bulletin lists a code for each organization that can receive scores. You should list the code for each certification agency or college you want to receive your scores. The scores must usually be sent directly to the agencies from ETS.

You may feel that you should wait until you know you have gotten a passing score before sending it in, but that's not necessary. You will just slow down the process and incur extra expense. Certification agencies do not use these scores for evaluative purposes. They just need to see a passing score, and ETS reports only your highest score.

You will receive your own report, and you are entitled to have four score reports sent to the certification agency or colleges you choose. Any extra reports will be sent to you.

Special Test Arrangements

ETS offers special arrangements or considerations for the following categories. If you qualify for special test arrangements, take advantage of the opportunity. Special arrangements can be made for both the Paper-Based PPST and the Computer-Based PPST. Go to *www.ets.org/disability* for complete documentation.

Do You Have a Disability (a Learning Disability or a Physical, Visual, or Hearing Impairment)?

You may qualify for additional time to complete the test, for someone to read the test to you, or for other special circumstances to accommodate your disability. You must use the Certification of Disability form from the Registration Bulletin or write directly to ETS to receive these special considerations. Your letter should describe your disability and the special arrangements you desire. Also enclose a note from a school counselor or employer to verify that these arrangements have previously been made for you, or a note from a health professional documenting your disability. Contact ETS if you have any questions.

Do You Celebrate Your Sabbath on Saturday? Do Your U.S. Military Duties Prevent You from Taking the Test on a Saturday?

You may qualify to take the test on the Monday following the Saturday administration. Complete the PPST registration form indicating this special situation. If you are unable to take a test for religious reasons, include a note from the head of the religious group where you worship, on that group's letterhead, stating that your Sabbath is on Saturday. If you cannot take a test for military reasons, include a copy of your orders.

PASSING THE PPST

This section reviews PPST scoring and gives you some information about what it takes to get a passing score.

RAW SCORES AND SCALE SCORES

Your raw score is the number of items you answer correctly, or the number of points you actually earn. Your scale score converts your raw score to a score that can be compared to those of everyone else who has taken that test.

It works this way. Test items, test sections, and different forms of the test have different difficulty levels. For example, an item on one form might be harder than a comparable item on another form. To make up for this difference in difficulty, the harder item might earn a 0.9 scale point, while the easier item might earn a 0.8 scale point. A scale score can be compared to the scale score on all forms of a test.

This is the fair way to do it. To maintain this fairness, PPST scores are reported to you as scale scores. All the scores discussed here are scale scores.

PPST Scale Scoring

The scoring for each PPST test is summarized on the following pages. The tables show the scale score range and score interval for each test, along with the scale scores at the first quartile, second quartile, and third quartile. An explanation of quartiles is given below.

	Percent of test takers who scored <u>at or below</u> this scale score	Percent of test takers who scored <u>above</u> this scale score
First quartile	25%	75%
Second quartile	50%	50%
Third quartile	75%	25%

Paper-Based PPST and Computer-Based PPST scores range from 150 to 190 for about 40 scale points, respectively. You will find below a table with PPST scale score percentiles.

PPST Scale Scores

	First Quartile	Median	Third Quartile	Your State's Passing Scores
Paper-Based PPST Mathematics (0730)	174	179	184	
Computer-Based PPST Mathematics (5730)	174	178	183	
Paper-Based PPST Reading (0710)	174	178	181	
Computer-Based PPST Reading (5710)	173	177	181	
Paper-Based PPST Writing (0720)	173	176	178	
Computer-Based PPST Writing (5732)	173	175	178	

These quartiles are for the tests taken over several years. The quartile scores on the test you take will probably be different. The same scale score on two different tests (such as Reading and Mathematics) does not mean the same level of performance.

Look at the state passing scores in this section on pages 11–18 to find your passing scores. Write those scores in the boxes on the table. Refer back to your passing scores as you read the rest of this section.

PASSING SCALE SCORES

Passing scores vary from test to test and for each state and program, as you can see from the State Passing Score section on pages 11–18. The passing score is the same, regardless of whether you take the computer-based or paper-based version of the PPST.

PASSING RAW SCORES

It is tricky to figure out the raw score you'll need to get a passing scale score. That's because the raw scores vary from one test version to another. Even ETS does not know the conversion of a raw score to a scale score until after the test has been given. And the passing raw scores on tests released by ETS vary widely.

This means we have to be cautious. But this is information readers often request, so we will help as best we can. Please remember that these are just estimates. ETS may adjust their scaling, or the PPST versions they design may be harder or easier. The test you take may be a harder or easier version. Any of these things will significantly reduce the meaning of these estimates.

Of course, the idea is to do your best. And remember that you can pick up raw score points by using the fundamental test strategies. Eliminate every answer you know is incorrect. Never leave an answer blank. You will also see that a good essay score can significantly reduce the English multiple-choice raw score you'll need.

We use percentages to describe raw scores because the Paper-Based PPST and the Computer-Based PPST have a different number of items. So here it is—ESTIMATES. There is absolutely no assurance that they will apply to the test you take. The best approach is to assume you will have to do better than these guidelines indicate.

Generally speaking, a multiple-choice raw score of 70% correct is generally a good score for most test takers. An essay score of 8 points out of 12 points is also a good score for most test takers. Here are our recommended goals for most state passing score requirements:

> **Mathematics** — 65% correct
> **Reading** — 75% correct
> **Writing** — 8 of 12 essay points and 65% of the multiple-choice points

We give indicators below for each test, with a focus on common required passing scale scores. You can estimate your raw score goal if your passing scale score is not specifically listed.

Mathematics

SCALE SCORE OF 171 Your goal could be about 50% correct. It may be possible on some versions to correctly answer about 40% of the items and earn a scale score of 171.

SCALE SCORE OF 174 Your goal could be about 60% correct. It may be possible on some versions to correctly answer about 50% of the items and still earn a scale score of 174.

SCALE SCORE OF 178 Your goal could be about 65% to 70% correct. It may be possible on some versions to correctly answer about 50% to 55% of the items and still earn a scale score of 178.

Reading

SCALE SCORE OF 172 Your goal could be about 70% correct. It may be possible on some versions to correctly answer about 60% of the items and earn a scale score of 172.

SCALE SCORE OF 174 Your goal could be about 75% correct. It may be possible on some versions to correctly answer about 65% of the items and earn a scale score of 174.

SCALE SCORE OF 178 Your goal could be about 80% correct. It may be possible on some versions to correctly answer about 75% of the items and earn a scale score of 178.

Writing

The Writing PPST scale score combines points from the multiple-choice items and points from the essay. That makes setting raw score goals a little more difficult.

SCALE SCORE OF 171 One goal is 6 of 12 points from the essay and about 65% correct multiple-choice items. You may be able to earn 8 of 12 points from the essay and get 55% of the multiple-choice points. It may be possible on some versions of the test to earn 4 essay points and about 70% of the multiple-choice items, or 6 essay points and 55% of the multiple-choice items and still earn a scale score of 171.

SCALE SCORE OF 173 One goal is about 6 of 12 points from the essay and about 75% of the multiple-choice items. Another goal is 8 of 12 points from the essay and 65% of the multiple-choice items. It may be possible on some versions of the test to earn 4 essay points and about 80% of the multiple-choice items, or 6 essay points and about 65% of the multiple-choice items, and still earn a scale score of 173.

SCALE SCORE OF 176 One goal is 6 of 12 points from the essay and about 85% of the multiple-choice items. Another goal is 8 of 12 essay points and 75% of the multiple-choice items. It may be possible on some versions of the test to earn 4 essay points and 95% of the multiple-choice items, or 6 essay points and 75% of the multiple-choice items, and still earn a scale score of 176.

State-by-State Certification

This section lists all the state education departments, Internet sites, and shows the PPST passing scores required in each state.

This listing is current. However, state contact information and certification requirements change constantly. Go to *www.ets.org/praxis/* and click on state-by-state requirements for the most recent testing requirements and contact information.

> A blank box indicates there is no current required score.

ALABAMA

Alabama Department of Education
www.alsde.edu

Paper-Based PPST and Computer-Based PPST

- ❑ **Reading**
- ❑ **Writing**
- ❑ **Mathematics**

ATTP Basic Skills Testing Program Follow the PPST study plan in reading, mathematics, and writing.

ALASKA

Alaska Department of Education
www.educ.state.ak.us

Paper-Based PPST and Computer-Based PPST

- 175 **Reading**
- 174 **Writing**
- 173 **Mathematics**

ARIZONA

Arizona Department of Education
www.ade.state.az.us

Paper-Based PPST and Computer-Based PPST
- ❏ Reading
- ❏ Writing
- ❏ Mathematics

ARKANSAS

Arkansas Department of Education
www.arkansased.org

Paper-Based PPST and Computer-Based PPST

- 172 Reading
- 173 Writing
- 171 Mathematics

CALIFORNIA

California Commission on Teacher Credentialing
www.ctc.ca.gov

Paper-Based PPST and Computer-Based PPST
- ❏ Reading
- ❏ Writing
- ❏ Mathematics

See Barron's *How to Prepare for the CBEST* and *How to Prepare for the CSET.*

COLORADO

Colorado Department of Education
www.cde.state.co.us

Paper-Based PPST and Computer-Based PPST
- ❏ Reading
- ❏ Writing
- ❏ Mathematics

CONNECTICUT

Connecticut State Department of Education
www.ctcert.org

Paper-Based PPST and Computer-Based PPST

- 172 Reading
- 171 Writing
- 171 Mathematics

DELAWARE

Delaware Department of Education
www.deeds.doe.state.de.us

Paper-Based PPST and Computer-Based PPST

- 175 Reading
- 173 Writing
- 174 Mathematics

You are exempt from the Reading Test if you submit an SAT I Verbal score of at least 560, or a GRE Verbal score of at least 490. You are exempt from the Mathematics test if you submit an SAT I Mathematics score of 540 or a GRE quantative score of at least 540.

DISTRICT OF COLUMBIA

Office of the State Superintendent of Education
www.K12.dc.us

Paper-Based PPST and Computer-Based PPST

- 172 Reading
- 171 Writing
- 174 Mathematics

FLORIDA

Florida Department of Education
www.fldoe.org/EdCert

**Paper-Based PPST and
Computer-Based PPST**

- ❑ **Reading**
- ❑ **Writing**
- ❑ **Mathematics**

GEORGIA

Georgia Professional Standards
Commission
www.gapsc.com

**Paper-Based PPST and
Computer-Based PPST**

- ❑ **Reading**
- ❑ **Writing**
- ❑ **Mathematics**

The GACE Skills Assessment. Follow
the PPST study plan.

HAWAII

Hawaii Teacher Standards Board
www.htsb.org

**Paper-Based PPST and
Computer-Based PPST**

- 172 **Reading**
- 171 **Writing**
- 173 **Mathematics**

You may submit a composite score of 516,
as each individual score is 170 or above.

IDAHO

Idaho Department of Education
www.sde.idaho.gov

**Paper-Based PPST and
Computer-Based PPST**

- ❑ **Reading**
- ❑ **Writing**
- ❑ **Mathematics**

ILLINOIS

Illinois State Board of Education
www.isbe.state.il.us

**Paper-Based PPST and
Computer-Based PPST**

- ❑ **Reading**
- ❑ **Writing**
- ❑ **Mathematics**

ILLINOIS CERTIFICATION TESTING SYSTEM

Basic Skills Test

Follow the PPST study plan.

INDIANA

Indiana Department of Education
www.state.in.us/psb/

**Paper-Based PPST and
Computer-Based PPST**

176 Reading
172 Writing
175 Mathematics

IOWA

Iowa Department of Education
www.state.ia.us/educate/

**Paper-Based PPST and
Computer-Based PPST**

❏ Reading
❏ Writing
❏ Mathematics

KANSAS

Kansas Department of Education
www.ksde.org

**Paper-Based PPST and
Computer-Based PPST**

❏ Reading
❏ Writing
❏ Mathematics

KENTUCKY

Kentucky Education Professional
Standards Board
www.kyepsb.net

**Paper-Based PPST and
Computer-Based PPST**

173 Reading
172 Writing
173 Mathematics

Illustrative scores: Scores for entry into
teacher certification programs are set by
the program.

LOUISIANA

Louisiana Department of Education
www.teachlouisiana.net

**Paper-Based PPST and
Computer-Based PPST**

174 Reading
173 Writing
172 Mathematics

You may also submit an ACT composite
score of 22, or an SAT verbal/math score
of 1030.

MAINE

Maine Department of Education
www.state.me.us/education

**Paper-Based PPST and
Computer-Based PPST**

176 Reading
175 Writing
175 Mathematics

You may also submit a composite score
of 526, as long as your individual scores
meet these requirements: R—173, W—
172, M—175.

MARYLAND

Maryland Department of Education
www.certification.msde.state.md.us

**Paper-Based PPST and
Computer-Based PPST**

177 Reading
173 Writing
177 Mathematics

*You may also meet the testing require-
ment by submitting a composite score
of 527.

You may also submit some SAT, ACT,
and CRE scores. Visit the web site for
full information.

MASSACHUSETTS

Massachusetts Department of Education
www.doe.mass.edu

**Paper-Based PPST and
Computer-Based PPST**
- ❑ Reading
- ❑ Writing
- ❑ Mathematics

MICHIGAN

Michigan Department of Education
www.mde.state.mi.us

**Paper-Based PPST and
Computer-Based PPST**
- ❑ Reading
- ❑ Writing
- ❑ Mathematics

MICHIGAN TESTS FOR TEACHER CERTIFICATION

Basic Skills Examination

Follow the PPST study plan.

MINNESOTA

Minnesota Department of Children,
Families, and Learning
www.education.state.mn.us

**Paper-Based PPST and
Computer-Based PPST**
- 173 Reading
- 172 Writing
- 171 Mathematics

MISSISSIPPI

Mississippi Department of Education
www.mde.k12.ms.us

**Paper-Based PPST and
Computer-Based PPST**
- 170 Reading
- 172 Writing
- 169 Mathematics

MISSOURI

Missouri Department of Elementary
and Secondary Education
www.dese.state.mo.us

**Paper-Based PPST and
Computer-Based PPST**
- ❑ Reading
- ❑ Writing
- ❑ Mathematics

MONTANA

Montana Office of Public Instruction
www.metnet.state.mt.us

**Paper-Based PPST and
Computer-Based PPST**
- 170 Reading
- 170 Writing
- 170 Mathematics

NEBRASKA

Nebraska Department of Education
www.nde4.nde.state.ne.us

**Paper-Based PPST and
Computer-Based PPST**
- 170 Reading
- 172 Writing
- 171 Mathematics

NEVADA

Nevada Department of Education
www.nvteachorg.doe.nv.gov

**Paper-Based PPST and
Computer-Based PPST**
- 174 Reading
- 172 Writing
- 172 Mathematics

NEW HAMPSHIRE

New Hampshire Department of Education
www.ed.state.nh.us

Paper-Based PPST and Computer-Based PPST

174 Reading
172 Writing
172 Mathematics

You may also meet the PPST requirement with a total PPST score of 518 and minimum scores of R—172, W—170, and M—170.

NEW JERSEY

New Jersey Office of Licensing and Academic Credentials
www.state.nj.us

Paper-Based PPST and Computer-Based PPST

❑ Reading
❑ Writing
❑ Mathematics

NEW MEXICO

New Mexico Department of Education
www.sde.state.nm.us

Paper-Based PPST and Computer-Based PPST

❑ Reading
❑ Writing
❑ Mathematics

NEW YORK

New York Department of Education
www.highered.gov.tcert

Paper-Based PPST and Computer-Based PPST

❑ Reading
❑ Writing
❑ Mathematics

Use *Barron's NYSTCE*.

NORTH CAROLINA

North Carolina Department of Public Instruction
www.ncpublicschools.org

Paper-Based PPST and Computer-Based PPST

176 Reading
173 Writing
173 Mathematics

You may also submit a composite score of 522.

NORTH DAKOTA

North Dakota Department of Public Instruction
www.nd.gov/espb

Paper-Based PPST and Computer-Based PPST

173 Reading
173 Writing
170 Mathematics

You may also submit a composite score of 516, as long as two of your three scores meets the requirements above.

OHIO

Ohio Department of Education
www.ode.state.oh.us

Paper-Based PPST and Computer-Based PPST

❑ Reading
❑ Writing
❑ Mathematics

OKLAHOMA

Oklahoma Department of Education
www.ok.gov/octp

Paper-Based PPST and Computer-Based PPST

173* Reading
172* Writing
171* Mathematics

*Required for admission to teacher certification programs.

OREGON

Oregon Teacher Standards and Practices Commission
www.tspc.state.or.us

Paper-Based PPST and Computer-Based PPST

174 Reading
171 Writing
175 Mathematics

PENNSYLVANIA

Pennsylvania Department of Education
www.pde.state.pa.us

Paper-Based PPST and Computer-Based PPST

172 Reading
173 Writing
173 Mathematics

You may submit a composite score of 521, if your individual scores are at or above these scores: R—169, W—170, M—170.

RHODE ISLAND

Rhode Island Department of Education
www.ridoe.net

Paper-Based PPST and Computer-Based PPST

❑ Reading
❑ Writing
❑ Mathematics

SOUTH CAROLINA

South Carolina Department of Education
www.scteachers.org

Paper-Based PPST and Computer-Based PPST

175 Reading
173 Writing
172 Mathematics

SOUTH DAKOTA

South Dakota Department of Education
www.state.sd.us

Paper-Based PPST and Computer-Based PPST

❑ Reading
❑ Writing
❑ Mathematics

TENNESSEE

Tennessee Department of Education
www.tennessee.gov

Paper-Based PPST and Computer-Based PPST

174 Reading
173 Writing
173 Mathematics

TEXAS

Texas Education Agency
www.sbec.state.tx.us

Paper-Based PPST and Computer-Based PPST

❑ Reading
❑ Writing
❑ Mathematics

UTAH

Utah Board of Education
www.usue.k12.ut.gov

Paper-Based PPST and Computer-Based PPST

❑ Reading
❑ Writing
❑ Mathematics

VERMONT

Vermont Department of Education
www.state.vt.us/educ/

**Paper-Based PPST and
Computer-Based PPST**

177 Reading
174 Writing
175 Mathematics
You may also submit a composite score of 526 or SAT and ACT scores.

VIRGINIA

Virginia Department of Education
www.per.k12.va.us/go/udoe

**Paper-Based PPST and
Computer-Based PPST**

178 Reading
176 Writing
178 Mathematics
You may also submit a composite score of 532.

WASHINGTON

State Superintendent of Instruction
www.k12.wa.us

**Paper-Based PPST and
Computer-Based PPST**

❑ Reading
❑ Writing
❑ Mathematics

WEST VIRGINIA

Office of Professional Preparation
www.wvde.state.wv.us

**Paper-Based PPST and
Computer-Based PPST**

174 Reading
172 Writing
172 Mathematics
If you hold a master's degree, you may qualify for an exemption based on your SAT or ACT score.

WISCONSIN

Department of Public Instruction
www.dpi.state.wi.us

**Paper-Based PPST and
Computer-Based PPST**

175 Reading
174 Writing
173 Mathematics

WYOMING

Wyoming Department of Education
www.k12.wy.us

**Paper-Based PPST and
Computer-Based PPST**

❑ Reading
❑ Writing
❑ Mathematics

DEPARTMENT OF DEFENSE SCHOOLS

www.dodea.edu

**Paper-Based PPST and
Computer-Based PPST**

177 Reading
174 Writing
175 Mathematics

GUAM

Guam Department of Education

**Paper-Based PPST and
Computer-Based PPST**

173 Reading
170 Writing
170 Mathematics

Test Preparation and Test-Taking Strategies

CHAPTER 2

TEST INFO BOX

This chapter shows you how to set up a test preparation schedule and shows you some test-taking strategies that will help you improve your score. The important strategies are discussed below.

MULTIPLE CHOICE

Eliminate and then guess. There is no penalty for wrong answers. Never leave any answer blank.

Suppose a multiple-choice test has 40 items with four answer choices. Eliminate two incorrect answer choices on all the items, guess every answer, and, on average, you would get 20 correct.

ESSAY

Write an outline first, then write the essay. Handwrite your outline for the Computer-Based PPST.

Topic Paragraph: Begin the written assignment with an introduction to orient the reader to the topic. The first paragraph should clearly state the main idea of your entire written assignment.

Topic Sentence: Begin each paragraph with a topic sentence that supports the main idea.

Details: Provide details, examples, and arguments to support the topic sentence.

Grammar, Punctuation, Spelling: Edit sentences to conform to standard usage.

Avoid Passive Construction: Write actively and avoid the passive voice.

Conclusion: End the written assignment with a paragraph that summarizes your main points.

Words Matter: Longer essays get better scores. Plan to write at least 350 words. Highest scores go to good essays that have 450–500 words.

Preparing for the Tests

This section describes how to prepare for certification tests, and the next section describes test-taking strategies. Before we go on, let's think about what you are preparing for.

Wait! Why Test Me? I'm a Good Person!

Why indeed? Life would be so much easier without tests. If anyone tells you that they like to take tests, don't believe him or her. Nobody does. Tests are imperfect. Some people "pass" when they should have failed, while others "fail" when they should have passed. It may not be fair, but it is very real. So sit back and relax. You're just going to have to do it. And this book will show you how.

Who Makes Up These Tests and How Do They Get Written?

Consider the following scenario. It is late in the afternoon in Princeton, New Jersey. Around a table sit teachers, deans of education, parents, and representatives of state Education Departments. In front of each person is a preliminary list of skills and knowledge that teachers should possess. The list comes from comments by an even larger group of teachers and other educational professionals.

Those around the table are regular people just like the ones you might run into in a store or on the street. They all care about education. They also bring to the table their own strengths and weaknesses—their own perspectives and biases. What's that? An argument just broke out. People are choosing up sides and, depending on the outcome, one item on the list will stay or go.

This goes on for a few days until this group has drawn up a final list. Thousands of teachers and national teacher organizations receive the list. Each rates the importance of every item. The items rated important will be measured by the test.

The final list goes to professional test writers to prepare test items. These items are tried out, refined, and put through a review process. Eventually the test question bank is established, and a test is born. These test writers are not geniuses. They just know how to write questions. You might get a better score on this test than some of them would.

The test writers want to write a test that measures important concepts. They try not to ask silly or obscure questions that have strange answers. For the most part, they are successful. You can count on the test questions to cover concepts that you should know.

You can also be sure that the test writers will ask questions that will make you think. Their questions will ask you to use what you know and apply it.

Keep those people around the table and the test writers in mind as you use this book. You are preparing for their test. Soon, you will be like one of those people around the table. You may even contribute to a test like this one.

Proven Test-Preparation Strategies

Here are several strategies and steps to follow as you prepare for the test. These strategies take you right up to test day.

Get Yourself Ready for the Test

Most people are less tense when they exercise. Set up a *reasonable* exercise program for yourself. The program should involve exercising in a way that is appropriate for you 30 to 45 minutes each day. This exercise may be just as important as other preparation.

Prepare with another person. You will feel less isolated if you have a friend or colleague to study with.

Follow This Study Plan

Begin working four to ten weeks before the test. Review the description of each test you have to take and then take each appropriate review quiz. Use the answer key to mark the review quiz. Each incorrect answer will point you to a specific portion of the review.

Use the subject matter review indicated by the review quiz. Don't spend your time reviewing things you already know.

Take the targeted test after the review of each chapter is complete. It will let you know what further review may be necessary. Complete your review two weeks before the test. Then, complete the practice test. Take the test under exact test conditions.

Grade your own test or have someone do it for you. Either way, review each incorrect answer and read all the explanations. Every answer is explained in detail.

TIP

To simulate actual testing conditions, we recommend that you take the practice test on the same day of the week and during the same time period that you will take the actual test.

TWO WEEKS TO GO

During this week look over those areas you answered incorrectly on the practice test. Go over the answer explanations and go back to the review sections. For the Computer-Based PPST, practice using a computer mouse, a keyboard, and a word processor.

ONE WEEK TO GO

Get up each day at the time you will have to get up the following Saturday. Sit down at the time the test will start and spend about one hour answering questions on targeted tests or practice tests even if you've answered these questions before.

Follow this schedule for the week leading up to test day.

FIVE DAYS TO GO

Monday

Make sure you

- have your admission ticket.
- know where the test is given.
- know how you're getting there.

Tuesday

Visit the test site, if you haven't done so already.

Wednesday

Get some sharpened no. 2 pencils, a digital watch or pocket clock, and an eraser.

Friday

- Complete any forms you have to bring to the test.
- Prepare any snacks or food you want to bring with you.
- Talk to someone who makes you feel good or do something enjoyable and relaxing.
- Have a good night's sleep.

Saturday

- Dress comfortably.
- Eat the same kind of breakfast you've been eating each morning.
- Get together things to bring to the test, including: registration ticket, identification forms, pencils, eraser, and snacks.
- Get to the test room about 10 to 15 minutes before the start time. Remember to leave time for parking and walking to the test site.
- Hand in your forms.
- Follow the test-taking strategies in the next section.

TIP

Test Day Necessities

- Admission Ticket
- Completed forms
- Identification
- Sharpened No. 2 pencils
- Eraser
- A digital watch or pocket clock
- Snacks

Proven Test-Taking Strategies

Testing companies like to pretend that test-taking strategies don't help that much. They act like that because they want everyone to think that their tests only measure your knowledge of the subject. Of course, they are just pretending; test-taking strategies can make a big difference.

However, there is nothing better than being prepared for the subject matter on the test. These strategies will do you little good if you lack this fundamental knowledge. If you are prepared, then these strategies can make a difference. Use them. Other people will. Not using them may very well lower your score.

Be Comfortable

Get a good seat for the PPST. Don't sit near anyone or anything that will distract you. Stay away from your friends. If you don't like where you are sitting, move or ask for another seat. You paid money for this test, and you have a right to favorable test conditions. For the Computer-Based PPST, make sure that your chair is comfortably adjusted and that the computer is working properly.

You Will Make Mistakes

You are going to make mistakes on this test. The people who wrote the test expect you to make them.

You Are Not Competing with Anyone

Don't worry about how anyone else is doing. Your score does not depend on theirs. When the score report comes out it doesn't say, "Nancy got a 661, but Blaire got a 670."

You just want to get the score required for your certificate. Stay focused. Remember your goal.

Specific Strategies for Each Test

These strategies are for all of the PPST Tests. This book also has strategies for each individual test.

Multiple-Choice Strategies

It's Not What You Know That Matters, It's Just Which Answer You Mark

No one you know or care about will see your test. An impersonal machine scores every item except the essay. The machine just senses whether the correct answer is marked. That is the way the test makers want it. If that's good enough for them, it should be good enough for you. Concentrate on marking the correct answer.

Do Your Work in the Test Booklet (Paper-Based PPST)
Do Your Work on Scrap Paper (Computer-Based PPST)

TIP

You Can Be Right But Be Marked Wrong

If you get the right answer but mark the wrong answer, the machine will mark it wrong. We told you that marking the right answer was what mattered. We strongly recommend that you follow this tip.

On the Paper-Based PPST, write the letter for your answer big in the test booklet next to the number for the problem. If you change your mind about an answer, cross off the "old" letter and write the "new" one. At the end of each section, transfer all the answers together from the test booklet to the answer sheet.

You can write anything you want in your test booklet. The test booklet is not used for scoring and no one will look at it. You can't bring scrap paper to the Paper-Based PPST but it's available for the Computer-Based PPST.

Some Questions are Traps

Some questions include the words "not," "least," or "except." You are being asked for the answer that doesn't fit with the rest. Be alert for these types of questions.

Work Backward from the Answers

Back solving is particularly useful for answering mathematics questions. This strategy is discussed in detail in the mathematics section pages 151–154.

They Show You the Answer

Every multiple-choice test shows you the correct answer for each question. The answer is staring right at you. You just have to figure out which one it is.

Some Answers are Traps

When someone writes a test question, he or she often includes distracters. Distracters are traps—incorrect answers that look like correct answers. It might be an answer to an addition problem when you should be multiplying. It might be a correct answer to a different question. It might just be an answer that catches your eye. Watch out for this type of incorrect answer.

Eliminate the Incorrect Answers

If you can't figure out which answer is correct, then decide which answers can't be correct. Choose the answers you're sure are incorrect. Cross them off in the test booklet on the Paper-Based PPST. Only one left? That's the correct answer.

Guess, Guess, Guess

If there are still two or more answers left, then guess. Guess the answer from those remaining. Never leave any item blank. There is no penalty for guessing.

Computer-Based PPST Strategies

Use the Tutorial

There is an untimed tutorial before each test that shows you how to use the computer, how to indicate your answer, and how to use the "mark tool" and review page. Pay careful attention to the tutorial. It will speed things up when you take the test. Take as much time as you need.

You Have More Time

Take your time as you answer each item. You have a little more time to answer a Computer-Based PPST item than you have to answer a Paper-Based PPST item. Let's compare the time you have for each item.

PPST Tests
Multiple-Choice Items Time Comparison

	Paper-Based PPST			Computer-Based PPST		
	Time in Minutes	Items	Time per Item	Time in Minutes	Items	Time per Item
Reading	60	40	1.5 minutes	75	46	1.64 minutes
Writing	30	38	0.79 minutes	38	44	0.86 minutes
Mathematics	60	40	1.5 minutes	75	46	1.64 minutes

You have almost 9 seconds longer for each Computer-Based PPST reading and mathematics item, and just 4 seconds longer for each writing item. This may not seem like much, but every little bit helps.

Mark Every Item You Might Come Back To

Before you skip an item, mark it with the "mark tool." Mark each item you answer if you think you may want to come back to it.

Use the Review Screen

Before you finish the test, check the review page to be sure you have answered each item. You can use the review screen to check your progress during the test. Be sure to answer every item.

Use the Scratch Paper

Use the scratch paper provided at the test center. Use it to do calculations, to jot down possible answers, and to write reminder notes.

> **Don't Use a Word Processor**
>
> You won't have the spell and grammar checking and other word processing features available when you write your essay. Don't use these features when you practice.

Essay Strategies

Your Responses Are Graded Holistically

Holistic scoring means the raters assign a score based on their informed sense about your writing. Raters have a lot of answers to look at and they do not do a detailed analysis. The ETS sends your essay to readers over the Internet. Representatives of ETS show the readers the topics for the test and review the types of responses that should be rated 1–6. The rating guidelines are on page 36. The readers are trained to evaluate the responses according to the ETS guidelines.

Each written assignment is evaluated twice, without the second reader knowing the evaluation given by the first reader. If the two evaluations differ by more than one point, other readers review the assignment.

Readers have a tedious, tiring assignment. Think about those readers as you write. Write a response that makes it easy for them to give you a high score.

You will find detailed steps for writing essays on pages 75–78.

PART II

SUBJECT MATTER PREPARATION

CHAPTER 3

Writing

```
┌─────────────────────────────────────────────────────────────────────┐
│                       TEST INFO BOX                                   │
│ Paper-Based PPST      38 Multiple-Choice Items          30 minutes    │
│                          Usage                 21 Items              │
│                          Sentence Correction   17 Items              │
│                       1 Handwritten Essay               30 minutes    │
│                                                                       │
│ Computer-Based PPST   44 Multiple-Choice Items          38 minutes    │
│                          Usage                 24 Items              │
│                          Sentence Correction   20 Items              │
│                       1 Typed Essay                     30 minutes    │
└─────────────────────────────────────────────────────────────────────┘
```

Using This Chapter

This chapter prepares you to take the multiple-choice writing section and the essay section of the Paper-Based PPST and the Computer-Based PPST. You will need to find an English professor, teacher, or tutor to mark the essay portion of the review test. This person may also be able to help you prepare for the essay section of the test. Choose one of these approaches.

- **I want all the writing help I can get.** Skip the review quiz and read the writing review. Then take the English review quiz. Correct the test and reread the indicated parts of the writing review. Take the targeted test at the end of the chapter.

- **I want writing help.** Take the review quiz. Correct the quiz and review the indicated parts of the English review. Take the targeted test at the end of the chapter.

- **I want a quick writing review.** Take the review quiz. Correct the quiz. Then take the targeted test at the end of the chapter.

- **I want to practice a writing test.** Take the targeted test at the end of the chapter.

English Review Quiz

The English Review Quiz assesses your knowledge of the English topics included in the PPST. The quiz also provides an excellent way to refresh your memory about these topics. The first part of the quiz consists of sentences to mark or correct. Make your marks or corrections right on the sentences. In the second part of the quiz, you are asked to write a brief essay.

This quiz will be more difficult than the questions on the actual certification test. It's not important to answer all these questions correctly and don't be concerned if you miss many of them.

The answers are found immediately after the quiz. It's to your advantage not to look until you have completed the quiz. Once you have completed and marked this review quiz, use the checklist to decide which sections to study.

PART I—SENTENCE CORRECTION

Directions: Correct the sentence. Some sentences may not contain errors.

1. Ron and James fathers each sent them to players camp to learn the mysterys of sport.

2. They go to the camp, ridden horses while they were there, and had write letters home.

3. James went to the water and goes skiing.

4. Ron and James called his coach. The operator never answered, and they wondered what happened to her.

5. Bob and Liz went to the store and got some groceries.

6. Dad want me to do my homework. My sisters try their best to help me.

Directions: Underline the subject in each sentence.

7. Chad's project that he showed the teacher improved his final grade.

8. The legs pumped hard, and the racer finished in first place.

9. Through the halls and down the stairs ran the harried student.

10. Where is the dog's leash

Directions: Correct the sentence. Some sentences may not contain errors.

11. Chad was sure correct, the food tastes bad and the singer sang bad but Ryan played really well. Ryan was more happy than Chad who sat closer to the stage than Ryan.

12. The larger table in the restaurant was full.

13. The waiter brought food to the table on a large tray. The waiter wanted a job in the suburbs that paid well.

14. Waiting for the food to come, the complaining began.

15. The food arrived, the eating began. The waiter stood by he was tired.

Directions: Correct the sentence. Some sentences may not contain errors.

16. The coach realized that new selection rules to go into effect in May. She also knew what it would take for Ryan to be selected. Ryan winning every game. But the coach and Ryan had a common goal. To see Ryan on the team.

17. Ryan's parents wanted a success rather than see him fail. They knew he stayed in shape by eating right and exercising daily. Ryan was a person who works hard and has talent.

18. Chad was dog tired after soccer practice. He became a coach for the purpose of helping the college to the soccer finals. During the rein of the former coach, the team had miserable seasons. Chad would stay at the job until such time as he could except the first place trophy.

19. Chad was satisfied but the players were grumbling. The players wanted to practice less have more free time. The players didn't like their light blue uniforms! The finals began in May 1996. The first game was scheduled for Tuesday May 9 at 1:00 P.M. The time for the game was here the players were on the field. Chad had the essential materials with him player list score book soccer balls and a cup of hope.

PART II—ESSAY

Directions: Time yourself for 30 minutes. Use the lined page to write a brief essay that answers this question.

Should high school students have to pass a standardized test before they graduate?

Write a brief outline here.

STUDY CHECKLIST

PART I—SENTENCE CORRECTION

The answers are organized by review sections. Check your answers. If you miss any item in a section, check the box and review that section.

❏ *Nouns, page 37*
    1. <u>Ron's</u> and <u>James's</u> fathers each sent them to <u>players'</u> camp to learn the <u>mysteries</u> of sport.

❏ *Verbs, page 39*
    2. They <u>went</u> to the camp, <u>rode</u> horses while they were there, and <u>wrote</u> letters home.

❏ *Tense Shift, page 40*
    3. James <u>went</u> to the water and <u>went</u> skiing. James <u>goes</u> to the water and <u>goes</u> skiing.

❏ *Pronouns, page 42*
    4. Ron and James called (<u>Ron's, James's, their</u>) coach. The operator never answered, and they wondered what happened to <u>him or her</u>.

❏ *Subject-Verb Agreement, page 44*
    5. No error
    6. Dad <u>wants</u> me to do my homework. My sisters try their best to help me.
    7. Chad's <u>project</u> that he showed the teacher improved his final grade.
    8. The <u>legs</u> pumped hard, and the <u>racer</u> finished in first place.

    9. Through the halls and down the stairs ran the harried <u>student.</u>
    10. Where is the dog's <u>leash?</u>

❏ *Adjectives and Adverbs, page 46*
    11. Chad was <u>surely</u> correct, the food tastes bad and the singer sang <u>badly</u> but Ryan played really well. Ryan was <u>happier</u> than Chad who sat closer to the singer than Ryan <u>did.</u>

❏ *Comparison, page 47*
    12. The <u>largest</u> table in the restaurant was full.

❏ *Misplaced and Dangling Modifiers, page 48*
    13. The waiter brought food <u>on a large tray</u> to the <u>table.</u> The waiter wanted a <u>well-paying job</u> in the <u>suburbs.</u>
    14. Waiting for the food to come, the (<u>patrons, diners</u>) complained. The (<u>patrons, diners</u>) complained about waiting for the food to come.

❏ *Comma Splices and Run-on Sentences, page 49*
    15. The food arrived. The eating began.
    The food arrived; the eating began.
    The food arrived, and the eating began. The waiter stood by. He was tired.

The waiter stood by; he was tired.
The waiter stood by, and he was tired.

❏ *Sentence Fragments, page 50*

16. The coach realized that new selection rules <u>would</u> go into effect in May. She also knew what it would take for Ryan to be selected. Ryan <u>would have to win</u> every game. But the coach and Ryan had a common goal. <u>They wanted</u> to see Ryan on the team.

❏ *Parallelism, page 52*

17. Ryan's parents wanted <u>a success</u> rather than <u>a failure</u> (wanted success rather than failure). They knew he stayed in shape by eating right and <u>by</u> exercising daily. Ryan was a person who works hard and <u>who</u> has talent. (Ryan is hardworking and talented.)

❏ *Diction, page 53*

18. Chad was [delete "dog"] tired after soccer practice. He became a coach <u>to help</u> the college <u>ascend</u> to the soccer finals. During the <u>reign</u> of the former coach, the team had miserable seasons. Chad would stay at the job until [delete "such time as"] he could <u>accept the first place trophy.</u>

❏ *Punctuation, page 56*

19. Chad was satisfied<u>,</u> but the players were grumbling. The players wanted to practice less <u>and</u> have more free time. The players didn't like their light blue uniforms. The finals began in May 1996. The first game was scheduled for Tuesday<u>,</u> May 9<u>,</u> at 1:00 P.M. The time for the game was here; the players were on the field. Chad had the essential materials with him<u>:</u> player list, score book, soccer balls<u>,</u> (optional) and a cup of hope.

PART II—ESSAY
Evaluation Guidelines

Find an English professor or a high school English teacher and ask that person to correct your essay and to rate it rigorously 6 through 1 using these criteria.

A rating of 6 or 5 indicates that your writing is acceptable. A rating of 4 or 3 shows you need to work on the errors identified by the raters. A rating of 2 or 1 indicates that you will benefit from English tutoring or additional English coursework.

RATING SCALE

6 This essay is extremely well written. It is the equivalent of an A on an in-class assignment. The essay addresses the question and provides clear supporting arguments, illustrations, or examples. The paragraphs and sentences are well organized and show a variety of language and syntax. The essay may contain some minor errors.

5 This essay is well written. It is the equivalent of a B+ on an in-class assignment. The essay addresses the question and provides some supporting arguments, illustrations, or examples. The paragraphs and sentences are fairly well organized and show a variety of language and syntax. The essay may contain some minor mechanical or linguistic errors.

4 This essay is fairly well written. It is the equivalent of a B on an in-class assignment. The essay adequately addresses the question and provides some supporting arguments, illustrations, or examples for some points. The paragraphs and sentences are acceptably organized and show a variety of language and syntax. The essay may contain mechanical or linguistic errors but is free from an identifiable pattern of errors.

3 This essay may demonstrate some writing ability, but it contains obvious errors. It is the equivalent of a C or C+ on an in-class assignment. The essay may not clearly address the question and may not give supporting arguments or details. The essay may show problems in diction including inappropriate word choice. The paragraphs and sentences may not be acceptably developed. There will be an identifiable pattern or grouping of errors.

2 This essay shows only the most limited writing ability. It is the equivalent of a C on an in-class assignment. It contains serious errors and flaws. This essay may not address the question, be poorly organized, or provide no supporting arguments or detail. It usually shows serious errors in diction, usage, and mechanics.

1 This essay does not demonstrate minimal writing ability. It is the equivalent of a D or F on an in-class assignment. This essay may contain serious and continuing errors, or it may not be coherent.

English Review

This review section targets the skills and concepts you need to know in order to pass the English parts of the PPST.

NOUNS AND VERBS

Every sentence has a subject and a predicate. Most sentences are statements. The sentence usually names something (subject). Then the sentence describes the subject or tells what that subject is doing (predicate). Sentences that ask questions also have a subject and a predicate. Here are some examples.

Subject	Predicate
The car	moved.
The tree	grew.
The street	was dark.
The forest	teemed with plants of every type and size.

Many subjects are nouns. Every predicate has a verb. A list of the nouns and verbs from the preceding sentences follows.

Noun	Verb
car	moved
tree	grew
street	was
forest, plants	teemed

Nouns

Nouns name a person, place, thing, characteristic, or concept. Nouns give a name to everything that is, has been, or will be. Here are some simple examples.

Person	Place	Thing	Characteristic	Concept(Idea)
Abe Lincoln	Lincoln Memorial	beard	mystery	freedom
judge	courthouse	gavel	fairness	justice
professor	college	chalkboard	intelligence	number

SINGULAR AND PLURAL NOUNS

Singular nouns refer to only one thing. Plural forms refer to more than one thing. Plurals are usually formed by adding an *s* or dropping a *y* and adding *ies*. Here are some examples.

Singular	Plural
college	colleges
professor	professors
Lincoln Memorial	Lincoln Memorials
mystery	mysteries

POSSESSIVE NOUNS

Possessive nouns show that the noun possesses a thing or a characteristic. Make a singular noun possessive by adding *'s*. Here are some examples.

The *child's* sled was in the garage ready for use.
The *school's* mascot was loose again.

The rain interfered with *Jane's* vacation.

Ron's and *Doug's* fathers were born in the same year.
Ron and *Doug's* teacher kept them after school.

Make a singular noun ending in *s* possessive by adding *'s* unless the pronunciation is too difficult.

The teacher read *James's* paper several times.
The angler grabbed the *bass'* fin.

Make a plural noun possessive by adding an apostrophe (') only.

The *principals'* meeting was delayed.
The report indicated that *students'* scores had declined.

Practice

Directions: Write the plural of each singular noun.

1. sheaf

2. deer

3. fry

4. lunch

5. knee

6. lady

7. octopus

8. echo

9. foot

10. half

Answers on page 60.

VERBS

Some verbs are action verbs. Other verbs are linking verbs that link the subject to words that describe it. Here are some examples.

Action Verbs	Linking Verbs
Blaire *runs* down the street.	Blaire *is* tired.
Blaire *told* her story.	The class *was* bored.
The crowd *roared*.	The players *were* inspired.
The old ship *rusted*.	It *had been* a proud ship.

Tense

A verb has three principal tenses: present tense, past tense, and future tense. The present tense shows that the action is happening now. The past tense shows that the action happened in the past. The future tense shows that something will happen. Here are some examples.

Present: I *enjoy* my time off.
Past: I *enjoyed* my time off.
Future: I *will enjoy* my time off.
Present: I *hate* working late.
Past: I *hated* working late.
Future: I *will hate* working late.

Regular and Irregular Verbs

Regular verbs follow the consistent pattern noted previously. However, a number of verbs are irregular. Irregular verbs have their own unique forms for each tense. A partial list of irregular verbs follows. The past participle is usually preceded by *had, has,* or *have.*

Some Irregular Verbs

Present Tense	Past Tense	Past Participle
am, is, are	was, were	been
begin	began	begun
break	broke	broken
bring	brought	brought
catch	caught	caught
choose	chose	chosen
come	came	come

continued

Some Irregular Verbs *(continued)*

Present Tense	Past Tense	Past Participle
do	did	done
eat	ate	eaten
give	gave	given
go	went	gone
grow	grew	grown
know	knew	known
lie	lay	lain
lay	laid	laid
raise	raised	raised
ride	rode	ridden
see	saw	seen
set	set	set
sit	sat	sat
speak	spoke	spoken
take	took	taken
tear	tore	torn
throw	threw	thrown
write	wrote	written

TENSE SHIFT

Verbs in a sentence should reflect time sequence. If the actions represented by the verbs happened at the same time, the verbs should have the same tense.

Incorrect: Beth sits in the boat while she wore a life jacket.
Correct: Beth sits in the boat while she wears a life jacket.
[Both verbs are present tense.]
Correct: Beth sat in the boat while she wore a life jacket.
[Both verbs are past tense.]
Correct: Beth wears the life jacket she wore last week.
[The verbs show time order.]

Practice

Directions: Correct the tense errors. Some sentences may be correct.

1. Ryan driven to Florida.

2. Refereeing soccer games is not work.

3. Chad ride to the game with his team last week.

4. Why did Mary ran her errands now?

5. I have speak to my teacher about the grade.

6. Carl paddled across the river every Saturday.

7. Blaire thrown out the ball for the players to use.

8. Joann will lost her bag if she leaves it in the store.

9. Bob is standing on a stool next to the green table.

10. Liz begun to grasp the depth of her happiness.

Answers on pages 60–61.

Practice

Directions: Correct the tense shifts. Some sentences may be correct.

1. Lisa already went to the North Pole but she is not going there again.

2. Dennis will take his airline tickets with him because he is leaving for his flight.

3. The runner gasped as she crosses the finish line.

4. I like to hear music so I played the clarinet.

5. Chris wanted to be a producer so he puts in long hours every day.

6. Bertha sews five hours a day because she will need her dress by next month.

7. The car turns over and then bounced down the hill.

8. Lois handed over her money because she wants to buy the computer.

9. The captain wandered out on the deck as she calls to her friends on shore.

10. The sun sets in the west as the moon rose in the east.

Answers on page 61.

PRONOUNS

Pronouns take the place of nouns or noun phrases and help avoid constant repetition of the noun or phrase. Here is an example.

> *Blaire* is in law school. *She* studies in *her* room every day.
> [The pronouns *she* and *her* refer to the noun *Blaire*.]

Pronoun Cases

Pronouns take three case forms: subjective, objective, and possessive. The personal pronouns *I, he, she, it, we, they, you* refer to an individual or individuals. The relative pronoun *who* refers to these personal pronouns as well as to an individual or individuals. These pronouns change their case form depending on their use in the sentence.

SUBJECTIVE PRONOUNS: *I, WE, HE, IT, SHE, THEY, WHO, YOU*

Use the subjective form if the pronoun is, or refers to, the subject of a clause or sentence.

> *He* and *I* studied for the PPST.
> The proctors for the test were *she* and *I*.
> [*She* and *I* refer to the subject *proctors*.]
> She is the woman *who* answered every question correctly.
> I don't expect to do as well as *she*.
> [*She* is the subject for the understood verb *does*.]

OBJECTIVE PRONOUNS: *ME, US, HIM, IT, HER, THEM, WHOM, YOU*

Use the objective form if the pronoun is the object of a verb or preposition.

> Cathy helps both *him* and *me*.
> She wanted *them* to pass.
> I don't know *whom* she helped most.

POSSESSIVE PRONOUNS: *MY, OUR, HIS, ITS, HER, THEIR, WHOSE, YOUR*

Use the objective form if the pronoun shows possession.

> I recommended they reduce the time they study with *their* friends.
> He was the person *whose* help they relied on.

CLEAR REFERENCE

The pronoun must clearly refer to a particular noun or noun phrase. Here are some examples.

> *Unclear*
>
> Chris and Blaire took turns feeding *her* cat.
> [We can't tell which person *her* refers to.]
>
> Chris gave *it* to Blaire.
> [The pronoun *it* refers to a noun that is not stated.]

Clear

> Chris and Blaire took turns feeding Blaire's cat.
> [A pronoun doesn't work here.]

> Chris got the book and gave it to Blaire.
> [The pronoun works once the noun is stated.]

AGREEMENT

Each pronoun must agree in number (singular or plural) and gender (male or female) with the noun it refers to. Here are some examples.

Nonagreement in Number

> The children played all day, and *she* came in exhausted.
> [*Children* is plural, but *she* is singular.]

> The child picked up the hat and brought *them* into the house.
> [*Hat* is singular, but *them* is plural.]

Agreement

> The children played all day, and *they* came in exhausted.
> The child picked up the hat and brought *it* into the house.

Nonagreement in Gender

> The lioness picked up *his* cub.
> [*Lioness* is female, and *his* is male.]

> A child must bring in a doctor's note before *she* comes to school.
> [The child may be a male or female but *she* is female.]

Agreement

> The lioness picked up *her* cub.
> A child must bring in a doctor's note before *he* or *she* comes to school.

Practice

Directions: Correct the clear reference and case and number errors in these sentences. Some sentences may not have errors.

1. His was the best table tennis player.

2. Whom was the worst table tennis player?

3. Where are the table tennis balls?

4. Before the game everyone are going to choose teams.

5. The names of the winning team are sent to we.

6. Them are the best table tennis team.

7. Ron and Jeff wanted to use his skates.

8. Jeff went to get them.

9. The couch looked different, depending on how they were arranged.

10. Bob won most of his table tennis games.

11. The student waited for their school bus to come.

12. Either of the buses can arrive on time if they don't break down.

13. The book was most interesting near her beginning.

14. She read the book to find her most interesting parts.

15. I am the winner; victory is ours.

16. His friends got out of the car, and he went over to talk to them.

17. The rain clouds moved toward the pool, and the swimmers tried to wish it away.

18. Was Les disappointed that him team did not win?

19. Whom has more experience than Nicky does?

20. You play better after you have experience.

Answers on pages 61–63.

SUBJECT-VERB AGREEMENT

Singular and Plural

Singular nouns take singular verbs. Plural nouns take plural verbs. Singular verbs usually end in *s*, and plural verbs usually do not. Here are some examples.

Singular:	My father wants me home early.
Plural:	My parents want me home early.
Singular:	Ryan runs a mile each day.
Plural:	Ryan and Chad run a mile each day.
Singular:	She tries her best to do a good job.
Plural:	Liz and Ann try their best to do a good job.

Correctly Identify Subject and Verb

The subject may not be in front of the verb. In fact, the subject may not be anywhere near the verb. Say the subject and the verb to yourself. If it makes sense, you probably have it right.

- Words may come between the subject and the verb.

    Chad's final exam score, which he showed to his mother, improved his final grade.

The verb is *improved*. The word *mother* appears just before *improved*.

Is this the subject? Say it to yourself. [Mother improved the grade.]

That can't be right. *Score* must be the subject. Say it to yourself. [Score improved the grade.] That's right. *Score* is the subject, and *improved* is the verb.

The racer running with a sore arm finished first.

Say it to yourself. [Racer finished first.] *Racer* is the noun, and *finished* is the verb.

It wouldn't make any sense to say the arm finished first.

• The verb may come before the subject.

Over the river and through the woods romps the merry leprechaun.

Leprechaun is the subject, and *romps* is the verb. [Think: Leprechaun romps.]

Where are the car keys?

Keys is the subject, and *are* is the verb. [Think: The car keys are where?]

Examples of Subject-Verb Agreement

Words such as *each, neither, everyone, nobody, someone,* and *anyone* are singular pronouns. They always take a singular verb.

Everyone needs a good laugh now and then.
Nobody knows more about computers than Bob.

Words that refer to number such as *one-half, any, most,* and *some* can be singular or plural.

One-fifth of the students were absent. [*Students* is plural.]
One-fifth of the cake was eaten. [There is only one cake.]

Practice

Directions: Correct any subject-verb agreement errors. Some sentences may be correct.

1. The chess set are still on the shelf.

2. The shortest route to the college are shown in the catalog.

3. The golf pro drive a golf cart every day.

4. Derek and Ann walks every morning.

5. The tropical birds in the tree adds a festive air to the occasion.

6. No one, not even Rick or Ronnie, walk to school today.

7. Do you know who they is?

8. Ron prepare a paper for submission to the committee.

9. The 15 employees of the coffee house shows up each day at 6:00 A.M.

10. Each person who takes the 12 steps improve his or her view.

Answers on page 63.

ADJECTIVES AND ADVERBS

Adjectives

Adjectives modify nouns and pronouns. Adjectives add detail and clarify nouns and pronouns. Frequently, adjectives come immediately before the nouns or pronouns they are modifying. At other times, the nouns or pronouns come first and are connected directly to the adjectives by linking verbs. Here are some examples.

Direct	With a Linking Verb
That is a *large* dog.	That dog is *large*.
He's an *angry* man.	The man seems *angry*.

Adverbs

Adverbs are often formed by adding *ly* to an adjective. However, many adverbs don't end in *ly* (e.g., *always*). Adverbs modify verbs, adjectives, and adverbs. Adverbs can also modify phrases, clauses, and sentences. Here are some examples.

Modify verb:	Ryan *quickly* sought a solution.
Modify adjective:	That is an *exceedingly* large dog.
Modify adverb:	Lisa told her story *quite* truthfully.
Modify sentence:	*Unfortunately*, all good things must end.
Modify phrase:	The instructor arrived *just* in time to start the class.

AVOIDING ADJECTIVE AND ADVERB ERRORS

- Don't use adjectives in place of adverbs.

Correct	Incorrect
Lynne read the book quickly.	Lynne read the book quick.
Stan finished his work easily.	Stan finished his work easy.

- Don't confuse the adjectives *good* and *bad* with the adverbs *well* and *badly*.

Correct	Incorrect
Adverbs	
She wanted to play the piano well.	She wanted to play the piano good.
Bob sang badly.	Bob sang bad.
Adjectives	
The food tastes good.	The food tastes well.
The food tastes bad.	The food tastes badly.

• Don't confuse the adjectives *real* and *sure* with the adverbs *really* and *surely*.

Correct	Incorrect
Chuck played really well.	Chuck played real well.
He was surely correct.	He was sure correct.

COMPARISON

Adjectives and adverbs can show comparisons. Avoid clumsy modifiers.

Correct	Incorrect
Jim is more clingy than Ray.	Jim is clingier than Ray.
Ray is much taller than Jim.	Ray is more taller than Jim.
Jim is more interesting than Ray.	Jim is interesting than Ray.
Ray is happier than Jim.	Ray is more happy than Jim.

Word comparisons carefully to be sure that the comparison is clear.

Unclear:	Chad lives closer to Ryan than Blaire.
Clear:	Chad lives closer to Ryan than Blaire does.
Clear:	Chad lives closer to Ryan than he does to Blaire.
Unclear:	The bus engines are bigger than cars.
Clear:	The bus engines are bigger than cars' engines.

Practice

Directions: Correct the adjective and adverb errors. Some sentences may contain no errors.

1. The view of the Grand Canyon was real spectacular.

2. The trainer said the dog behaved very good today.

3. Unfortunate, the tickets for the concert were sold out.

4. Things went smooth.

5. The judge took extremely exception to the defendant's actions.

6. The accident was silly, particularly since driving more careful would have avoided the whole thing.

7. But the reviews said the performance was truly horrible.

8. The manager conveniently forgot that she promised the employee a raise.

9. The bonus was a welcome surprise; it was a real large check.

10. I didn't do good, but didn't do bad either.

Answers on page 64.

Practice

Directions: Correct the comparison errors. Some sentences may be correct.

1. Leon was the happier chef in the restaurant.

2. But some of the people eating in the restaurant were happier than Leon.

3. The jet was the faster plane at the airport.

4. John was the fastest of the twins.

5. The taller of the apartment buildings is under repair.

6. The lightest of the two weights is missing.

7. Lonnie was among the most creative students in the school.

8. Ron is the least able of the two drivers.

9. His shoe size is the smallest in his class.

10. She was the more capable of the two referees.

Answers on pages 64–65.

MISPLACED AND DANGLING MODIFIERS

Modifiers may be words or groups of words. Modifiers change or qualify the meaning of another word or group of words. Modifiers belong near the words they modify.

Misplaced modifiers appear to modify words in a way that doesn't make sense.

The modifier in the following sentence is *in a large box*. It doesn't make sense for *in a large box* to modify *house*. Move the modifier near *pizza* where it belongs.

Misplaced: Les delivered pizza to the house in a large box.
Revised: Les delivered pizza in a large box to the house.

The modifier in the next sentence is *paid well*. *Paid well* can't modify *city*. Move it next to *the job* where it belongs.

Misplaced: Gail wanted the job in the city that paid well.
Revised: Gail wanted the well-paying job in the city.

Dangling modifiers modify words not present in the sentence. The modifier in the following sentence is *waiting for the concert to begin*.

This modifier describes the audience, but audience is not mentioned in the sentence. The modifier is left dangling with nothing to attach itself to.

Dangling:	Waiting for the concert to begin, the chanting started.
Revised:	Waiting for the concert to begin, the audience began chanting.
Revised:	The audience began chanting while waiting for the concert to begin.

The modifier in the next sentence is *after three weeks in the country*. The modifier describes the person, not the license. But the person is not mentioned in the sentence. The modifier is dangling.

Dangling:	After three weeks in the country, the license was revoked.
Revised:	After he was in the country for three weeks, his license was revoked.
Revised:	His license was revoked after he was in the country three weeks.

Practice

Directions: Correct the misplaced modifiers. Some sentences may be correct.

1. Les was reading his book through glasses with dirty lenses.

2. Jim left work early to go to the doctor on the train.

3. The first train car was crowded; which had to go to the next car.

4. Ron's car ran out of gas when on the way to the store.

5. Zena was jogging, when caused her to fall.

6. Derek wrapped the flowers and put them in the delivery van with colorful paper.

7. Which bus stops at the corner where the stop sign is?

8. Fran is going on the plane, which is just pulling up to the gate.

9. Lisa bought a shirt in the store, which was expensive.

10. The car turned around and the headlights shone quickly into the garage.

Answers on pages 65–66.

COMMA SPLICES AND RUN-ON SENTENCES

An *independent clause* is a clause that could be a sentence.

Independent clauses should be joined by a semicolon, or by a comma and a conjunction.

A *comma splice* consists of two independent clauses joined by just a comma.

A *run-on* sentence consists of two independent clauses incorrectly joined.

Correct: The whole family went on vacation; the parents took turns driving.
[Two independent clauses are joined by a semicolon.]

The whole family went on vacation, and the parents took turns driving.
[Two independent clauses are joined by a comma and a conjunction.]

Incorrect: The whole family went on vacation, the parents took turns driving.
[Comma splice. Two independent clauses are joined by just a comma.]

The whole family went on vacation the parents took turns driving.
[Run-on sentence. Two independent clauses are incorrectly joined.]

Practice

Directions: Correct the run-on sentences and comma splices. Some sentences may be correct.

1. It will be tomorrow before the sea is calm enough to go out.

2. It started to rain unexpectedly the boaters were soaked.

3. But right now my sneakers are soaking wet the towel is too wet to help me.

4. The Marine Police sounded the siren the boat stopped immediately.

5. I put the sneakers next to the fire to dry, although they started to steam after a while.

6. The Coast Guard monitors boats as they enter the river they use the data to monitor water pollution.

7. I like to use my compass when I go out on the boat.

8. When the boat breaks down, Liz calls Sea Tow.

9. The fire went out the sun came up.

10. Splashing through the waves, the water skier was covered with salt spray.

Answers on page 66.

SENTENCE FRAGMENTS

English sentences require a subject and a predicate (see page 37). Fragments are parts of sentences written as though they were sentences. Fragments are writing mistakes that lack a subject, a predicate, or both subject and predicate. Here are some examples.

Since when.
To enjoy the summer months.

Because he isn't working hard.

If you can fix old cars.

What the principal wanted to hear.

Include a subject and/or a verb to rewrite a fragment as a sentence.

Fragment	Sentence
Should be coming up the driveway now.	The *car* should be coming up the driveway now.
Both the lawyer and her client.	Both the lawyer and her client *waited* in court.
Which is my favorite subject.	*I took math*, which is my favorite subject.
If you can play.	If you can play, *you'll improve with* practice.

Verbs such as *to be, to go, winning, starring,* etc., need a main verb.

Fragment	Sentence
The new rules to go into effect in April.	The new rules *will* go into effect in April.
The team winning every game.	The team *was* winning every game.

Often, a fragment is related to a complete sentence. Combine the two to make a single sentence.

Fragment: Reni loved vegetables. *Particularly corn, celery, lettuce, squash, and eggplant.*

Revised: Reni loved vegetables, particularly corn, celery, lettuce, squash, and eggplant.

Fragment: *To see people standing on Mars.* This could happen in the 21st century.

Revised: To see people standing on Mars is one of the things that could happen in the 21st century.

Sometimes short fragments can be used for emphasis. However, you should not use fragments in your essay. Here are some examples.

Stop! Don't take one more step toward that apple pie.

I need some time to myself. *That's why.*

Practice

Directions: Correct the sentence fragments. Some items may be correct.

1. A golf bag, golf clubs, and golf balls. That's what she needed to play.

2. As the rocket prepared for blast-off. Mary saw birds flying in the distance.

3. Jim is mowing the lawn. Then, the mower stopped.

4. The lawn looked lush and green. Like a golf course.

5. The polar bears swept across the ice. Like white ghosts in fur jackets.

6. Jim looked across at the igloo. Like an ice fort, it stood a lonely vigil.

7. Astronauts and their equipment went by. These were the people who would go into space.

8. This was what Joe had been waiting for. To graduate from college.

9. To be finished with this test. That's what I'm waiting for.

10. The test finished and done. The papers graded and good.

Answers on pages 60–67.

PARALLELISM

When two or more ideas are connected, use a parallel structure. Parallelism helps the reader follow the passage more clearly. Here are some examples.

Not Parallel:	Toni stayed in shape by eating right and exercising daily.
Parallel:	Toni stayed in shape by eating right and *by* exercising daily.
Not Parallel:	Lisa is a student who works hard and has genuine insight.
Parallel:	Lisa is a student who works hard and *who* has genuine insight.
Not Parallel:	Art had a choice either to clean his room or take out the garbage.
Parallel:	Art had a choice either to clean his room or *to* take out the garbage.
Not Parallel:	Derek wanted a success rather than failing.
Parallel:	Derek wanted a success rather than a failure.
Parallel:	Derek wanted success rather than failure.

Practice

Directions: Correct any parallel form errors. Some sentences may not have errors.

1. I have to get to work, but first I have to find my way to breakfast.

2. The road was dry; the day was hot and sultry.

3. Jane likes to eat and go shopping when she is at the mall.

4. April chose to be a cameraperson rather than to be a technician who works the sound board.

5. Since I have not heard from you, I decided to write this letter.

6. Although she had driven the road before, Sally proceeded slowly, keeping her eye on the yellow line.

7. The tree withstood the hurricane, but the branches on the tree snapped off.

8. His work on the Board of Education revealed his dedication to the community.

9. Cars, taxis, and buses were my transportation to the airport.

10. The subject matter and the preparation for class created an excellent lesson.

Answers on pages 67–68.

DICTION

Diction is choosing and using appropriate words. Good diction conveys a thought clearly without unnecessary words. Good diction develops fully over a number of years; however, there are some rules and tips you can follow.

- Do not use slang, colloquialisms, or other non-standard English. One person's slang is another person's confusion. Slang is often regional, and slang meanings change rapidly. We do not give examples of slang here for that very reason. Do not use slang words in your formal writing.

  Colloquialisms are words used frequently in spoken language. This informal use of terms such as *dog tired*, *kids*, and *hanging around* is not generally accepted in formal writing. Save these informal terms for daily speech and omit or remove them from your writing except as quotations.

  Omit any other non-standard English. Always choose standard English terms that accurately reflect the thought to be conveyed.

- Avoid wordy, redundant, or pretentious writing. Good writing is clear and economical.

  Wordy: I chose my career as a teacher because of its high ideals, the truly self-sacrificing idealism of a career in teaching, and for the purpose of receiving the myriad and cascading recognition that one can receive from the community as a whole and from its constituents.

Revised: I chose a career in teaching for its high ideals and for community recognition.

Given below is a partial list of wordy phrases and the replacement word.

Wordy Phrases and Replacements

at the present time	now	because of the fact that	because
for the purpose of	for	in the final analysis	finally
in the event that	if	until such time as	until

HOMONYMS

Homonyms are words that sound alike but do not have the same meaning. These words can be confusing and you may use the incorrect spelling of a word. If words are homonyms, be sure you choose the correct spelling for the meaning you intend.

Homonyms

accept (receive)	ascent (rise)
except (other than)	assent (agreement)
board (wood)	fair (average)
bored (uninterested)	fare (a charge)
led (guided)	lessen (make less)
lead (metal)	lesson (learning experience)
past (gone before)	peace (no war)
passed (moved by)	piece (portion)
rain (precipitation)	to (toward)
reign (rule)	too (also)
rein (animal strap)	two (a number)
their (possessive pronoun)	its (shows possession)
there (location)	it's (it is)
they're (they are)	

IDIOMS

Idioms are expressions with special meanings and often break the rules of grammar. Idioms are acceptable in formal writing, but they must be used carefully. Here are some examples.

Idioms

in accordance with	inferior to
angry with	occupied by (someone)
differ from (someone)	occupied with (something)
differ about (an issue)	prior to
independent of	rewarded with (something)

Practice

Directions: Write the word or phrase that fits best in the blank.

1. Many _____ diseases, including pneumonia and swelling in cuts, are caused by bacteria.

   innocuous   unfortunate
   infectious   ill-fated

2. Sigmund Freud's views of sexuality had become _____, and the country entered the sexual revolution.

   well known   all knowing
   universal   inculcated

3. After crossing the land bridge near the Bering Strait, groups of Native Americans _____ spread throughout all of North, Central, and South America.

   inclusively   eventually
   regardless   remotely

4. During the early 1500s Cortez and Pizarro opened up Central America to the Spanish who began _____ slaves from Africa.

   importing   exporting
   imparting   immigrating

5. The Stamp Act requiring every legal paper to carry a tax stamp was vehemently _____ and eventually repealed by England.

   denied   deported
   proclaimed   protested

Directions: Circle the underlined portion that is unnecessary in the passage.

6. No goal is more noble—no feat more revealing—than the strikingly brave exploration of space.

7. As many as a ton of bananas may have spoiled when the ship was stuck and delayed in the Panama Canal.

8. He <u>was concerned</u> about <u>crossing</u> the bridge, <u>but the officer</u> said that it was all right to cross <u>and he need not worry</u>.

9: A <u>professional</u> golfer told the <u>novice</u> beginning golfer that <u>professional instruction</u> or more practice <u>improves most</u> <u>golfers' scores</u>.

10. The soccer player's <u>slight</u> strain from the shot on goal <u>that won</u> <u>the game</u> led to a <u>pulled</u> muscle that <u>would</u> keep her from <u>playing</u> the next match.

Directions: Circle the word or words used incorrectly in the sentence.

---

11. He went to the bird's nest near the river, only too realize he missed its assent.

12. The rider pulled back on the horse's reign before the whether turned rainy.

13. The whether turned rainy as he led the hikers on there ascent.

14. The lessen was clear; it was fare, but not easy to accept.

15. They're board relatives were not fare too her father.

Directions: Correct the idiom errors. Some sentences may not have errors.

---

16. Her grades had everything to do of her efforts.

17. Joanie expected him to wait to the house until she arrived home.

18. She could spend months absorbed in her studies.

19. The two coaches differ significantly with each other's style.

20. That person is wearing the same coat from you.

Answers on pages 68–69.

PUNCTUATION

The Comma (,)

The comma may be the most used punctuation mark. This section details a few of these uses.

A clause is part of a sentence that could be a sentence itself. If a clause begins with a conjunction, use a comma before the conjunction.

> Incorrect: I was satisfied with the food but John was grumbling.
> Correct: I was satisfied with the food, but John was grumbling.

Incorrect: Larry was going fishing or he was going to paint his house.
Correct: Larry was going fishing, or he was going to paint his house.

A clause or a phrase often introduces a sentence. Introductory phrases or clauses should be set off by a comma. If the introductory element is very short, the comma is optional. Here are some examples.

However, there are other options you may want to consider.
When the deicer hit the plane's wing, the ice began to melt.
To get a driver's license, go to the motor vehicle bureau.
It doesn't matter what you want, you have to take what you get.

Parenthetical expressions interrupt the flow of a sentence. Set off the parenthetical expression with commas. Do not set off expressions that are essential to understanding the sentence. Here are some examples.

Tom, an old friend, showed up at my house the other day.

I was traveling on a train, in car 8200, on my way to Florida.

John and Ron, who are seniors, went on break to Florida.
[Use a comma. The phrase "who are seniors" is extra information.]

All the students who are seniors take an additional course.
[Don't use a comma. The phrase "who are seniors" is essential information.]

Commas are used to set off items in a list or series. Here are some examples.

Jed is interested in computers, surfing, and fishing.
[Notice the comma before the conjunction *and*.]

Mario drives a fast, red car.
[The sentence would make sense with *and* in place of the comma.]

Andy hoped for a bright, sunny, balmy day.
[The sentence would make sense with *and* in place of the commas.]

Lucy had a pale green dress.
[The sentence would not make sense with *and*. The word *pale* modifies *green*. Don't use a comma.]

Randy will go to the movies, pick up some groceries, and then go home.

Practice

1. I had a slow day yesterday, but I worked hard in my junior year.

2. Passing calculus seems a difficult, but achievable, result.

3. After making the sandwich, I looked for some pickles, but the jar was empty.

4. Write an outline first and be sure to leave enough time to write the essay.

5. In the attic I found some old clothes, an old trunk, and a shoe.

6. Chad, Blaire, and Ryan have advanced degrees but they are still children at heart.

7. Using a computer the Computer-Based PPST tests reading, writing, and arithmetic.

8. Either walk the dog or wash the dishes.

9. Every pilot, who has flown over 20 missions, receives an award.

10. Each time I ate lunch at home, my mother made liverwurst sandwiches.

Answers on pages 69–70.

Semicolon and Colon

THE SEMICOLON (;)

Use the semicolon to connect main clauses not connected by a conjunction. Include a semicolon with very long clauses connected by a conjunction. Here are some examples.

> The puck was dropped; the hockey game began.
> The puck was dropped, and the hockey game began.
> The general manager of the hockey team was not sure what should be done about the player who was injured during the game; but he did know that the player's contract stipulated that his pay would continue whether he was able to play or not.

THE COLON (:)

Use the colon after a main clause to introduce a list. Here are some examples.

> Liz kept these items in her car: spare tire, jack, flares, and a blanket.
> Liz kept a spare tire, jack, flares, and a blanket in her car.

Practice

Directions: Correct any semicolon or colon errors. Some sentences may be correct.

1. Pack these other things for camp; a bathing suit, some socks, and a shirt.

2. In your wallet put: your camp information card and your bus pass.

3. I have one thing left to do; say good-bye.

4. We went to the store; and the parking lot was filled with cars.

5. We fought our way through the crowds, the store was even more crowded than the parking lot.

Answers on page 70.

Period, Question Mark, Exclamation Point

THE PERIOD (.)

Use a period to end every sentence, unless the sentence is a direct question, a strong command, or an interjection.

You will do well on the PPST test.

THE QUESTION MARK (?)

Use a question mark to end every sentence that is a direct question.

What is the passing score for the PPST test?

THE EXCLAMATION POINT (!)

Use an exclamation point to end every sentence that is a strong command or interjection. Do not overuse exclamation points.

Interjection: Pass that test!
Command: Avalanche, head for cover!

Practice

Directions: Correct any punctuation errors.

1. I was so worn out after swimming!

2. Avalanche.

3. Who said that!

4. Warning. The danger signal blared in the background.

5. I can't believe this is the last day of camp?

Answers on pages 70–71.

Answers for English Practice

Nouns, page 38

1. sheaves
2. deer
3. fries
4. lunches
5. knees
6. ladies
7. octopi
8. echoes
9. feet
10. halves

Verbs, page 41

    drove
1. Ryan ~~driven~~ to Florida.

2. Refereeing soccer games is not work.
   [No tense errors.]

    rode
3. Chad ~~ride~~ to the game with his team last week.
   [The words *last week* indicate that the verb must be past tense.]

    run
4. Why did Mary ~~ran~~ her errands now?

    spoken
5. I have ~~speak~~ to my teacher about the grade.

    paddles
6. Carl ~~paddled~~ across the river every Saturday.
   [Use the present tense because it is a regular event.]

    had thrown
7. Blaire ~~thrown~~ out the ball for the players to use.

    lose
8. Joann will ~~lost~~ her bag if she leaves it in the store.

9. Bob is standing on a stool next to the green table.
   [No tense errors.]

   began
10. Liz ~~begun~~ to grasp the depth of her happiness.

Tense Shift, page 41

1. Lisa already went to the North Pole but she is not going there again.
   [No tense shift errors.]

   took
2. Dennis ~~will take~~ his airline tickets with him because he is leaving for his flight.

3. The runner gasped as she crosses the finish line.

   The runner gasped as she crossed the finish line.
   The runner gasps as she crosses the finish line.

   play
4. I like to hear music so I ~~played~~ the clarinet.

   wants
5. Chris ~~wanted~~ to be a producer so he puts in long hours every day.

6. Bertha sews five hours a day because she will need her dress by next month.
   [No tense shift errors.]

7. The car turns over and then bounced down the hill.

   The car turned over and then bounced down the hill.
   The car turns over and then bounces down the hill.

8. Lois handed over her money because she wants to buy the computer.

   Lois hands over her money because she wants to buy the computer.
   Lois handed over her money because she wanted to buy the computer.

9. The captain wandered out on the deck as she calls to her friends on shore.

   The captain wandered out on the deck as she called to her friends on shore.
   The captain wanders out on the deck as she calls to her friends on shore.

10. The sun sets in the west as the moon rose in the east.

    The sun set in the west as the moon rose in the east.
    The sun sets in the west as the moon rises in the east.

Pronouns, pages 43–44

   He
1. ~~His~~ was the best table tennis player.

Who
2. ~~Whom~~ was the worst table tennis player?

3. Where are the table tennis balls?
   [No errors.]

is
4. Before the game everyone ~~are~~ going to choose teams.

us
5. The names of the winning team are sent to ~~we~~.

They
6. ~~Them~~ are the best table tennis team.

Ron's
7. Ron and Jeff wanted to use ~~his~~ skates.
   [Jeff's, or any other name, could be used in place of Ron's.]

the skates
8. Jeff went to get ~~them~~.
   [Other nouns that make sense in this context could be used in place of skates.]

the pillows
9. The couch looked different, depending on how ~~they~~ were arranged.

10. Bob won most of his table tennis games.
    [No errors.]

her or his
11. The student waited for ~~their~~ school bus to come.

it doesn't
12. Either of the buses can arrive on time if ~~they don't~~ break down.

its
13. The book was most interesting near ~~her~~ beginning.

the
14. She read the book to find ~~her~~ most interesting parts.

15. I am the winner; victory is ours.

    I am the winner; victory is mine.
    We are the winners; victory is ours.

16. His friends got out of the car, and he went over to talk to them.
    [No errors.]

17. The rain clouds moved toward the pool, and the swimmers tried to wish it away.

   The rain cloud moved toward the pool, and the swimmers tried to wish it away.
   The rain clouds moved toward the pool, and the swimmers tried to wish them away.

        his
18. Was Les disappointed that ~~him~~ team did not win?

    Who
19. ~~Whom~~ has more experience than Nicky does?

20. You play better after you have experience.
   [No errors.]

Subject-Verb Agreement, page 45

      is
1. The chess set ~~are~~ still on the shelf.

           is
2. The shortest route to the college ~~are~~ shown in the catalog.

      drives
3. The golf pro ~~drive~~ a golf cart every day.

      walk
4. Derek and Ann ~~walks~~ every morning.

        add
5. The tropical birds in the tree ~~adds~~ a festive air to the occasion.

        walks
6. No one, not even Rick or Ronnie, ~~walk~~ to school today.

       are
7. Do you know who they ~~is~~?

    prepares
8. Ron ~~prepare~~ a paper for submission to the committee.

          show
9. The 15 employees of the coffee house ~~shows~~ up each day at 6:00 A.M.

         improves
10. Each person who takes the 12 steps ~~improve~~ his or her view.

Adjectives and Adverbs, pages 47–48

                                       really
1. The view of the Grand Canyon was ~~real~~ spectacular.

                                       well
2. The trainer said the dog behaved very ~~good~~ today.

Unfortunately
3. ~~Unfortunate~~, the tickets for the concert were sold out.

               smoothly
4. Things went ~~smooth~~.

                 extreme
5. The judge took ~~extremely~~ exception to the defendant's actions.

                                                               carefully
6. The accident was silly, particularly since driving more ~~careful~~ would have avoided the whole thing.

7. But the reviews said the performance was truly horrible.
[No adjective or adverb errors.]

8. The manager conveniently forgot that she promised the employee a raise.
[No adjective or adverb errors.]

                                     really
9. The bonus was a welcome surprise; it was a ~~real~~ large check.

                well   **badly**
10. I didn't do ~~good~~, but didn't do ~~bad~~ either.

Comparison, page 48

               happiest
1. Leon was the ~~happier~~ chef in the restaurant.

2. But some of the people eating in the restaurant were happier than Leon.
[No error.]

               fastest
3. The jet was the ~~faster~~ plane at the airport.

               faster
4. John was the ~~fastest~~ of the twins.

               tallest
5. The ~~taller~~ of the apartment buildings is under repair.

lighter
6. The ~~lightest~~ of the two weights is missing.

7. Lonnie was among the most creative students in the school.
   [No error.]

   less
8. Ron is the ~~least~~ able of the two drivers.

9. His shoe size is the smallest in his class.
   [No error.]

10. She was the more capable of the two referees.
    [No error.]

Misplaced and Dangling Modifiers, page 49

1. Les was reading his book through glasses with dirty lenses.
   [No modifier errors.]

2. Jim left work early to go to the doctor on the train.

   Jim left work early to go on a train to the doctor.

3. The first train car was crowded; which had to go to the next car.

   The first train car was crowded; someone (he) (she) had to go to the next car.

4. Ron's car ran out of gas when on the way to the store.

   Ron's car ran out of gas when he was on the way to the store.
   [Many other substitutions are possible for *he was*.]

5. Zena was jogging, when caused her to fall.

   Zena was jogging, when a hole caused her to fall.
   [Many other substitutions are possible for *a hole*.]

6. Derek wrapped the flowers and put them in the delivery van with colorful paper.

   Derek wrapped the flowers with colorful paper and put them in the delivery van.

7. Which bus stops at the corner where the stop sign is?
   [No modifier errors.]

8. Fran is going on the plane, which is just pulling up to the gate.
   [No modifier errors.]

9. Lisa bought a shirt in the store, which was expensive.

   Lisa bought an expensive shirt in the store.
   Lisa bought a shirt in an expensive store.
   Lisa bought an expensive shirt in an expensive store.

10. The car turned around and the headlights shone quickly into the garage.

    The car turned around quickly and the headlights shone into the garage.

Run-On Sentences and Comma Splices, page 50

There are three ways to remedy run-on sentence errors and comma splice errors. You can create two sentences, put a comma and a conjunction between the clauses, or put a semicolon between the two clauses. Only one of these options is shown in the answers.

1. It will be tomorrow before the sea is calm enough to go out.
   [No errors.]

2. It started to rain unexpectedly; the boaters were soaked.

3. But right now my sneakers are soaking wet; the towel is too wet to help me.

4. The Marine Police sounded the siren; the boat stopped immediately.

5. I put the sneakers next to the fire to dry, although they started to steam after a while.
   [No errors.]

6. The Coast Guard monitors boats as they enter the river; they use the data to monitor water pollution.

7. I like to use my compass when I go out on the boat.
   [No errors.]

8. When the boat breaks down, Liz calls Sea Tow.
   [No errors.]

9. The fire went out; the sun came up.

10. Splashing through the waves, the water skier was covered with salt spray.
    [No errors.]

Sentence Fragments, page 52

1. A golf bag, golf clubs, and golf balls. That's what she needed to play.

   A golf bag, golf clubs, and golf balls were what she needed to play.

2. As the rocket prepared for blast-off. Mary saw birds flying in the distance.

   The rocket prepared for blast-off. Mary saw birds flying in the distance.
   As the rocket prepared for blast-off, Mary saw birds flying in the distance.

3. Jim is mowing the lawn. Then, the mower stopped.
   [No sentence fragment errors.]

4. The lawn looked lush and green. Like a golf course.

   The lawn looked lush and green, like a golf course.

5. The polar bears swept across the ice. Like white ghosts in fur jackets.

   The polar bears swept across the ice, like white ghosts in fur jackets.

6. Jim looked across at the igloo. Like an ice fort, it stood a lonely vigil.
   [No sentence fragment errors.]

7. Astronauts and their equipment went by. These were the people who would go into space.
   [No sentence fragment errors.]

8. This was what Joe had been waiting for. To graduate from college.

   This was what Joe had been waiting for, to graduate from college.

9. To be finished with this test. That's what I'm waiting for.

   To be finished with this test is what I'm waiting for.

10. The test finished and done. The papers graded and good.

    The tests were finished and done.
    The papers were graded and good.

Parallelism, page 53

                                      get
1. I have to get to work, but first I have to ~~find my way~~ to breakfast.

2. The road was dry; the day was hot and sultry.
   [No parallel form errors.]

3. Jane likes to eat and go shopping when she is at the mall.
   [No parallel form errors.]

                                             sound technician
4. April chose to be a cameraperson rather than to be a ~~technician who works the sound board.~~

5. Since I have not heard from you, I decided to write this letter.
   [No parallel form errors. The conjunction *since* shows subordination.]

6. Although she had driven the road before, Sally proceeded slowly, keeping her eye on the yellow line.
   [No parallel form errors. The conjunction *although* shows subordination.]

                                                                               tree branches

7. The tree withstood the hurricane, but ~~the branches on the tree~~ snapped off.

8. His work on the Board of Education revealed his dedication to the community.
   [No parallel form errors.]

9. Cars, taxis, and buses were my transportation to the airport.
   [No parallel form errors.]

                                                                 class preparation

10. The subject matter and the ~~preparation for class~~ created an excellent lesson.

Diction, pages 55–56

1. Many <u>infectious</u> diseases, including pneumonia and swelling in cuts, are caused by bacteria.
   Infectious means a disease caused by bacteria. While the disease may be unfortunate, the context of the sentence calls for a word that means *caused by bacteria*.

2. Sigmund Freud's views of sexuality had become <u>well known</u>, and the country entered the sexual revolution.
   Well known means known by many people. *Universal* means known everywhere, which does not fit the context of this sentence.

3. After crossing the land bridge near the Bering Strait, groups of Native Americans <u>eventually</u> spread throughout all of North, Central, and South America.
   Eventually means over a period of time. The other words do not make sense in this context.

4. During the early 1500s Cortez and Pizarro opened up Central America to the Spanish who began <u>importing</u> slaves from Africa.
   Importing means to bring in. Exporting means to send out, which does not fit the context of the sentence.

5. The Stamp Act requiring every legal paper to carry a tax stamp was vehemently <u>protested</u> and eventually repealed by England.
   The act could only be *protested* in this context. It was not *denied*, and it does not make sense to say it was *vehemently* denied.

The circled phrases make the sentence too wordy.

6. <u>No goal is more noble</u>—<u>no feat more revealing</u>—than the (strikingly) brave <u>exploration of space.</u>

7. As many as a ton of bananas may have spoiled when the ship was stuck (and delayed) in the Panama Canal.

8. He was concerned about crossing the bridge, but the officer said that it was all right to cross (and he need not worry).

9. A professional golfer told the (novice) beginning golfer that professional instruction or more practice improves most golfers' scores.

10. The soccer player's slight strain from the shot on goal (that won the game) led to a pulled muscle that would keep her from playing the next match.

The circled words are homonym errors.

11. He went to the bird's nest near the river, only (too) realize he missed its (assent).

12. The rider pulled back on the horse's (reign) before the (whether) turned rainy.

13. The (whether) turned rainy as he led the hikers on (there) ascent.

14. The (lessen) was clear; it was (fare), but not easy to accept.

15. (They're) (board) relatives were not (fare) (too) her father.

Refer to page 55 for a list of idioms.

with
16. Her grades had everything to do ~~of~~ her efforts.

at
17. Joanie expected him to wait ~~to~~ the house until she arrived home.

18. She could spend months absorbed in her studies.
    [No idiom error.]

from
19. The two coaches differ significantly ~~with~~ each other's style.

as
20. That person is wearing the same coat ~~from~~ you.

Commas, page 58

1. I had a slow day yesterday, but I worked hard in my junior year.
   [No comma errors.]

2. Passing calculus seems a difficult, but achievable, result.
   [No comma errors.]

3. After making the sandwich, I looked for some pickles, but the jar was empty.
   [No comma errors.]

4. Write an outline first, and be sure to leave enough time to write the essay.
   [Add a comma before the conjunction to separate the two clauses.]

5. In the attic I found some old clothes, an old trunk, and a shoe.
   [No comma errors.]

6. Chad, Blaire, and Ryan have advanced degrees, but they are still children at heart.
   [Add a comma to separate the clauses.]

7. Using a computer, the Computer-Based PPST tests reading, writing, and arithmetic.
   [Add a comma to set off the introductory phrase.]

8. Either walk the dog or wash the dishes.
   [No comma errors.]

9. Every pilot who has flown over 20 missions receives an award.
   [Remove the commas.]

10. Each time I ate lunch at home my mother made liverwurst sandwiches.
    [Remove the comma.]

Semicolons and Colons, page 59

1. Pack these other things for camp: a bathing suit, some socks, and a shirt.
   [Replace the semicolon with a colon.]

2. In your wallet put your camp information card and your bus pass.
   [Remove the colon.]

3. I have one thing left to do: say good-bye.
   [Replace the semicolon with a colon.]

4. We went to the store, and the parking lot was filled with cars.
   [Replace the semicolon with a comma.]

5. We fought our way through the crowds; the store was even more crowded than the parking lot.
   [Replace the comma with a semicolon.]

Period, Question Mark, and Exclamation Point, page 60

1. I was so worn out after swimming.
   [Change the exclamation point to a period.]

2. Avalanche!
   [Change the period to an exclamation point.]

3. Who said that?
   [Change the exclamation point to a question mark.]

4. Warning! The danger signal blared in the background.
   [Change the period to an exclamation point.]

5. I can't believe this is the last day of camp.
   [Change the question mark to a period.]

Strategies for Taking the Multiple-Choice Writing Test

This section shows you how to pass the multiple-choice writing portion of the Paper-Based PPST and Computer-Based PPST writing test.

TYPES OF QUESTIONS

The multiple-choice writing test gives you a chance to show what you know about grammar, sentence structure, and word usage. You should be familiar with the subjects covered in the English Review section.

The following topics may be particularly important:

- subject-verb and noun-pronoun agreement
- correct verb tense
- the best word or phrase for a sentence
- parallel verb forms and parallel sentence structure
- sentence fragments and wordy sentences
- distinguishing clear and exact sentences from awkward or ambiguous ones

You may be able to get the correct answer from your sense or feel about the sentence. If you are someone who has an intuitive grasp of English usage, you should rely on your intuition as you complete this section of the tests.

There are two types of questions on the Paper-Based PPST and the Computer-Based PPST. These examples are from the Review Questions that follow.

Usage

You are shown a sentence with four parts underlined and lettered (A), (B), (C), and (D). There is a fifth choice: (E) No error. You choose the letter of the flawed part or E if there is no error. You do not have to explain what the error is or what makes the other parts correct. No sentence contains more than one error. You just have to recognize the error or realize that there is no error.

EXAMPLE

Every week, Doug took a child from the
    (A)   (B)

class on a visit to the art room until he
             (C)   (D)

got tired. No error.
          (E)

Sentence Correction

You are shown a sentence with one part underlined. Choice (A) repeats the underlined selection exactly. Choices (B) through (E) give suggested changes for the underlined part. You choose the letter of the best choice that does not change the meaning of the original sentence. If the original is best, choose (A). Otherwise, select one of the suggested changes.

EXAMPLE

Many times a shopper will prefer value to price.

- (A) to price
- (B) instead of price
- (C) rather than price
- (D) more than price
- (E) than price

STRATEGIES FOR PASSING THE MULTIPLE-CHOICE TEST

Read Carefully

In this section, it is often small details that count. Read each sentence carefully. Read the whole sentence, and not just the underlined sections. Remember that an underlined section by itself can look fine but be incorrect in the whole sentence or passage. Read each sentence a few times until you get a sense for its rhythm and flow.

This Is a Test of Written English

Evaluate each sentence as written English. Do not apply the more informal rules of spoken English.

Don't Focus on Punctuation

Use the English rules discussed in the English Review section. However, don't be overly concerned about punctuation. Punctuation rules are seldom tested.

Eliminate and Guess

Eliminate the answers you know are incorrect. If you can't pick out the correct answer, guess from among the remaining choices.

TIP

Remember, the test booklet is yours. You can write on the passage as well as on the question and answers. If you are taking the Computer-Based PPST, be sure to make good use of the scrap paper provided.

Review Questions

USAGE

Directions: Choose the letter that indicates an error, or choose (E) for no error.

1. Every week, Doug took a child from
    (A)   (B)
    the class on a visit to the art room
               (C)
    until he got tired. No error.
      (D)   (E)

2. Doug walks two miles every day
         (A)   (B)
    and he rubbed off the dirt on
                (C)
    his shoes as he went. No error.
     (D)   (E)

3. Jim and Tom, the salesman,
              (A)
    was doing a good job directing the
     (B)   (C)
    under twelve soccer league. No error.
     (D)   (E)

4. The students were greatly effected
       (A)   (B)   (C)
    by the retirement of a very popular
                (D)
    teacher. No error.
        (E)

5. The Rathburn is a high rated and
               (A)
    singularly successful
        (B)
    Italian restaurant near the beach in
       (C)   (D)
    Avalon. No error.
       (E)

SENTENCE CORRECTION

Directions: Choose the letter of the best choice for the underlined section, without changing the meaning of the sentence. If the original is best, choose (A). Otherwise, select one of the suggested changes.

6. Many times a shopper will prefer value to price.

    (A) to price
    (B) instead of price
    (C) rather than price
    (D) more than price
    (E) than price

7. The tug boat strained against the ship, revved up its engines and was able to maneuver the ship into the middle of the channel.

    (A) and was able to maneuver the ship into the middle of the channel.
    (B) and moves the ship into the middle of the channel.
    (C) moving the ship into the middle of the channel.

   (D) and moved the ship into the middle of the channel.
   (E) with the ship moved into the middle of the channel.

8. After it had snowed steadily for days, the snow plows and snow blowers <u>most important priorities</u>.

   (A) most important priorities.
   (B) were ready for action.
   (C) concentrated on the most important priorities.

   (D) most significant priorities.
   (E) most frequent difficulties.

9. The zoo opened for <u>the day, the children ran</u> to the exhibits.

   (A) the day, the children ran
   (B) the day. the children ran
   (C) the day; the children ran
   (D) the day: the children ran
   (E) the day the children ran

Answers Explained

USAGE

1. **(D)** Pronoun error—it is not clear which noun the pronoun *he* refers to.

2. **(A)** Verb tense error—the verb *walks* should be *walked* to agree with the verb *rubbed*.

3. **(B)** Number error—the subject, *Jim and Tom*, is plural. The verb *was* should be the plural verb *were*.

4. **(C)** Diction error—the word *effected* should be replaced by the word *affected*.

5. **(A)** Adjective-adverb error—the adjective *high* should be changed to the adverb *highly*.

SENTENCE CORRECTION

6. **(A)** No error—Always choose (A) if there is no error.

7. **(D)** Parallelism error—Choice (D) maintains the parallel development of the sentence.

8. **(C)** Sentence fragment error—The original choice is a sentence fragment. There is no verb for the subject *snow plows and snow blowers*. Choice (B) is grammatically correct but changes the meaning of the sentence.

9. **(C)** Run-on sentence error—Use a semicolon to separate two independent clauses.

Strategies for Taking the Essay Writing Test

FORM OF THE TEST

You will be given one essay topic. You will have 30 minutes to write the essay. Your essay is graded holistically by two raters using the six-point scale described on page 36. Holistic grading means that the raters grade you based on their informed sense about your writing and not on a detailed analysis of the essay.

STRATEGIES FOR PASSING THE ESSAY TEST

Read the Topic

Take a few minutes to read and understand the topic. Part of your rating will depend on how well you address the topic.

Make Notes and Sketch a Brief Outline

On the Paper-Based PPST, the page listing the topic has room for notes. On the Computer-Based PPST, use the scrap paper. Think for a few minutes and take up to five more minutes to write a brief outline showing how you will structure each of the three or four paragraphs in the essay.

Use the time writing the outline to plan your essay. Use the time working on the essay to write well.

Follow These Rules as You Write

You should have a little more than 15 minutes to write your essay. Plan to write three or four paragraphs. Essays scored 6 are usually longer than those scored 5 or less. Your essay should be a maximum of 350 words.

This does not mean that longer is necessarily better. It does mean that you will need at least four well-written paragraphs to receive a 6 and three or four well-written paragraphs to receive a 5.

Compose and write the topic sentence for your first paragraph. Write two more sentences that develop the topic sentence. These sentences may contain examples, illustrations, and other supporting facts or arguments. You can close your paragraph with a summary sentence.

If you follow this plan for the remaining paragraphs, you should be able to get a 4 or higher.

Refer to your outline as you write.

TIP

Use the rules of grammar as you write your essay. Punctuate as carefully as you can but do not spend an inordinate amount of time on punctuation. Raters will often ignore minor grammatical or spelling errors if the essay is well developed.

Steps for Writing Passing Essays

Follow these steps to write a passing essay. Remember, you have 30 minutes for both the Paper-Based PPST essay and for the Computer-Based PPST essay.

1. **Understand the topic** (2 minutes).
    A topic is introduced and then described in more detail. Read the topic carefully to ensure that you understand it completely.

2. **Choose a thesis statement. Write it down** (2 minutes).
Readers expect you to have a point of view about the topic. Choose yours; make sure it addresses the entire topic, and stick to it.

3. **Use the Paper-Based PPST test booklet or the Computer-Based PPST scrap paper to write a brief outline** (4 minutes).
Write a brief outline summarizing the following essay elements.

- Thesis statement
- Introduction
- Topic sentence and details for each paragraph
- Conclusion

Use this time to plan your essay.

4. **Write or type the essay** (18 minutes).
Essays rated in the upper third typically have three or four paragraphs totaling 150 to 250 words. Writing an essay this long does not guarantee a passing score, but most passing essays are about this long. Use this time to write well.

5. **Proofread and edit** (4 minutes).
Leave four minutes to read your essay over and correct any errors in usage, spelling, or punctuation. The readers understand that your essay is a first draft and they expect to see corrections on the Paper-Based PPST essay.

Apply the Steps

Let's see how to apply these steps for a particular essay topic. Remember, there are many different thesis statements and essays that would receive a passing score.

ESSAY TOPIC

Some people say that machines cause difficulty for people. Others say that machines help people.

Choose one of these positions. Give a specific example of a machine that causes difficulty or one that helps people. Write an essay that explains how the machine you chose causes difficulty for people or helps people.

1. **Understand the topic.**
The topic is about machines. I have to decide whether to write about machines that cause difficulty for people OR about machines that help people. I have to give a specific example of a machine that causes difficulty or a machine that helps.

I've got to stick to this topic.

For this essay, I'm going to choose machines that help people.

A complete response to the topic is an essay about a machine that helps people. There are many machines to choose from. An incomplete response will significantly lower the score.

2. **Choose a thesis statement. Write it down.**
This important step sets the stage for your entire essay. Work through this section actively. Write down the names of several machines that help people. There is no one correct answer, so it does not have to be an exhaustive list.

>Computers
>Escalator
>Car
>Heart-lung machine
>Fax machine

Add your own machines to this list.

_____

_____

_____

_____

I'll choose <u>heart-lung machines</u>.

Now I write how, what, and why heart-lung machines help people.

>How: Circulate blood in place of the heart.
>What: Replaces the heart during heart surgery.
>Why: The heart is unable to pump blood when it is being operated on.

Write the choice from your list of machines. _____

Write how, what, and why the machine you chose helps people.

>How: _____
>What: _____
>Why: _____

Thesis statement

My thesis statement is:

>**Heart-lung machines are machines that help people by taking the place of the heart during heart surgery.**

The thesis statement identifies the heart-lung machine as a machine that helps people and explains the basis for my choice of the heart-lung machine. Both parts are needed for an effective thesis statement.

3. **Write a brief outline.**
   Here is my outline.

   - Introduction, including the thesis statement.
   - A heart-lung machine saves lives.
   - People would die if the machines were not available.
   - The machine circulates and filters blood during operations.
     Special membranes filter the blood, removing impurities.
   - The heart can literally stop while the heart-lung machine is in use.
     Doctors have to restart the heart.
   - Conclusion.

   My outline consists of an introduction, topic sentences and supporting details for three paragraphs, and a conclusion. That's five paragraphs in all.

   Now write your own thesis statement and an outline on the heart-lung machine and how it helps people.

   _____

   _____

   _____

   _____

   _____

4. **Write or type the essay.**
   I wrote an outline to plan my essay. I am going to rely on that plan as I concentrate on writing well.

   Use a separate piece of paper, or a word processor.

   Write your own essay about the heart-lung machine—a machine that helps people.

5. **Proofread and edit.**
   Revise, proofread, and edit your essay.

   Remember that readers expect to see changes on the handwritten Paper-Based PPST essay.

Review Sample Essays

You will find four rated sample essays on this topic on pages 79–81. Compare your essay to the samples.

Practice

Write, proofread, and edit an essay on this topic, but for the machine you chose on page 76. Show your essay to an English professor or an experienced essay evaluator. Ask that person to evaluate your essay using the samples and the rating scale on page 36 and make recommendations for improving your writing.

Sample Essays

ESSAY 1

This essay would likely receive a total score of 1 or 2 out of 6. The essay shows limited writing ability, and it is only long enough to support a rating above the lower third. The essay is not adequately developed, and it does not always address the question. This essay does not provide adequate supporting details, and it contains serious and repeated errors in grammar and usage.

> I think that machines are mostly helpful to people,
> Look at the heart-lung machine which were a medical miracle. Heart lung machines are use in hospitals all over the place. Doctors use this machine while doing surgery. Heart lung machines keep people alive during surgery and they use them to do surgry. A hospital is not a nice place to be at.
> Some people say that their are too many bypass surgerys done every year and this may cause more problems than it fixes. However, lots of people would die without the machine. Its a good thing that the heart lung machine was invented.

ESSAY 2

This essay would likely receive a total score of 2 or 3 out of 6. The essay shows some writing ability, but it is not long enough to support a rating in the middle third. The essay is somewhat well developed, and it does provide some supporting details. But the essay contains many errors in grammar, usage, and mechanics.

> Overall, machines are mostly helpful to people. A heart lung machine is an examples of a machine that helped. Heart lung machines are use in hospitals all over the world. They get use every day. People are hook up to them when they are having surgery like if they are having open heart surgery.
> I will now present one way heart lung machines are in use. Once we didn't have heart lung machines to help a doctor. When the machine was invent we see lots of changes in surgry that a doctor can do. The doctor can operate during the person heart not work. My grandmother went to the hospital for have surgry and they use the machine. Where she would been without the machine.
> And the machine keep blood move through the body. The doctor can take their time to fix a person heart while they are laying their on the operating room. I know someone who work in a hospital and they say didn't know how it was possible befour machine.
> Last, that machine clean a bodies blood as it floes through. The blood won't poison the person whose blood it is. But it wood be better if body clean its own blood. A body better machine. I did tell you how the machine work and what it did. The machine can save a lifes.

ESSAY 3

This essay would likely receive a total score of 4, or perhaps 5, out of 6. The essay is fairly well written, and it is long enough to support a rating in the upper third. The essay is fairly well developed, and it directly addresses the question with a number of appropriate supporting details. There are significant errors in grammar and usage. The writer intended the heading to be helpful, but it does not help the rater understand the essay topic.

   This is what this essay looked like after editing. Note the editorial changes the student made during the editing process. This is the essay that raters would actually see. The raters expect to see these changes and marks.

MACHINES AND PEOPLE

Overall, machines are helpful to people. I have chosen the heart lung machine as an example of a machine that helps people. Heart lung machined are a ~~medicine~~ ^{Medical} miracle. They are used in hospitals all over the world. Heart lung machines are used during open heart surgry_e to circulate a patient's blood and clean the blood. These machines can save lots of ~~lifes~~ lives.

   Heart-lung machines have made open heart surgery possible. Before they were invented, many people died of disaese or during surgery. Surgery would not have been impossible before then. And many people are alive today because of them. Besides surgery can now go on for hours. Sometimes the surgry can last as long as 12 hours. The heart lung machine makes things ~~very~~ possible and saves lives.

   Heart lung machines circulate blood ~~thru~~ ^{through} the body. It pumps like a heart. The heart can stop and the heart lung machine will pump instead. Then the blood moving through the body just like the heart ~~is~~ pumping. So the blood gets to all the veins.

   It is ~~how~~ unbelievable ~~why~~ ^{how} the heart lung machine can work and keep people from dying. The heart lung machine can clean a person's blood. All the bad stuff gets taken out of the blood before it goes back into the body. That way the body won't get poison. I know of someone who had their blood cleaned by the machine while they were operated on.

   The person was ~~unconscience~~ ^{unconscious}. The doctor fixed his heart. Since the machine was going the persons heart was stopped. The doctor had to start it up again. It was pretty scary to think about that happening to a person. But the machine took the bad stuff out of the blood and the person lives today.

   To conclu~~sion~~^{de}, I believe that the heart lung machine is great for people who need open heart surgery. It pumps and cleans their blood too. They are a medical miracle.

ESSAY 4

This essay would likely receive a total score of 5 or 6 out of 6. This essay is very well written, and it is long enough to support a rating in the upper third. The essay is very well developed, and it directly addresses the question. It provides excellent supporting details and is free of all but the most minor errors. The heading helps the rater understand the essay topic.

THE HEART LUNG MACHINE – PROOF THAT OVERALL MACHINES HELP PEOPLE

In my opinion, machines are more likely to help people than to cause trouble. I chose the heart-lung machine as an example of a helpful machine. In this essay I will explain what the heart-lung machine does and how it is helpful.

Every day the heart-lung machine saves someone's life. The heart-lung machine is a wonderful machine that makes open-heart surgery possible by pumping and cleaning a person's blood. Surgeons use the machine during open heart surgery. Each day we walk by someone who is alive because of the heart-lung machine. Each day throughout the world skilled surgeons perform difficult surgery with the aid of a heart-lung machine.

The heart-lung machine makes open-heart surgery possible. Open-heart surgery means the doctor is operating inside of the heart. In order to operate on the inside of the heart, the flow of blood must be stopped. But without blood flow the patient would die. Researchers worked for decades to find a way to keep a patient alive while the hearty was stopped. They were eventually successful and they named the machine a heart-lung machine. The first heart lung machines were probably very primitive, but today's machines are very sophisticated.

The heart-lung machine circulates blood while the heart is not pumping. The blood is taken from the body into one side of the machine and pumped back into the body though the other side. The blood pumped back into the body travels through the circulatory system.

However, just pumping blood is not enough. As blood passes through a person's body, the body uses oxygen stored in the blood. Blood starts from the heart full of oxygen and returns to the heart without much oxygen. The lungs take in oxygen and pass that oxygen on to the blood. But during surgery the heart-lung machine does the lung's work and puts oxygen in the blood as the blood passes through the machine.

The heart-lung machine makes open-heart surgery possible. The machine circulates and oxygenates a person's blood while the heart is stopped. Without the machine, many people would die from heart disease or would die during surgery. The heart-lung machine is a machine that helps people by keeping them alive and holds the promise of even more amazing machines to come.

Targeted Writing Test

This targeted test is designed to help you practice the strategies presented in this chapter. For that reason, questions may have a different emphasis than the actual test, and the actual test will certainly be more complete.

Mark your choice, then check your answers.

Use the strategies on pages 71–72.

PART A

Directions: Choose the letter that indicates an error, or choose (E) for no error.

1. Kitty and Harry's anniversary will fall on
    (A)   (B)
   Father's Day this year. No error.
    (C)   (D)   (E)

2. The trees leaves provide a fall festival
    (A)   (B)
   called "Fall Foliage"
        (C)
   in most New England states. No error.
        (D)   (E)

3. Most colleges require
    (A)   (B)
   a specific number
        (C)
   of academic credits for admission.
                (D)
   No error.
    (E)

4. My brother Robert
    (A)
   loves to read novels but would enjoy
        (B)   (C)
   good mystery's more. No error.
        (D)   (E)

5. Louise had lay her mitt on the bench
    (A)   (B)   (C)
   when she got a glass of water.
            (D)
   No error.
    (E)

6. It seems to me that I had spoke to my
            (A)   (B)
   landlord about the crack in the ceiling
                (C)
   about two months ago. No error.
            (D)   (E)

7. The committee on fund-raising
        (A)   (B)
   gathers in the hall,
        (C)
   but Joe went to the room. No error.
            (D)   (E)

8. The administrator wanted
        (A)   (B)
   all lesson plan books
            (C)
   handed in by Friday. No error.
            (D)   (E)

9. Behind the tree, she was reading a book,
            (A)   (B)
   eating a banana, and she waited for the
            (C)   (D)
   sunset. No error.
        (E)

10. Is Washington, D. C. closer to Arlington
    (A)   (B)   (C)
    Cemetery than Charleston? No error.
            (D)   (E)

11. The student <u>would not</u> <u>do nothing</u>
          (A)   (B)
<u>to redeem</u> himself
   (C)
<u>in the eyes of the principal.</u> <u>No error.</u>
        (D)   (E)

12. <u>Good teachers</u> are <u>distinguished</u> by
      (A)   (B)
their <u>enthusiasm</u> and <u>organization.</u>
       (C)   (D)
<u>No error.</u>
 (E)

13. The <u>principle</u> of the middle school
     (A)   (B)
<u>wanted</u> to reorganize
 (C)
the lunch schedule. <u>No error.</u>
     (D)   (E)

14. <u>Grandmother's shopping list</u> <u>consisted of</u>
        (A)   (B)
mustard, green beans, <u>buttermilk,</u> and
              (C)
<u>included some eggs.</u> <u>No error.</u>
    (D)   (E)

15. Unless <u>you arm yourself</u> with
        (A)
insect <u>repellent,</u> you <u>will get</u> a <u>bight.</u>
     (B)   (C)   (D)
<u>No error.</u>
 (E)

16. Graduation <u>exercises</u> will be <u>held on</u> __
           (A)   (B)
<u>Friday</u> __ June 19th, at <u>7:00</u> P.M. <u>No error.</u>
  (C)   (D)   (E)

17. <u>With a quick glance</u> the <u>noisy room</u>
   (A)   (B)   (C)
<u>was silenced.</u> <u>No error.</u>
  (D)   (E)

18. <u>Without even trying,</u> <u>the sprinter</u>
     (A)   (B)
<u>passed</u> the world record
 (C)
<u>by five tenths</u> of a second. <u>No error.</u>
   (D)   (E)

19. <u>Prior to</u> the <u>passage of PL 94-142,</u>
   (A)   (B)
special education <u>students</u>
       (C)
<u>were not unrepresented legally.</u>
         (D)
<u>No error.</u>
 (E)

20. <u>Combine</u> the <u>sugar,</u> <u>waters,</u> cornstarch,
   (A)   (B)   (C)
and <u>eggs.</u> <u>No error.</u>
  (D)   (E)

PART B

Directions: Choose the letter of the best choice for the underlined section, without changing the meaning of the sentence. If the original is best, choose (A). Otherwise, select one of the suggested changes.

21. Postman's talents were missed <u>not any more</u> as a student but also in his extracurricular activities on campus.

    (A) not any more
    (B) not
    (C) not only
    (D) never any
    (E) any

22. <u>Piled on the table, the students started sorting through their projects.</u>

    (A) Piled on the table, the students started sorting through their projects.
    (B) The students started sorting through their projects, which were piled on the table.
    (C) Piled on the table, the students sorted through their projects.
    (D) The students sorted through their projects as they piled on the table.
    (E) Students started sorting through the table piled with projects.

23. All the soccer players, <u>who are injured,</u> must not play the game.

    (A) , who are injured,
    (B) , who are injured
    (C) who are injured,
    (D) who are injured
    (E) (who are injured)

24. The plumber kept these tools in his <u>truck; plunger, snake, washers and faucets.</u>

    (A) truck; plunger, snake, washers and faucets
    (B) truck (plunger, snake, washers and faucets
    (C) truck: plunger; snake; washers and faucets
    (D) truck; plunger, snake, washers, and faucets
    (E) truck: plunger, snake, washers, and faucets.

25. The two <u>attorneys meet</u> and agreed on an out-of-court settlement.

    (A) attorneys meet
    (B) attorney's meet
    (C) attorney's met
    (D) attorneys met
    (E) attorney meets

PART C

Directions: Use the lined pages to write a brief essay based on this topic.

> **Elementary school teachers provide a model of appropriate and inappropriate classroom practices that their students can in turn learn from when they become teachers.**

Describe the extent to which you agree or disagree with this statement. Support your response with specific details, examples, and experiences.

Write a brief outline first.

Answers Explained

Part A

1. **(E)** The underlined sections are all correct.

2. **(A)** Replace the word *trees* with the possessive *tree's*.

3. **(E)** The underlined sections are all correct.

4. **(D)** Replace the word *mystery's* with the plural *mysteries*.

5. **(A)** Replace the words *had lay* with *laid* to show the past tense.

6. **(B)** Replace the words *had spoke* with *spoke* or *had spoken* to show the past tense.

7. **(C)** Replace *gathers* with *gathered* to show past tense and agree with the plural *committee*.

8. **(E)** The underlined sections are all correct.

9. **(D)** Replace the phrase with *and waiting* to maintain the parallel form.

10. **(D)** Replace the phrase with *than to Charleston* to maintain the parallel form.

11. **(B)** Replace the phrase with *would do nothing*, or similar phrases to eliminate the double negative.

12. **(E)** The underlined sections are all correct.

13. **(A)** Replace the word *principle* with the correct spelling *principal*.

14. **(D)** Replace the phrase with *eggs* to maintain the parallel form.

15. **(D)** Replace the phrase with *bitten* to show the future tense.

16. **(C)** Replace the blank space with a comma.

17. **(E)** The underlined sections are all correct.

18. **(D)** Replace *five tenths* with the hyphenated *five-tenths*.

19. **(D)** Replace *unrepresented* with *represented* to eliminate the double negative.

20. **(C)** Replace the word *waters* with the singular *water*.

Part B

21. **(C)** The conjunction pair *not only . . . but also* is the correct coordination for this sentence.

22. **(B)** This wording conveys the meaning of students sorting through projects, which are piled on the table.

23. **(D)** The phrase *who are injured* is essential to the sentence, and it is not set off by commas.

24. **(E)** This choice shows the correct combination of punctuation, a colon and three commas.

25. **(D)** This choice shows the correct combination of a plural noun and a past tense verb.

Part C

Compare your essay to the sample essays that follow. You may want to show your essay to an English expert for further evaluation.

SAMPLE ESSAY

The first two essays would likely earn less than 3 points. An essay that earns less than 3 points means that you will have to do very well on the multiple-choice items to earn a passing score.

This essay would likely earn 1 out of 6 points.

> Teachers can make a big difference in everything about adult lives, and certainly what someone would be like as a teacher. Teachers should certainly be aware of that as they teach the pupils in their classes.

This essay would likely earn 2 out of 6 points (142 words).

> Teaching is probably the most important profession. I remember that someone famous said something like "the best of us would be teachers and everyone else would have to be something else." I agree with that statement.
>
> A teacher is one of the most important people in a young child's life. They should treat that special place of trust carefully and be aware as they teach that they are so important.
>
> A teacher can change lives. Just by showing an interest in a child a teacher can make the world different for that child. Many teachers do not realize how important they are when it comes to that.
>
> In conclusion, a teacher may be like one of their own teachers. We can only hope that the teacher they are like was a good teacher who though about the teacher their student would be.

This essay would likely receive a score of 3 or possibly 4 out of 6 (294 words).

You want to write an essay at least at this level. The first paragraph clearly states the position on the statement, even though it misses the mark a little. The following paragraphs more or less follow the point made in the first paragraph. The sentences are fairly well written and there are no glaring grammatical mistakes. The essay ends with a conclusion. Perhaps most importantly, there are 294 words in this essay and you're probably going to have to write that many coherent words to get a score of 3. Another 150 or 200 useful words that better developed the writer's theme, and better alignment with the topic might earn this essay a 5 or a 6.

I disagree that what elementary school teachers do in the classroom is important because young children are so impressionable. The way teachers act can make a difference but the difference is not as much as their parents may make or their friends either.

I remember that my teachers had rules about the way we had to act in class. But once we were outside of class things changed. It was mainly the way your parents had raised you, and who your friends were. If you got in with the wrong group there was no way that a teacher was going to have anything to do with the way you behaved. I always remember that I was much more interested outside of school, where I was most of the time. About what my friends thought than what my parents thought. So I think for behavior the teacher is not the most important person.

Then there is achievement in school. Teachers had a lot more to do with that than with behavior. But I always thought that what I could learn depended more on how smart I was or whether things came easily to me than what the teacher did. I know that I have read articles that it was your parents that made the biggest difference in what you learned. If you read a lot at home is more important than if you read in school. I don't think that the teacher is the most important person when it comes to learning. They are important but not the most important.

But I guess if I ever became a teacher then the way my teachers acted might make a difference in how I was as a teacher. But I do not think it would make the biggest difference.

This essay would likely receive a total score of 5 out of 6. This well-written essay is long enough to earn a rating in the upper third. The essay is very well developed and it directly addresses each point in the essay prompt. The essay provides excellent supporting details, including extra details about the essay writer and the teacher discussed in the essay. The heading helps the reader understand the essay topic and prepares the reader for the essay to follow. But this essay is a little short on words.

Miss Stendel – The Teacher I Want to be Like

I agree completely that elementary school teachers can shape what their students will be like as teachers. Miss Dorothea T. Stendel is the teacher I want to be like. She was my fifth grade teacher in Emerson School. She liked to visit Native American reservations. She used to spend a lot of time in the western states.

The main appropriate technique she used was to be very nice to me. She seemed to understand boys, which many teachers do not. I worked hard because she was nice to me and I would try to use that same approach in my classroom. This may not be a scientific approach but it certainly was a very appropriate approach for me.

The approach motivated me. I guess you would call it intrinsic motivation. I did not want to work hard for grades. I was interested. I wanted to work hard just for the work itself.

Miss Stendel used an approach that I thought was not appropriate. She had piles of mathematics worksheets all around the windowsill. You had to work your way around the windowsill to do the math program. When you reached the last window, you were done.

The approach was inappropriate because it did not it did not show real world applications of mathematics and did not show how mathematical ideas were connected. The sheets were boring and you really got nothing out of them. There were just a lot of exercises and skill problems on the sheets. You could do the entire windowsill and not learn anything.

In my classroom, I would try to make sure students mastered mathematics concepts and be sure to show how to transfer the learning to real world situations. I would emphasize the meaning of mathematics and show students how mathematics ideas were connected.

I do not know where Miss Stendel is today, but I would like to thank her for helping me so much. It seems motivating someone to learn is more important than teaching them mathematics. The more I think about it, the more I realize how much she understood and how strategic she was. I want to be like that.

CHAPTER 4

Mathematics

TEST INFO BOX

Paper-Based PPST	40 Multiple-Choice Items	60 minutes
Computer-Based PPST	46 Multiple-Choice Items	75 minutes

Using This Chapter

This chapter prepares you to take the mathematics part of the Paper-Based PPST and Computer-Based PPST. Choose one of these approaches to the information in this chapter.

- **I want all the math help I can get.** Skip the review quiz and read the mathematics review section. Then take the mathematics review quiz. Correct the quiz and reread the indicated parts of the mathematics review. Take the targeted test at the end of the chapter.

- **I want math help.** Take the mathematics review quiz. Correct the quiz and review the indicated parts of the mathematics review. Take the targeted test at the end of the chapter.

- **I want a quick math review.** Take the mathematics review quiz. Correct the quiz. Take the targeted test at the end of the chapter.

- **I want to practice math items.** Take the targeted test at the end of the chapter.

Mathematics Review Quiz

This quiz is not like the PPST. It uses a short-answer format to help you find out what you know about the mathematics topics reviewed in this chapter. The quiz results direct you to the portions of the chapter you should review.

This quiz will also help focus your thinking about mathematics, and these questions and answers are a good review in themselves. It's not important to answer all these questions correctly, and don't be concerned if you miss many of them.

The answers are found immediately after the quiz. It's to your advantage not to look at them until you have completed the quiz. Once you have completed and corrected this review quiz, use the answer checklist to decide which sections of the review to study.

Directions: Write the answers in the space provided or on a separate sheet of paper.

1. Which number is missing from this sequence?

    3 6 _____ 12

Questions 2–4: Use symbols for less than, greater than, and equal to, and compare these numbers:

2. 23 _____ 32

3. 18 _____ 4 + 14

4. 9 _____ 10 _____ 11

5. Write the place value of the digit 7 in the numeral 476,891,202,593.

_____

6. Write this number in words:

    6,000,000,000,000.

_____

7. $2{,}826 + 13{,}874 =$

8. $9{,}030 - 6{,}231 =$

9. $23 \times 689 =$

10. $14{,}832 \div 72 =$

11. $4^3 = $ _____

12. $2^2 \times 2^3 = $ _____

13. $6^9 \div 6^7 = $ _____

14. $3^2 \times 2^3 = $ _____

15. Simplify this square root:
    $\sqrt{98} = $ _____

16. $5 + 7 \times 3^2$ _____

17. $5 \times 8 - (15 - 7 \times 2)$ _____

18. Write the place value of the digit 4 in the numeral 529.354.

_____

Questions 19–20: Use symbols for less than, greater than, and equal to, and compare these numbers:

19. 9.879 _____ 12.021

20. 98.1589 _____ 98.162

Questions 21–24

Round 234,489.0754 to the:

21. thousands place

_____

22. hundredths place

    _____

23. tenths place

    _____

24. hundreds place

    _____

25. $203.61 + 9.402 + 0.78 =$ _____

26. $30.916 - 8.72$ _____

27. 3.4×0.0021 _____

28. $0.576 \div 0.32$ _____

29. Write these fractions from least to greatest.

    $$\frac{7}{8}, \qquad \frac{11}{12}, \qquad \frac{17}{20}$$

    _____ , _____ , _____

30. $1\frac{2}{3} \times 3\frac{3}{4} =$ _____

31. $1\frac{2}{3} \div \frac{3}{8} =$ _____

32. $1\frac{4}{9} + \frac{5}{6} =$ _____

33. $4\frac{5}{6} - 2\frac{3}{5} =$ _____

34. Write a seven-digit number divisible by 4.

    _____

35. Write the GCF and LCM of 6 and 14.

    _____

36. Complete the following ratio so that it is equivalent to 4 : 5

    28 : _____

37. Use a proportion and solve this problem. Bob uses jelly and peanut butter in a ratio of 5 : 2. He uses 10 teaspoons of jelly. How much peanut butter will he use?

    _____

Questions 38–43: Change among decimals, percents, and fractions to complete the table.

Decimal	Percent	Fraction
0.56	38. _____	39. _____
40. _____	15.2%	41. _____
42. _____	43. _____	$\frac{3}{8}$

44. What is 35 percent of 50?

    _____

45. What percent of 120 is 40?

    _____

46. 15 percent of what number is 6? _____

47. A $68 sweater is on sale for 15% off. What is the sale price?

    _____

48. A store marks up their prices 45% over the wholesale cost and adds a 6% sales tax. What is the final cost of an item with a $30 wholesale price? _____

49. What is the probability of rolling one die and getting a 7? _____

50. You flip a fair coin five times in a row and it comes up heads each time. What is the probability that it will come up tails on the next flip?

    _____

51. You pick one card from a deck. Then you pick another one without replacing the first. Are these dependent or independent events? Explain.

_____

Questions 52–54: Find the mean, median, and mode of this set of data.

10, 5, 2, 1, 8, 5, 3, 0

52. Mean _____

53. Median _____

54. Mode _____

55. A librarian picks two books out of three books. How many different groups of two books are there? _____

56. There are four seats next to one another at the movies. In how many ways could four students arrange themselves in the seats? _____

57. $^-8 + {}^+4 =$ _____

58. $^+85 + {}^-103 =$ _____

59. $^-12 - {}^+7 =$ _____

60. $^-72 - {}^-28 =$ _____

61. $^-9 \times {}^+8 =$ _____

62. $^-12 \times {}^-6 =$ _____

63. $^-28 \div {}^+7 =$ _____

64. $^-72 \div {}^-9 =$ _____

65. Write 3,982 in scientific notation.

_____

66. Write 0.976 in scientific notation.

_____

Write the value of the variable.

67. $x - 35 = 26$ _____

68. $x + 81 = 7$ _____

69. $y \div 8 = 3$ _____

70. $3z = 54$ _____

71. $4y - 9 = 19$ _____

72. $k \div 6 + 5 = 17$ _____

Questions 73–79: Draw a model of:

73. a point

74. a line

75. a ray

76. an acute angle

77. complementary angles

78. an isosceles triangle

79. a rectangle

80. Use this coordinate grid and plot these points: A (3,2) B (−4,−2).

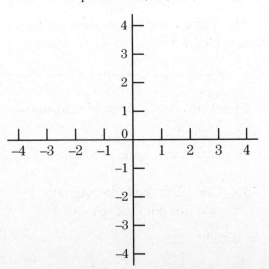

81. What is the difference between the mass of an object on earth and the mass of the same object on the moon?

_____

82. How many inches would it take to make 5 yards? _____

83. How many cups would it take to make 3 quarts? _____

84. A kilogram is how many grams? _____

85. A centimeter is how many meters? _____

86. Find the area of a triangle with a base of 3 and a height of 2.

_____

87. Find the area of a square with a side of 5.

_____

88. Find the area of a circle with a radius of 6.

_____

89. Find the volume of a cube with a side of 5.

_____

90. It's 1:00 P.M. in Los Angeles. What time is it in New York? _____

91. It's 32° Celsius. How would you describe a day with that temperature? _____

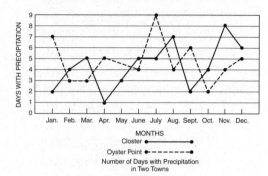

Number of Days with Precipitation
in Two Towns

Use the graph above to answer questions 92 and 93.

92. In which months were the Closter precipitation days twice the Oyster Point precipitation days? _____

93. What is the sum of the precipitation days in September? _____

94. Draw a stem and leaf plot that shows these data: 12, 12, 23, 25, 36, 38.

_____

95. Draw a flow chart that "prints" even whole numbers but does not "print" odd whole numbers.

_____

96. Draw a diagram to show that all vowels (*a, e, i, o, u*) are letters and that all consonants are letters, but that no vowels are consonants.

_____

STUDY CHECKLIST

The answers are organized by review sections. Check your answers. If you miss any questions in a section, check the box and review that section. Review the Problem Solving section on pages 152–165.

❑ *Understanding and Ordering Whole Numbers, page 101*
   1. 9
   2. <
   3. =
   4. <, <
   5. 10 billion
   6. six trillion

❑ *Whole Number Computation, page 102*
   7. 16,700
   8. 2,799
   9. 15,847
   10. 206

❑ *Positive Exponents, page 104*
   11. 64
   12. 32
   13. 36
   14. 72

❑ *Square Roots, page 105*
   15. $7\sqrt{2}$

❑ *Order of Operations, page 106*
   16. 68
   17. 39

❑ *Understanding and Ordering Decimals, page 107*
   18. thousandths
   19. <
   20. <

❑ *Rounding Whole Numbers and Decimals, page 108*
   21. 234,000
   22. 234,489.08
   23. 234,489.1
   24. 234,500

❑ *Add, Subtract, Multiply, and Divide Decimals, page 109*
   25. 213.792
   26. 22.196
   27. 0.00714
   28. 1.8

❑ *Understanding and Ordering Fractions, page 111*
   29. $\dfrac{17}{20}, \dfrac{7}{8}, \dfrac{11}{12}$

❑ *Multiply, Divide, Add, and Subtract Fractions and Mixed Numbers, page 113*
   30. $6\dfrac{1}{4}$
   31. $4\dfrac{4}{9}$
   32. $2\dfrac{5}{18}$
   33. $2\dfrac{7}{30}$

❑ *Number Theory, page 114*
   34. The last 2 digits have to be divisible by 4.
   35. GCF is 2. LCM is 42.

❑ *Ratio and Proportion, page 117*
   36. 35
   37. 4

❑ *Percent, page 118*

Decimal	Percent	Fraction
0.56	**38.** 56%	**39.** 14/25
40. 0.152	15.2%	**41.** 19/125
42. 0.375	**43.** 37.5%	3/8

❑ *Three Types of Percent Problems, page 120*
    44. 17.5
    45. $33\frac{1}{3}\%$
    46. 40

❑ *Percent of Increase and Decrease, page 121*
    47. $57.80
    48. $46.11

❑ *Probability, page 122*
    49. Zero
    50. $\frac{1}{2}$
    51. Dependent. The outcome of one event affects the probability of the other event.

❑ *Statistics, page 124*
    52. 4.25
    53. 4
    54. 5

❑ *Permutations and Combinations, page 125*
    55. 3
    56. 24

❑ *Integers, page 126*
    57. −4
    58. −18
    59. −19
    60. −44

    61. −72
    62. +72
    63. −4
    64. +8

❑ *Scientific Notation, page 128*
    65. 3.982×10^3
    66. 9.76×10^{-1}

❑ *Equations, page 129*
    67. 61
    68. −74
    69. 24
    70. 18
    71. 7
    72. 72
    73. ·
    74. ↔
    75. →

❑ *Geometry, page 131*

76. Acute angle

77. Complementary angles

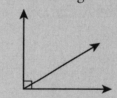
78. Isosceles triangle

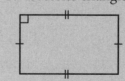
79. Rectangle

Coordinate Grid, page 134

80.

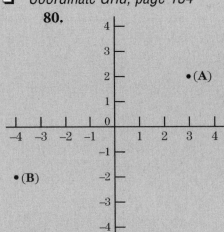

Measurement, page 137

81. None. Mass remains constant.

Customary (English) Units, page 138

82. 180 inches

83. 12

Metric System, page 138

84. 1,000

85. 0.01

Formulas, page 140

86. 3

87. 25

88. about 113 (113.097...)

89. 125

Time and Temperature, page 144

90. 4:00 P.M.

91. Hot—about 90°F.

Graphs, page 146

92. October, November

93. 8

Stem-and-Leaf and Box-and-Whisker Plots, page 149

94.

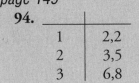

1	2,2
2	3,5
3	6,8

Flow Charts, page 150

95.

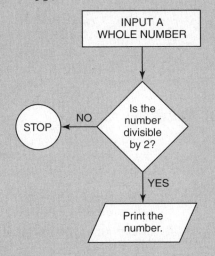

Logic, page 151

96.

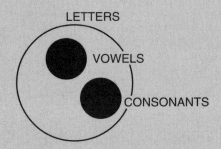

☑ *Problem Solving, page 152*

Everyone should review this section.

Mathematics Review

This review section targets the skills and concepts you need to know to pass the Mathematics part of the Paper-Based PPST and the Computer-Based PPST.

UNDERSTANDING AND ORDERING WHOLE NUMBERS

Whole numbers are the numbers you use to tell how many. They include 0, 1, 2, 3, 4, 5, 6 . . . The dots tell us that these numbers keep going on forever. There are an infinite number of whole numbers, which means you will never reach the last one.

Cardinal numbers such as 1, 9, and 18 tell how many. There are 9 players on the field in a baseball game. Ordinal numbers such as 1st, 2nd, 9th, and 18th tell about order. For example, Lynne batted 1st this inning.

You can visualize whole numbers evenly spaced on a number line.

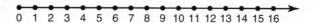

You can use the number line to compare numbers. Numbers get smaller as we go to the left and larger as we go to the right. We use the terms *equal to* (=), *less than* (<), *greater than* (>), and *between* to compare numbers.

12 equals 10 + 2	2 is less than 5	9 is greater than 4	6 is between 5 and 7
12 = 10 + 2	2 < 5	9 > 4	5 < 6 < 7

Place Value

We use ten digits, 0–9, to write out numerals. We also use a place value system of numeration. The value of a digit depends on the place it occupies. Look at the following place value chart.

millions	hundred thousands	ten thousands	thousands	hundreds	tens	ones
3	5	7	9	4	1	0

The value of the 9 is 9,000. The 9 is in the thousands place. The value of the 5 is 500,000. The 5 is in the hundred thousands place. Read the number three million, five hundred seventy-nine thousand, four hundred ten.

Some whole numbers are very large. The distance from Earth to the dwarf planet Pluto is about six trillion (6,000,000,000,000) yards. The distance from Earth to the nearest star is about 40 quadrillion (40,000,000,000,000,000) yards.

EXAMPLES

(A)   What is the value of 8 in the numeral 47,829?

The value of the 8 is 800; this is because the 8 is in the hundreds place.

(B)   Use >, <, or = to compare 2 and 7.

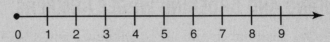

Use the number line to see that 2 < 7 (2 is less than 7).

Practice

Directions: Fill in the space with =, <, or > to make each statement true.

1.   2 _____ 3

2.   4 _____ 1

3.   8 _____ 9

4.   1 _____ 1

5.   7 _____ 6

6.   Write a numeral in which the value of 7 is seven, the value of 9 is nine thousand, the value of 3 is thirty, and the 0 is in the hundreds place.

7.   Write a numeral in which the value of 5 is fifty, the value of 2 is two thousand, the value of 1 is one, and the value of 8 is eight hundred.

8.   What place values in the numeral 65,747 contain the same digit?

9.   Write the whole numbers between 0 and 15.

10.   How many whole numbers are there between 0 and 50?

Answers on page 171.

WHOLE NUMBER COMPUTATION

Follow these steps to add, subtract, multiply, and divide whole numbers. Estimate first and then check to be sure your answer is reasonable.

Add: 24,262 + 8,921.

Estimate first.

24,262 rounded to the nearest ten thousand is 24,000.
8,921 rounded to the nearest thousand is 9,000.
24,000 + 9,000 = 33,000. The answer should be close to 33,000.

Add.

```
    2 4 2 6 2          1 1
  +   8 9 2 1        2 4 2 6 2
                   +   8 9 2 1
                     3 3 1 8 3
```

Align digits.   Add.

33,183 is close to 33,000 so the answer is reasonable.

Subtract: 20,274 − 17,235.

Estimate first.

20,274 rounded to the nearest thousand is 20,000.
17,235 rounded to the nearest thousand is 17,000.
20,000 − 17,000 = 3,000.
The answer should be close to 3,000.

Subtract.

```
                   1 10   6 14
  2 0 2 7 4         2 0 2 7 4
- 1 7 2 3 5       - 1 7 2 3 5
                    3 0 3 9
```

Align digits.   Subtract.

3,039 is close to 3000, so the answer seems reasonable.

Multiply: 32 × 181.

Estimate first.

Multiplication answers may look correct but may be wrong by a multiple of 10.

32 rounded to the nearest ten is 30.
181 rounded to the nearest hundred is 200.

30 × 200 = 6,000

The answer should be near 6,000.

Multiply.

```
    181              181
  ×  32            ×  32
    362              362
    543              543
                    5792
```

Find the partial products.   Add the partial products.

The answer is close to 6,000.
The answer seems reasonable.

Divide: 927 ÷ 43.

Estimate first.

You may make a division error if you misalign digits.

927 rounded to the nearest hundred is 900.
43 is close to 45 and 45 evenly divides 90.

$900 \div 45 = 20$

The answer should be somewhere near 20.

Divide.

$$43\overline{)927}$$

$$\begin{array}{r} 21 \ \ R24 \\ 43\overline{)927} \\ 86 \ \ \ \\ \hline 67 \\ 43 \\ \hline 24 \end{array}$$

Divide.   Find the quotient and the remainder.

The answer is close to 20.
The answer seems reasonable.

Practice

Directions: Find the answer for each problem below.

1. 97,218
    + 1,187

2. 23,045
    + 4,034

3. 67,914
    + 27,895

4. 48,549
    + 17,635

5. 20,591
    − 4,578

6. 34,504
    − 405

7. 57,895
    − 23,207

8. 84,403
    − 42,194

9. 240
    × 57

10. 302
    × 91

11. 725
    × 41

12. 146
    × 36

13. $328 \div 41 =$

14. $240 \div 59 =$

15. $754 \div 26 =$

16. $2,370 \div 74 =$

Answers on page 171.

POSITIVE EXPONENTS

You can show repeated multiplication as an exponent. The exponent shows how many times the factor appears.

[Exponent]
$$\text{Base} \rightarrow 3^5 = 3 \times 3 \times 3 \times 3 \times 3 = 243$$
[Factors]

Rules for Exponents

$$a^0 = 1 \qquad a^1 = a$$

Use these rules to multiply and divide exponents with the *same base*.

$7^8 \times 7^5 = 7^{13}$ $a^n \times a^m = a^{m+n}$ $7^8 \div 7^5 = 7^3$ $a^n \div a^m = a^{n-m}$
Multiply with the same base.   Divide with the same base.
Keep the base.   Keep the base.
Add the exponents.   Subtract the exponents.

EXAMPLES

(A) $4^3 + 6^2$ $= 4 \times 4 \times 4 + 6 \times 6$ $= 64 + 36 = 100$
(B) $(2^3)(4^2) = (2 \times 2 \times 2) \times (4 \times 4) = 8 \times 16$ $= 128$
(C) $(3^2)^2$ $= 3^4$ $= 3 \times 3 \times 3 \times 3 = 81$
(D) $(10 - 9)^2 = 1^2$ $= 1$

Practice

Directions: Find the answer.

1. $5^2 \times 6^3 =$

2. $(3^2)^2 =$

3. $(8 - 6)^3 =$

4. $(5^2)(6^2) =$

5. $3^3 + 2^3 =$

6. $10^2 - 7^2 =$

7. $(4^3)^2 =$

8. $(2^1)^5 =$

9. $6^2 + 2^3 =$

10. $(25 - 15)^3 =$

11. $(4^2)^2 =$

12. $(2^3)(3^2) =$

Answers on pages 171–172.

SQUARE ROOTS

The square root of a given number, when multiplied by itself, equals the given number. This symbol ($\sqrt{25}$) means the square root of 25. The square root of 25 is 5. $5 \times 5 = 25$.

Some Square Roots Are Whole Numbers

The numbers with whole-number square roots are called perfect squares.

$\sqrt{1} = 1$ $\sqrt{4} = 2$ $\sqrt{9} = 3$ $\sqrt{16} = 4$ $\sqrt{25} = 5$ $\sqrt{36} = 6$

$\sqrt{49} = 7$ $\sqrt{64} = 8$ $\sqrt{81} = 9$ $\sqrt{100} = 10$ $\sqrt{121} = 11$ $\sqrt{144} = 12$

Use This Rule to Write a Square Root in Simplest Form

$$\sqrt{a \times b} = \sqrt{a} \times \sqrt{b} \qquad \sqrt{5 \times 3} = \sqrt{5} \times \sqrt{3}$$

Simplify $\sqrt{72}$

If possible, write 72 as a product with a perfect square.

36 is a perfect square. Write $\sqrt{72}$ as $\sqrt{36 \times 2}$.

Use the rule. Write $\sqrt{36 \times 2} = \sqrt{36} \times \sqrt{2}$.

$\sqrt{36} \times \sqrt{2} = 6 \times \sqrt{2}$ or $6\sqrt{2}$.

$\sqrt{72}$ in simplest form is $6\sqrt{2}$.

EXAMPLES

(A) Write the square root of 162 in simplest form.

$\sqrt{162} = \sqrt{81 \times 2} = \sqrt{81} \times \sqrt{2} = 9\sqrt{2}$

(B) Write the square root of 51 in simplest form.

$\sqrt{51}$ is in simplest form because 51 cannot be written as a product with a perfect square.

Practice

Directions: Simplify.

1. $\sqrt{256}$
2. $\sqrt{400}$
3. $\sqrt{576}$
4. $\sqrt{900}$
5. $\sqrt{1225}$
6. $\sqrt{48}$
7. $\sqrt{245}$
8. $\sqrt{396}$
9. $\sqrt{567}$
10. $\sqrt{832}$

Answers on page 172.

ORDER OF OPERATIONS

Use this phrase to remember the order in which we do operations:

Please Excuse My Dear Aunt Sally

(1) **P**arentheses (2) **E**xponents (3) **M**ultiplication or **D**ivision (4) **A**ddition or **S**ubtraction.

For example,

$$4 + 3 \times 7^2 = 4 + 3 \times 49 = 4 + 147 = 151$$
$$(4 + 3) \times 7^2 = 7 \times 7^2 = 7 \times 49 = 343$$
$$(6 - 10 \div 5) + 6 \times 3 = (6 - 2) + 6 \times 3 = 4 + 6 \times 3 = 4 + 18 = 22$$

EXAMPLE

$7 + 3 \times 6 + 4^2 - (8 + 4) = 7 + 3 \times 6 + 4^2 - \underline{12} =$

$7 + 3 \times 6 + \underline{16} - 12 \quad = 7 + \underline{18} + 16 - 12 \quad = 29$

Practice

Directions: Find the answer for each problem below.

1. $4 \times 5 + 4 \div 2 =$

2. $(5 + 7 - 9) \times 8^2 + 2 =$

3. $((7 + 4) - (1 + 4)) \times 6 =$

4. $6^2 + 3(9 - 5 + 7)^2 =$

5. $(12 + 5) \times 3 - 6^2 =$

6. $8 \times 5 + 4 - 8 \div 2 =$

7. $100 - 30 \times 5 + 7 =$

8. $((5 + 2)^2 + 16) \times 8 =$

Answers on page 172.

UNDERSTANDING AND ORDERING DECIMALS

Decimals are used to represent numbers between 0 and 1. Decimals can also be shown on a number line.

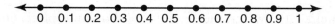

We also use ten digits, 0–9, and a place value system of numeration to write decimals. The value of a digit depends on the place it occupies. Look at the following place value chart.

ones	tenths	hundredths	thousandths	ten thousandths	hundred thousandths	millionths	ten millionths	hundred millionths	billionths
0 .	3	6	8	7					

The value of 3 is three tenths. The 3 is in the tenths place. The value of 8 is eight thousandths. The 8 is in the thousandths place.

Comparing Whole Numbers and Decimals

To compare two numbers, compare the value of the digits in each place.

Compare   9,879 and 16,459   23,801 and 23,798   58.1289 and 58.132

9,879	23,801	58.1289
16,459	23,798	58.132
9,879 < 16,459	23,801 > 23,798	58.1289 < 58.132
Less than	Greater than	Less than

EXAMPLES

(A) What is the value of the digit 2 in the decimal 35.6829?

The 2 is in the thousandths place. $2 \times 0.001 = 0.002$.
The value of the 2 is 0.002 or 2 thousandths.

(B) Use <, >, or = to compare 1248.9234 and 1248.9229

1248.9234   1248.9229 The digits in the numerals are the same until you reach
the thousandths place where 3 > 2. Since 3 > 2, then 1248.9234 > 1248.9229.

Practice

Directions: Use <, >, or = to compare.

1. 0.02 _____ 0.003

2. 4.6 _____ 1.98

3. 0.0008 _____ 0.00009

4. 1.0 _____ 1

5. 7.6274 _____ 7.6269

Directions: Solve for each problem below.

6. Write a numeral in which the value of 5 is five tenths, the value of 2 is two, the value of 6 is six thousandths, and the value of 8 is eight hundredths.

7. Write a numeral in which the value of 4 is in the ten thousandths place, the value of 3 is three hundred, the 7 is in the hundredths place, the 1 is in the tens place, the 9 is in the ten thousands place, and the rest of the digits are zeros.

8. In the numeral 6.238935, which place values contain the same digit?

9. Using only the tenths place, write all the decimals from 0 to 1.

10. If you used only the tenths and hundredths places, how many decimals are between 0 and 1?

Answers on page 172.

ROUNDING WHOLE NUMBERS AND DECIMALS

Follow these steps to round a number to a place.

- Look at the digit to the right of a specific place.

- If the digit to the right is 5 or more, round up. If the digit is less than 5, round down.

EXAMPLES

(A) *Round 859,465 to the nearest hundred thousand.*
Underline the hundred thousands place.
Look at the digit to the right of 8. The digit is 5 or more, so you round up.
859,465 rounded to the *nearest hundred thousand* is 900,000.

(B) *Round 8.6<u>4</u>7 to the nearest hundredth.*
Underline the hundredths place.
Look at the digit to the right of 4. The digit 7 is 5 or more, so you round up.
8.647 rounded to the *hundredths* place is 8.65.
8.647 rounded to the *tenths* place is 8.6.

Practice

1. Round 23,465 to the hundreds place.

2. Round 74.1508 to the thousandths place.

3. Round 975,540 to the ten thousands place.

4. Round 302.787 to the tenths place.

5. Round 495,244 to the tens place.

6. Round 1508.75 to the hundreds place.

7. Round 13.097 to the hundredths place.

8. Round 198,704 to the hundred thousands place.

9. Round 51.8985 to the ones place.

10. Round 23,457 to the hundreds place.

Answers on page 172.

ADD, SUBTRACT, MULTIPLY, AND DIVIDE DECIMALS

Estimate first. Then add, subtract, multiply, or divide.

Add and Subtract Decimals

Line up the decimal points

Add: $14.9 + 3.108 + 0.16$ Subtract: $14.234 - 7.14$

$$\begin{array}{r} 14.9 \\ 3.108 \\ +\ 0.16 \\ \hline 18.168 \end{array}$$

$$\begin{array}{r} 14.234 \\ -\ 7.14 \\ \hline 7.094 \end{array}$$

Multiply Decimals

Multiply decimals as you would whole numbers. Count the total number of decimal places in the factors. Put that many decimal places in the product. You may have to write leading zeros.

Multiply: 17.4×1.3 Multiply: 0.016×1.7

$$
\begin{array}{r}
17.4 \\
\times\ \underline{1.3} \\
522 \\
\underline{174} \\
22.62
\end{array}
$$
$$
\begin{array}{r}
0.016 \\
\times\ \underline{1.7} \\
112 \\
\underline{16} \\
.0272
\end{array}
$$

Divide Decimals

Move the decimal point to make the divisor a whole number. Move the decimal point in the dividend the same number of places. Then divide.

$$0.16)\overline{1.328} \qquad 016.)\overline{132.8} \qquad
\begin{array}{r}
8.3 \\
16)\overline{132.8} \\
\underline{128} \\
48 \\
\underline{48} \\
0
\end{array}
$$

Practice

1. $\begin{array}{r} 12.79 \\ 8.1 \\ +\ \underline{5.2} \end{array}$
2. $\begin{array}{r} 40.267 \\ 23.2 \\ +\ \underline{9.15} \end{array}$
3. $\begin{array}{r} 940.17 \\ 36.15 \\ +\ \underline{12.07} \end{array}$
4. $\begin{array}{r} 5290.3 \\ 167.8 \\ +\ \underline{15.09} \end{array}$

5. $\begin{array}{r} 37.9 \\ -\ \underline{29.7} \end{array}$
6. $\begin{array}{r} 136.804 \\ -\ \underline{65.7944} \end{array}$
7. $\begin{array}{r} 513.72 \\ -\ \underline{59.75} \end{array}$
8. $\begin{array}{r} 2451.06 \\ -\ \underline{683.19} \end{array}$

9. $\begin{array}{r} 0.249 \\ \times\ \underline{2.5} \end{array}$
10. $\begin{array}{r} 46.7 \\ \times\ \underline{3.5} \end{array}$
11. $\begin{array}{r} 56.2 \\ \times\ \underline{65.49} \end{array}$
12. $\begin{array}{r} 93.57 \\ \times\ \underline{40.2} \end{array}$

13. $10.08 \div 2.1 =$ 14. $16.32 \div 1.7 =$

15. $248.64 \div 7.4 =$ 16. $653.276 \div 5.2 =$

Answers on page 172.

UNDERSTANDING AND ORDERING FRACTIONS

A fraction names a part of a whole or of a group. A fraction has two parts, a numerator and a denominator. The denominator tells how many parts in all. The numerator tells how many parts you identified.

$$\frac{3}{4} \quad \begin{array}{l} \text{Numerator} \\ \text{Denominator} \end{array}$$

Mixed Numbers and Improper Fractions

Change an improper fraction to a mixed number:

$$\frac{23}{8} = 8\overline{)23}^{\,2\frac{7}{8}} \atop {\frac{16}{7}}$$

Change a mixed number to an improper fraction:

$$3\frac{2}{5} = \frac{17}{5}$$

Multiply denominator and whole number. Then add the numerator.

$$\frac{(3 \times 5) + 2}{5} = \frac{15 + 2}{5} = \frac{17}{5}$$

Equivalent Fractions

Two fractions that stand for the same number are called equivalent fractions. Multiply or divide the numerator and denominator by the same number to find an equivalent fraction.

$$\frac{2 \times 3}{5 \times 3} = \frac{6}{15} \qquad \frac{6 \div 3}{9 \div 3} = \frac{2}{3} \qquad \frac{6 \times 4}{8 \times 4} = \frac{24}{32} \qquad \frac{8 \div 2}{10 \div 2} = \frac{4}{5}$$

Fractions can also be written and ordered on a number line. You can use the number line to compare fractions. Fractions get smaller as we go to the left and larger as we go to the right. We use the terms equivalent to (=), less than (<), greater than (>), and between to compare fractions.

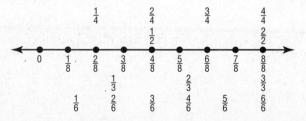

$\frac{1}{2}$ is equivalent to $\frac{2}{4}$ | $\frac{2}{3}$ is less than $\frac{3}{4}$ | $\frac{5}{8}$ is greater than $\frac{1}{2}$ | $\frac{1}{3}$ is between $\frac{1}{4}$ and $\frac{3}{8}$

$\frac{1}{2}=\frac{2}{4}$ | $\frac{2}{3}<\frac{3}{4}$ | $\frac{5}{8}>\frac{1}{2}$ | $\frac{1}{4}<\frac{1}{3}<\frac{3}{8}$

Compare Two Fractions

Use this method to compare two fractions. For example, compare $\frac{13}{18}$ and $\frac{5}{7}$. First, write the two fractions and cross multiply as shown. The larger cross product appears next to the larger fraction. If cross products are equal, then the fractions are equivalent.

$$91 = \qquad = 90$$

$$\frac{13}{18} \times \frac{5}{7}$$

$$91 > 90 \text{ so } \frac{13}{18} > \frac{5}{7}$$

EXAMPLES

(A) Compare $\frac{5}{7}$ and $\frac{18}{19}$.

Use cross multiplication.

$\frac{5}{7} \times \frac{18}{19}$, $5 \times 19 = 95$ and $7 \times 18 = 126$, therefore $\frac{5}{7} < \frac{18}{19}$.

(B) Write $\frac{27}{7}$ as a mixed number.

$$\begin{array}{r} 3 \text{ R6} \\ 7\overline{)27} \\ \underline{21} \\ 6 \end{array}$$

$\frac{27}{7} = 3\frac{6}{7}$

(C) Write $6\frac{5}{8}$ as a fraction.

$6 \times 8 = 48$. Multiply the denominator and the whole number.
$48 + 5 = 53$. Add the numerator to the product.

$6\frac{5}{8} = \frac{53}{8}$

Practice

Directions: Write the improper fraction as a mixed number.

1. $\frac{5}{3}$ 2. $\frac{15}{7}$ 3. $\frac{24}{9}$

Directions: Write the mixed number as an improper fraction.

4. $8\frac{1}{5}$ 5. $6\frac{7}{8}$ 6. $9\frac{5}{7}$

Directions: Use >, <, = to compare the fractions.

7. $\frac{3}{7}, \frac{4}{9}$ 8. $\frac{5}{6}, \frac{25}{30}$ 9. $\frac{4}{5}, \frac{7}{8}$

Answers on pages 172–173.

MULTIPLY, DIVIDE, ADD, AND SUBTRACT FRACTIONS AND MIXED NUMBERS

Multiply Fractions and Mixed Numbers

To write any mixed number as an improper fraction, multiply the numerator and the denominator. Write the product in simplest form. For example, multiply $\frac{3}{4}$ and $\frac{1}{6}$.

$$\frac{3}{4} \times \frac{1}{6} = \frac{3}{24} = \frac{1}{8}$$

Now, multiply $3\frac{1}{3}$ by $\frac{3}{5}$.

$$3\frac{1}{3} \times \frac{3}{5} = \frac{10}{3} \times \frac{3}{5} = \frac{30}{15} = 2$$

Divide Fractions and Mixed Numbers

To divide $1\frac{4}{5}$ by $\frac{3}{8}$:

$$1\frac{4}{5} \div \frac{3}{8} = \frac{9}{5} \div \frac{3}{8} \quad = \quad \frac{9}{5} \times \frac{8}{3} = \frac{72}{15} \quad = \quad 4\frac{12}{15} \quad = \quad 4\frac{4}{5}$$

Write mixed numbers as improper fractions.   Invert the divisor and multiply.   Write the product.   Write the quotient in simplest form.

Add Fractions and Mixed Numbers

To add, write fractions with common denominators. Then write in simplest form.

Add: $\frac{3}{8} + \frac{1}{4}$ Add: $\frac{7}{8} + \frac{5}{12}$ Add: $2\frac{1}{3} + \frac{5}{7}$

$$\frac{3}{8} = \frac{3}{8} \qquad\qquad \frac{7}{8} = \frac{21}{24} \qquad\qquad 2\frac{1}{3} = 2\frac{7}{21}$$

$$+ \frac{1}{4} = \frac{2}{8} \qquad\qquad + \frac{5}{12} = \frac{10}{24} \qquad\qquad + \frac{5}{7} = \frac{15}{21}$$

$$\frac{5}{8} \qquad\qquad\qquad \frac{31}{24} = 1\frac{7}{24} \qquad\qquad 2\frac{22}{21} = 3\frac{1}{21}$$

Subtract Fractions and Mixed Numbers

Write fractions with common denominators. Subtract and then write in simplest form.

Subtract: $\dfrac{5}{6} - \dfrac{1}{3}$

$$\dfrac{5}{6} = \dfrac{5}{6}$$
$$-\ \dfrac{1}{3} = \dfrac{2}{6}$$
$$\overline{\dfrac{3}{6} = \dfrac{1}{2}}$$

Subtract: $\dfrac{3}{8} - \dfrac{1}{5}$

$$\dfrac{3}{8} = \dfrac{15}{40}$$
$$-\ \dfrac{1}{5} = \dfrac{8}{40}$$
$$\overline{\dfrac{7}{40}}$$

Subtract: $3\dfrac{1}{6} - 1\dfrac{1}{3}$

$$3\dfrac{1}{6} = 3\dfrac{1}{6} = 2\dfrac{7}{6}$$
$$-\ 1\dfrac{1}{3} = 1\dfrac{2}{6} = 1\dfrac{2}{6}$$
$$\overline{1\dfrac{5}{6}}$$

Practice

1. $\dfrac{1}{3} \times \dfrac{5}{9} =$

2. $\dfrac{2}{3} \times \dfrac{1}{4} =$

3. $3\dfrac{3}{8} \times 4\dfrac{1}{8} =$

4. $3\dfrac{1}{5} \times 2\dfrac{4}{7} =$

5. $\dfrac{3}{4} \div \dfrac{7}{8} =$

6. $\dfrac{2}{5} \div \dfrac{7}{9} =$

7. $9\dfrac{5}{7} \div 4\dfrac{1}{3} =$

8. $2\dfrac{4}{5} \div 7\dfrac{3}{5} =$

9. $\dfrac{5}{9} + \dfrac{2}{3} =$

10. $\dfrac{7}{10} + \dfrac{2}{4} =$

11. $1\dfrac{6}{7} + 2\dfrac{3}{14} =$

12. $5\dfrac{2}{3} + 6\dfrac{5}{6} =$

13. $\dfrac{2}{7} - \dfrac{5}{21} =$

14. $\dfrac{2}{5} - \dfrac{3}{8} =$

15. $3\dfrac{4}{5} - 3\dfrac{2}{15} =$

16. $8\dfrac{1}{7} - 4\dfrac{2}{9} =$

Answers on page 173.

NUMBER THEORY

Number theory explores the natural numbers [1, 2, 3, 4, . . .]. We'll review just a few important number theory concepts.

Factors

The factors of a number evenly divide the number with no remainder. For example, 2 is a factor of 6, but 2 is not a factor of 5.

The number 1 is a factor of every number. Each number is a factor of itself.

1	The only factor is 1	6	1, 2, 3, 6
2	Factors 1, 2	7	1, 7
3	1, 3	8	1, 2, 4, 8
4	1, 2, 4	9	1, 3, 9
5	1, 5	10	1, 2, 5, 10

Prime Numbers and Composite Numbers

A prime number has exactly two factors, itself and 1.

2 is prime. The only factors are 1 and 2.

3 is prime. Factors: 1, 3

5 is prime. Factors: 1, 5

7 is prime. Factors: 1, 7

A composite number has more than two factors.

4 is composite. The factors are 1, 2, 4.

6 is composite. Factors: 1, 2, 3, 6

8 is composite. Factors: 1, 2, 4, 8

9 is composite. Factors: 1, 3, 9

10 is composite. Factors: 1, 2, 5, 10

> The number 1 has only one factor, itself. The number 1 is neither prime nor composite.

Least Common Multiple (LCM), Greatest Common Factor (GCF)

Multiples. The multiples of a number are all the numbers you get when you count by that number. Here are some examples.

Multiples of 1: 1, 2, 3, 4, 5, . . .

Multiples of 2: 2, 4, 6, 8, 10, . . .

Multiples of 3: 3, 6, 9, 12, 15, . . .

Multiples of 4: 4, 8, 12, 16, 20, . . .

Multiples of 5: 5, 10, 15, 20, 25, . . .

Least common multiple is the smallest multiple shared by two numbers.

The least common multiple of 6 and 8 is 24.

List the multiples of 6 and 8. Notice that 24 is the smallest multiple common to both numbers.

Multiples of 6: 6, 12, 18, **24**, 30, 36

Multiples of 8: 8, 16, **24**, 32, 40

Greatest common factor is the largest factor shared by two numbers.

The greatest common factor of 28 and 36 is 4.

List the factors of 28 and 36.

Factors of 28: 1, 2, **4**, 7, 28

Factors of 36: 1, 2, 3, **4**, 6, 9, 12, 18, 36

Divisibility Rules

Use these rules to find out if a number is divisible by the given number. Divisible means the given number divides evenly with no remainder.

2   Every even number is divisible by 2.

3   If the sum of the digits is divisible by 3, the number is divisible by 3.

347   $3 + 4 + 7 = 14$ 14 is not divisible by 3, so 347 is not divisible by 3.

738   $7 + 3 + 8 = 18$ 18 is divisible by 3, so 738 is divisible by 3.

4   If the last two digits are divisible by 4, the number is divisible by 4.

484,8<u>42</u>   42 is not divisible by 4, so 484,842 is not divisible by 4.

371,9<u>56</u>   56 is divisible by 4, so 371,956 is divisible by 4.

5   If the last digit is 0 or 5, then the number is divisible by 5.

6   If the number meets the divisibility rules for both 2 *and* 3, then it is divisible by 6.

8   If the last three digits are divisible by 8, then the number is divisible by 8.

208,513,<u>114</u>   114 is not divisible by 8, so 208,513,114 is not divisible by 8.

703,628,<u>920</u>   920 is divisible by 8, so 703,628,920 is divisible by 8.

9   If the sum of the digits is divisible by 9, then the number is divisible by 9.

93,163 $9 + 3 + 1 + 6 + 3 = 22$ 22 is not divisible by 9, so 93,163 is not divisible by 9.

86,715 $8 + 6 + 7 + 1 + 5 = 27$ 27 is divisible by 9, so 86,715 is divisible by 9.

10   If a number ends in 0, the number is divisible by 10.

EXAMPLES

(A)   Find the factors of 24.

The factors are 1, 2, 3, 4, 6, 8, 12, and 24.
These are the only numbers that divide 24 with no remainder.

(B)   Find the GCF of 14 and 22.

Write out the factors of each number.
14: 1, 2, 7, 14
22: 1, 2, 11, 22
The greatest common factor is 2.

(C)   Find the LCM of 6 and 9.

List some of the multiples of each number.
6: 6, 12, 18, 24, . . .
9: 9, 18, 27, . . .
The least common multiple is 18.

Practice

Directions: Write the factors of each number.

1. 13

2. 26

3. 40

4. 23

Directions: Find the LCM of the two numbers.

5. 6 and 8

6. 5 and 12

7. 7 and 35

8. 4 and 14

Directions: Find the GCF of the two numbers.

9. 24 and 30

11. 32 and 64

10. 15 and 40

12. 56 and 84

Answers on page 173.

RATIO AND PROPORTION
Ratio

A ratio is a way of comparing two numbers with division. It conveys the same meaning as a fraction. There are three ways to write a ratio.

Using 3 to 4   As a fraction $\frac{3}{4}$ Using a colon 3:4

Proportion

A proportion shows two ratios that have the same value; that is, the fractions representing the ratios are equivalent. Use cross multiplication. If the cross products are equal, then the two ratios form a proportion.

$\frac{3}{8}$ and $\frac{27}{72}$ form a proportion. The cross products are equal. ($3 \times 72 = 8 \times 27$)

$\frac{3}{8}$ and $\frac{24}{56}$ do not form a proportion. The cross products are not equal.

Writing a Proportion: You may have to write a proportion to solve a problem. For example, the mason mixes cement and sand using a ratio of 2:5. Twelve bags of cement will be used. How much sand is needed? To solve, use the numerator to stand for cement. The denominator will stand for sand.

$$\frac{2}{5} = \frac{12}{S}$$
$$2 \times S = 5 \times 12$$
$$2S = 60$$
$$S = 30$$

Cross multiply to solve.

Thirty bags of sand are needed.

EXAMPLE

The problem compares loaves of whole wheat bread with loaves of rye bread. Let the numerators stand for loaves of whole wheat bread. The denominators stand for loaves of rye bread.

Ratio of whole wheat to rye. $\frac{3}{7}$ Ratio of whole wheat to rye for 51 loaves of whole wheat. $\frac{51}{R}$

Write a proportion. $\frac{3}{7} = \frac{51}{R}$

Solution: $3R = 357$ $R = 119$

There are 119 loaves of rye bread.

Practice

1. A salesperson sells 7 vacuum cleaners for every 140 potential buyers. If there are 280 potential buyers, how many vacuums are sold?

2. There is one teacher for every 8 preschool students. How many teachers are needed if there are 32 preschool students?

3. There are 3 rest stops for every 20 miles of highway. How many rest stops would there be on 140 miles of highway?

4. Does $\frac{7}{9}$ and $\frac{28}{36}$ form a proportion? Explain.

Answers on page 173.

PERCENT

Percent comes from *per centum*, which means per hundred. Whenever you see a number followed by a percent sign it means that number out of 100.

Decimals and Percents

To write a decimal as a percent, move the decimal point two places to the right and write the percent sign.

$$0.34 = 34\% \qquad 0.297 = 29.7\% \qquad 0.6 = 60\% \qquad 0.001 = 0.1\%$$

To write a percent as a decimal, move the decimal point two places to the left and delete the percent sign.

$$51\% = 0.51 \qquad 34.18\% = 0.3418 \qquad 0.9\% = 0.009$$

Fractions and Percents

WRITING FRACTIONS AS PERCENTS

- Divide the numerator by the denominator. Write the answer as a percent.

Write $\frac{3}{5}$ as a percent.   Write $\frac{5}{8}$ as a percent.

$$5)\overline{3.0} \;\; 0.6 \qquad 0.6 = 60\%$$

$$8)\overline{5.00} \;\; 0.625 \qquad 0.625 = 62.5\%$$

- Write an equivalent fraction with 100 in the denominator. Write the numerator followed by a percent sign.

Write $\frac{13}{25}$ as a percent.

$$\frac{13}{25} = \frac{52}{100} = 52\%$$

- Use these equivalencies.

$$\frac{1}{4}=25\% \qquad \frac{1}{2}=50\% \qquad \frac{3}{4}=75\% \qquad \frac{4}{4}=100\%$$

$$\frac{1}{5}=20\% \qquad \frac{2}{5}=40\% \qquad \frac{3}{5}=60\% \qquad \frac{4}{5}=80\%$$

$$\frac{1}{6}=16\frac{2}{3}\% \qquad \frac{1}{3}=33\frac{1}{3}\% \qquad \frac{2}{3}=66\frac{2}{3}\% \qquad \frac{5}{6}=83\frac{1}{3}\%$$

$$\frac{1}{8}=12\frac{1}{2}\% \qquad \frac{3}{8}=37\frac{1}{2}\% \qquad \frac{5}{8}=62\frac{1}{2}\% \qquad \frac{7}{8}=87\frac{1}{2}\%$$

WRITING PERCENTS AS FRACTIONS

Write a fraction with 100 in the denominator and the percent in the numerator. Simplify.

$$18\%=\frac{18}{100}=\frac{9}{50} \qquad 7.5\%=\frac{7.5}{100}=\frac{18}{1000}=\frac{9}{40}$$

EXAMPLES

(A) Write 0.567 as a percent.

Move the decimal two places to the right and write a percent sign, therefore, 0.567 = 56.7%.

(B) Write $\frac{1}{4}$ as a percent.

Write $\frac{1}{4}$ as a decimal (1 ÷ 4) = 0.25

Write 0.25 as a percent 0.25 = 25%

(C) Write 26% as a fraction.

Place the percent number in the numerator and 100 in the denominator.

$26\%=\frac{26}{100}=\frac{13}{50}.$

Simplify: $\frac{26}{100}=\frac{13}{50}$

Practice

Directions: Write the decimal as a percent.

1. 0.359

2. 0.78

3. 0.215

4. 0.041

Directions: Write the fraction as a percent.

5. $\frac{1}{9}$

6. $\frac{5}{8}$

7. $\frac{3}{10}$

8. $\frac{4}{9}$

Directions: Write the percents as fractions in simplest form.

9. 58%   11. 85.2%

10. 79%   12. 97.4%

Answers on page 173.

THREE TYPES OF PERCENT PROBLEMS

Finding a Percent of a Number

To find a percent of a number, write a number sentence with a decimal for the percent and solve.

$$\text{Find } 40\% \text{ of } 90.$$
$$0.4 \times 90 = 36$$

It may be easier to write a fraction for the percent.

$$\text{Find } 62\frac{1}{2}\% \text{ of } 64.$$
$$\frac{5}{8} \times 64 = 5 \times 8 = 40$$

Finding What Percent One Number Is of Another

To find what percent one number is of another, write a number sentence and solve to find the percent.

$$\text{What percent of 5 is 3?}$$
$$n \times 5 = 3$$
$$n = \frac{3}{5} = 0.6 = 60\%$$

Finding a Number When a Percent of It Is Known

To find a number when a percent of it is known, write a number sentence with a decimal or a fraction for the percent and solve to find the number.

$$\text{5\% of what number is 2?}$$
$$0.05 \times n = 2$$
$$n = 2 \div 0.05$$
$$n = 40$$

EXAMPLES

(A) What percent of 70 is 28?

$$\square \times 70 = 28$$
$$\square = \frac{28}{70} = \frac{4}{10}$$
$$\square = 40\%$$

(B) 30% of 60 is what number?

$30\% \times 60 = \square$
$0.3 \times 60 = \square$
$\square = 18$

(C) 40% of what number is 16?

$0.40 \times \square = 16$
$\square = \dfrac{16}{0.4}$
$\square = 40$

Practice

1. 120 is what percent of 240?

2. 15% of 70 is what number?

3. 60% of 300 is what number?

4. What percent of 60 is 42?

5. What percent of 25 is 2.5?

6. 40% of what number is 22?

7. 70% of what number is 85?

8. 25% of 38 is what number?

9. 35% of what number is 24?

10. 24 is what percent of 80?

Answers on page 174.

PERCENT OF INCREASE AND DECREASE

Percent of Increase

A price increases from $50 to $65. What is the percent of increase?

Subtract to find the amount of increase.	$65 - $50 = $15 $15 is the amount of increase
Write a fraction. The amount of increase is the numerator. The original amount is the denominator.	$\dfrac{\$15}{\$50}$ Amount of increase Original amount
Write the fraction as a percent. The percent of increase is 30%.	$\begin{array}{r} 0.3 \\ 50\overline{)15.00} \end{array}$ $0.3 = 30\%$

Percent of Decrease

A price decreases from $35 to $28. What is the percent of decrease?

Subtract to find the amount of decrease.	$35 - $28 = $7 $7 is the amount of decrease
Write a fraction. The amount of decrease is the numerator. The original amount is the denominator.	$\dfrac{\$7}{\$35}$ Amount of decrease Original amount
Write the fraction as a percent. The percent of decrease is 20%.	$\dfrac{7}{35} = \dfrac{1}{5} = 20\%$

EXAMPLES

(A) The price increased from \$30 to \$36. What is the percent of increase?

\$36 − \$30 = \$6

$$\frac{6}{30} = \frac{1}{5} = 20\%$$

(B) An \$80 item goes on sale for 25% off. What is the sale price?

\$80 × 25% = \$80 × 0.25 = \$20

\$80 − \$20 = \$60. \$60 is the sale price.

Practice

1. The price increased from \$25 to \$35. What is the percent of increase?

2. A sale marks down a \$100 item 25%. What is the sale price?

3. The price decreases from \$80 by 15%. What is the new price?

4. The price increased from \$120 to \$150. What is the percent of increase?

5. A sale marks down a \$75 item 10%. What is the sale price?

6. The price decreases from \$18 to \$6. What is the percent of decrease?

7. A sale marks down a \$225 item to \$180. What is the percent of decrease?

8. A sale price of \$150 was 25% off the original price. What was the original price?

Answers on page 174.

PROBABILITY

The probability of an occurrence is the likelihood that it will happen. Most often, we write probability as a fraction.

Flip a fair coin and the probability that it will come up heads is $\frac{1}{2}$. The same is true for tails. Write the probability this way.

$$P(\text{H}) = \frac{1}{2} \qquad\qquad P(\text{T}) = \frac{1}{2}$$

If something will never occur the probability is 0. If something will always occur, the probability is 1. Therefore, if you flip a fair coin,

$$P(7) = 0 \qquad\qquad P(\text{H or T}) = 1$$

Write the letters A, B, C, D, and E on pieces of paper. Pick them randomly without looking. The probability of picking any letter is $\frac{1}{5}$.

| A | B | C | D | E |

$$P(\text{vowel}) = \frac{2}{5} \qquad P(\text{consonant}) = \frac{3}{5}$$

Rules for Computing Probability

$$P(A \text{ or } B) = P(A) + P(B) = \frac{1}{5} + \frac{1}{5} = \frac{2}{5}$$

when A and B have no common elements

$$P(A \text{ and } B) = P(A) \times P(B) = \frac{1}{5} \times \frac{1}{5} = \frac{1}{25}$$

$$P(\text{not } C) = 1 - P(C) = 1 - \frac{1}{5} = \frac{4}{5}$$

EXAMPLE

In one high school, 40% of the students go on to college. Two graduates of the high school are chosen at random. What is the probability that they both went to college?

Write the probabilities you know.

$$P(\text{college}) = \frac{40}{100} = \frac{2}{5}$$

Solve the problem.

$P(A \text{ and } B)$ probability the two students went to college.

$$P(A \text{ and } B) = P(A) \times P(B) = \frac{2}{5} \times \frac{2}{5} = \frac{4}{25}$$

The probability that they both went to college is $\frac{4}{25}$.

Practice

1. There are 3 black, 2 white, 2 gray, and 3 blue socks in a drawer. What is the probability of drawing a sock that is not black?

2. Six goldfish are in a tank; 4 are female and 2 are male. What is the probability of scooping out a male?

3. A standard deck of 52 playing cards is spread facedown on a table. What is the probability of choosing a card that is a king or a queen?

4. Six names are written on pieces of paper. The names are Aaron, Ben, Carl, Edith, Elizabeth, and Phyllis. One name is picked and replaced. Then another name is picked. What is the probability that the names were Carl and Phyllis?

5. A fair die having six sides is rolled. What is the probability that the side facing up is a prime number?

6. A fair coin is tossed in the air 5 times. What is the probability of getting five tails?

Answers on pages 174–175.

STATISTICS

Descriptive statistics are used to explain or describe a set of numbers. Most often we use the mean, median, or mode to describe these numbers.

Mean (Average)

The mean is a position midway between two extremes. To find the mean:

1. Add the items or scores.
2. Divide by the number of items.

For example, find the mean of 23, 17, 42, 51, 37.

$$23 + 17 + 42 + 51 + 37 = 170 \quad 170 \div 5 = 34$$

The mean or average is 34.

Median

The median is the middle number. To find the median:

1. Arrange the numbers from least to greatest.
2. If there are an odd number of scores, then find the middle score.
3. If there is an even number of scores, average the two middle scores.

For example, find the median of these numbers.

$$6, 9, 11, 17, 21, 33, 45, 71$$

There are an even number of scores.

$$17 + 21 = 38 \quad 38 \div 2 = 19$$
The median is 19.

Don't forget to arrange the scores in order before finding the middle score!

Mode

The mode is the number that occurs most often. For example, find the mode of these numbers.

$$6, 3, 7, 6, 9, 3, 6, 1, 2, 6, 7, 3$$
The number 6 occurs most often, so 6 is the mode.

Not all sets of numbers have a mode. Some sets of numbers may have more than one mode.

EXAMPLE

What is the mean, median, and mode of 7, 13, 18, 4, 14, 22?

Mean	Add the scores and divide by the number of scores.	
	$7 + 13 + 18 + 4 + 14 + 22 = 78 \div 6 = 13$	The mean is 13.
Median	Arrange the scores in order. Find the middle score.	
	$4, 7, 13, 14, 18, 22 \quad 13 + 14 = 27 \div 2 = 13.5$	The median is 13.5.
Mode	Find the score that occurs most often.	
	Each score occurs only once.	There is no mode.

Practice

1. A group of fourth graders received the following scores on a science test.

   80, 87, 94, 100, 75, 80, 98, 85, 80, 95, 92

   Which score represents the mode?

2. What is the mean of the following set of data?

   44, 13, 84, 42, 12, 18

3. What is the median of the following set of data?

   8, 9, 10, 10, 8, 10, 7, 6, 9

4. What measure of central tendency does the number 16 represent in the following data?

   14, 15, 17, 16, 19, 20, 16, 14, 16

5. What is the mean of the following set of scores?

   100, 98, 95, 70, 85, 90, 94, 78, 80, 100

6. What is the mode of the following data?

   25, 30, 25, 15, 40, 45, 30, 20, 30

Answers on page 175.

PERMUTATIONS, COMBINATIONS, AND THE FUNDAMENTAL COUNTING PRINCIPLE

Permutations

A permutation is the way a set of things can be arranged in order. There are 6 permutations of the letters A, B, and C.

ABC	ACB	BAC	BCA	CAB	CBA

Permutation Formula

The formula for the number of permutations of *n* things is **n! (n factorial)**.

$$6! = 6 \times 5 \times 4 \times 3 \times 2 \times 1 \qquad 4! = 4 \times 3 \times 2 \times 1 \qquad 2! = 2 \times 1$$

There are 120 permutations of 5 things.

$$n! = 5! = 5 \times 4 \times 3 \times 2 \times 1 = 120$$

Combinations

A combination is the number of ways of choosing a given number of elements from a set. The order of the elements does not matter. There are 3 ways of choosing 2 letters from the letters A, B, and C.

AB AC BC

Fundamental Counting Principle

The fundamental counting principle is used to find the total number of possibilities. Multiply the number of possibilities from each category.

EXAMPLE

An ice cream stand has a sundae with choices of 28 flavors of ice cream, 8 types of syrups, and 5 types of toppings. How many different sundae combinations are available?

28	×	8	×	5	=	1,120
flavors		syrups		toppings		sundaes

There are 1,120 possible sundaes.

Practice

1. There are 2 chairs left in the auditorium, but 4 people are without seats. In how many ways could 2 people be chosen to sit in the chairs?

2. The books *Little Women, Crime & Punishment, Trinity, The Great Santini, Pygmalion, The Scarlet Letter,* and *War and Peace* are on a shelf. In how many different ways can they be arranged?

3. A license plate consists of 2 letters and 2 digits. How many different license plates can be formed?

4. There are four students on line for the bus, but there is only room for three students on this bus. How many different ways can 3 of the 4 students get on the bus?

Answers on page 175.

INTEGERS

The number line can also show negative numbers. There is a negative whole number for every positive whole number. Zero is neither positive nor negative. The negative whole numbers, the positive whole numbers, and zero, together, are called integers.

$$-10 \quad -9 \quad -8 \quad -7 \quad -6 \quad -5 \quad -4 \quad -3 \quad -2 \quad -1 \quad 0 \quad +1 \quad +2 \quad +3 \quad +4 \quad +5 \quad +6 \quad +7 \quad +8 \quad +9 \quad +10$$

Add and Subtract Integers

ADD

When the signs are the same, keep the sign and add.

$$\begin{array}{r} ^+7 \\ + \; ^+8 \\ \hline ^+15 \end{array} \qquad \begin{array}{r} ^-3 \\ + \; ^-11 \\ \hline ^-14 \end{array}$$

When the signs are different, disregard the signs, subtract the numbers, and keep the sign of the larger number.

$$\begin{array}{r} ^+28 \\ + \; ^-49 \\ \hline ^-21 \end{array} \qquad \begin{array}{r} ^-86 \\ + \; ^+135 \\ \hline ^+49 \end{array}$$

SUBTRACT

Change the sign of the number being subtracted. Then add using the preceding rules.

$$
\begin{array}{cccc}
^+13 & ^-43 & ^+29 & ^-92 \\
-\ ^-18 & -\ ^-17 & -\ ^-49 & -\ ^+135 \\
\Downarrow & \Downarrow & \Downarrow & \Downarrow \\
^+13 & ^-43 & ^+29 & ^-92 \\
+\ ^+18 & +\ ^+17 & +\ ^+49 & +\ ^-135 \\
\hline
^+31 & ^-26 & ^+78 & ^-227
\end{array}
$$

Multiply and Divide Integers

MULTIPLY

Multiply as you would whole numbers. The product is *positive* if there are an even number of negative factors. The product is *negative* if there are an odd number of negative factors.

$$^-2 \times {}^+14 \times {}^-6 \times {}^+3 = {}^+144 \qquad {}^-2 \times {}^-4 \times {}^+6 \times {}^-3 = {}^-144$$

DIVIDE

Forget the signs and divide. The quotient is *positive* if both integers have the same sign. The quotient is *negative* if the integers have different signs.

$$^+24 \div {}^+4 = {}^+6 \qquad {}^-24 \div {}^-4 = {}^+6 \qquad {}^+24 \div {}^-4 = {}^-6 \qquad {}^-24 \div {}^+4 = {}^-6$$

Practice

1. $6 + 9 =$
2. $18 + {}^-17 =$
3. $^-24 + {}^-45 =$
4. $^-38 + 29 =$
5. $7 - 6 =$
6. $15 - {}^-39 =$
7. $^-36 - {}^-58 =$
8. $^-27 - 53 =$
9. $9 \times 11 =$
10. $26 \times {}^-25 =$
11. $^-31 \times {}^-59 =$
12. $^-42 \times 35 =$
13. $120 \div 8 =$
14. $68 \div {}^-4 =$
15. $^-352 \div {}^-8 =$
16. $^-66 \div 3 =$

Answers on page 175.

SCIENTIFIC NOTATION

Scientific notation uses powers of 10. The power shows how many zeros to use.

$10^0 = 1$ $10^1 = 10$ $10^2 = 100$ $10^3 = 1,000$ $10^4 = 10,000$ $10^5 = 100,000$
$10^{-1} = 0.1$ $10^{-2} = 0.01$ $10^{-3} = 0.001$ $10^{-4} = 0.0001$ $10^{-5} = 0.00001$

Write whole numbers and decimals in scientific notation. Use a decimal with one numeral to the left of the decimal point.

$2,345 = 2.345 \times 10^3$ The decimal point moved three places to the left. Use 10^3.

$176.8 = 1.768 \times 10^2$ The decimal point moved two places to the left. Use 10^2.

$0.0034 = 3.4 \times 10^{-3}$ The decimal point moved three places to the right. Use 10^{-3}.

$2.0735 = 2.0735 \times 10^0$ The decimal is in the correct form. Use 10^0 to stand for 1.

EXAMPLES

(A) Write 7,952 in scientific notation.

Move the decimal point three places to the left and write $7,952 = 7.952 \times 10^3$.

(B) Write 0.03254 in scientific notation.

Move the decimal point two places to the right and write 3.254×10^{-2}.

Practice

Directions: Rewrite using scientific notation.

1. 0.0564
2. 0.00897
3. 0.06501
4. 0.000354
5. 545
6. 7,790
7. 289,705
8. 1,801,319

Answers on page 175.

EQUATIONS

The whole idea of solving equations is to isolate the variable on one side of the equal sign. The value of the variable is what's on the other side of the equal sign. Substitute your answer in the original equation to check your solution.

Solving Equations by Adding or Subtracting

$$\text{Solve: } y + 19 = 23$$

Subtract 19 $\quad y + 19 - 19 = 23 - 19$

$$y = 4$$

Check: Does $4 + 19 = 23$? Yes. It checks.

$$\text{Solve: } x - 23 = 51$$

Add 23 $\quad x - 23 + 23 = 51 + 23$

$$x = 74$$

Check: Does $74 - 23 = 51$? Yes. It checks.

Solving Equations by Multiplying or Dividing

$$\text{Solve: } \frac{z}{7} = 6$$

Multiply by 7 $\quad \frac{z}{7} \times 7 = 6 \times 7$

$$z = 42$$

Check: Does $\frac{42}{7} = 6$? Yes. It checks.

$$\text{Solve: } 21 = -3x$$

Divide by –3 $\quad \frac{21}{-3} = \frac{-3x}{-3}$

$$-7 = x$$

Check: Does $21 = (-3)\,(-7)$? Yes. It checks.

Solving Two-Step Equations

Add or subtract before you multiply or divide.

$$\text{Solve: } 3x - 6 = 24$$

$$3x - 6 + 6 = 24 + 6$$

$$3x = 30$$

Divide by 3 $\quad \frac{3x}{3} = \frac{30}{3}$

$$x = 10$$

Check: Does $3 \times 10 - 6 = 24$? Yes. It checks.

Solve: $\frac{y}{7} + 4 = 32$

Subtract 4 $\qquad\qquad \frac{y}{7} + 4 - 4 = 32 - 4$

$$\frac{y}{7} = 28$$

Multiply by 7 $\qquad\qquad \frac{y}{7} \times 7 = (28)(7)$

$$y = 196$$

Check: Does $\frac{\mathbf{196}}{7} + 4 = 32$? Yes. It checks.

Check: Does $28 + 4 = 32$? Yes. It checks.

Practice

Directions: Solve for each problem below.

1. $w - 3 = 5$
2. $x + 9 = 24$
3. $y - 10 = 60$
4. $z + 50 = 46$
5. $3w = 12$
6. $\frac{x}{18} = 7$
7. $^{-}9y = 45$

8. $\frac{z}{6} = {}^{-}11$
9. $5w + 6 = 41$
10. $^{-}3 - 2x = 23$
11. $\frac{y}{19} + 11 = 35$
12. $26z - 13 = 65$

Answers on page 175.

GEOMETRY

We can think of geometry in two or three dimensions. A two-dimensional model is this page. A three-dimensional model is the room you'll take the test in.

Definition	Model	Symbol
Point—a location	· A	*A*
Plane—a flat surface that extends infinitely in all directions		plane *ABC*
Space—occupies three dimensions and extends infinitely in all directions		space *xyz*
Line—a set of points in a straight path that extends infinitely in two directions		$\overleftrightarrow{AB}$
Line segment—part of a line with two endpoints		*AB*
Ray—part of a line with one endpoint		*AB*
Parallel lines—lines that stay the same distance apart and never touch		
Perpendicular lines—lines that meet at right angles		
Angle—two rays with a common endpoint, which is called the vertex.		∠*ABC*
Acute angle—angle that measures between 0° and 90°		
Right angle—angle that measures 90°		
Obtuse angle—angle that measures between 90° and 180°		
Complementary angles—angles that have a total measure of 90°		

(continued)

Definition	Model	Symbol
Supplementary angles—angles that have a total measure of 180°		
Polygon—a closed figure made up of line segments; if all sides are the same length, the figure is a regular polygon		
Pentagon	Five Sides	
Hexagon	Six Sides	
Octagon	Eight Sides	
Triangle—polygon with three sides and three angles; the sum of the angles is always 180°		
Equilateral triangle—all the sides are the same length; all the angles are the same size, 60°		
Isosceles triangle—two sides the same length; two angles the same size		

(continued)

Definition	Model	Symbol

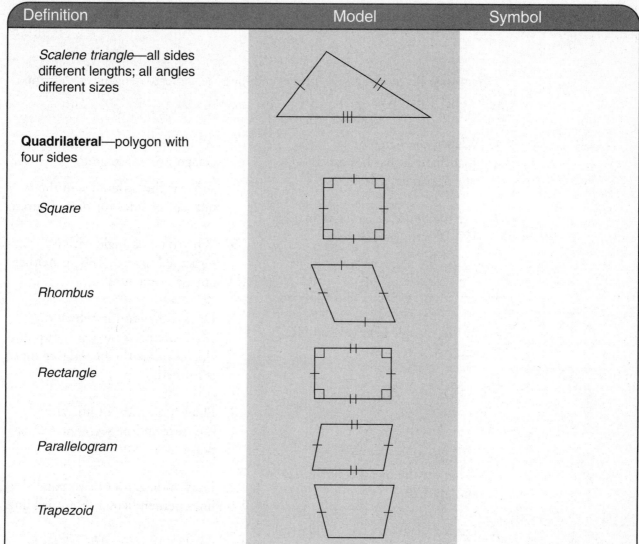

Scalene triangle—all sides different lengths; all angles different sizes

Quadrilateral—polygon with four sides

Square

Rhombus

Rectangle

Parallelogram

Trapezoid

EXAMPLE

Which types of quadrilaterals can be constructed using four congruent line segments *AB*, *BC*, *CD*, and *DA*?

You can create a square and a rhombus.

Practice

1. What is the name of a quadrilateral that has exactly one pair of parallel sides?

2. Use the figure below. The m∠1 = 45°. What is m∠2?

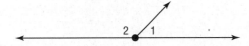

3. In the triangle below, $AB = AC$ and m∠$BAC = 80°$.

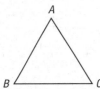

   What are the measures of ∠ABC and ∠ACB?

4. Draw a diagram of an equilateral triangle.

5. Which has more sides, an octagon or a hexagon?

   What is the difference in the number of sides for these figures?

6. What type of angle with a measure less than 180° is neither obtuse nor acute?

7. Draw a diagram in which ray (*AB*) intersects ray (*AC*) at point *A*, and name the new figure that is formed.

8. Draw a diagram of line *AB* intersecting line segment *CD* at point *E*.

9. Draw a diagram of two parallel lines perpendicular to a third line.

10. Given a triangle *ABC*, describe the relationship among the measures of the three angles.

Answers on page 176.

COORDINATE GRID

You can plot ordered pairs of numbers on a coordinate grid.

The *x*-axis goes horizontally from left to right. The first number in the pair tells how far to move left or right from the origin. A minus sign means move left. A plus sign means move right.

The *y*-axis goes vertically up and down. The second number in the pair tells how far to move up or down from the origin. A minus sign means move down. A plus sign means move up.

Pairs of numbers show the *x*-coordinate first and the *y*-coordinate second (*x*, *y*). The origin is point (0, 0) where the *x*-axis and the *y*-axis meet.

Plot these pairs of numbers on the grid.

A (⁺3, ⁻7)   B (⁺5, ⁺3)   C (⁻6, ⁺2)   D (⁻3, ⁻6)

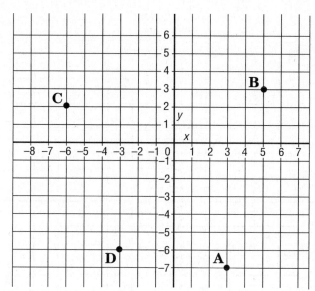

Practice

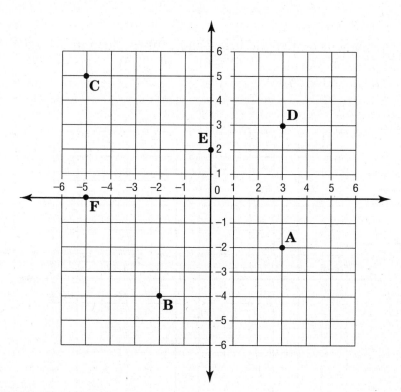

1. Write the coordinates of the points on the grid.

   A _____   D _____
   B _____   E _____
   C _____   F _____

2. Plot these points on the grid below.

   G (3, −1) H (2, −3) I (5, 6) J (−4, 0) K (−5, −2) L (−1, 6)

   M (0, 3) N (−5, 2)

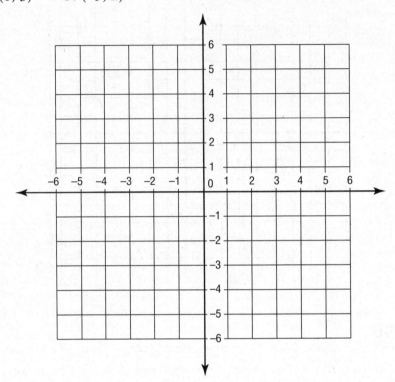

3. Plot these points on the grid below and connect them in the order shown.

   Z (−5, 5) Y (−2, 0) X (2, −6) W (3, 5) V (−6, −2) U (2, 0)

   T (6, 1) S (−5, 5)

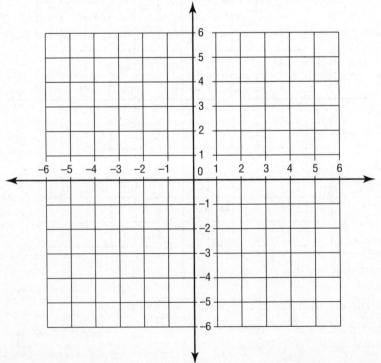

Answers on page 176.

MEASUREMENT

Measuring with a Ruler and a Protractor

You may use a ruler that shows inches, halves, quarters, and sixteenths, or you may use a ruler that shows centimeters and millimeters.

CUSTOMARY RULERS

Measure the length of a line segment to the nearest $\frac{1}{16}$ of an inch. Put one end of the line segment at the 0 point on the ruler. Read the mark closest to the end of the line.

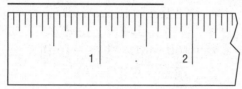

The line segment is $1\frac{11}{16}$ inches long.

METRIC RULERS

Measure the length of the line segment to the nearest millimeter. Put one end of the line segment at the 0 point on the ruler. Read the mark closest to the end of the line.

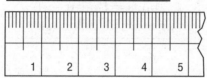

The line segment is 45 mm long.

PROTRACTORS

Most protractors are half circles and show degrees from 0° to 180°.

Put the center of the protractor on the vertex of the angle. Align one ray of the angle on the inner or outer 0° point on the scale. Read the measure of the angle on that scale.

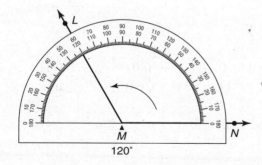
120°

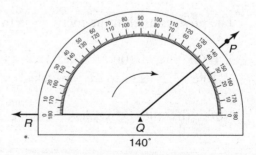
140°

Weight and Mass

Mass is the amount of matter in a body. Weight is a measure of the force of gravity on a body. Mass is the same everywhere, but weight depends on its location in a gravitational field. That is, an object has the same mass whether on the moon or on earth. However, the object weighs less on the moon than on earth.

Customary (English) Units

Length

12 inches (in.) = 1 foot
3 feet = 1 yard (yd)
36 inches = 1 yard
1,760 yards = 1 mile (mi)
5,280 feet = 1 mile

Weight

16 ounces (oz) = 1 pound (lb)
2,000 pounds = 1 ton (T)

Capacity

2 cups = 1 pint (pt)
2 pints = 1 quart (qt)
4 quarts = 1 gallon (gal)

Metric System

The metric system uses common units of measure. The system uses prefixes that are powers of 10 or 0.1.

The common units used in the metric system follow:

Length—meter
Mass—gram
Capacity—liter

The prefixes used in the metric system follow:

1000	100	10	Unit	0.1	0.01	0.001
Kilo	Hecto	Deka		Deci	Centi	Milli

Notice that the prefixes less than one end in *i*.

References for commonly used metric measurements

Unit Length	Description
Meter	A little more than a yard
Centimeter (0.01 meter)	The width of a paper clip (About 2.5 per inch)
Millimeter (0.001 meter)	The thickness of the wire on a paper clip
Kilometer (1,000 meters)	About 0.6 of a mile
Mass	
Gram	The weight of a paper clip
Kilogram (1,000 grams)	About 2.2 pounds
Capacity	
Liter	A little more than a quart
Milliliter	The amount of water in a cubic centimeter

EXAMPLE

Use your protractor and a ruler to construct an angle measuring 45°.

First construct a ray *AB*. Next place the center of the protractor at point *A*. Find the 45° measure and place a mark there. Call it point *C*. Now use the straight edge of the protractor and create ray *AC*.

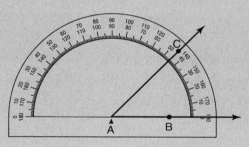

Practice

1. 220 centimeters is equal to how many decameters?

2. How many feet equal 5.5 miles?

3. What is the length of the segment below to the nearest $\frac{1}{4}$ of an inch?

4. How many pounds equal 8 ounces?

5. How many ounces equal 2 tons?

6. What is the length of the segment below to the nearest centimeter?

7. How many inches in 3 miles?

8. 2.367 hectoliters is how many milliliters?

9. How many quarts are in $\frac{1}{2}$ gallon?

10. What is the approximate measure of $\angle ABC$ below?

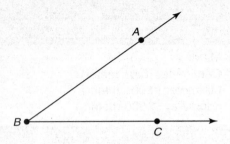

Answers on page 176.

FORMULAS

Evaluating an Expression or Formula

Evaluate an expression by replacing the variables with values. Remember to use the correct order of operations. For example, evaluate

$$3x - \frac{y}{z} \text{ for } x = 3, y = 8, \text{ and } z = 4$$

$$3(3) - \frac{8}{4} = 9 - 2 = 7$$

EXAMPLE

Principle (P) is the amount borrowed. Interest (I) is the simple interest rate. Time (T) is the length of the loan in **years.** (If the loan is for 6 months, $T = \frac{1}{2}$.) Find the simple interest earned on $2,000 invested at 9% for 3 years.

$I = PRT$
$I = (2000)\,(0.09)\,(3)$
$I = 180 \times 3 = 540$

The investment earns $540 in interest.

Distance and Area

Perimeter   The distance around a figure. The perimeter of a circle is called the circumference.

Area   The amount of space occupied by a two-dimensional figure.

Formulas for Perimeter and Area

Figure	Formula	Description
Triangle	Area $= \frac{1}{2}bh$ Perimeter $= s_1 + s_2 + s_3$	
Square	Area $= s^2$ Perimeter $= 4s$	
Rectangle	Area $= lw$ Perimeter $= 2l + 2w$	
Parallelogram	Area $= bh$ Perimeter $= 2b + 2h$	
Trapezoid	Area $= \frac{1}{2}h(b_1 + b_2)$ Perimeter $= b_1 + b_2 + s_1 + s_2$	
Circle	Area $= \pi r^2$ Circumference $= 2\pi r$ or $= \pi d$	

PYTHAGOREAN THEOREM

The Pythagorean Theorem for right triangles states that the sum of the square of the legs equals the square of the hypotenuse.

$$a^2 + b^2 = c^2$$

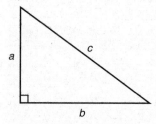

Other Polygons

Pentagon	5 sides	Octagon	8 sides
Hexagon	6 sides	Nonagon	9 sides
Heptagon	7 sides	Decagon	10 sides

Regular Polygon—All sides are the same length.

EXAMPLES—DISTANCE AND AREA

Let's solve distance and area problems.

(A) How many meters is it around a regular hexagon with a side of 87 centimeters?

A hexagon has 6 sides. It's a regular hexagon, so all the sides are the same length. $6 \times 87 = 522$. The perimeter is 522 centimeters, which equals 5.22 meters.

(B) What is the area of this figure?

The formula for the area of a circle is πr^2.
The diameter is 18, so the radius is 9. Use 3.14 for π.
$A = 3.14 \times (9)^2 = 3.14 \times 81 = 254.34$ or about 254.

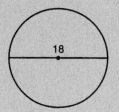

Volume

Volume—The amount of space occupied by a three-dimensional figure.

Formulas for Volume

Figure	Formula	Description
Cube	Volume = s^3	
Rectangular Prism	Volume = lwh	
Sphere	Volume = $\frac{4}{3}\pi r^3$	
Cone	Volume = $\frac{1}{3}\pi r^2 h$	

(continued)

Formulas for Volume *(continued)*

Figure	Formula	Description
Cylinder	Volume = $\pi r^2 h$ Surface Area = $2\pi r(h + r)$	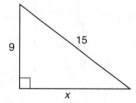

EXAMPLE—VOLUME

A circular cone has a radius of 8 cm and a height of 10 cm. What is the volume?

Formula for the volume of a cone $= \frac{1}{3}\pi r^2 h$.

$V = \left(\frac{1}{3}\right)(3.14)(8^2)(10) = \left(\frac{1}{3}\right)(3.14)(64)(10) = \left(\frac{1}{3}\right)(3.14)(640) = 669.87$

The volume of the cone is 669.87 cubic centimeters or about 670 cubic centimeters.

Practice

1. A circle has a radius of 9 meters. What is the area?

2. The faces of a pyramid are equilateral triangles. What is the surface area of the pyramid if the sides of the triangles equal 3 inches and the height is 2.6 inches?

3. A regular hexagon has one side 5 feet long. What is the distance around its edge?

4. What is the surface area of the side of a cylinder (not top and bottom) with a height of 10 cm and a diameter of 2.5 cm?

5. A rectangle has a width x and a length $(x + 5)$. If the perimeter is 90 feet, what is the length?

6. The perimeter of one face of a cube is 20 cm. What is the surface area?

7. What is the length of the third side in the right triangle below?

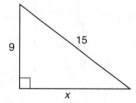

8. What is the area of a trapezoid whose height is 5 inches, the length of one base is 5 inches, and the length of the other base is 8 inches?

9. What is the volume of a sphere that has a diameter of length 20 cm?

10. What is the volume of a cube having a side length of 15 inches.

Answers on page 177.

TIME AND TEMPERATURE

Time

Each of the 24 hours in a day is partitioned into 60 minutes. Each minute is partitioned into 60 seconds. In the United States we use a 12-hour clock. The time between midnight and noon is called A.M., while the time between noon and midnight is called P.M. In other countries and in the scientific and military communities, a 24-hour clock is used. Both analog and digital clocks are used to keep track of time.

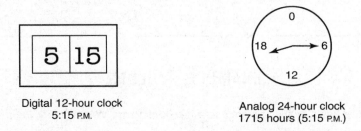

Digital 12-hour clock
5:15 P.M.

Analog 24-hour clock
1715 hours (5:15 P.M.)

There are 24 time zones in the world and four time zones in the continental United States. The U.S. time zones are shown in the following map. As you travel west, the sun rises later and the time gets earlier—10 A.M. in New York is 7 A.M. in Los Angeles.

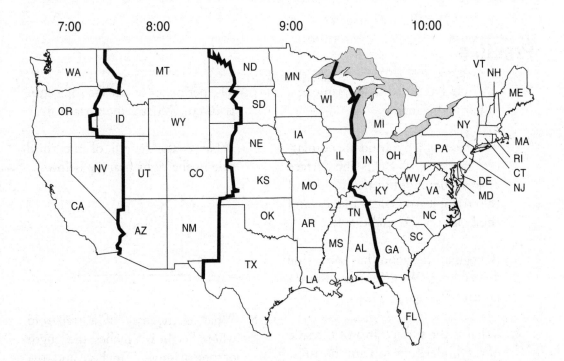

Temperature

Temperature is the degree of warmth or cold. We use Fahrenheit and Celsius thermometers to measure warmth. On a Fahrenheit thermometer water freezes at 32° and boils at 212°. A temperature of 98.6° Fahrenheit is normal body temperature and 90° Fahrenheit is a hot day. On the Celsius thermometer water freezes at 0° and boils at 100°. A temperature of 37° is normal body temperature and about 32° is a hot day.

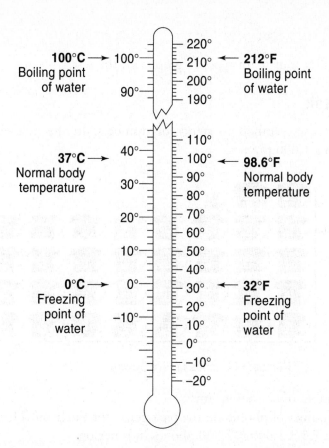

100°C → 100° — 220°
Boiling point   210° ← **212°F**
of water   200°   Boiling point
                90° — 190°   of water

                    — 110°
37°C → 40° — 100° ← **98.6°F**
Normal body   90°   Normal body
temperature   30° — 80°   temperature
                    — 70°
            20° — 60°
                    — 50°
            10° — 40°
                    — 30° ← **32°F**
0°C → 0° — 20°   Freezing
Freezing   10°   point of
point of   −10° — 0°   water
water   — −10°
                    — −20°

EXAMPLE

If it is 4:00 P.M. in North Carolina, what time is it in Nebraska?

Nebraska lies in two different time zones. If you are in the eastern Nebraska time zone, it is 3:00 P.M. If you are in the western Nebraska time zone, it is 2:00 P.M.

Practice

1. What is colder, 0°C or 0°F?

2. If it is 10:00 A.M. in Washington State, what time is it in Maine?

3. Draw a picture of an analog 24-hour clock displaying 6:30 P.M.

4. If it is 9:00 A.M. in Minnesota, what time is it in Georgia?

5. 10°C is approximately how many degrees Fahrenheit?

6. 220°F is approximately how many degrees Celsius?

Answers on page 177.

GRAPHS

You will encounter four main types of graphs on the test.

The Pictograph

The pictograph uses symbols to stand for numbers. In the following graph, each picture represents 1,000 phones.

Number of Phones in Five Towns

Find the number of phones in Emerson.

Count the number of phones on the pictograph for Emerson. There are $7\frac{1}{2}$. That means there are $7.5 \times 1,000 = 7,500$ phones in Emerson.

The Bar Graph

The bar graph represents information by the length of a bar.

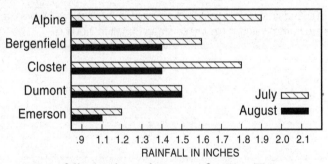

Rainfall in July and August for Five Towns

Find the August rainfall for Emerson and the July rainfall for Closter.

Follow the bar across and then read down to find that 1.1 inches of rain fell in Emerson during August.

Read down from the striped bar for Closter to find that 1.8 inches of rain fell in Closter during July.

The Line Graph

The line graph plots information against two axes.

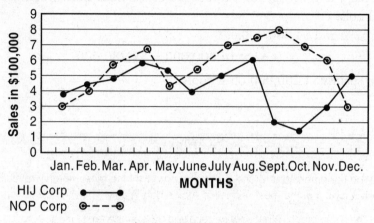

Sales for Two Companies During the Year

Find the June sales for HIJ Corp.

Read up from June and across from Sales to find that the HIJ Corp. had $400,000 in sales during June.

The Circle Graph

The circle represents an entire amount. Each wedge-shaped piece of the graph represents some percent of that whole.

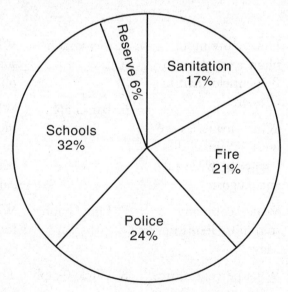

Percent of Tax Money Spent for Town Services

Multiply the percent and the entire budget amount to find the amount spent in a budget area.

For example, the town spends $4,000,000 on services. How much does the town spend on schools?

Multiply 32% and $4,000,000.

$$0.32 \times \$4,000,000 = \$1,280,000$$

The town spends $1,280,000 on schools.

EXAMPLES

A. Use the bar graph. Where and in which month was the most monthly rainfall? The graph shows that the most rain fell in Alpine during July.

B. Use the circle graph. What service received 32% of the tax revenue? Education received 32% of the tax revenue.

Practice

Directions: Use the graphs shown earlier in this section to answer these practice items.

1. Pictograph How many more phones are there in Bergenfield than in Closter?

2. Bar Graph Which town has the greatest rainfall difference between July and August?

3. Line Graph Which company sold more items in May?

4. Circle Graph What percent more tax money is spent on police than on fire?

5. Pictograph Which town has the smallest number of phones?

6. Bar Graph Which town has the most consistent amount of rainfall between July and August?

7. Line Graph What were the sales for the NOP Corp. in September?

8. Circle Graph The town collects $1,400,000 in taxes. How much money will be placed in reserve?

Answers on page 177.

STEM-AND-LEAF AND BOX-AND-WHISKER PLOTS

Stem-and-Leaf Plots

Stem-and-leaf plots represent data in place value–oriented plots. Each piece of data is shown in the plot. The following stem-and-leaf plot shows test scores. The stem represents 10, and the leaves represent 1. You can read each score. In the 50s the scores are 55, 55, and 58. There are no scores in the 60s. You can find the lowest score, 40, and the highest score, 128.

Stem	Leaves
4	0, 7
5	5, 5, 8
6	
7	1, 4, 4, 6
8	2, 3, 4, 5
9	9, 9
10	
11	
12	3, 4, 8

Example: 7 | 4 means 74

Box-and-Whisker Plots

Box-and-whisker plots show the range and quartiles of scores. The plot is a box divided into two parts with a whisker at each end. The ends of the left and right whiskers show the lowest and highest scores. Quartiles partition scores into quarters. The left and right parts of the box show the upper and lower quartiles; the dividing line shows the median.

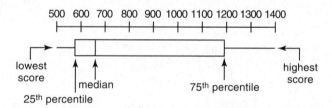

The median of these scores is about 660, while the highest score is about 1,390.

Practice

1. Create a stem-and-leaf plot using the following test scores.

   15, 19, 94, 10, 56, 23, 106, 28, 36, 38, 42, 48, 45, 26, 42, 105, 55, 53, 76, 47, 77, 29, 79, 49, 92, 96, 17, 13, 101, 75, 33

   Check the answer before continuing.

Answers on page 177.

Use the stem-and-leaf graph from exercise 1.

2. Which score is between 56 and 75?

3. What is the median of these test scores?

4. What is the mode of these test scores?

FLOW CHARTS

A flow chart shows the steps for completing a task. The flow chart uses these special symbols.

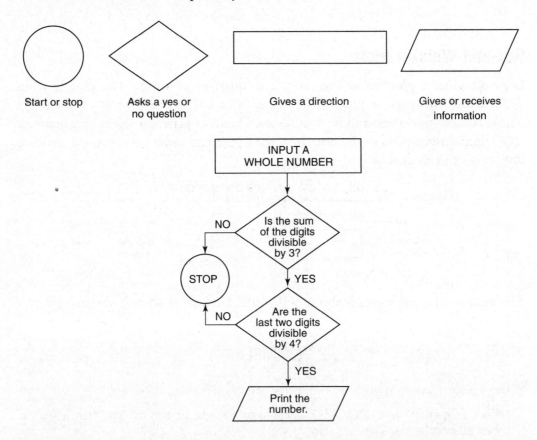

Start or stop

Asks a yes or no question

Gives a direction

Gives or receives information

INPUT A WHOLE NUMBER

NO — Is the sum of the digits divisible by 3?

STOP

YES

NO — Are the last two digits divisible by 4?

YES

Print the number.

According to the steps in the flow chart, the number printed will always be any number that gets a yes answer from both decision boxes and is divisible by both 3 and 4. These numbers are divisible by 12.

Practice

Directions: Use the flow chart below for exercises 1–3.

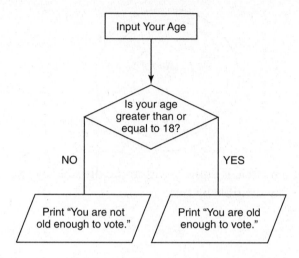

1. What information must be provided to use the flow chart?

2. What information does the above flow chart output?

3. How many phrases could be printed?

4. Create a flow chart that will display only prime numbers.

Answers on page 177.

LOGIC

Using Diagrams

ALL, SOME, AND NONE

Diagrams can show the logical connectives all, some, and none. View the following diagrams for an explanation.

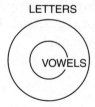

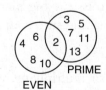

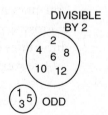

All—
All vowels are letters.

Some—
Some prime numbers are even.

None—
No odd numbers are divisible by two.

DEDUCTIVE REASONING

Deductive reasoning draws conclusions from statements or assumptions. Diagrams may help you draw a conclusion. Consider this simple example.

Assume that all even numbers are divisible by two and that all multiples of ten are even. Draw a diagram:

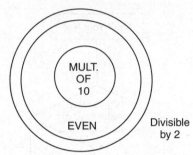

The multiple of ten circle is entirely within the divisible by two circle. Conclusion: All multiples of ten are divisible by two.

Practice

Directions: Write whether the statement is true or false. Explain your answer.

1. A ball is used in all sports.

2. Some numbers divisible by 5 are also divisible by 7.

3. There are no even numbers divisible by 3.

4. Some prime numbers are divisible by 2.

Answers on page 178.

PROBLEM SOLVING

Use these problem-solving strategies.

Estimate to Be Sure Your Answer is Reasonable

You can use estimation and common sense to be sure that the answer is reasonable. You may make a multiplication error or misalign decimal points. You may be so engrossed in a problem that you miss the big picture because of the details. These difficulties can be headed off by making sure your answer is reasonable.

A few examples follow.

- A question involves dividing or multiplying. Multiply: 28×72.
- Estimate first: $30 \times 70 = 2,100$. Your answer should be close to 2,100. If not, then your answer is not reasonable. A mistake was probably made in multiplication.
- A question involves subtracting or adding. Add: $12.9 + 0.63 + 10.29 + 4.3$.

- Estimate first: $13 + 1 + 10 + 4 = 28$. Your answer should be close to 28. If not, then your answer is not reasonable. The decimal points may not have been aligned.

- A question asks you to compare fractions to $\frac{11}{10}$.

- Think: $\frac{11}{10}$ is more than 1. Any number 1 or less will be less than $\frac{11}{10}$. Any number $1\frac{1}{8}$ or larger will be more than $\frac{11}{10}$. You have to look closely only at numbers between 1 and $1\frac{1}{8}$.

- A question asks you to multiply two fractions or decimals.

- The fractions or decimals are less than 1. The product of two fractions or decimals less than one is less than either of the two fractions or decimals. If not, you know that your answer is not reasonable.

Stand back for a second after you answer each question and ask, "Is this reasonable? Is this at least approximately correct? Does this make sense?"

TIP

Check answers to computation, particularly division and subtraction. When you have completed a division or subtraction example, do a quick, approximate check. Your check should confirm your answer. If not, your answer is probably not reasonable.

Circle Important Information and Key Words Eliminate Extra Information

This approach will draw your attention to the information needed to answer the question. A common mistake is to use from the question information that has nothing to do with the solution.

EXAMPLE

In the morning, a train travels at a constant speed over an 800 kilometer distance. In the afternoon the train travels back over this same route. There is less traffic and the train travels four times as fast as it did that morning. However, there are more people on the train during the afternoon. Which of the following do you know about the train's afternoon trip?

(A) The time is divided by four
(B) The time is multiplied by four
(C) The rate and time are divided by four
(D) The rate is divided by four
(E) The distance is the same, so the rate is the same

To solve the problem you just need to know that the speed is constant, four times as fast, and the same route was covered. Circle this information you need to solve the problem.

The distance traveled or that there were more people in the afternoon is extra information. Cross off this extra information, which may interfere with your ability to solve the problem.

In the morning, a train travels at a ~~constant speed~~ over an 800-kilometer distance. In the afternoon the train travels back over this ~~same route.~~ ~~There is less traffic~~ and the train travels ~~four times as fast~~ as it did that morning. ~~However, there are more people on the train during the afternoon.~~ Which of the following do you know about the train's afternoon trip?

The correct answer is (A), the time is divided by four. The route is the same, but the train travels four times as fast. Therefore, the time to make the trip is divided by four. Rate means the same thing as speed, and we know that the speed has been multiplied by four.

Words to Symbols Problems

Before you solve a problem, you may have to decide which operation to use. You can use key words to help you decide which operation to use.

KEY WORDS	
Addition	sum, and, more, increased by
Subtraction	less, difference, decreased by
Multiplication	of, product, times
Division	per, quotient, shared, ratio
Equals	is, equals

You can't just use these key words without thinking. You must be sure that the operation makes sense when it replaces the key word. For example,

19 and 23 is 42	16 is 4 more than 12	30% of 19 is 5.7?
$19 + 23 = 42$	$16 = 4 + 12$	$0.3 \times 19 = 5.7$

three more than y	$y + 3$	The product of 3 and y	$3y$
y increased by 3	$y + 3$	3 times y	$3y$
y more than 3	$3 + y$	3% of y	$0.03y$
3 less than y	$y - 3$	3 divided by y	$\dfrac{3}{y}$
y decreased by 3	$y - 3$	y divided by 3	$\dfrac{y}{3}$
3 decreased y	$3 - y$	ratio of 3 to y	$\dfrac{3}{y}$
The opposite of y	$-y$	The reciprocal of y	$\dfrac{1}{y}$

EXAMPLES

A. 18 divided by what number is 3?

$18 \div y = 3$ $\qquad$ $18 = 3y$ $\qquad$ $y = 6$

B. 25 less 6 is what number?

$25 - 6 = y$ $\qquad$ $y = 19$

C. A student correctly answered 80% of 120 mathematics problems. How many mathematics problems did he answer correctly?

$0.8 \times 120 = y$ $\qquad$ $y = 96$

The student correctly answered 96 problems.

D. The product of a number and its opposite is –25. What is the number?

$(y) \times (-y) = 25$ $\qquad$ $y = 5$ or $y = -5$

The number is 5 or –5.

Practice

Directions: Solve the problems.

1. What number decreased by 9 is 25?

2. What is 60% of 90?

3. Bob lives $\frac{2}{3}$ mile from Gina and $\frac{1}{2}$ mile from Sam. Bob's walk to the school is three times the sum of these distances. How far is Bob's walk to school?

4. The ratio of two gears is 20 to y. If the ratio equals 2.5, what is the value of y?

5. The sum of 5 and the reciprocal of another number is $5\frac{1}{8}$. What is the other number?

6. Car A travels at a constant speed of 60 mph for 2.5 hours. Car B travels at a constant speed of 70 mph for 2 hours. What is the total distance traveled by both cars?

Answers on page 178.

FINDING AND INTERPRETING PATTERNS
Sequences

Arithmetic Sequence

A sequence of numbers formed by adding the same nonzero number.

3, 11, 19, 27, 35, 42, 50 $\qquad$ Add 8 to get each successive term
52, 48, 44, 40, 36, 32 $\qquad$ Add (–4) to get each successive term

Geometric Sequence

A sequence of numbers formed by multiplying the same nonzero number.

3, 15, 75, 375   Multiply by 5 to get each successive term.

$160, 40, 10, 2\frac{1}{2}$ Multiply by $\frac{1}{4}$ to get each successive term.

Harmonic Sequence

A sequence of fractions with a numerator of 1 in which the denominators form an arithmetic sequence.

$\frac{1}{2} \quad \frac{1}{9} \quad \frac{1}{16} \quad \frac{1}{23} \quad \frac{1}{30}$ Each numerator is 1. The denominators form an arithmetic sequence.

Relationships

Linear Relationships

Linear relationships are pairs of numbers formed by adding or multiplying the same number to the first term in a pair. Here are some examples.

(3, 12), (5, 14), (11, 20), (15, 24)   Add 9 to the first term to get the second.

(1, 6), (2, 12), (3, 18), (4, 24), (5, 30)   Multiply the first term by 6 to get the second.

(96, 12), (72, 9), (56, 7), (24, 3), (16, 2)   Multiply the first term by $\frac{1}{8}$ to get the second.

EXAMPLES

A. What term is missing in this number pattern?

2   5   10   17   _____
  +3 +5   +7   +9

26 is the missing term.

B. These points are all on the same line.
Find the missing term.

$(-7, -15) \left(\frac{2}{3}, \frac{1}{3}\right) (2, 3) (4, 7) (8, \underline{\quad\quad})$

Multiply the first term by 2 and subtract 1.
The missing term is (8, 15).

Practice

Directions: Find the missing term in each pattern below.

1. 4, 2, 0, –2, –4, _____ –8, –10

2. 4, 6.5, 9, 11.5, _____

3. 120, 60, 30, 15, _____

4. 1, 2, 6, 24, 120, _____

5. 5 9 13 17 _____

Directions: The points in each sequence below are on the same line. Find the missing term.

6. (4, 12), (2, 10), (10, 18), (18, 26), (22, _____)

7. (100, 11), (70, 8), (90, 10), (40, 5), (30, _____)

8. (3, 9), (7, 49), (2, 4), (100, 10,000), (5, _____)

9. A meteorologist placed remote thermometers at sea level and up the side of the mountain at 1,000, 2,000, 5,000, and 6,000 feet. Readings were taken simultaneously and entered in the following table. What temperatures would you predict for the missing readings?

Temperature

0	1,000	2,000	3,000	4,000	5,000	6,000	7,000	8,000	9,000	10,000
52°	49°	46°			37°	34°				

10. Consider another example. A space capsule is moving in a straight line and is being tracked on a grid. The first four positions on the grid are recorded in the following table. Where will the capsule be on the grid when the x position is 13?

x-value	1	2	3	4
y-value	1	4	7	10

Answers on page 178.

ESTIMATION PROBLEMS

Follow these steps.

1. Round the numbers.
2. Use the rounded numbers to estimate the answer.

EXAMPLE

It takes a person about $7\frac{1}{2}$ minutes to run a mile. The person runs 174 miles in a month.

What is a reasonable estimate of the time it takes for the person to run that distance?

Round $7\frac{1}{2}$ to 8.

Round 174 to 180.

$180 \times 8 = 1,440$ minutes or 24 hours.

24 hours is a reasonable estimate of the answer.

Practice

1. A class took a spelling quiz and the grades were 93, 97, 87, 88, 98, 91. What is a reasonable estimate of the average of these grades?

2. To build a sandbox, you need lumber in the following lengths: 12 ft, 16 ft, 18 ft, and 23 ft. What is a reasonable estimate of the total length of the lumber?

3. Each batch of cookies yields 11 dozen. You need 165 dozen. What is a reasonable estimate for the number of batches you will need?

4. It takes 48 minutes for a commuter to travel back and forth from work each day. If the commuter drives back and forth 26 days a month, what is a reasonable estimate of the number of hours that are spent driving?

Answers on pages 178–179.

CHART PROBLEMS

Follow these steps:

1. Identify the data in the chart.
2. Add when necessary to find the total probability.

EXAMPLE

TABLE 1

	Air Express	Rail	Truck
5 pounds and over	0.07	0.34	0.18
Under 5 pounds	0.23	0.02	0.16

The table shows the percent of packages shipped by the method used and the weight classes.

What is the probability that a package picked at random was sent Air Express?

Add the two proportions for Air Express.
0.07 + 0.23 = 0.30
The probability that a randomly picked package was sent Air Express is 0.3.

What is the probability that a package picked at random weighed under five pounds?

Add the three proportions for under five pounds.
0.23 + 0.02 + 0.16 = 0.42.
The probability that a randomly chosen package weighed under five pounds is 0.42.

What is the probability that a package picked at random weighing under five pounds was sent by rail?

Look at the cell in the table where *under five pounds* and *rail* intersect.
That proportion is 0.02.
The probability that a randomly chosen package under five pounds was sent by rail is 0.02.

Practice

Directions: Use Table 1 above.

1. What is the probability that a package was sent by truck?

2. What is the probability of a package five pounds and over being randomly chosen?

3. What is the probability that a package five pounds and over picked at random was sent by Air Express?

4. What is the probability of randomly choosing a package under five pounds that was sent other than by rail?

Answers on page 179.

FREQUENCY TABLE PROBLEMS

Percent

Percent tables show the percent or proportion of a particular score or characteristic. We can see from Table 1 that 13% of the students got a score from 90 through 100.

EXAMPLE

TABLE 1

Scores	Percent of Students
0–59	2
60–69	8
70–79	39
80–89	38
90–100	13

Which score interval contains the median?

The cumulative percentage of 0–79 is 49%.
The median is in the interval in which the cumulative percentage of 50% occurs. The score interval 80–89 contains the median.

What percent of the students scored above 79?

Add the percentiles of the intervals above 79.   38 + 13 = 51
51% of the students scored above 79.

Percentile Rank

The percentile rank shows the percent of scores below a given value. We can see from Table 2 that 68% of the scores fell below 60.

EXAMPLE

TABLE 2

Standardized Score	Percentile Rank
80	99
70	93
60	68
50	39
40	22
30	13
20	2

What percent of the scores are below 50?

The percentile rank next to 50 is 39. That means 39% of the scores are below 50.

What percent of the scores are between 30 and 70?

Subtract the percentile rank for 30 from the percentile rank for 70.
93% – 13% = 80%. 80% of the scores are between 30 and 70.

What percent of the scores are at or above 60?

Subtract the percentile rank for 60 from 100%.
100% – 68% = 32%. 32% of the scores are at or above 60.

Practice

Directions: Use Table 1 and Table 2 on page 160.

Table 1

1. What percent of the scores are below 70?

2. In which score interval is the median?

3. What percent of the scores are from 80 to 100?

Table 2

4. The lowest passing score is 50. What percent of the scores are passing?

5. What percent of the scores are from 20 to 50?

Answers on page 179.

FORMULA PROBLEMS

Concentrate on substituting values for variables. If you see a problem to be solved with a proportion, set up the proportion and solve.

EXAMPLES

A. A mechanic uses this formula to estimate the displacement (P) of an engine. $P = 0.8 \ (d^2)(s)(n)$ where **d** is the diameter, **s** is the stroke length of each cylinder, and **n** is the number of cylinders. Estimate the displacement of a 6-cylinder car whose cylinders have a diameter of 2 inches and a stroke length of 4 inches.

1. Write the formula. $P = 0.8 \ (d^2)(s)(n)$

2. Write the values of the variables. $d = 2, \ s = 4, \ n = 6$

3. Substitute the values for the variables. $P = 0.8(2^2)(4)(6)$

4. Solve. $P = 0.8(4)(24) = (3.2)(24)$

   $P = 76.8$

The displacement of the engine is about 76.8 cubic inches.

B. The accountant calculates that it takes $3 in sales to generate $0.42 in profit. How much cost does it take to generate a profit of $5.46?

1. Write a proportion
   Use s for sales. $\dfrac{3}{0.42} = \dfrac{s}{5.46}$

2. Cross multiply. $0.42s = 16.38$

3. Solve. $s = \dfrac{16.38}{0.42}$

   $s = 39$

It will take $39 in sales to generate $5.46 in profits.

Practice

1. A retail store makes a profit of $3.75 for each $10 of goods sold. How much profit would the store make on a $45 purchase?

2. The formula for calculating average speed is $d/(T_2 - T_1)$. If T_1 (start time) is 5:00 P.M. and T_2 (end time) is midnight the same day, and 287 miles were traveled, what was the average speed?

3. A car purchased for $12,000 ($O$) depreciates 10% ($P$) a year ($Y$). If the car is sold in 3 years, what is its depreciated value if $V = O - POY$?

4. There is a square grid of dots. A figure is made of line segments that connect the dots. The formula for the area of a figure on the grid is $\dfrac{T-2}{2} + I$.

   T is the number of dots touching the figure, and I is the number of dots inside. What is the area of a figure with 14 dots touching and 5 dots inside?

Answers on page 179.

PYTHAGOREAN THEOREM PROBLEMS

Follow these steps to solve this type of problem.

1. Sketch and label the right triangle.

2. Use the Pythagorean formula.

3. Solve the problem.

EXAMPLE

A radio tower sticks 40 feet straight up into the air. Engineers attached a wire with no slack from the top of the tower to the ground 30 feet away from the tower. If it costs $95 a foot to attach the wire, how much did the wire cost?

1. Sketch and label the right triangle.

2. Use the Pythagorean formula.
   $a^2 + b^2 = c^2$
   $(40)^2 + (30)^2 = c^2$
   $1{,}600 + 900 = c^2$
   $2{,}500 = c^2$
   $50 = c$
   The wire is 50 feet long.

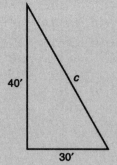

3. Solve the problem.
   50 feet at $95 a foot.
   $50 \times 95 = 4{,}750$. The wire costs $4,750 to install.

Practice

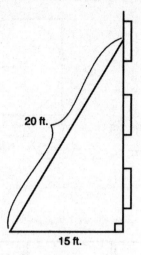

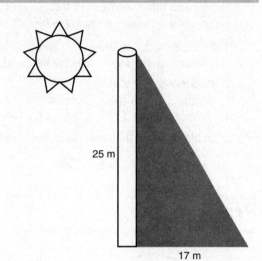

1. A 20-foot ladder is leaning against the side of a tall apartment building. The bottom of the ladder is 15 feet from the wall. At what height on the wall does the top of the ladder touch the building?

2. A 25-meter telephone pole casts a shadow. The shadow ends 17 meters from the base of the pole. How long is it straight from the top of the pole to the end of the shadow?

4. A truck ramp is shaped like a right triangle. The base of the ramp is 300 feet long. The ramp itself is 340 feet long. How high is the third side of the ramp?

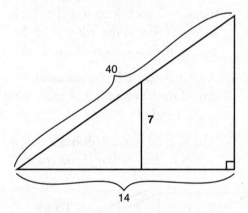

3. You are building a staircase. The wall is 14 feet wide and the stairs are 40 feet long. How high is the wall where it touches the top of the stairs?

Answers on pages 179–180.

GEOMETRIC FIGURE PROBLEMS

Follow these steps to solve this type of problem.

1. Identify the figure or figures involved.

2. Use the formulas for these figures.

3. Use the results of the formulas to solve the problem.

EXAMPLE

A circular pool with a radius of 10 feet is inscribed inside a square wall. What is the area of the region outside the pool but inside the fence?

1. There is a square with $s = 20$ and a circle with $r = 10$.
   The side of the square is twice the radius of the circle.

2. Find the areas.
   Square: $(A = s^2)$ $(20) \times (20) = 400$
   Circle: $(A = \pi r^2)$ $3.14 \times 10^2 = 3.14 \times 100 = 314$

3. Subtract to find the area inside the square but outside the circle.
   $400 - 314 = 86$

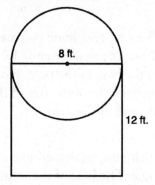

Practice

1. The dimensions of part of a basket-ball court are shown in the diagram above. One pint of paint covers 35 square feet. How much paint would it take to paint the inside region of this part of the court?

2. A roofer uses one bushel of shingles to cover 1200 square feet. How many bushels of shingles are needed to cover these three rectangular roofs?

   Roof 1: 115 ft by 65 ft
   Roof 2: 112 ft by 65 ft
   Roof 3: 72 ft by 52 ft

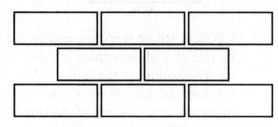

3. The bricks in the wall pictured here measure 2 inches by 4 inches by 8 inches. What is the volume of the bricks in this section of the wall?

4. A circular cone has a radius of 4 cm. If the volume is 134 cm³, what is the height?

5. The official basketball has a radius of 6.5 inches. What is the volume?

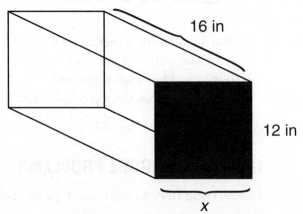

6. The rectangular solid shown here has a volume of 1,920 in³. What is the area of the shaded side?

INTERPRETING REMAINDER PROBLEMS

When you divide to solve a problem there may be both a quotient and a remainder. You may need to (1) use only the quotient, (2) round the quotient to the next greater whole number, or (3) use only the remainder.

EXAMPLE

Stereo speakers are packed 4 to a box. There are 315 stereo speakers to be packed.

Questions:

1. How many boxes can be filled?

2. How many boxes would be needed to hold all the stereo speakers?

3. How many stereo speakers will be in the box that is not completely full?

Divide 315 by 4.

```
      78 R3
  4)315
     28
     35
     32
      3
```

Answers:

1. Use only the quotient—78 of the boxes can be filled.

2. Round the quotient to the next higher number. It would take 79 boxes to hold all the stereo speakers.

3. Use only the remainder. Three stereo speakers would be in the partially filled box.

Practice

At the quarry, workers are putting 830 pounds of sand into bags that hold 25 pounds.

1. How much sand is left over after the bags are filled?

2. How many bags are needed to hold all the sand?

3. How many bags can be filled with sand?

Answers on page 180.

Strategies for Taking the Mathematics Test

The mathematics tested is the kind you probably had in high school and in college. It is the kind of mathematics you will use as you teach and go about your everyday life. Computational ability, alone, is expected but is held to a minimum. Remember to use the general test strategies discussed in the Introduction.

WRITE IN THE TEST BOOKLET

It is particularly important to write in the test booklet while taking the mathematics portion of the test. Use these hints for writing in the test booklet.

Do Your Calculations in the Test Booklet

Do all your calculations in the Paper-Based PPST test booklet to the right of the question or on the Computer-Based PPST scrap paper. This makes it easy to refer to the calculations as you choose the correct answer.

This example should make you feel comfortable about writing in the test booklet.

What number times 0.00708 is equal to 70.8

(A) 100,000 × *0.00708 = 700.8*
(B) 10,000 × *0.00708 = 70.8*
(C) 1,000
(D) 0.01
(E) 0.0001

The correct answer is (B) 10,000.

Draw Diagrams and Figures in the Test Booklet or on Scrap Paper

When you come across a geometry problem or related problem, draw a diagram in the Paper-Based PPST test booklet or on the Computer-Based PPST scrap paper to help.

All sides of a rectangle are shrunk in half. What happens to the area?

(A) Divided by two
(B) Divided by four
(C) Multiplied by two
(D) Multiplied by six
(E) Does not change

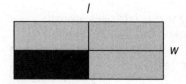

Answer (B), divided by 4, is the correct answer. The original area is evenly divided into four parts.

Work from the Answers

If you don't know how to solve a formula or relation, try out each answer choice until you get the correct answer. Look at this example.

What percent times $\frac{1}{4}$ is $\frac{1}{5}$?

(A) 25%
(B) 40%
(C) 80%
(D) 120%
(E) None of the above

Just take each answer in turn and try it out.

$$0.25 \times \frac{1}{4} = \frac{1}{4} \times \frac{1}{4} = \frac{1}{16}$$ That's not it.

$$0.40 \times \frac{1}{4} = \frac{4}{10} \times \frac{1}{4} = \frac{4}{40} = \frac{1}{10}$$ That's not it either.

$$0.8 \times \frac{1}{4} = \frac{4}{5} \times \frac{1}{4} = \frac{4}{20} = \frac{1}{5}$$

You know that 0.8 is the correct answer, and so choice (C) is correct.

Try Out Numbers

Look at the preceding question.

Work with fractions at first. Ask: What number times $\frac{1}{4}$ equals $\frac{1}{5}$?

Through trial and error you find out that $\frac{4}{5} \times \frac{1}{4} = \frac{1}{5}$.

The answer in fractions is $\frac{4}{5}$.

$$\frac{4}{5} = 0.8 = 80\%$$

The correct choice is (C).

In this example, we found the answer without ever solving an equation. We just tried out numbers until we found the one that works.

Eliminate and Guess

Use this approach when all else has failed. Begin by eliminating the answers you know are wrong. Sometimes you know with certainty that an answer is incorrect. Other times, an answer looks so unreasonable that you can be fairly sure that it is not correct.

Once you have eliminated incorrect answers, a few will probably be left. Just guess among these choices. There is no method that will increase your chances of guessing correctly.

Targeted Mathematics Test

This targeted test is designed to help you practice the problem-solving and test-taking strategies presented in this chapter. For that reason, questions may have a different emphasis than the actual test, and the actual test will certainly be more complete. Answers are on pages 180–181.

Directions: Mark your choice, then check your answers.
Use the strategies on pages 166–167 and 152–154.

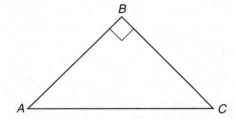

1. This is an isosceles triangle. What is the measure of angle *A*?

   (A) 10°
   (B) 40°
   (C) 90°
   (D) 45°
   (E) 180°

2. After a discount of 25%, the savings on a pair of roller blades was $12.00. What was the sale price?

   (A) $48.00
   (B) $36.00
   (C) $24.00
   (D) $25.00
   (E) $60.00

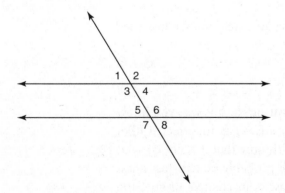

3. Which two angles are supplementary?

   (A) 6 & 7
   (B) 1 & 4

   (C) 3 & 6
   (D) 2 & 4
   (E) 4 & 8

4. Chad rolls a fair die. The sides of the die are numbered from 1 to 6. Ten times in a row he rolls a 5. What is the probability that he will roll a 5 on his next roll?

   (A) $\frac{1}{5}$

   (B) $\frac{1}{6}$

   (C) $\frac{1}{50}$

   (D) $\frac{1}{11}$

   (E) $\frac{1}{10}$

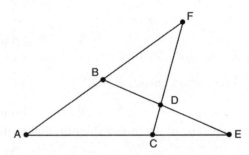

5. Which of the following set of points do not form an angle in the diagram?

   (A) ABF
   (B) ABE
   (C) AFC
   (D) ABC
   (E) CDE

6. An apple costs (*C*). You have (*D*) dollars. What equation would represent the amount of apples you could buy for the money you have?

    (A) *C/D*
    (B) *CD*
    (C) *C* + *D*
    (D) *D/C*
    (E) *C* + 2*D*

7. If a worker gets $144.00 for 18 hours' work, how much would that worker get for 32 hours' work?

    (A) $200.00
    (B) $288.00
    (C) $400.00
    (D) $432.00
    (E) $256.00

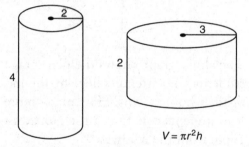

$V = \pi r^2 h$

8. Find the difference between the volumes of these two cylinders?

    (A) 2 π
    (B) 4 π
    (C) 9 π
    (D) 16 π
    (E) 18 π

9. *r* = regular price
   d = discount
   s = sale price

   What equation would represent the calculations for finding the discount?

    (A) *d* = *r* − s
    (B) *d* = *s* − r
    (C) *d* = *sr*
    (D) *d* = *s* + *r*
    (E) $d = \frac{1}{2}r$

10. A printing company makes pamphlets that cost $.75 per copy plus $5.00 as a setter's fee. If $80 were spent printing a pamphlet, how many pamphlets were ordered?

    (A) 50
    (B) 75
    (C) 100
    (D) 150
    (E) 225

11. Which is furthest from $\frac{1}{2}$ on a number line?

    (A) $\frac{1}{12}$

    (B) $\frac{7}{8}$

    (C) $\frac{3}{4}$

    (D) $\frac{2}{3}$

    (E) $\frac{5}{6}$

12. Which of the following could be about 25 centimeters long?

    (A) a human thumb
    (B) a doorway
    (C) a car
    (D) a house
    (E) a notebook

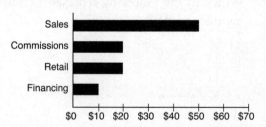

13. The sales department staff draws its salary from four areas of the company's income. Using the above graph, determine what percentage is drawn from the retail fund.

    (A) 10%
    (B) 20%
    (C) 25%
    (D) 30%
    (E) 15%

14. If 250 is lowered by 40%, what percent of the new number is 30?

   (A) 5%
   (B) 10%
   (C) 20%
   (D) 25%
   (E) 50%

15. For a fund-raiser the Science and Technology Club is selling raffles at the cost of six raffles for $5.00. It cost the club $250.00 for the prizes and tickets that will be given away. How many raffles will the club have to sell in order to make $1,000.00?

   (A) 300
   (B) 600
   (C) 750
   (D) 1200
   (E) 1500

16. What value for n makes the number sentence true?

   $5.3 \times 10^4 = 0.0053 \times 10^n$

   (A) 4
   (B) 5
   (C) 6
   (D) 7
   (E) 8

17. Which of the following represents complementary angles?

   (A)

   (B)

   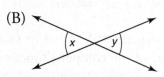

   (C)

   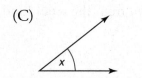

(D)

(E)

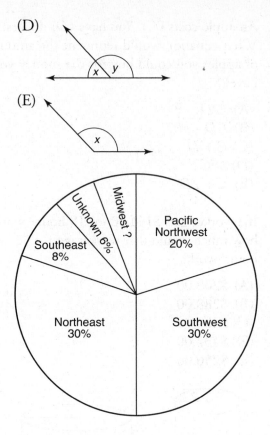

18. The above graph shows the percentage of students who attend college by the location of their home towns. How many more college students come from the Northeast than come from the Midwest?

   (A) twice as many
   (B) three times as many
   (C) half as many
   (D) five times as many
   (E) ten times as many

19. Each rectangle has a total area of 1 square unit. What number represents the area of the shaded regions?

   (A) $\dfrac{5}{6}$ square units

   (B) $\dfrac{7}{8}$ square units

   (C) $1\dfrac{3}{4}$ square units

(D) $1\dfrac{1}{3}$ square units

(E) $1\dfrac{5}{24}$ square units

20. Which diagram shows both the set of whole numbers between 1 and 20 and multiples of 5 between 1 and 20?

(A)
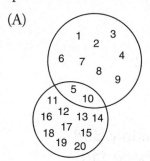

(B)
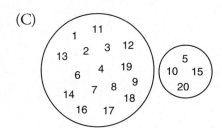

(C)
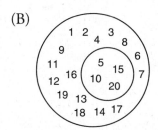

(D)
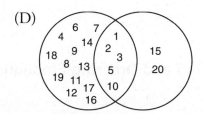

(E)
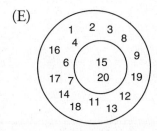

Answers on pages 180–181.

Answers for Mathematics Practice

Understanding and Ordering Whole Numbers, page 102

1. $2 < 3$
2. $4 > 1$
3. $8 < 9$
4. $1 = 1$
5. $7 > 6$
6. 9,037
7. 2,851
8. The hundreds place and the ones place each contain a 7.
9. 1, 2, 3, 4, 5, 6, 7, 8, 9, 10, 11, 12, 13, 14
   The problem asks for the numbers between 0 and 15, so 0 and 15 are not included.
10. There are 49. (1, 2, 3, . . . , 47, 48, 49)

Whole Number Computation, page 104

1. 98,405
2. 27,079
3. 95,809
4. 66,184
5. 16,013
6. 34,099
7. 34,688
8. 42,209
9. 13,680
10. 27,482
11. 29,725
12. 5,256
13. 8
14. 4 R4
15. 29
16. 32 R2

Positive Exponents, page 105

1. 5,400
2. 81
3. 8
4. 900
5. 35
6. 51

7. $4^6 = 4,096$
8. $2^5 = 32$
9. 44
10. 1,000
11. $4^4 = 256$
12. 72

Square Roots, page 106

1. $\sqrt{256} = 16$
2. $\sqrt{400} = 20$
3. $\sqrt{576} = 24$
4. $\sqrt{900} = 30$
5. $\sqrt{1225} = 35$
6. $\sqrt{48} = \sqrt{16 \times 3} = 4\sqrt{3}$
7. $\sqrt{245} = \sqrt{49 \times 5} = 7\sqrt{5}$
8. $\sqrt{396} = \sqrt{36 \times 11} = 6\sqrt{11}$
9. $\sqrt{567} = \sqrt{81 \times 7} = 9\sqrt{7}$
10. $\sqrt{832} = \sqrt{64 \times 13} = 8\sqrt{13}$

Order of Operations, page 107

1. $4 \times 5 + 4 \div 2 = 20 + 2 = 22$
2. $(5 + 7 - 9) \times 8^2 + 2 = 3 \times 8^2 + 2 = 194$
3. $((7 + 4) - (1 + 4)) \times 6 = (11 - 5) \times 6 = 36$
4. $6^2 + 3(9 - 5 + 7)^2 = 36 + 3 \times 11^2 = 399$
5. $51 - 36 = 15$
6. $40 + 4 - 4 = 40$
7. $^-50 + 7 = {}^-43$
8. $(49 + 16) \times 8 = 520$

Understanding and Ordering Whole Numbers and Decimals, page 108

1. $0.02 > 0.003$
2. $4.6 > 1.98$
3. $0.0008 > 0.00009$
4. $1.0 = 1$
5. $7.6274 > 7.6269$
6. 2.586
7. 90310.0704
8. The hundredths place and the hundred thousandths place each contain a 3.
9. 0, 0.1, 0.2, 0.3, 0.4, 0.5, 0.6, 0.7, 0.8, 0.9, 1.0
10. There are 99—0.01, 0.02, 0.03, . . . , 0.50, 0.51, 0.52, . . . , 0.97, 0.98, 0.99

Rounding Whole Numbers and Decimals, page 109

1. 23,500
2. 74.151
3. 980,000
4. 302.8
5. 495,240
6. 1500
7. 13.1
8. 200,000
9. 52
10. 23,500

Add, Subtract, Multiply, and Divide Decimals, page 110

1. 26.09
2. 72.617
3. 988.39
4. 5473.19
5. 8.2
6. 71.0096
7. 453.97
8. 1767.87
9. .6225
10. 163.45
11. 3680.538
12. 3761.514
13. 4.8
14. 9.6
15. 33.6
16. 125.63

Understanding and Ordering Fractions, pages 112–113

1. $1\frac{2}{3}$
2. $2\frac{1}{7}$
3. $2\frac{2}{3}$
4. $\frac{41}{5}$
5. $\frac{55}{8}$
6. $\frac{68}{7}$

7. $\frac{3}{7} < \frac{4}{9}$

8. $\frac{5}{6} = \frac{25}{30}$

9. $\frac{4}{5} < \frac{7}{8}$

Multiply, Divide, Add, and Subtract Fractions and Mixed Numbers, page 114

1. $\frac{5}{27}$

2. $\frac{1}{6}$

3. $13\frac{59}{64}$

4. $8\frac{8}{35}$

5. $\frac{6}{7}$

6. $\frac{18}{35}$

7. $2\frac{22}{91}$

8. $\frac{7}{19}$

9. $1\frac{2}{9}$

10. $1\frac{1}{5}$

11. $4\frac{1}{14}$

12. $12\frac{1}{2}$

13. $\frac{1}{21}$

14. $\frac{1}{40}$

15. $\frac{2}{3}$

16. $3\frac{58}{63}$

Number Theory, pages 116–117

1. 13: 1 and 13
2. 26: 1, 2, 13, and 26
3. 40: 1, 2, 4, 5, 8, 10, 20, 40
4. 23: 1 and 23
5. 24
6. 60
7. 35
8. 28
9. 6
10. 5
11. 32
12. 28

Ratio and Proportion, page 118

1. 14 vacuum cleaners for 280 houses
2. 4 teachers for 32 children
3. 21 rest stops for 140 miles
4. Yes. $\frac{7}{9} = \frac{28}{36}$ because $7 \times 36 = 252 = 9 \times 28$

Percent, pages 119–120

1. 35.9%
2. 78%
3. 21.5%
4. 4.1%
5. $11\frac{1}{9}\%$
6. 62.5%
7. 30%
8. $44\frac{4}{9}\%$
9. $\frac{29}{50}$
10. $\frac{79}{100}$
11. $\frac{213}{250}$
12. $\frac{487}{500}$

Three Types of Percent Problems, page 121

1. $\square \times 240 = 120$

   $\square = \dfrac{120}{240}$

   $\square = .5 = 50\%$

2. $.15 \times 70 = \square$

   $.15 \times 70 = 10.5$

   $\square = 10.5$

3. $.6 \times 300 = \square$

   $.6 \times 300 = 180$

   $\square = 180$

4. $\square \times 60 = 42$

   $\square = \dfrac{42}{60}$

   $\square = 70\%$

5. $\square\% \times 25 = 2.5$

   $\square\% = \dfrac{2.5}{25}$

   $\square = 10\%$

6. $40\% \times \square = 22$

   $\square = \dfrac{22}{.4}$

   $\square = 55$

7. $.7 \times \square = 85$

   $\square = \dfrac{85}{.7}$

   $\square = 121\dfrac{3}{7}$

8. $25\% \times 38 = \square$

   $.25 \times 38 = 9.5$

   $\square = 9.5$

9. $.35 \times \square = 24$

   $\square = \dfrac{24}{.35}$

   $\square = 68\dfrac{4}{7}$

10. $24 = \square \times 80$

    $\dfrac{24}{80} = \square$

    $\square = 30\%$

Percent of Increase and Decrease, page 122

1. Amount of increase $35 − $25 = $10

   $\dfrac{10}{25} = 0.4 = 40\%$

   Percent of increase = 40%

2. Discount: $100 × .25 = $25

   $100 − $25 = $75

   Sale price = $75

3. Discount $80 × 15% = $12

   $80 − $12 = $68

   New price = $68

4. Amount of increase $150 − $120 = $30

   $\dfrac{30}{120} = \dfrac{1}{4} = 25\%$

   Percent of increase = 25%

5. Discount $75 × 10% = $7.50

   $75 − $7.50 = $67.50

   Sale price = $67.50

6. Amount of decrease $18 − $6 = $12

   $\dfrac{12}{18} = \dfrac{2}{3} = 66\dfrac{2}{3}\%$

   Percent of decrease = $66\dfrac{2}{3}\%$

7. Amount of decrease $225 − $180 = $45

   $\dfrac{45}{225} = 0.2 = 20\%$

   Percent of decrease = 20%

8. Discount $150 = x − 0.25x$

   $150 = 0.75x$

   $x = $200

   Original price: $200

Probability, page 123

1. There are 10 socks in the drawer. 7 of the 10 are not black.

   $P\text{ (not black)} = \dfrac{7}{10}$

2. There are 6 goldfish; 2 of the 6 are male

   $P\text{ (male)} = \dfrac{2}{6} = \dfrac{1}{3}$

3. There are 52 cards in a deck. There are 4 kings and 4 queens.

P (king or queen) = P (king) + P (queen) =

$$\frac{4}{52} + \frac{4}{52} = \frac{8}{52} = \frac{2}{13}$$

4. There are 6 different names.
P (Carl and Phyllis) =
P (Carl) $\times$ P (Phyllis) =

$$\frac{1}{6} \times \frac{1}{6} = \frac{1}{36}$$

5. $\dfrac{1}{2}$

6. This is an "and" problem. Multiply the probability.

$$\left(\frac{1}{2}\right)\left(\frac{1}{2}\right)\left(\frac{1}{2}\right)\left(\frac{1}{2}\right)\left(\frac{1}{2}\right) = \frac{1}{32}$$

Statistics, page 125

1. mode 80
2. mean (average) 35.5
3. median 9 (Remember to arrange the numbers in order.)
4. 16 is the median, the mode, and very close to the mean.
5. mean 89
6. mode 30

Permutations and Combinations, page 126

1. There are 6 combinations of 2 people to sit in the chairs.
2. There are 5,040 possible arrangements of the 7 books on the shelf.
3. 67,600 ($26 \times 26 \times 10 \times 10$)
4. The positions on the bus are not specified. Order does not matter. This is a combination problem.

Four students   A   B   C   D
ABC   ABD   ACD   BCD

There are four ways for three of four students to board the bus.

Integers, page 127

1. 15
2. 1
3. −69
4. −9
5. 1
6. 54
7. 22
8. −80
9. 99
10. −650
11. 1829
12. −1470
13. 15
14. −17
15. 44
16. −22

Scientific Notation, page 128

1. $0.0564 = 5.64 \times 10^{-2}$
2. $0.00897 = 8.97 \times 10^{-3}$
3. $0.06501 = 6.501 \times 10^{-2}$
4. $0.000354 = 3.54 \times 10^{-4}$
5. $545 = 5.45 \times 10^{2}$
6. $7{,}790 = 7.79 \times 10^{3}$
7. $289{,}705 = 2.89705 \times 10^{5}$
8. $1{,}801{,}319 = 1.801319 \times 10^{6}$

Equations, page 130

1. $w = 8$
2. $x = 15$
3. $y = 70$
4. $z = -4$
5. $w = 4$
6. $x = 126$
7. $y = -5$
8. $z = -66$
9. $w = 7$
10. $x = -13$
11. $y = 456$
12. $z = 3$

Geometry, page 134

1. trapezoid
2. m∠2 = 135°
3. m∠ABC = 50° = m∠ACB
4.

5. An octagon (8 sides) has two more sides than a hexagon (6 sides).
6. A right angle, which has a measure of 90°.
7. (Picture may vary)

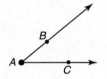

The new figure is ∠BAC.

8.

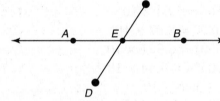

(Picture may vary)

9. (Picture may vary)

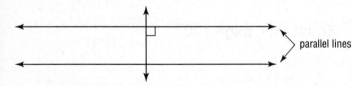

parallel lines

10. The sum of the measures is 180° (m∠A + m∠B + m∠C = 180°).

Coordinate Grid, pages 135–136

1. A(3, −2)
   B(−2, −4)
   C(−5, 5)
   D(3, 3)
   E(0, 2)
   F(−5, 0)

2.

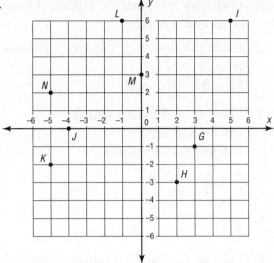

3.

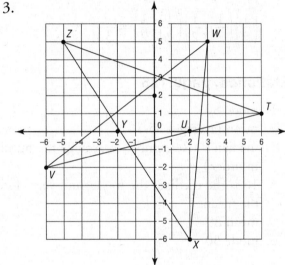

Measurement, pages 139–140

1. 0.22 decameters
2. 29,040 feet
3. $2\frac{1}{2}$ inches
4. $\frac{1}{2}$ pound
5. 64,000 ounces
6. 4 centimeters
7. 190,080 inches
8. 236,700 milliliters
9. 2 quarts
10. About 35°

Formulas, page 143

1. πr^2
   $3.14 \times (9)^2 =$
   $3.14 \times 81 = 254.34 \text{ m}^2$
2. $b = 3$, $h = 2.6$
   $\left(\dfrac{1}{2}\right)(3)(2.6) = 3.9$
   $4 \times 3.9 = 15.6 \text{ in}^2$
3. Hexagon is 6-sided
   $6 \times 5 \text{ ft} = 30 \text{ ft perimeter}$
4.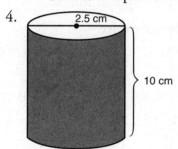
   $\begin{array}{cccc} 2 & \pi & r & h \end{array}$
   $2\,(3.14)(1.25)(10)$
   $= 78.5 \text{ cm}^2$
5. $(x + 5) + (x + 5) + x + x = 90$
   $4x + 10 = 90$
   $4x = 80 \quad x = 20$
   length $= x + 5$
   length $= 25 \text{ ft}$
6. Area of each side $= 25 \text{ cm}^2$
   Cube is 6-sided
   $6 \times 25 = 150 \text{ cm}^2$
7. $x = 12$
8. $A = 32.5 \text{ in.}^2$
9. $V = 4186.\overline{6}\left(4186\,\dfrac{2}{3}\right) \text{ cm}^3$
10. $V = 3375 \text{ in}^3$

Time and Temperature, page 145

1. 0°F (0°C is 32°F)
2. 1:00 P.M.
3.

   (clock showing hands)

4. 10:00 A.M.
5. 50°F
6. 104°C

Graphs, page 148

1. 1,000 phones
2. Alpine
3. HIJ Corp.
4. 3%
5. Alpine
6. Dumont
7. $800,000
8. $84,000

Stem-and-Leaf and Box-and- Whisker Plots, page 150

1.

Stem	Leaf
1	0, 3, 5, 7, 9
2	3, 6, 8, 9
3	3, 6, 8,
4	2, 2, 5, 7, 8, 9
5	3, 5, 6,
6	
7	5, 6, 7, 9
8	
9	2, 4, 6,
10	1, 5, 6

2. There is no score between 56 and 75.
3. 47
4. 42

Flow Charts, page 151

1. A person's age
2. The flow chart outputs whether or not an individual is old enough to vote.
3. There are two possible sentences: "You are old enough to vote." *or* "You are not old enough to vote."

4.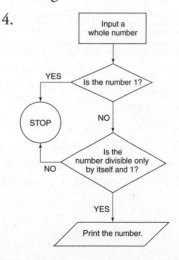

Logic, page 152

1. False—Some sports, such as hockey, do not use a ball.
2. True—For example, 35 is divisible by both 5 and 7.
3. False—For example, 12 is divisible by 3.
4. True—For example, 2 is both prime and divisible by 2.

Words to Symbols Problems, page 155

1. 34; $34 - 9 = 25$
2. $0.6 \times 90 = 54$
3. Add: $\dfrac{2}{3} + \dfrac{1}{2} = \dfrac{7}{6}$

   Multiply: $\dfrac{7}{6} \times 3 = \dfrac{21}{6}$

   Divide: $\dfrac{21}{6} \div 3\dfrac{3}{6} = 3\dfrac{1}{2}$.

   Bob's walk to school is $3\dfrac{1}{2}$ miles.
4. $\dfrac{20}{y} = 2.5 \quad 20 = 2.5y \quad y = 8$
5. $5\dfrac{1}{x} = 5\dfrac{1}{8} \qquad x = 8$

   The number is 8.
6. Multiply: $60 \times 2.5 = 150$
   $ 70 \times 2 = 140$
   Add: $150 + 140 = 290$
   The cars traveled a total distance of 290 miles.

Finding and Interpreting Patterns, page 157

1. **–6** is the missing term. Subtract 2 from each term.
2. **14** is the missing term. Add 2.5 to each term.
3. **7.5** is the missing term. Divide each term by 2 to get the next term.
4. **720** is the missing term. The sequence follows the pattern $(1 \times 1)(1 \times 2)(1 \times 2 \times 3)$ $(1 \times 2 \times 3 \times 4) \ldots$
5. **21** is the missing term. Add 4 to find the next term.
6. **(22, 30)** is the missing term. Add 8 to the first term to find the second term.
7. **(30, 4)** is the missing term. Divide the first term by 10 and add 1 to find the second term.
8. **(5, 25)** is the missing term. Square the first term to get the second term.
9. The temperature drops 3° from 52° to 49° and from 49° to 46°. If it drops at the same rate, the temperature drop at 3,000 feet would be 43° and 4,000 feet would be 40° (followed by 37° and 34°). Continue to fill in the table accordingly, as follows.

   Temperature

0	1,000	2,000	3,000	4,000	5,000
52°	49°	46°	43°	40°	37°

6,000	7,000	8,000	9,000	10,000
34°	31°	28°	25°	22°

10. Multiply three times the x value, subtract 2, and that gives the y value. The rule is y equals three times $x - 2$ so that the equation is $y = 3x - 2$. Substitute 13 for x:

    $$y = 3(13) - 2 = 39 - 2 = 37$$

    The capsule will be at position (13, 37).

Estimation Problems, page 158

1. Round all the scores and add the rounded scores.

   $90 + 100 + 90 + 90 + 100 + 90 = 560$

   Divide by the number of scores.
   $560 \div 6 = 93.3$
   93 is a reasonable estimate of the average.

2. Round the lengths and add the rounded lengths.

   $10 + 20 + 20 + 20 = 70$

   70 feet is a reasonable estimate of the amount of wood needed.

3. Round the number of dozens to the nearest 10.

   Divide the rounded numbers.

   $\dfrac{170}{10} = 17$

   17 is a reasonable estimate of the number of batches needed.

4. Round the number of minutes and number of days to the nearest 10.

Multiply the rounded numbers.

$50 \times 30 = 1,500$
Divide to find hours.

$1,500 \div 60 = 25$
25 is a reasonable estimate of the number of hours.

Chart Problems, page 159

1. Add two proportions for truck.

$0.18 + 0.16 = 0.34$

The probability that a package picked at random was sent by truck is 34%.

2. Add the three proportions for 5 pounds and over.

$0.07 + 0.34 + 0.18 = 0.59$

3. The proportion for Air Express over 5 pounds is 0.07.

4. Add proportions for under 5 pounds by Air Express and under 5 pounds by truck.

$0.23 + 0.16 = 0.39$

Frequency Table Problems, page 161

1. Add the percentiles of the intervals below 70.

$2 + 8 = 10$ 10% of the students scored below 70.

2. The median score is in the interval 80–89.

3. The percent of scores from 80 to 100 is $38 + 13 = 51$

51% of the students scored from 80 to 100.

4. The question is asking for the number of scores that are above 50. The percentile rank next to 50 is 39. So 39% of the scores are below 50, 39% failed. $100 - 39 = 61$. 61% passed.

5. The percent of the scores from 20 to 50 is the percentile rank for 50, less the percentile rank for 20.

$39 - 2 = 37$

37% of the scores are from 20 to 50.

Formula Problems, page 162

1. $P =$ about $16.88
2. $s = 41$ mph
3. $V = \$8,400$
4. $A = 11$

Pythagorean Theorem Problems, page 163

1.
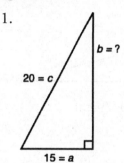

$a^2 + b^2 = c^2$
$(15)^2 + b^2 = (20)^2$
$225 + b^2 = 400$
$b^2 = 400 - 225 = 175$
$b =$ approximately 13.2 ft.

2.
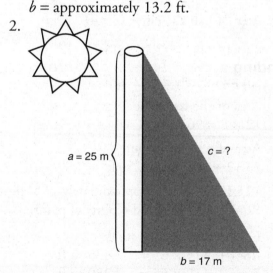

$a^2 + b^2 = c^2$
$(25)^2 + (17)^2 = c^2$
$625 + 289 = c^2$
$c^2 = 914$, $c =$ approximately 30.2 m.

3.

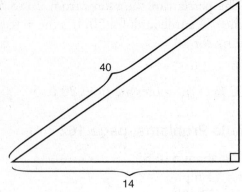

$a^2 + b^2 = c^2$
$(14)^2 + b^2 = (40)^2$
$196 + b^2 = 1,600$
$b^2 = 1,404$
$b =$ approximately 37.5

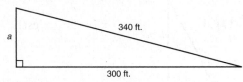

The height is about 37.5 feet.

4. $a^2 + b^2 = c^2$
   $a^2 + (300)^2 = (340)^2$
   $a^2 = 115,600 - 90,000 = 25,600$
   $a = 160$ ft
   The ramp is 160 feet high.

Geometric Figure Problems, page 164

1. Area of half the circle ($r = 4$)

   $\frac{1}{2}(3.14)(16) = (3.14)(8)$ is

   approximately 25.12 sq ft

   Area of the rectangle
   $12 \times 8 = 96$ sq ft

   Area of the entire figure
   $25.12 + 96 = 121.12$ sq ft

   $121.12 \div 35$ is approximately 3.5 pints
   Round up. You need 4 pints of paint.

2. Find the area of the roofs.
   Roof 1: $115 \times 65 =$ 7,475 sq ft
   Roof 2: $112 \times 65 =$ 7,280 sq ft
   Roof 3: $72 \times 52 =$ 3,744 sq ft
   TOTAL   18,499 sq ft
   $18,499 \div 1,200 = 15.4$
   Round up. You need 16 bushels.

3. Volume of a brick = lwh

   $V = 2 \times 4 \times 8 = 64$ in^3

   8×64 in$^3 = 512$ in^3

4. Volume of a cone = $\frac{1}{3}\pi r^2 h$

   $134 \approx \frac{1}{3}(3.14)(4)^2\, h$

   $134 \approx 16.7\, h$
   $h \approx 8$ cm

5. Volume of a sphere = $\frac{4}{3}\pi r^3$

   $V = \frac{4}{3}(3.14)(274.6)$

   $V = 1149.76$ in^3

6. Volume of a rectangular solid = lwh
   $1920 = (16)(12)\, w$
   $1920 = 192\, w \quad w = 10$

   Shaded area = $12 \times 10 = 120$ in^2

Interpreting Remainder Problems, page 165

1. 5 pounds
2. 34 bags
3. 33 bags

Targeted Mathematics Test, page 168

1. **(D)** $(180 - 90) \div 2 = 45°$. There is a total of $180°$ in a triangle. If it is an isosceles right triangle, that means one angle is $90°$ and the other two are equivalent.

2. **(B)** 25% of $48 = $12
   $48 - $12 = $36.

3. **(D)** Supplementary angles total $180°$, which is the number of degrees on this line.

4. **(B)** The probability of rolling a "5" is $\frac{1}{6}$, regardless of what happened on previous rolls.

5. **(D)** An angle is not formed because point B and Point C are not connected in this diagram.

6. **(D)** Divide the money by the cost of an item to find the number of items you can afford.

7. **(E)** Estimate. 32 hours is not twice 18 hours, so eliminate (B), (C), and (D). 32 hours is about 75% more than 18 hours. 75% more than $144 is about $250. Answer E must be correct.

8. **(A)** $\pi(3^2 \times 2) - \pi(2^2 \times 4) =$ $(9 \times 2 - 4 \times 4)\pi = 2\pi$.

9. **(A)** The discount is the regular price less the sale price.

10. **(C)** $80 - $5 = $75 $75 \div $0.75 = 100$.

11. **(A)** The fraction furthest from $\frac{1}{2}$ will be closest to 0 or closest to 1. The answer is $\frac{1}{12}$ from 0. The other answers are greater than $\frac{1}{2}$ but further than $\frac{1}{12}$ from 1.

12. **(E)** 25 centimeters is about 10 inches, a reasonable length for a notebook.

13. **(B)** The total spent was $100. Retail was $20. $20 \div 100 = .2 = 20\%$.

14. **(C)** $250 - .4 \times 250 = 150$. 30 out of $150 = 30 \div 150 = .2 = 20\%$.

15. **(E)** $1,000 + $250 = $1,250, needed to make $1000. $1250 \div $5 = 250$ $250 \times 6 = 1500$ tickets

16. **(D)** $5.3 \times 10^4 = 53,000$. 0.0053 needs to have the decimal moved right 7 places.

17. **(A)** Complementary angles total 90°, the number of degrees in this right angle.

18. **(D)** $100\% - 94\% = 6\%$ (Midwest). Northeast = 30%. $6\% \times 5 = 30\%$.

19. **(E)** $\frac{1}{2} + \frac{1}{3} + \frac{3}{8} = \frac{12}{24} + \frac{8}{24} + \frac{3}{8} = \frac{27}{24} = 1\frac{5}{24}$.

20. **(B)** The outer circle and the inner circle show the whole numbers from 1 to 20. The inner circle shows the multiples of 5 from 1 to 20.

Reading

TEST INFO BOX		
Paper-Based PPST	40 Multiple-Choice Items	60 minutes
Computer-Based PPST	46 Multiple-Choice Items	75 minutes

Using This Chapter

This chapter prepares you to take the Paper-Based PPST and Computer-Based PPST reading comprehension tests. Choose one of these approaches.

- **I want vocabulary and reading help.** Review the entire chapter and take the targeted test at the end.

- **I just want reading help.** Read Strategies for Passing the Reading Test beginning on page 191. Take the targeted test at the end of the chapter.

- **I want to practice reading items.** Take the targeted test at the end of the chapter.

Vocabulary Review

You can't read if you don't know the vocabulary. But you don't have to know every word in the dictionary. Follow this reasonable approach to developing a good vocabulary for these tests.

CONTEXT CLUES

Many times you can figure out a word from its context. Look at these examples. Synonyms, antonyms, examples, or descriptions may help you figure out the word.

1. The woman's mind wandered as her two friends **prated** on. It really did not bother her though. In all the years she had known them, they had always <u>babbled</u> about their lives. It was almost comforting.

2. The wind **abated** in the late afternoon. Things were different yesterday when the wind had <u>picked up</u> toward the end of the day.

3. The argument with her boss had been her **Waterloo**. She wondered if the <u>defeat</u> suffered by Napoleon <u>at this famous place</u> had felt the same.

4. The events swept the politician into a **vortex** of controversy. The politician knew what it meant to be spun around like a toy boat in the <u>swirl of water</u> that swept down the bathtub drain.

Passage 1 gives a synonym for the unknown word. We can tell that *prated* means babbled. *Babbled* is used as a synonym of *prated* in the passage.

Passage 2 gives an antonym for the unknown word. We can tell that *abated* means slowed down or diminished because *picked up* is used as an antonym of *abated.*

Passage 3 gives a description of the unknown word. The description of Waterloo tells us that the word means defeat.

Passage 4 gives an example of the unknown word. The example of a *swirl of water* going down the bathtub drain gives us a good idea of what a *vortex* is.

ROOTS

A root is the basic element of a word. The root is usually related to the word's origin. Roots can often help you figure out the word's meaning. Here are some roots that may help you.

Root	Meaning	Examples
bio	life	biography, biology
circu	around	circumference, circulate
frac	break	fraction, refract
geo	earth	geology, geography
mal	bad	malicious, malcontent
matr, mater	mother	maternal, matron
neo	new	neonate, neoclassic
patr, pater	father	paternal, patron
spec	look	spectacles, specimen
tele	distant	telephone, television

PREFIXES

Prefixes are syllables that come at the beginning of a word. Prefixes usually have a standard meaning. They can often help you figure out the word's meaning. Here is a list of prefixes that may help you figure out a word.

Prefix	Meaning	Examples
a-	not	amoral, apolitical
il-, im-, ir-	not	illegitimate, immoral, irreversible
un-	not	unbearable, unknown
non-	not	nonbeliever, nonsense
ant-, anti-	against	antiwar, antidote
de-	opposite	defoliate, declaw
mis-	wrong	misstep, misdeed
ante-	before	antedate, antecedent
fore-	before	foretell, forecast
post-	after	postfight, postoperative
re-	again	refurbish, redo
super-	above	superior, superstar
sub-	below	subsonic, subpar

THE VOCABULARY LIST

Here is a list of a few hundred vocabulary words. The list includes everyday words and a few specialized education terms. Read through the list and visualize the words and their definitions. After a while you will become very familiar with them.

Of course, this is not anywhere near all the words you need to know for the exams. But they will give you a start. These words also will give you some idea of the kinds of words you may encounter on the examinations.

abhor To regard with horror
I abhor violence.

abstain To refrain by choice
Ray decided to abstain from fattening foods.

abstract Not related to any object; theoretical
Mathematics can be very abstract.

acquisition An addition to an established group or collection
The museum's most recent acquisition was an early Roman vase.

admonish To correct firmly but kindly
The teacher admonished the student not to chew gum in class.

adroit Skillful or nimble in difficult circumstances
The nine year old was already an adroit gymnast.

adversary A foe or enemy
The wildebeest was ever-alert for its ancient adversary, the lion.

advocate To speak for an idea; a person who speaks for an idea
Lou was an advocate of gun control.

aesthetic Pertaining to beauty
Ron found the painting a moving aesthetic experience.

affective To do with the emotional or feeling aspect of learning
Len read the Taxonomy of Educational Objectives: Affective Domain.

alias An assumed name
The check forger had used an alias.

alleviate To reduce or make more bearable
The hot shower helped alleviate the pain in her back.

allude To make an indirect reference to, hint at
Elaine only alluded to her previous trips through the state.

ambiguous Open to many interpretations
That is an ambiguous statement.

TIP

A great way to develop a vocabulary is to read a paper every day and a news magazine every week, in addition to the other reading you are doing. There are also several inexpensive books, including *1100 Words You Need to Know* and *Pocket Guide to Vocabulary* from Barron's, which may help you develop your vocabulary further.

apathy Absence of passion or emotion
The teacher tried to overcome their apathy toward the subject.

apprehensive Fear or unease about possible outcomes
Bob was apprehensive about visiting the dentist.

aptitude The ability to gain from a particular type of instruction
The professor pointed out that aptitude, alone, was not enough for success in school.

articulate To speak clearly and distinctly, present a point of view
Chris was chosen to articulate the group's point of view.

assess To measure or determine an outcome or value
There are many informal ways to assess learning.

attest To affirm or certify
I can attest to Cathy's ability as a softball pitcher.

augment To increase or add to
The new coins augmented the already large collection.

belated Past time or tardy
George sent a belated birthday card.

benevolent Expresses goodwill or kindly feelings
The club was devoted to performing benevolent acts.

biased A prejudiced view or action
The judge ruled that the decision was biased.

bolster To shore up, support
The explorer sang to bolster her courage.

candid Direct and outspoken
Lee was well known for her candid comments.

caricature Exaggerated, ludicrous picture, in words or a cartoon
The satirist presented world leaders as caricatures.

carnivorous Flesh eating or predatory
The lion is a carnivorous animal.

censor A person who judges the morality of others; act on that judgment
Please don't censor my views!

censure Expression of disapproval, reprimand
The senate acted to censure the congressman.

cessation The act of ceasing or halting
The eleventh hour marked the cessation of hostilities.

chronic Continuing and constant
Asthma can be a chronic condition.

clandestine Concealed or secret
The spy engaged in clandestine activities.

cogent Intellectually convincing
He presented a cogent argument.

cognitive Relates to the intellectual area of learning
Lou read the Taxonomy of Educational Objectives: Cognitive Domain.

competency Demonstrated ability
Bert demonstrated the specified mathematics competency.

complacent Unaware self-satisfaction
The tennis player realized she had become complacent.

concept A generalization
The professor lectured on concept development.

congenital Existing at birth but non-hereditary
The baby had a small congenital defect.

contemporaries Belonging in the same time period, about the same age
Piaget and Bruner were contemporaries.

contempt Feeling or showing disdain or scorn
She felt nothing but contempt for their actions.

contentious Argumentative
Tim was in a contentious mood.

corroborate To make certain with other information, to confirm
The reporter would always corroborate a story before publication.

credence Claim to acceptance or trustworthiness
They did not want to lend credence to his views.

cursory Surface, not in depth
Ron gave his car a cursory inspection.

daunt To intimidate with fear
Harry did not let the difficulty of the task daunt him.

debacle Disastrous collapse or rout
The whole trip had been a debacle.

debilitate To make feeble
He was concerned that the flu would debilitate him.

decadent Condition of decline/decay
Joan said in frustration, "We live in a decadent society."

deductive Learning that proceeds from general to specific
He proved his premise using deductive logic.

demographic Population data
The census gathers demographic information.

denounce To condemn a person or idea
The diplomat rose in the United Nations to denounce the plan.

deter To prevent or stop an action, usually by some threat
The president felt that the peace conference would help deter aggression.

diligent A persistent effort; a person who makes such an effort
The investigator was diligent in her pursuit of the truth.

discern To perceive or recognize, often by insight
The principal attempted to discern which student was telling the truth.

discord Disagreement or disharmony
Gail's early promotion led to discord in the office.

discriminate To distinguish among people or groups based on their characteristics
It is not appropriate to discriminate based on race or ethnicity.

disdain To show or act with contempt
The professional showed disdain for her amateurish efforts.

disseminate To send around, scatter
The health organization will disseminate any new information on the flu.

divergent Thinking that extends in many directions, is not focused
Les was an intelligent but divergent thinker.

diverse Not uniform, varied
Alan came from a diverse neighborhood.

duress Coercion
He claimed that he confessed under duress.

eccentric Behaves unusually, different from the norm
His long hair and midnight walks made Albert appear eccentric.

eclectic Drawing from several ideas or practices
Joe preferred an eclectic approach to the practice of psychology.

eloquent Vivid, articulate expression
The congregation was held spellbound by the eloquent sermon.

emanate To flow out, come forth
How could such wisdom emanate from one so young?

embellish To make things seem more than they are
Art loved to embellish the facts.

empirical From observation or experiment
The scientist's conclusions were based on empirical evidence.

employment A job or professional position (paid)
You seek employment so you can make the big bucks.

enduring Lasting over the long term
Their friendship grew into an enduring relationship.

enhance To improve or build up
The mechanic used a fuel additive to enhance the car's performance.

enigma A mystery or puzzle
The communist bloc was an "enigma wrapped inside a mystery." (Churchill)

equity Equal attention or treatment
The workers were seeking pay equity with others in their industry.

equivocal Uncertain, capable of multiple interpretations
In an attempt to avoid conflict the negotiator took an equivocal stand.

expedite To speed up, facilitate
Hal's job at the shipping company was to expedite deliveries.

exploit Take maximum advantage of, perhaps unethically
Her adversary tried to exploit her grief to gain an advantage.

extrinsic Coming from outside
The teacher turned to extrinsic motivation.

farce A mockery
The attorney objected, saying that the testimony made the trial a farce.

feign To pretend, make a false appearance of
Some people feign illness to get out of work.

fervent Marked by intense feeling
The spokesman presented a fervent defense of the company's actions.

fiasco Total failure
They had not prepared for the presentation, and it turned into a fiasco.

formidable Difficult to surmount
State certification requirements can present a formidable obstacle.

fracas A noisy quarrel or a scrap
The debate turned into a full-fledged fracas.

gamut Complete range or extent
Waiting to take the test, her mind ran the gamut of emotions.

glib Quickness suggesting insincerity
The glib response made Rita wonder about the speaker's sincerity.

grave Very serious or weighty
The supervisor had grave concerns about the worker's ability.

guile Cunning, craftiness, duplicity
When the truth failed, he tried to win his point with guile.

handicapped Having one or more disabilities
The child study team classified Loren as handicapped.

harass Bother persistently
Some fans came to harass the players on the opposing team.

heterogeneous A group with normal variation in ability or performance
Students from many backgrounds formed a heterogeneous population.

homogeneous A group with little variation in ability or performance
The school used test scores to place students in homogeneous groups.

hypocrite One who feigns a virtuous character or belief
Speaking against drinking and then driving drunk made him a hypocrite!

immune Protected or exempt from disease or harm
The vaccination made Ray immune to measles.

impartial Fair and objective
The contestants agreed on an objective, impartial referee.

impasse Situation with no workable solution
The talks had not stopped, but they had reached an impasse.

impede To retard or obstruct
Mason did not let adversity impede his progress.

implicit Understood but not directly stated
They never spoke about the matter, but they had an implicit understanding.

indifferent Uncaring or apathetic
The teacher was indifferent to the student's pleas for an extension.

indigenous Native to an area
The botanist recognized it as an indigenous plant.

inductive Learning that proceeds from specific to general
Science uses an inductive process, from examples to a generalization.

inevitable Certain and unavoidable
After the rains, the collapse of the dam was inevitable.

infer To reach a conclusion not explicitly stated
The viewer could infer that this product is superior to all others.

inhibit To hold back or restrain
The hormone was used to inhibit growth.

innovate To introduce something new or change established procedure
Mere change was not enough, they had to innovate the procedure.

inquiry Question-based Socratic learning
Much of science teaching uses inquiry-based learning.

intrinsic Inherent, the essential nature
The teacher drew on the meaning of the topic for an intrinsic motivation.

inundate To overwhelm, flood
It was December, and mail began to inundate the Post Office.

jocular Characterized by joking or good nature
The smiling man seemed to be a jocular fellow.

judicial Relating to the administration of justice
His goal was to have no dealings with the judicial system.

knack A talent for doing something
Ron had a real knack for mechanical work.

languid Weak, lacking energy
The sunbather enjoyed a languid afternoon at the shore.

liaison An illicit relationship or a means of communication
The governor appointed his chief aid liaison to the senate.

lucid Clear and easily understood
The teacher answered the question in a direct and lucid way.

magnanimous Generous in forgiving
Loretta is magnanimous to a fault.

malignant Very injurious, evil
Crime is a malignant sore on our society.

malleable Open to being shaped or influenced
He had a malleable position on gun control.

meticulous Very careful and precise
Gina took meticulous care of the fine china.

miser A money hoarder
The old miser had more money than he could ever use.

monotonous Repetitive and boring
Circling the airport, waiting to land, became dull and monotonous.

mores Understood rules of society
Linda made following social mores her goal in life.

motivation Something that creates interest or action
Most good lessons begin with a good motivation.

myriad Large indefinite number
Look skyward and be amazed by the myriad of stars.

naive Lacking sophistication
Laura is unaware, and a little naive, about the impact she has on others.

nemesis A formidable rival
Lex Luthor is Superman's nemesis.

novice A beginner
Her unsteady legs revealed that Sue was a novice skater.

nullified Removed the importance of
The penalty nullified the 20-yard gain made by the running back.

objective A goal
The teacher wrote an objective for each lesson.

oblivious Unaware and unmindful
Les was half asleep and oblivious to the racket around him.

obscure Vague, unclear, uncertain
The lawyer quoted an obscure reference.

ominous Threatening or menacing
There were ominous black storm clouds on the horizon.

palatable Agreeable, acceptable
Sandy's friends tried to make her punishment more palatable.

panorama A comprehensive view or picture
The visitors' center offered a panorama of the canyon below.

pedagogy The science of teaching
Parts of certification tests focus on pedagogy.

perpetuate To continue or cause to be remembered
A plaque was put up to perpetuate the memory of the retiring teacher.

pompous Exaggerated self-importance
Rona acted pompous, but Lynne suspected she was very empty inside.

precarious Uncertain, beyond one's control
A diver sat on a precarious perch on a cliff above the water.

precedent An act or instance that sets the standard
The judge's ruling set a precedent for later cases.

preclude To act to make impossible or impracticable
Beau did not want to preclude any options.

precocious Very early development
Chad was very precocious and ran at six months.

prognosis A forecast or prediction
The stockbroker gave a guarded prognosis for continued growth.

prolific Abundant producer
Isaac Asimov was a prolific science fiction writer.

provoke To stir up or anger
Children banging on the cage would provoke the circus lion to growl.

psychomotor Relates to the motor skill area of learning
I read the Taxonomy of Behavioral Objectives: Psychomotor Domain.

quagmire Predicament or difficult situation
The regulations were a quagmire of conflicting rules and vague terms.

qualm Feeling of doubt or misgiving
The teacher had not a single qualm about giving the student a low grade.

quandary A dilemma
The absence of the teacher aide left the teacher in a quandary.

quench To put out, satisfy
The glass of water was not enough to quench his thirst.

rancor Bitter continuing resentment
A deep rancor had existed between the two friends since the accident.

rationale The basis or reason for something
The speeder tried to present a rationale to the officer who stopped her.

reciprocal Mutual interchange
Each person got something out of their reciprocal arrangement.

refute To prove false
The lawyer used new evidence to refute claims made by the prosecution.

remedial Designed to compensate for learning deficits
Jim spent one period a day in remedial instruction.

reprove Criticize gently
The teacher would reprove students for chewing gum in class.

repudiate To reject or disown
The senator repudiated membership in an all-male club.

resolve To reach a definite conclusion
A mediator was called in to resolve the situation.

retrospect Contemplation of the past
Ryan noted, in retrospect, that leaving home was his best decision.

revere To hold in the highest regard
Citizens of the town revere their longtime mayor.

sanction To issue authoritative approval or a penalty
The boxing commissioner had to sanction the match.

scrutinize To inspect with great care
You should scrutinize any document before signing it.

siblings Brothers or sisters
The holidays give me the chance to spend time with my siblings.

skeptical Doubting, questioning the validity
The principal was skeptical about the students' reason for being late.

solace Comfort in misfortune
Her friends provided solace in her time of grief.

solitude Being alone
Pat enjoyed her Sunday afternoon moments of solitude.

stagnant Inert, contaminated
In dry weather the lake shrank to a stagnant pool.

stereotype An oversimplified generalized view or belief
We are all guilty of fitting people into stereotypes.

subsidy Financial assistance
Chris received a subsidy from her company so she could attend school.

subterfuge A deceptive strategy
The spy used a subterfuge to gain access to the secret materials.

subtle Faint, not easy to find or understand
Subtle changes in the teller's actions alerted the police to the robbery.

superficial Surface, not profound
The inspector gave the car a quick, superficial inspection.

tacit Not spoken, inferred
They had a tacit agreement.

taxonomy Classification of levels of thinking or organisms
I read each Taxonomy of Educational Objectives.

tenacious Persistent and determined
The police officer was tenacious in pursuit of a criminal.

tentative Unsure, uncertain
The athletic director set up a tentative basketball schedule.

terminate To end, conclude
He wanted to terminate the relationship.

transition Passage from one activity to another
The transition from college student to teacher was not easy.

trepidation Apprehension, state of dread
Erin felt some trepidation about beginning her new job.

trivial Unimportant, ordinary
The seemingly trivial occurrence had taken on added importance.

ubiquitous Everywhere, omnipresent
A walk through the forest invited attacks from the ubiquitous mosquitoes.

ultimatum A final demand
After a trying day, the teacher issued an ultimatum to the class.

usurp To wrongfully and forcefully seize and hold, particularly power
The association vice president tried to usurp the president's power.

vacillate To swing indecisively
He had a tendency to vacillate in his stance on discipline.

valid Logically correct
The math teacher was explaining a valid mathematical proof.

vehement Forceful, passionate
The child had a vehement reaction to the teacher's criticism.

vestige A sign of something no longer there or existing
Old John was the last vestige of the first teachers to work at the school.

vicarious Experience through the activities or feelings of others
He had to experience sports in a vicarious way through his students.

virulent Very poisonous or noxious
The coral snake has a particularly virulent venom.

vital Important and essential
The school secretary was a vital part of the school.

waffle To write or speak in a misleading way
The spokesperson waffled as she tried to explain away the mistake.

wary Watchful, on guard
The soldiers were very wary of any movements across the DMZ.

Xanadu An idyllic, perfect place
All wished for some time in Xanadu.

yearned Longed or hoped for
Liz yearned for a small class.

zeal Diligent devotion to a cause
Ron approached his job with considerable zeal.

Strategies for Passing the Reading Test

TIP

Let me repeat, do not begin by reading the passage in detail. In fact, that kind of careful reading will almost certainly get you into trouble. Only read in detail after you've read a question and you're looking for the answer. This section shows you how to do that.

This section gives an integrated approach to answering the literal and figurative reading items on the Paper-Based PPST and the Computer-Based PPST.

The reading test consists of passages followed by multiple-choice items. You do not have to understand the entire passage. In fact, the most common error is to read the entire passage before reading the questions. Don't do that. It just wastes time. You only have to know enough to get the correct answer. Less than half, often less than 25%, of the details in a passage are needed to answer a question.

THE READING COMPREHENSION STUDY PLAN

First we discuss the different PPST reading comprehension question types. There are examples and tips for answering each type. Then you will learn about the five steps for taking the PPST reading test.

Next come passages and questions to try out. All the questions have explained answers. Don't skip anything. Don't look at the answers until you've answered all of the questions.

PPST Reading Comprehension Question Types

There are two categories of reading questions—literal comprehension and figurative comprehension. Literal questions typically ask directly about the passage. Figurative questions typically ask you to interpret, extend, and apply ideas in the passage. There are four types of literal questions and eight types of figurative questions.

REMEMBERING THE QUESTION TYPES

This section helps familiarize you with each question type. But each question type has many different forms, and identifying each question type under testing time pressure may not be realistic. On the actual test, try to at least identify whether a question calls for literal comprehension, or figurative comprehension. If you can more than that, that's great. By then, answering questions will be a more natural

CORRECT ANSWERS

It all comes down to finding the correct answer. The correct answer will be the best choice available among the choices listed, even if there is a better answer. The correct answer will be based on the passage, not on something not in the passage that you may know is true or think is true.

Literal Comprehension

MAIN IDEA (MAIN PURPOSE)

These questions are the main focus of reading comprehension. Main idea and main purpose questions ask you to identify the topic of the passage or part of the passage, or the main reason the author wrote the passage or part of that passage.

Main idea questions often include the words "main idea":

Which of the following describes the main idea of the passage?

Main purpose questions also often include the words "primary purpose":

The primary purpose of this passage is . . .

Find the central idea of the passage to answer these questions. What was the author really trying to get at? Why did the author write the passage?

Some main ideas may not be directly stated in the passage. But the main idea or purpose must be from the passage. It can't be what you think the author might have in mind.

SUPPORTING DETAILS

Authors give details to support the main idea. These details may be facts, opinions, experiences, or discussions.

Here are some examples of supporting details questions:

Which of the following does the author use to support the main idea in the passage?

Which of the following details is not found in this passage?

To explain [a statement] in the passage the author writes. . .

When the passage describes the outcomes of [an event] it mentions. . .

The answer choices will usually include statements or summaries of statements found in the passage. Read the question carefully to be sure what details are asked for.

Answer choices frequently include details you know to be true, but details that are not found in the passage. Eliminate those. The correct answer will be found in the passage.

VOCABULARY QUESTIONS

A passage has lots of words and phrases. Vocabulary questions typically ask you to show that you know the meaning of one of those words or phrases.

Here are some examples of vocabulary questions:

> Which of the following words is a synonym for (the word) in line 99 of the passage?
>
> Which of the following gives the best definition of (word) in line 99 of the passage?
>
> All of the following gives the best meaning for the (phrase/word) in line 99 EXCEPT. . .

The vocabulary section of this book (pages 183–191) gives a vocabulary review. It also includes ways to identify words from their context. A word in context is not always a strict dictionary definition. Word meaning can be literal or figurative.

Here's an easy example. The author writes, "Stand up for what you believe in." The question asks about the meaning of "stand up." One of the answer choices is (A) "stand up straight." Another choice is (B) "take a position." The main dictionary definition is "stand up straight." But that is not what these words mean in context. The words mean "take a position." That's the correct answer.

That's not to say that a literal definition will always be wrong, or often wrong. It does mean that you should think about the word's meaning in context.

ORGANIZATION

These questions ask you about the way a passage or part of a passage is organized. It sounds hard, but the answer choices are just plain language descriptions. It's usually more a matter of common sense than any specialized knowledge.

Organization questions are just what you'd think they would be:

> Which of the following choices best describes the way the passage is organized?

There may be some moderately difficult words in the choices for these types of questions. Use the vocabulary skills you'll learn on pages 183–191 to tackle those words if they occur.

Figurative Comprehension

INFERENCE

An inference question asks you to identify something that can be reasonably implied or inferred from a passage. The answers to inference questions will not be directly stated in the passage.

Inference questions look like this:

> Which choice below can be inferred from this passage?
>
> What can be inferred about [name or event] from lines ___–___ in the passage?

Test writers try to write five choices for which only one is clearly the "most correct" inference. They usually do a good job. But sometimes other apparently reasonable inferences slip in. Choose the inference a test writer would choose.

TIP

Choose an inference based on the passage. Don't make a choice just because it is true—you'll find choices like that. Don't make a choice because it has some other emotional appeal. The inference has to be based on information in the passage.

EVALUATE SUPPORTING DETAILS

Some of these questions may ask you to decide whether details support the main idea. Other times, the questions introduce other details and ask you to determine if they would strengthen or weaken the author's argument.

Evaluating supporting details questions look like this:

> Which of the following statements, if added to the passage, would best support (weaken) the author's argument?
>
> Which of the following information would be needed to fully support the author's claim?

A main idea, a position, or a claim needs appropriate support from details. Think about the author's claim or argument. Think about what in the argument convinces you, and about what information is questionable or missing.

Strengthening or weakening an argument does not mean to prove or disprove that argument. Here is an example:

> An author writes, "All my shoes are black." Then someone says, "Did I see you wearing brown shoes the other day?" The second statement weakens the first. But it does not disprove it. The second statement may be wrong, or it may be meant as a joke, or lots of other things. But the second statement is enough to make us think, and enough to weaken the author's statement.

FACT OR OPINION

These questions usually ask you to identify a part of the passage that is a fact or an opinion. All of the answer choices are right from the passage. Let's review a little bit about facts and opinions.

> **Fact**—A fact can be either true or false. It is a common mistake to think that a fact must be true.

Something is true only if it is always true. The statement "trees shed their leaves in fall and winter" sounds true. But it's not. For example, there are tress in the southern climates that never shed their leaves. The statement would be false if there was just one tree with leaves that did not shed them in fall or winter.

> TRUE FACT—Most of Africa is in the Northern Hemisphere.
>   A map shows that over 60% of Africa is in North America.
>
> FALSE FACT—Mexico is in South America.
>   A map shows that Mexico is actually in North America.
>
> **Opinion**—An opinion is a personal belief or opinion not based on proof. An opinion cannot be proven true or shown to be false.
>
> OPINION—It's great to vacation near the ocean.

This is someone's personal view. There is no way to prove it always true or always false. It is a matter of opinion.

> OPINION—It's best to go swimming when it is cold.

This just does not seem right, and most people would probably disagree. But there is no way to prove it true or false. It's an opinion.

Fact or opinion questions look like this:

Which of these statements from the passage is a fact rather than an opinion?

The best way to approach this question is to think about a fact. Remember that a fact can always be proven true or shown to be false. If a statement can't be proven true or shown to be false, it's an opinion.

ATTITUDE QUESTIONS

By attitude, these questions mean a position or point of view the author holds that is revealed in a passage. Author's tone may also be used to describe these questions. These questions typically have one-word answers. The idea is to figure out how someone feels about something and then find the vocabulary word that matches the feeling.

Attitude questions are pretty much what you would expect.

What is the author's attitude about [some idea or fact]?

Look for a statement in the passage that includes judgment terms such as "bad," "guide," "well-thought-out," "I guess" or "questionable," and the like.

MAKING PREDICTIONS

These questions ask you to identify predictions that can be made from the information in the passage. A prediction is a statement about something that will happen. The questions may also ask you to identify something that a person may say or do, based on information in the passage.

Here is an example that could lead to a prediction:

Derek loves to go out on his boat, but he did not go out yesterday because the waves were over three feet. It's reasonable to predict that Derek would not go out on his boat in the future if the waves were over three feet.

Making predictions questions look like this:

Which of the statements below is the author most likely to agree with?

Do not choose an answer because it is correct or because you agree with it. The answer must be predictable from information in the passage.

DRAWING CONCLUSIONS

These questions ask you to assume that everything in the passage is correct, and then to draw a conclusion from that information. Drawing a conclusion usually means drawing a logical conclusion based on two pieces of information. These two pieces of information may not appear near one another in the passage.

 TIP

Making a prediction is not the same as saying you are absolutely sure. In the example, Derek might go out on the boat in special circumstances. The waves might be over three feet, but a friend might be out on a boat and need help. It's possible that Derek would go out on his boat under those circumstances. But we would not predict that based on the information in the passage.

Here is a simple example that could lead to a conclusion:

> Whenever Liz meets someone she knows she always talks to him or her. (The first bit of information means talking.) Later we could read that when Liz talks to someone she knows she always shakes his or her hand.

We can conclude that if Liz met someone she knows she would shake his or her hand. We can't conclude that if she shakes hands with someone, then she knows him or her. That conclusion is not supported by the passage.

Drawing conclusions questions look like this:

> Based on the information in the passage, which of the following is the most reasonable conclusion?

Do not choose an answer just because it is correct or because you agree with it. The answer must flow logically from the information in the passage.

Application

This type of question asks you to apply a general principle or idea in a passage to a new situation. These questions typically have one-word answers.

Here is a simple example that might lead to an application:

> In the past, a manufacturer has always hired experienced workers whenever a new manufacturing process began.

A general idea of the sentence is that something new is best served by experience. You would look for that relationship to answer the question.

Application questions look like this:

> Which of the following choices shows a way to apply [some rule or test] to [a new situation]?

Remember to choose the word that summarizes the general principle in the passage. Do not choose an answer just because you agree with it.

Five Steps for Answering Reading Comprehension Questions

This section describes five steps for answering any PPST reading question. You'll learn how to apply the steps and then you'll see the steps applied to sample passages.

READING ABOUT READING

Reading seems to be a natural process. Reading about reading and about steps to taking reading tests can seem contrived and confusing. However, we know that these steps and techniques work. Once you apply the steps to the practice exercises, your reading ability and scores will improve.

Five Steps to Taking A Reading Test

During a reading test follow these steps:

1. Skim to find the topic of each paragraph.

2. Read the questions and the answers.

3. Identify the question type.

4. Eliminate incorrect answers.

5. Scan the details to find the answer.

1. **Skim to Find the Topic of Each Paragraph.** Your first job is to find the topic of each paragraph. The topic is what a paragraph or passage is about.

   The topic of a paragraph is usually found in the first and last sentences. Read the first and last sentences just enough to find the topic. You can write the topic in the margin next to the passage on the Paper-Based PPST; for the Computer-Based PPST, use scrap paper. Remember, the Paper-Based PPST test booklet is yours. The topic will help you know where to look for the answer.

Reading Sentences

Every sentence has a subject that tells what the sentence is about. The sentence also has a verb that tells what the subject is doing or links the subject to the complement. The sentence may also contain a complement that receives the action or describes what is being said about the subject. The words underlined in the following examples are the ones you would focus on as you preview.

1. The famous educator <u>John Dewey founded</u> an educational movement called <u>progressive education</u>.

2. Sad to say, we have learned <u>American school children</u> of all ages <u>are poorly nourished</u>.

You may occasionally encounter a paragraph or passage in which the topic can't be summarized from the first and last sentences. This type of paragraph usually contains factual information. If this happens, you will have to skim the entire paragraph.

2. **Read the Questions and the Answers.** Now read the questions—one at a time. Read the answers for the question you are working on. Be sure that you understand what each question and its answers mean.

   Before you answer a question, be sure you know whether it is asking for a fact or an inference. If the question asks for a fact, the correct answer will identify a main idea or supporting detail. We'll discuss more about main ideas and details later. The correct answer may also identify a cause and effect relationship among ideas or be a paraphrase or summary of parts of the passage. Look for these.

   If the question asks for an inference, the correct answer will identify the author's purpose, assumptions, or attitude and the difference between fact and the author's opinion. Look for these elements.

3. **Identify the question type.** There are twelve different types. That's a lot, and it may not be possible to identify the exact question type on the actual PPST.

But identify each question type on the practice questions. It will really help on the test.

4. **Eliminate Incorrect Answers.** Read the answers and eliminate the ones that you absolutely know are incorrect. Read the answers literally. Look for words such as *always, never, must, all.* If you can find a single exception to this type of sweeping statement, then the answer can't be correct. Eliminate it.

5. **Scan the Details to Find the Answer.** Once you have eliminated answers, compare the other answers to the passage. When you find the answer that is confirmed by the passage—stop. That is your answer choice. Follow these other suggestions for finding the correct answer.

Who Wrote This Answer?

People who write tests go to great lengths to choose a correct answer that cannot be questioned. That is what they get paid for. They are not paid to write answers that have a higher meaning or include great truths.

Test writers want to be asked to write questions and answers again. They want to avoid valid complaints from test takers like you who raise legitimate concerns about their answers.

Try to think like the person who wrote the test.

A Vague Answer Can Be Correct

How can a person write a vague answer that is correct? Think of it this way. If I wrote that a person is 6 feet 5 inches tall, you could get out a tape measure to check my facts. Since I was very specific, you are more likely to be able to prove me wrong.

On the other hand, if I write that the same person is over 6 feet tall you would be hard pressed to find fault with my statement. So my vague statement was hard to argue with. If the person in question is near 6 feet 5 inches tall, then my vague answer is most likely to be the correct one.

Don't choose an answer just because it seems more detailed or specific. A vague answer may just as likely be correct.

APPLYING THE STEPS

Let's apply the five steps to this passage and items 1 and 2.

> Many vocational high schools in the United States give off-site work experience to their students. Students usually work in local businesses part of the school day and attend high school the other part. These programs have
> *Line* made American vocational schools world leaders in making job experience
> *(5)* available to teenage students.

1. According to this paragraph, American vocational high schools are world leaders in making job experience available to teenage students because they

   (A) have students attend school only part of the day.
   (B) were quick to move their students to schools off-site.
   (C) require students to work before they can attend the school.
   (D) involve their students in cooperative education programs.
   (E) involve their students in after-school part time work.

Step 1: Skim to find the topic of each paragraph. Both the first and last sentences tell us that the topic is vocational schools and work experience.

Step 2: Read the questions and the answers. Why are American vocational education high schools the world leaders in offering job experience?

Step 3: Identify the question type. This is a details question.

Step 4: Eliminate incorrect answers. Answer (C) is obviously wrong. It has to do with work before high school. Answer (B) is also incorrect. This has to do with attending school off-site. This leaves answers (A), (D), and (E).

Step 5: Scan the details to find the answer. Scan the details and find that parts of answer (A) are found in the passage. In answer (D) you have to know that cooperative education is another name for off-site work during school. There is no reference to the after-school work found in answer (E).

It is down to answer (A) or answer (D). But answer (A) contains only part of the reason that vocational education high schools have gained such acclaim. Answer (D) is the correct answer.

Here's how to apply the steps to the following passage.

Problem Solving

Problem solving has become the main focus of mathematics learning. Students learn problem-solving strategies and then apply them to problems. Many tests now focus on problem solving and limit the number of computational problems. The problem-solving movement is traced to George Polya who wrote several problem-solving books for high school teachers.

Problem Solving Strategies

Problem-solving strategies include guess and check, draw a diagram, and make a list. Many of the strategies are taught as skills, which inhibits flexible and creative thinking. Problems in textbooks can also limit the power of the strategies. However, the problem-solving movement will be with us for some time, and a number of the strategies are useful.

2. According to this passage, a difficulty with teaching problem-solving strategies is:

(A) The strategies are too difficult for children.
(B) The strategies are taught as skills.
(C) The strategies are in textbooks.
(D) The strategies are part of a movement.
(E) Problem solving is for high school teachers.

Step 1: Skim to find the topic of each paragraph. The topic of the first paragraph is problem solving. You find the topic in both the first and last sentences. Write the topic next to the paragraph. The topic for the second paragraph is problem-solving strategies. Write the topic next to the paragraph if you are taking the paper-based test.

Now we are ready to look at the questions. If the question is about problem solving "in general" we start looking in the first paragraph for the answer. If the question is about strategies, we start looking in the second paragraph for the answer.

Step 2: Read the questions and the answers. The answer will be a difficulty with teaching problem solving.

Step 3: Identifying the question type. This is a details question.

Step 4: Eliminate incorrect answers. Answer (A) can't be right because difficulty is not mentioned in the passage. Choice (E) can't be correct because it does not mention strategies at all. That leaves (B), (C), and (D) for us to consider.

Step 5: Scan the details to find the answer. The question asks about strategies so we look immediately to the second paragraph for the answer. The correct answer is (B). Choice (C) is not correct because the passage does not mention strategies in textbooks. There is no indication that (D) is correct.

The correct choice is (B).

Try Them Out

Here are passages with at least one of each question type. There are many examples of each question type, and you may see completely different examples on the PPST you take.

Remember that you are looking for the best answer from among the ones listed, even if you can think of a better answer. Remember that the answer must be supported by the passage, and that you should not pick an answer choice just because it is true or because you agree with it.

Apply the five steps. You can look back to remind yourself what question type it is. You cannot look ahead at the answers. Looking ahead at the answers will deny you important experiences, and it may well hurt your performance on the PPST.

Cross off the answers you know are incorrect. Circle your choice of the correct answer.

Use this passage to answer items 3–7.

Apply the five steps to these practice passages. Mark the letter of the correct answer. Follow the directions given below. The answers to these questions are found on pages 207–213. Do not look at the answers until you complete your work.

Read the following passage. After reading the passage, choose the best answer to each question from among the five choices. Answer all the questions following the passage on the basis of what is stated or implied in the passage.

> Today's students have hand-held calculators that can graph one or even many equations. Students can even type in several equations and the calculator will "solve" them. This is the best way just to see a plotted graph quickly.
>
> *Line* This is the worst way to learn about graphing and equations. The calcu-
> *(5)* lator can't tell the students anything about the process of graphing and does not teach them how to plot a graph.
>
> Left to this electronic graphing process, students will not have the hands-on experience needed to see the patterns and symmetry that characterize graphing and equations. They may become too dependent on the calculator and be
> *(10)* unable to reason effectively about equations and the process of graphing.
>
> It may be true that graphing and solving equations is taught mechanically in some classrooms. There is also something to be said for these electronic

devices, which give students the opportunity to try out several graphs and solutions quickly before deciding on a final solution.

(15)   For all their electronic accuracy and patience, these graphing calculators cannot replace the process of graphing and solving equations on your own. For mastery of equations and graphing comes not just from seeing the graph automatically displayed on a screen, but also comes from a hands-on involvement with graphing.

3. The main idea of the passage is that:

(A) a child can be good at graphing equations only through hands-on experience.
(B) teaching approaches for graphing equations should be improved.
(C) accuracy and patience are the keys to effective graphing instruction.
(D) the new graphing calculators have limited ability to teach students about graphing.
(E) graphing calculators provide one of the best possible ways to practice graphing equations.

4. According to this passage, what negative impact will graphing calculators have on students who use them?

(A) They will not have experience with four-function calculators.
(B) They will become too dependent on the calculator.
(C) They can quickly try out several graphs before coming up with a final answer.
(D) They will get too much hands-on experience with calculators.
(E) The teachers will not know how to use the electronic calculator because they use mechanical aids.

5. According to the passage, which of the following is a major drawback of the graphing calculator?

(A) It graphs many equations with their solutions.
(B) It does not give students hands-on experience with graphing.
(C) It does not give students hands-on experience with calculators.
(D) This electronic method interferes with the mechanical method.
(E) It does not replace the patient teacher.

6. The passage includes information that would answer which of the following questions?

(A) What are the shortcomings of graphing and solving equations as it sometimes takes place?
(B) How many equations can you type into a graphing calculator?
(C) What hands-on experience should students have as they learn about graphing equations?
(D) What is the degree of accuracy and speed that can be attained by a graphing calculator?
(E) What level of ability is needed to show mastery of equations and graphing?

7. The description of a graphing calculator found in this passage tells about which of the following?

 I. The equations that can be graphed
 I. The approximate size of the calculator
 III. The advantages of the graphing calculator

 (A) I only
 (B) II only
 (C) I and II only
 (D) II and III only
 (E) I, II, and III

Use this passage to answer items 8–10.

On July 2, 1937, during her famed journey across the Pacific Ocean to complete flying around the world, noted aviator Amelia Earhart disappeared. *Line* Speculation remains about the cause and validity of (5) her elusive disappearance, and Earhart's whereabouts remain a mystery. As one of the first female aviators to attempt an around-the-world flight, Earhart solidified her reputation as one of the most daring women of her day. Having achieved a series of (10) record-breaking flights—such as surpassing the women's altitude record of 14,000 feet in 1922 and venturing solo across the Atlantic Ocean in 1932—this trailblazer not only paved the way for women aviators but advocated independence, (15) self-reliance, and equal rights for all women.

Billed as the "First Lady of the Air" or "Lady Lindy" (Charles A. Lindbergh's female counterpart), Earhart challenged gender barriers and influenced women's position in the nascent aviation industry. (20) She was a founding member and president of the Ninety-Nines, an international organization of women pilots. In 1932, after completing her solo flight across the Atlantic Ocean, President Herbert Hoover presented Earhart with the National (25) Geographic Society's gold medal, an honor never before bestowed to a woman. She was also the first woman to receive the National Aeronautical Association's honorary membership.

8. Which of the following is most likely an assumption made by the author of this passage?

    (A) Amelia Earhart was an American spy captured by Japanese forces.
    (B) Charles Lindbergh would not have disappeared had he been the pilot on this mission.
    (C) Amelia Earhart's daring nature caused her to crash on her flight.
    (D) Amelia Earhart may not have died when she disappeared.
    (E) Amelia Earhart may have flown too high and passed out, leading to her disappearance.

9. Which of the following statements, if added to the passage, would weaken the author's statement that Amelia Earhart's whereabouts are unknown?

    (A) A strong storm was reported by a ship along the flight route that Amelia Earhart was following.
    (B) The last person to see Amelia Earhart's plane, a Lockheed Vega, reported that the plane seemed very heavy as it lifted off.
    (C) A search pilot reported signs of recent human habitation on a deserted island along the flight route that Amelia Earhart took.

    (D) Further research on the radio in Amelia Earhart's plane revealed that all the radios in that version of the Lockheed Vega often failed.
    (E) Fred Noonan, a noted aviator and navigator, was with Amelia Earhart as she made this flight in the Pacific Ocean.

10. The author's attitude toward Amelia Earhart can best be described as

    (A) condescending.
    (B) reverential.
    (C) unsettled.
    (D) abhorrent.
    (E) impartial.

11. This passage indicates that Earhart would most likely agree with which of the following?

    (A) Good planning is the secret to any successful endeavor.
    (B) Experience is the quality that is most likely to serve you well in times of trouble.
    (C) Life is full of unexpected events and outcomes.
    (D) The recognition of America's leaders is the best reward for effort.
    (E) In this life, a woman is as capable of success and achievement as any man.

Use this passage to answer items 12–18.

Thousands of different types of rocks and minerals have been found on Earth. Most rocks at the Earth's surface are formed from only eight elements (oxygen,
Line silicon, aluminum, iron, magnesium, calcium, potassium,
(5) and sodium), but these elements are combined in a number of ways to make rocks that are very different.

Rocks are continually changing. Wind and water wear them down and carry bits of rock away; the tiny particles accumulate in a lake or ocean and harden into rock again.

(10) Scientists say the oldest rock ever found is more than 3.9 billion years old. The Earth itself is at least 4.5 billion years old, but rocks from the beginning of Earth's history have changed so much from their original form that they have become new kinds of rock.

(15) Rock-forming and rock-destroying processes have been active for billions of years. Today, in the Guadalupe Mountains of western Texas, you find limestone, a sedimentary rock, that was a coral reef in a tropical sea about 250 million years ago. Half Dome in Yosemite

(20) Valley, California, about 8,800 feet above sea level, is composed of quartz monzonite, an igneous rock that solidified several thousand feet within the Earth. A simple rock collection captures the enormous sweep of the history of our planet.

12. What is the main purpose of this passage?

(A) To provide information that rocks are continually changing

(B) To emphasize that the Earth is made of rock from the tallest mountains to the floor of the deepest ocean

(C) To examine that there are thousands of different types of rocks and minerals that have been found on Earth

(D) To prove that in a simple rock collection of a few dozen samples, one can capture an enormous sweep of the history of our planet and the process that formed it

(E) To provide information on the oldest rock that has ever been found more than 3.9 billion years ago

13. Which of the following words or phrases is the best substitute for the word *accumulate* in line 9?

(A) Disperse
(B) Renew
(C) Break down
(D) Gather
(E) Float

14. According to the passage, most rocks at the Earth's surface are formed from

(A) oxygen, silicon, calcium, and potassium.
(B) aluminum, iron, and magnesium.
(C) one of eight elements.
(D) elements combined in a number of ways.
(E) from what were once coral reefs.

15. What is the author's reason for mentioning that rocks are continually changing?

    (A) To make the reading more technical
    (B) To provide a visual description
    (C) To provide the reader with a physical description of rocks
    (D) To allow the reader to have a clearer understanding about the formation of rocks
    (E) To provide information to the reader as to why all rocks look different

16. Which of the following is the best description of the organization of this passage?

    (A) An overall description is followed by some specific examples.
    (B) A discussion of one topic ends up with a discussion of an entirely different topic.
    (C) Specific examples are given followed by an explanation of those examples.
    (D) A significant question is raised followed by possible answers to that question.
    (E) A theory is expressed and then examples and counter-examples of that theory are presented.

17. It can be reasonably inferred from the passage that the author

    (A) believes only what the author can personally observe.
    (B) is open to accepting theories presented by others.
    (C) believes science is a mixture of fact and fiction.
    (D) knows how the Earth itself was created.
    (E) has an advanced degree in geology.

18. Which of the following statements from the paragraph is most convincingly an opinion as opposed to a fact?

    (A) Thousands of different types of rocks and minerals have been found on Earth.
    (B) Today, in the Guadalupe Mountains of western Texas you find limestone, a sedimentary rock, that was a coral reef in a tropical sea about 250 million years ago.
    (C) Wind and water wear them down and carry bits of rock away; the tiny particles accumulate in a lake or ocean and again harden into rock.
    (D) The Earth itself is at least 4.5 billion years old.
    (E) A simple rock collection captures the enormous sweep of the history of our planet.

Use this passage to answer items 19 and 20.

The potential for instruction provided by cable television in the classroom is eclipsed by the number of educational practitioners who remain uninformed
Line about the concept or who lack proficiency in the
(5) use of protocols and strategies necessary to

optimize its benefits. Teachers, trainers, and
educational administrators nationwide would
benefit from structured opportunities, rather
than trial and error, to learn how to maximize

(10) the potential of the medium. Cable television in the
classroom can introduce real events into
instruction by reporting the news from a
perspective with which young people are
familiar. Broadcasts received by television

(15) satellite can present issues as opportunities in
which young people can play an active role,
rather than as overwhelming problems no one
can solve. By incorporating current events and
televised symposia learners are exposed to

(20) perspectives beyond their teacher's own view
and can explore truth without sensationalism
or condescension. Thus cable television access
in the classroom allows learners to make informed
judgments about the content under study.

19. Which of the following conclu-
    sions can reasonably be drawn
    from this passage?

    (A) The potential for television
        in the classroom is more
        important than the opposi-
        tion against it.
    (B) A lack of understanding of
        appropriate strategies is the
        reason cable television in the
        classroom has not been fully
        implemented.
    (C) The reason cable television
        in the classroom has not
        been accepted goes beyond
        being informed about this
        instructional tool.
    (D) Cable television in the
        classroom ensures that
        the teacher's views will
        receive his or her appropriate
        attention.

    (E) Learners have the ability and
        the capability, themselves, to
        make informed decisions
        about any content area that
        might be under study.

20. If the analysis of this passage were
    applied to introducing a com-
    pletely different type of vacuum
    cleaner, one might say that success
    would most likely be a function of

    (A) effectiveness.
    (B) cost.
    (C) name.
    (D) size.
    (E) advertising.

Practice Passage Explained Answers

Don't read this section until you have completed the practice passage. Here's how to apply the steps. Use this Step 1 for items 3–7. Complete your own Step 1 for the remaining passages.

Step 1: Skim to find the topic of each paragraph. You may have written a topic next to each paragraph. Suggested topics are shown next to the following selection. Your topics don't have to be identical, but they should accurately reflect the paragraph's content.

Graphing Calculators

Problem with Graphing Calculators

Why it's a Problem

Good Points

Today's students have hand-held calculators that can graph one or even many equations. Students can even type in several equations and the calculator will "solve" them. This is the best way to just see a plotted graph quickly.

This is the worst way to learn about graphing and equations. The calculator can't tell the students anything about the process of graphing and does not teach them how to plot a graph.

Left to this electronic graphing process, students will not have the hands-on experience needed to see the patterns and symmetry that characterize graphing and equations. They may become too dependent on the calculator and be unable to reason effectively about equations and the process of graphing.

It may be true that graphing and solving equations is taught mechanically in some classrooms. There is also something to be said for these electronic devices, which give students the opportunity to try out several graphs and solutions quickly before deciding on a final solution.

For all their electronic accuracy and patience, these graphing calculators cannot replace the process of graphing and solving equations on your own. Mastery of equations and graphing comes not just from seeing the graph automatically displayed on a screen, but also from a hands-on involvement with graphing.

Apply Steps 2 through 5 to each of the questions.

3. *Step 2:* Read the question and the answers. You have to identify the main idea of the passage. This is a very common question on reading tests. Remember that the main idea is what the writer is trying to say or communicate in the passage.

   Step 3: Identify the question type. This is a main idea question.

   Step 4: Eliminate incorrect answers. Answers (B) and (C) are not correct. Answer (C) is not at all correct based on the passage. Even though (B) may be true, it does not reflect what the writer is trying to say in this passage. Answer (E) is also not the correct answer. You might be able to imply this answer from the paragraph, but it is not the main idea.

Step 5: Scan the details to find the answer. As we review the details we see that both answer (A) and answer (D) are stated or implied in the passage. A scan of the details, alone, does not reveal which is the main idea. We must determine that on our own.

The correct answer is (D). The author certainly believes that (A) is true, but uses this point to support the main idea.

4. *Step 2:* Read the question and the answers. This is a straightforward comprehension question. What negative impact will calculators have on students who use them? The second and third paragraphs have topics related to problems with calculators. We'll probably find the answer there.

Step 3: Identify the question type. This is a main idea question.

Step 4: Eliminate incorrect answers. Answer (E) is obviously incorrect. The question asks about students. This answer is about teachers. Answer (C) is not a negative impact of graphing calculators. Scan the details to find the correct answer from (A), (B), and (D).

Step 5: Scan the details to find the answer. The only detail that matches the question is in paragraph 3. The author says that students may become too dependent on the calculators. That's our answer.

Answer (B) is the only correct choice.

5. *Step 2:* Read the question and the answers. This is another straightforward comprehension question. This question is somewhat different from Question 2. Notice that the question asks for a drawback of the calculator. It does not ask for something that is wrong with the calculator itself. The topics indicate that we will probably find the answer in paragraph 1 or paragraph 2.

Step 3: Identify the question type. This is a details question.

Step 4: Eliminate incorrect answers. Answer (C) is obviously wrong. Graphing calculators do give students hands-on experience with calculators. Be careful! It is easy to mix up (C) with (B). Answer (A) is a strength of the calculator and is also incorrect. Let's move on to the details.

Step 5: Scan the details to find the answer. Choices (B), (D), and (E) remain. The details in paragraph 2 reveal that the correct answer is (B).

Answer (B) is the only absolutely correct answer.

6. *Step 2:* Read the question and the answers. This is yet another type of reading comprehension question. You are asked to identify the questions that could be answered from the passage.

Step 3: Identify the question type. This is a details question.

Step 4: Eliminate incorrect answers. Choices (B), (D), and (E) are not correct. None of this information is included in the passage. This is not to say that these questions, particularly (E), are not important. Rather it means that the answers to these questions are not found in this passage.

Step 5: Scan the details to find the answer. Both (A) and (C) are discussed in the passage. However, a scan of the details reveals that the answer to (C) is not found in the passage. The passage mentions hands-on experience, but it does not mention what types of hands-on experience students should have. There is an answer for (A). Graphing is taught mechanically in some classrooms.

Answer (A) is the correct answer. This is the only question that can be answered from the passage. The answer is not related to the writer's main idea and this may make it more difficult to answer.

7. *Step 2:* Read the question and the answers. This is another classic type of reading comprehension question. You are given several choices. You must decide which combination of these choices is the absolutely correct answer.

   Step 3: Identify the question type. This is a details question.

   Step 4: Eliminate incorrect answers. If you can determine that Statement I, for example, is not addressed in the passage, you can eliminate ALL answer choices that include Statement I.

   Step 5: Scan the details to find which of the original three statements is (are) true.

   I. No, there is no description of which equations can be graphed.
   II. Yes, paragraph 1 mentions that the calculators are hand-held.
   III. Yes, paragraph 4 mentions the advantages.

Both II and III are correct. That's answer D.

8. *Step 2:* Read the question and the answers. You have to identify an assumption.

   Step 3: Identify the question type. This is an assumption question.

   Step 4: Eliminate incorrect answers. Always try to eliminate at least one answer. Eliminate (A). There is nothing here at all about this assumption.

   Step 5: Scan the details to find the answer. (D) is the correct answer. The author assumes that Amelia Earhart may not have died when she disappeared. The author never states it, but the author questions the validity of her disappearance and calls her whereabouts a mystery. (A) This choice was eliminated even though this is a popular theory among some people. But there is no mention of this assumption in this passage. (B) There is nothing to indicate anything about Lindbergh, except for a nickname for Earhart. (C) and (E) are incorrect because there is nothing in the passage to indicate any reason for her disappearance.

9. *Step 2:* Read the question and the answers. You have to find the statement that would weaken the author's argument that Earhart's whereabouts are unknown. Remember weaken does not mean disprove.

   Step 3: Identify the question type. This is a question about evaluating supporting details.

   Step 4: Eliminate incorrect answers. Eliminate (B) and (D) because each contains information about why Earhart's plane may have encountered trouble, but not about her whereabouts.

Step 5: Scan the details to find the answer. (C) The reports of human habitation on a deserted island is the only statement that would weaken that argument, although it would not by itself disprove the statement. The other statements are incorrect: (A) A strong storm, (B) a heavy plane, (D) a malfunctioning radio, and (E) a second member of her crew do not provide any information about her whereabouts. Don't be tempted by the specific information about Earhart's plane found in choices (B) and (D).

10. *Step 2:* Read the question and the answers. You have to understand how the author feels about Earhart.

    Step 3: Identify the question type. This is an attitude question—it says it is.

    Step 4: Eliminate incorrect answers. Eliminate (D) abhorrent. It's a negative word and the author thinks the world of Earhart.

    Step 5: Scan the details to find the answer. Choice (B) is correct. Reverential means to honor and respect. That's obviously how the author feels toward her. Choice (A) is incorrect because condescending means to look down on. Choice (C) is incorrect because the author was settled in his opinion of Earhart. Choice (D) was eliminated. Abhorrent means to have strong negative feelings. (E) is incorrect because impartial means to have no strong views about someone. This author had very positive feelings about Earhart.

11. *Step 2:* Read the question and the answers. You have to identify what Earhart would say about something.

    Step 3: Identify the question type. This is a prediction question.

    Step 4: Eliminate incorrect answers. Eliminate (D). This passage is mainly about Earhart's disappearance, not about recognition or rewards.

    Step 5: Scan the details to find the answer. Choice (C) is correct. This passage is about Earhart's disappearance and if she were able to draw anything from that, it would be the uncertainty of life. The other choices are incorrect because none of them meant anything on that fateful day that she likely crashed into the Pacific Ocean. Be careful of the emotional appeal of choice (E). This is true but it's not what we would predict from this passage.

12. *Step 2:* Read the question and the answers. You have to identify which answer best summarizes the main purpose of the passage. Why was it written? Save lots of time by reading the question and answers before looking at the details in the passage.

    Step 3: Identify the question type. This is a main purpose question.

    Step 4: Eliminate incorrect answers. Answer (D) is clearly wrong. The main purpose is not about rock collections. You might be able to eliminate more but you can be sure of this one. If you had to guess, eliminating just this one answer would increase the odds that you will guess correctly.

    Step 5: Scan the details to find the answer. The answer to this question is (C) because most of the passage examines that there are thousands of different types of rocks and minerals that have been found on Earth. (A) is incorrect because the passage was not written primarily to discuss that rocks continually change. (B) and (E) are incorrect because each states facts found in the passage that are too detailed to be the main purpose.

13. *Step 2:* Read the question and the answers. You have to determine the meaning of a word, perhaps from the context.

    Step 3: Identify the question type. This is a vocabulary question.

    Step 4: Eliminate incorrect answers. Eliminate (C) because "accumulate" does not mean "break down."

    Step 5: Scan the details to find the answer. (D) is the correct answer. If you accumulate something, you gather it. You can actually tell from the context that (A) is incorrect because disperse means the opposite of accumulate. It is an antonym. (B) is incorrect because bits of rock do not renew themselves; rather they combine with other bits of rock. (C) was eliminated because break down also means the opposite of accumulate. The rocks broke down before they accumulated. (E) is incorrect because floating is not related to accumulating. Some of the bits of rock may have floated on the surface of a lake when they first landed there, but that had nothing to do with the accumulation.

14. *Step 2:* Read the question and the answers. You have to find information in the passage.

    Step 3: Identify the question type. This is a question about details.

    Step 4: Eliminate incorrect answers. Eliminate (A) and (B) because each of them is just a partial list of the elements that most rocks are formed from. Correctly eliminating two choices means you would have a one-third chance of guessing correctly instead of a one-fifth chance. That's a big difference, if you had to guess.

    Step 5: Scan the details to find the answer. The correct answer is (D), because the passage states that elements are combined in a number of ways to form rocks. (A) and (B) were eliminated because they do not list all of the eight elements from the passage. (C) is incorrect because the passage says that rocks are a combination of elements. (E) is incorrect because a rock may have been formed from a coral reef, but that is not the way most rocks near the Earth's surface were formed.

15. *Step 2:* Read the question and the answers. You have to find the author's purpose for writing something in the passage.

    Step 3: Identify the question type. This is a purpose question.

    Step 4: Eliminate incorrect answers. Eliminate all the choices except for (E). If you know that all the other choices are incorrect, then you can be sure (E) is correct. Eliminate (A) because the author does not mention that all rocks are continually changing primarily to make the reading more technical. Eliminate (B) and (C) because telling us that rocks are continually changing does not give us a visual or a physical description of rocks. Eliminate (D) because the statement that rocks are continually changing does not give the reader a clearer understanding about the formation of rocks.

Step 5: Scan the details to find the answer. (E) is the correct answer. All the other answer choices were eliminated, and the author mentions that rocks are continually changing to explain why rocks look different.

16. *Step 2:* Read the question and the answers. You have to look at the overall structure of the passage to see how it is organized.

    Step 3: Identify the question type. This is an organization question.

    Step 4: Eliminate incorrect answers. Eliminate choice (D) because no significant question is raised in the passage.

    Step 5: Scan the details to find the answer. Choice (A) is correct. The author writes about how rocks are formed, and then discusses rocks formed deep in the Earth or from a coral reef. (B) is incorrect because the last sentence mentions Earth's history, but there is no discussion of Earth's history. (C) is incorrect because this is more or less the opposite of the actual structure of the passage. (D) was eliminated because the author never raises a significant question, although some scientists may have questions about the exact dates in the second paragraph. (E) is incorrect because the author never presents a theory and gives no counterexamples.

17. *Step 2:* Read the question and the answers. You have to draw an inference from the passage.

    Step 3: Identify the question type. This is an inference question.

    Step 4: Eliminate incorrect answers. Eliminate (C) because there is nothing here to suggest that science is a mixture of fact and fiction.

    Step 5: Scan the details to find the answer. (B) is correct. In the second paragraph the author presents a theory from other scientists about the age of rocks found on Earth. (A) is incorrect because most of what the author presents can't be personally observed. (C) was eliminated because there is nothing to indicate that the author has presented or believes that science includes both fact and fiction. (D) is incorrect because the author presents information about the age of rocks and the age of the Earth, but nothing about how the Earth was formed. (E) is incorrect because there is no evidence that the author has any advanced degree.

18. *Step 2:* Read the question and the answers. You have to identify the statement that is most likely an opinion.

    Step 3: Identify the question type. This is a fact or opinion question.

    Step 4: Eliminate incorrect answers. Eliminate the choices that are facts. There are a lot of facts in this passage so you should be able to eliminate many of the choices. The first three choices, (A), (B), and (C), are facts. That leaves choices (D) and (E).

Step 5: Scan the details to find the answer. (E) is the correct answer. It is clearly the author's opinion about a simple rock collection. It could never be proven true or false. (D) is tempting, but scientists have ways of proving this true or false. Besides, choice (E) is a much clearer example of an opinion, and the question asks for the most convincing example.

19. *Step 2:* Read the question and the answers. You have to look for several elements in the passage that will lead to a conclusion.

    Step 3: Identify the question type. This is a conclusion question.

    Step 4: Eliminate incorrect answers. Eliminate (D) because the passage says learners will be exposed to "perspectives beyond their teacher's own view."

    Step 5: Scan the details to find the answer. (C) is the correct answer. The first five lines of the passage mention both technical ability and familiarity as the reasons cable television in the classroom has not been accepted. We use those two bits of information to draw the conclusion. (A) is incorrect because the beginning of the passage says the opposite—that acceptance of cable television in the classroom is eclipsed by the number of educational practitioners who don't use it. (B) is incorrect because the passage mentions other reasons beyond strategies as why cable television in the classroom has not been accepted. (D) was eliminated because the passage mentions that cable television in the classroom will be exposed to views other than the teacher's view. (E) is incorrect because the passage says the opposite of this. "Cable television access in the classroom allows learners to make informed judgments about the content under study."

20. *Step 2:* Read the question and the answers. You have to decide how to use the information from the passage in a different setting.

    Step 3: Identify the question type. This is an application question.

    Step 4: Eliminate incorrect answers. Eliminate everything but choice (E). The main point of the passage is that teachers don't use cable television in the classroom because they don't know about it and don't know how to use it. One part of that message, applied to introducing a new vacuum cleaner, is that you have to get the word out. One way to do that is through advertising. You can eliminate all the other choices, which will probably be important when the new vacuum cleaner is introduced. Some of them may turn out to be more important than advertising. But none of those other choices are related to knowing about the vacuum or knowing how to use the new vacuum.

    Step 5: Scan the details to find the answer. (E) is the best answer. Advertising is the only choice from among those given that is supported by this passage.

Targeted Reading Test

This targeted test is designed to help you further practice the strategies presented in this chapter. The answers immediately follow the test.

Directions: Mark your choice, then check your answers. Use the strategies on pages 191–199.

While becoming a teacher, I spent most of my time with books. I read books about the subjects I would teach in school and books that explained how to teach the subjects. As a new teacher, I relied on books to help my students learn. But I learned, and now the basis for my teaching is to help students apply what they have learned to the real world.

21. We can predict that which of the following would most likely be the next line of this passage?

    (A) The world is a dangerous and intimidating place; be wary of it.
    (B) Children should be taught to seek whatever the world has to offer.
    (C) A teacher has to be in the world, not just study about the world.
    (D) But you can't forget about books.
    (E) Teaching is like learning.

22. Which of the following is best inferred from this passage?
    (A) Teaching art is very rewarding.
    (B) Children learn a lot from field trips.
    (C) There is much to be said for teachers who think of their students' experiences first.
    (D) Firsthand experiences are important for a teacher's development.
    (E) You never know what you will end up teaching.

The American alligator is found in Florida and Georgia, and has also been reported in other states, including North and South Carolina. Weighing in at more than 400 pounds, the length of an adult alligator is twice that of its tail. Adult alligators eat fish and small mammals while young alligators prefer insects, shrimp, and frogs.

An untrained person may mistake a crocodile for an alligator. Crocodiles are found in the same areas as alligators and both have prominent snouts with many teeth. The crocodile has a long thin snout with teeth in both jaws. The alligator's snout is wider with teeth only in the upper jaw.

23. Which of the following would be a good title for this passage?

    (A) Large Reptiles
    (B) Eating Habits of Alligators
    (C) The American Alligator
    (D) How Alligators and Crocodiles Differ
    (E) American Alligator: Endangered Species

24. Which of the following would be a way to distinguish an alligator from a crocodile?

    (A) Number of teeth
    (B) Shape of snout
    (C) Habitat
    (D) Diet
    (E) Mating rituals

25. Which of the following best describes the purpose of the passage?

    (A) All animals are noteworthy.
    (B) Reptiles are interesting animals.
    (C) To educate readers about differences in similar animals
    (D) To describe the life cycle of wetland creatures
    (E) To provide information about the American alligator

Remove the jack from the trunk. Set the jack under the car. Use the jack to raise the car. Remove the lug nuts. Remove the tire and replace it with the doughnut. Reset the lug nuts loosely and use the jack to lower the chassis to the ground. Tighten the lug nuts once the tire is touching the ground.

26. Which of the following is the main idea of this passage?

    (A) Using a jack
    (B) Changing a tire on a car
    (C) Maintaining a car
    (D) Following directions
    (E) Caring for a car

Farmers and animals are fighting over rain forests. The farmers are clearing the forests and driving out the animals to make room for crops. If this battle continues, the rain forest will disappear. Both the farmers and the animals will lose, and the soil in the cleared forest will form a hard crust.

Of course, there are global implications as well. Clearing the forests increases the amount of carbon dioxide in the atmosphere. The most promising solution to the problems caused by clearing the rain forests is the education of the local farmers.

27. Which information below is not provided in the passage?

    (A) Reasons the animals are being run out
    (B) Reasons the farmers need more land
    (C) Effects of lost rain forests
    (D) Ways that people can help globally
    (E) Ways that people can help locally

28. What most likely would the attitude of the author be about wildlife conservation?

    (A) All animals must fend for themselves.
    (B) Damage to the earth affects both people and animals.
    (C) Our greatest resource is education.
    (D) Testing products on animals is a practice that should be outlawed.
    (E) Animals and people should have equal rights.

I love gingerbread cookies, which are flavored with ginger and molasses. I can remember cold winter days when my brother and I huddled around the fire eating gingerbread cookies and sipping warm apple cider. In those days, gingerbread cookies came in many shapes and sizes. When you eat a gingerbread cookie today, you have to bite a "person's" head off.

29. Why did the author of the passage above put quotes around the word person?

    (A) To emphasize the difference between gingerbread cookies that appear as people rather than windmills
    (B) Because gingerbread cookies often don't look like people
    (C) To emphasize the most popular current shape of gingerbread cookies
    (D) To emphasize this word has a figurative meaning
    (E) To emphasize how our culture now puts more importance on people than on things

Use this fable attributed to Aesop to answer items 10 and 11.

The Frogs Who Wanted a King

The frogs lived a happy life in the pond. They jumped from lily pad to lily pad and sunned themselves without a care. But a few of the frogs were not satisfied with this relaxed and enjoyable life. These frogs thought that they needed a king to rule them. So they sent a note to the god Jupiter requesting that he appoint a king.

Jupiter was amused by this request. In a good-natured response, Jupiter threw a log into the pond, which landed with a big splash. All the frogs jumped to safety. Some time passed and one frog started to approach the log, which lay still in the pond. When nothing happened, the other frogs jumped on the floating giant, treating it with disdain.

The frogs were not satisfied with such a docile king. They sent another note to Jupiter asking for a strong king to rule over them. Jupiter was not amused by this second request and he was tired of the frogs' complaints.

So Jupiter sent a stork. The stork immediately devoured every frog in sight. The few surviving frogs gave Mercury a message to carry to Jupiter pleading for Jupiter to show them mercy.

Jupiter was very cold. He told Mercury to tell the frogs that they were responsible for their own problems. They had asked for a king to rule them and they would have to make the best of it.

30. Which of the following morals fits the passage?

   (A) Let well enough alone.
   (B) Familiarity breeds contempt.
   (C) Slow and steady wins the race.
   (D) Liberty is too high a price to pay for revenge.
   (E) Misery loves company.

31. Why did the frogs treat the log with contempt?

   (A) The log was sent by Jupiter.
   (B) The log floated in the pond.
   (C) The log was not alive.
   (D) The log could not speak.
   (E) The log was not assertive.

You may want to go to a park on a virgin prairie in Minnesota. The park borders Canada and is just west of the Mississippi River. The thousands of acres of park land are home to hundreds of species of birds and mammals. In the evening, a sotto wind sweeps across the prairie, creating wave-like ripples in the tall grasses. This prairie park is just one of the wonders you can see when you visit marvelous Minnesota.

32. We can infer that this passage is most likely from a

   (A) cookbook.
   (B) travel brochure.
   (C) hunting magazine.
   (D) national parks guide.
   (E) conservation organization mailing.

33. We can conclude that this part of the United States is in the

   (A) Midwest
   (B) Northeast
   (C) Southeast
   (D) Northwest
   (E) Southwest

34. What does the author mean by "virgin prairie"?

   (A) Desolate taiga
   (B) Untouched grasslands
   (C) Wooded plains
   (D) Indian reservation
   (E) Untainted meadows

There was a time in the United States when a married woman was expected to take her husband's last name. Most women still follow this practice, but things are changing. In fact, Hawaii is the only state with a law requiring a woman to take her husband's last name when she marries.

Many women look forward to taking their husband's surname. They may enjoy the bond it establishes with their husband, or want to be identified with their husband's professional status. Other women want to keep their own last name. They may prefer their original last name, or want to maintain their professional identity.

Some women resolve this problem by choosing a last name that hyphenates their surname and their husband's surname. This practice of adopting elements of both surnames is common in other cultures.

35. What would be the best title for this passage?

   (A) Women Have Rights
   (B) Determining a Woman's Name After Marriage
   (C) Determining a Woman's Name After Divorce
   (D) Legal Aspects of Surname Changing
   (E) Hawaii's Domestic Laws

36. What can we infer about the author's position on women's rights?

    (A) For women but against men
    (B) For women and against equality
    (C) For women and for men
    (D) Against women but for men
    (E) Against women and against men

37. This passage would LEAST likely be found in a

    (A) fashion magazine.
    (B) woman's corporate magazine.
    (C) teen magazine aimed at girls.
    (D) fitness magazine.
    (E) bridal magazine.

38. What is the main idea of this passage?

    (A) Women are at the mercy of the law.
    (B) Women in Hawaii have no options.
    (C) Women today have many options related to surnames.
    (D) Children should have the same name as their mother.
    (E) Men have stopped demanding that women change their names.

In recent years, cooperative learning, which involves students in small group activities, has gained popularity as an instructional approach. Cooperative learning provides students with an opportunity to work on projects presented by the teacher. This type of learning emphasizes group goals, cooperative learning, and shared responsibility. All students must contribute in order for the group to be successful.

39. What is the main idea of this passage?

    (A) To show different learning styles
    (B) To examine the best way to teach
    (C) To explain why cooperative learning is the best method for eliminating classrooms
    (D) To illustrate the method of cooperative learning
    (E) To show the role of the teacher in a cooperative learning environment

40. According to this passage what would be a good definition of cooperative learning?

    (A) An instructional arrangement in which children work in small groups in a manner that promotes student responsibility
    (B) An instructional arrangement in which the teacher pairs two students in a tutor–tutee relationship to promote learning of academic skills or subject content
    (C) An instructional arrangement consisting of three to seven students that represents a major format for teaching academic skills
    (D) An instructional arrangement that is appropriate for numerous classroom activities such as show and tell, discussing interesting events, taking a field trip, or watching a movie
    (E) An instructional arrangement in which the teaching responsibilities are shared

Answers Explained

Targeted Reading Answers

21. **(C)** The passage emphasizes the necessary balance of learning from books and learning from experience.

22. **(D)** The passage notes that firsthand experiences are an important part of a teacher's development.

23. **(D)** The passages gives some insight into how these two reptiles are different.

24. **(B)** The passage indicates that the alligator has a wider snout than the crocodile.

25. **(C)** The passage educates readers about differences between these similar animals.

26. **(B)** The passage gives directions for changing a tire on a car.

27. **(D)** The passage mentions global problems, but gives no advice for how people can help on a global scale.

28. **(C)** The author concludes that education of local farmers offers the most promising solution. (B) is incorrect because it is not an opinion about wildlife conservation.

29. **(D)** The quotes indicate the word person is not to be taken literally.

30. **(A)** Things would clearly have been better for the frogs if they had left well enough alone.

31. **(E)** The passage indicates the frogs were not satisfied with such a docile king.

32. **(B)** This passage has all the flowery and positive wording you would find in a travel guide.

33. **(A)** The passage indicates that the park is near the center of the country around the Mississippi River, so Midwest is best among the choices given to describe this area.

34. **(B)** In this context, virgin means pristine or untouched. The *prairie* is grassland.

35. **(B)** The entire passage discusses ways in which a woman can determine her name after marriage.

36. **(C)** The author is objective and takes a balanced view of women and men.

37. **(D)** The passage would be completely out of place in a fitness magazine.

38. **(C)** The passage describes a range of options for choosing a surname (last name).

39. **(D)** The passage describes cooperative learning without evaluating its effectiveness.

40. **(A)** This choice best paraphrases the passage's description of cooperative learning. The other choices include information about cooperative learning not found in the passsage.

PART III

PRACTICE TESTS

Chapter 6
Practice PPST 1

Chapter 7
Practice PPST 2

Chapter 8
Practice Computer-Based PPST

Practice PPST 1

TEST INFO BOX

Reading	40 items	60 minutes
Writing Multiple Choice	38 items	30 minutes
Writing Essay	1 essay	30 minutes
Mathematics	40 items	60 minutes

Take this test in a realistic, timed setting. You should not take this practice test until you have completed your review.

The setting will be most realistic if another person times the test and ensures that the test rules are followed exactly. If another person is acting as test supervisor, he or she should review these instructions with you and say "Start" when you should begin a section and "Stop" when time has expired.

Use the multiple-choice answer sheet on page 225.

Use a pencil to mark the answer sheet. The actual test will be machine scored, so completely darken in the answer space.

Once the test is complete, review the answers and explanations for each item as you correct the test.

Answer Sheet

PRACTICE PPST 1

Reading—60 minutes

1 Ⓐ Ⓑ Ⓒ Ⓓ Ⓔ	11 Ⓐ Ⓑ Ⓒ Ⓓ Ⓔ	21 Ⓐ Ⓑ Ⓒ Ⓓ Ⓔ	31 Ⓐ Ⓑ Ⓒ Ⓓ Ⓔ
2 Ⓐ Ⓑ Ⓒ Ⓓ Ⓔ	12 Ⓐ Ⓑ Ⓒ Ⓓ Ⓔ	22 Ⓐ Ⓑ Ⓒ Ⓓ Ⓔ	32 Ⓐ Ⓑ Ⓒ Ⓓ Ⓔ
3 Ⓐ Ⓑ Ⓒ Ⓓ Ⓔ	13 Ⓐ Ⓑ Ⓒ Ⓓ Ⓔ	23 Ⓐ Ⓑ Ⓒ Ⓓ Ⓔ	33 Ⓐ Ⓑ Ⓒ Ⓓ Ⓔ
4 Ⓐ Ⓑ Ⓒ Ⓓ Ⓔ	14 Ⓐ Ⓑ Ⓒ Ⓓ Ⓔ	24 Ⓐ Ⓑ Ⓒ Ⓓ Ⓔ	34 Ⓐ Ⓑ Ⓒ Ⓓ Ⓔ
5 Ⓐ Ⓑ Ⓒ Ⓓ Ⓔ	15 Ⓐ Ⓑ Ⓒ Ⓓ Ⓔ	25 Ⓐ Ⓑ Ⓒ Ⓓ Ⓔ	35 Ⓐ Ⓑ Ⓒ Ⓓ Ⓔ
6 Ⓐ Ⓑ Ⓒ Ⓓ Ⓔ	16 Ⓐ Ⓑ Ⓒ Ⓓ Ⓔ	26 Ⓐ Ⓑ Ⓒ Ⓓ Ⓔ	36 Ⓐ Ⓑ Ⓒ Ⓓ Ⓔ
7 Ⓐ Ⓑ Ⓒ Ⓓ Ⓔ	17 Ⓐ Ⓑ Ⓒ Ⓓ Ⓔ	27 Ⓐ Ⓑ Ⓒ Ⓓ Ⓔ	37 Ⓐ Ⓑ Ⓒ Ⓓ Ⓔ
8 Ⓐ Ⓑ Ⓒ Ⓓ Ⓔ	18 Ⓐ Ⓑ Ⓒ Ⓓ Ⓔ	28 Ⓐ Ⓑ Ⓒ Ⓓ Ⓔ	38 Ⓐ Ⓑ Ⓒ Ⓓ Ⓔ
9 Ⓐ Ⓑ Ⓒ Ⓓ Ⓔ	19 Ⓐ Ⓑ Ⓒ Ⓓ Ⓔ	29 Ⓐ Ⓑ Ⓒ Ⓓ Ⓔ	39 Ⓐ Ⓑ Ⓒ Ⓓ Ⓔ
10 Ⓐ Ⓑ Ⓒ Ⓓ Ⓔ	20 Ⓐ Ⓑ Ⓒ Ⓓ Ⓔ	30 Ⓐ Ⓑ Ⓒ Ⓓ Ⓔ	40 Ⓐ Ⓑ Ⓒ Ⓓ Ⓔ

Writing—30 minutes

1 Ⓐ Ⓑ Ⓒ Ⓓ Ⓔ	11 Ⓐ Ⓑ Ⓒ Ⓓ Ⓔ	21 Ⓐ Ⓑ Ⓒ Ⓓ Ⓔ	31 Ⓐ Ⓑ Ⓒ Ⓓ Ⓔ
2 Ⓐ Ⓑ Ⓒ Ⓓ Ⓔ	12 Ⓐ Ⓑ Ⓒ Ⓓ Ⓔ	22 Ⓐ Ⓑ Ⓒ Ⓓ Ⓔ	32 Ⓐ Ⓑ Ⓒ Ⓓ Ⓔ
3 Ⓐ Ⓑ Ⓒ Ⓓ Ⓔ	13 Ⓐ Ⓑ Ⓒ Ⓓ Ⓔ	23 Ⓐ Ⓑ Ⓒ Ⓓ Ⓔ	33 Ⓐ Ⓑ Ⓒ Ⓓ Ⓔ
4 Ⓐ Ⓑ Ⓒ Ⓓ Ⓔ	14 Ⓐ Ⓑ Ⓒ Ⓓ Ⓔ	24 Ⓐ Ⓑ Ⓒ Ⓓ Ⓔ	34 Ⓐ Ⓑ Ⓒ Ⓓ Ⓔ
5 Ⓐ Ⓑ Ⓒ Ⓓ Ⓔ	15 Ⓐ Ⓑ Ⓒ Ⓓ Ⓔ	25 Ⓐ Ⓑ Ⓒ Ⓓ Ⓔ	35 Ⓐ Ⓑ Ⓒ Ⓓ Ⓔ
6 Ⓐ Ⓑ Ⓒ Ⓓ Ⓔ	16 Ⓐ Ⓑ Ⓒ Ⓓ Ⓔ	26 Ⓐ Ⓑ Ⓒ Ⓓ Ⓔ	36 Ⓐ Ⓑ Ⓒ Ⓓ Ⓔ
7 Ⓐ Ⓑ Ⓒ Ⓓ Ⓔ	17 Ⓐ Ⓑ Ⓒ Ⓓ Ⓔ	27 Ⓐ Ⓑ Ⓒ Ⓓ Ⓔ	37 Ⓐ Ⓑ Ⓒ Ⓓ Ⓔ
8 Ⓐ Ⓑ Ⓒ Ⓓ Ⓔ	18 Ⓐ Ⓑ Ⓒ Ⓓ Ⓔ	28 Ⓐ Ⓑ Ⓒ Ⓓ Ⓔ	38 Ⓐ Ⓑ Ⓒ Ⓓ Ⓔ
9 Ⓐ Ⓑ Ⓒ Ⓓ Ⓔ	19 Ⓐ Ⓑ Ⓒ Ⓓ Ⓔ	29 Ⓐ Ⓑ Ⓒ Ⓓ Ⓔ	
10 Ⓐ Ⓑ Ⓒ Ⓓ Ⓔ	20 Ⓐ Ⓑ Ⓒ Ⓓ Ⓔ	30 Ⓐ Ⓑ Ⓒ Ⓓ Ⓔ	

Mathematics—60 minutes

1 Ⓐ Ⓑ Ⓒ Ⓓ Ⓔ	11 Ⓐ Ⓑ Ⓒ Ⓓ Ⓔ	21 Ⓐ Ⓑ Ⓒ Ⓓ Ⓔ	31 Ⓐ Ⓑ Ⓒ Ⓓ Ⓔ
2 Ⓐ Ⓑ Ⓒ Ⓓ Ⓔ	12 Ⓐ Ⓑ Ⓒ Ⓓ Ⓔ	22 Ⓐ Ⓑ Ⓒ Ⓓ Ⓔ	32 Ⓐ Ⓑ Ⓒ Ⓓ Ⓔ
3 Ⓐ Ⓑ Ⓒ Ⓓ Ⓔ	13 Ⓐ Ⓑ Ⓒ Ⓓ Ⓔ	23 Ⓐ Ⓑ Ⓒ Ⓓ Ⓔ	33 Ⓐ Ⓑ Ⓒ Ⓓ Ⓔ
4 Ⓐ Ⓑ Ⓒ Ⓓ Ⓔ	14 Ⓐ Ⓑ Ⓒ Ⓓ Ⓔ	24 Ⓐ Ⓑ Ⓒ Ⓓ Ⓔ	34 Ⓐ Ⓑ Ⓒ Ⓓ Ⓔ
5 Ⓐ Ⓑ Ⓒ Ⓓ Ⓔ	15 Ⓐ Ⓑ Ⓒ Ⓓ Ⓔ	25 Ⓐ Ⓑ Ⓒ Ⓓ Ⓔ	35 Ⓐ Ⓑ Ⓒ Ⓓ Ⓔ
6 Ⓐ Ⓑ Ⓒ Ⓓ Ⓔ	16 Ⓐ Ⓑ Ⓒ Ⓓ Ⓔ	26 Ⓐ Ⓑ Ⓒ Ⓓ Ⓔ	36 Ⓐ Ⓑ Ⓒ Ⓓ Ⓔ
7 Ⓐ Ⓑ Ⓒ Ⓓ Ⓔ	17 Ⓐ Ⓑ Ⓒ Ⓓ Ⓔ	27 Ⓐ Ⓑ Ⓒ Ⓓ Ⓔ	37 Ⓐ Ⓑ Ⓒ Ⓓ Ⓔ
8 Ⓐ Ⓑ Ⓒ Ⓓ Ⓔ	18 Ⓐ Ⓑ Ⓒ Ⓓ Ⓔ	28 Ⓐ Ⓑ Ⓒ Ⓓ Ⓔ	38 Ⓐ Ⓑ Ⓒ Ⓓ Ⓔ
9 Ⓐ Ⓑ Ⓒ Ⓓ Ⓔ	19 Ⓐ Ⓑ Ⓒ Ⓓ Ⓔ	29 Ⓐ Ⓑ Ⓒ Ⓓ Ⓔ	39 Ⓐ Ⓑ Ⓒ Ⓓ Ⓔ
10 Ⓐ Ⓑ Ⓒ Ⓓ Ⓔ	20 Ⓐ Ⓑ Ⓒ Ⓓ Ⓔ	30 Ⓐ Ⓑ Ⓒ Ⓓ Ⓔ	40 Ⓐ Ⓑ Ⓒ Ⓓ Ⓔ

Reading Test

You should not take this practice test until you have completed Chapter 5 and the targeted test at the end of that chapter.

The test rules allow you exactly 60 minutes for this test.

Keep the time limit in mind as you work. Answer the easier questions first. Be sure you answer all the questions. There is no penalty for guessing. You may write on the test booklet and mark up the questions.

Each question or statement on the multiple-choice portions of the test has five answer choices. Exactly one of these choices is correct. Mark your choice on the answer sheet provided for this test.

Your score is based on the spaces you fill in on the answer sheet. Make sure that you mark your answer on the answer sheet in the correct space next to the correct question number.

Once the test is complete, review the answers and explanations for each item as you correct the test.

When you are ready, turn the page and begin.

READING

40 ITEMS   60 MINUTES

Directions: You will read selections followed by one or more questions with five answer choices. Select the best answer choice based on what the selection states or implies and mark that letter on the answer sheet.

1. The computers in the college dormitories are actually more sophisticated than the computers in the college computer labs, and they cost less. It seems that the person who bought the dormitory computers looked around until she found powerful computers at a low price. The person who runs the labs just got the computers offered by the regular supplier.

   The best statement of the main idea of this paragraph is

   (A) it is better to use the computers in the dorms.
   (B) it is better to avoid the computers in the labs.
   (C) the computers in the dorms are always in use so, for most purposes, it is better to use the computers in the labs.
   (D) it is better to shop around before you buy.
   (E) wholesale prices are usually better than retail prices.

Questions 2–4 are based on this passage.

   Researchers were not sure at first what caused AIDS or how it was transmitted. They did know early on that everyone who developed AIDS died. Then researchers began to understand that the disease is caused by the HIV virus, which could be transmitted through blood and blood products. Even after knowing this, some blood companies resisted testing blood for the HIV virus. Today we know that the HIV virus is transmitted through blood and other bodily fluids. Women may be more susceptible than men, and the prognosis hasn't changed.

2. The main purpose of this passage is to

   (A) show that blood companies can't be trusted.
   (B) detail the history of AIDS research.
   (C) detail the causes and consequences of AIDS.
   (D) warn women that they are susceptible to AIDS.
   (E) raise awareness about AIDS.

3. Which of the following questions could be answered from this passage?

   (A) How do intravenous drug users acquire AIDS?
   (B) Is AIDS caused by a germ or a virus?
   (C) Through what mediums is AIDS transmitted?
   (D) How do blood companies test for AIDS?
   (E) What does AIDS mean?

4. Which of the following would be the best conclusion for this passage?

   (A) AIDS research continues to be underfunded in the United States.
   (B) Sexual activity and intravenous drug use continue to be the two primary ways that AIDS is transmitted.
   (C) People develop AIDS after being HIV positive.
   (D) Our understanding of AIDS has increased significantly over the past several years, but we are no closer to a cure.
   (E) It is better to be transfused with your own blood, if possible.

5. The retired basketball player said that, while modern players were better athletes because there was so much emphasis on youth basketball and increased focus on training, he still believed that the players of his day were better because they were more committed to the game, better understood its nuances, and were more dedicated to team play.

   In this passage, the retired basketball player believed that which of the following factors led to today's basketball players being better athletes?

   (A) More dedication
   (B) Increased salaries
   (C) Better nutrition
   (D) Youth basketball
   (E) More commitment

6. The way I look at it, Robert E. Lee was the worst general in the Civil War—he was the South's commanding general, and the South lost the war.

   What assumption does the writer of this statement make?

   (A) War is horrible and should not be glorified.
   (B) Pickett's charge at Gettysburg was a terrible mistake.
   (C) A general should be judged by whether he wins or loses.
   (D) The South should have won the Civil War.
   (E) Slavery is wrong.

7. Advances in astronomy and space exploration during the past twenty-five years have been significant, and we now know more answers to questions about the universe than ever before, but we still cannot answer the ultimate question, "How did our universe originate?"

   Which of the following best characterizes the author's view of how the advances in astronomy and space exploration affect our eventual ability to answer the ultimate question?

   (A) We now know more answers than ever before.
   (B) All the questions have not been answered.
   (C) Eventually we will probably find out.
   (D) The question can't be answered.
   (E) We will have the answer very soon.

Questions 8–12 are based on this passage.

The Board of Adjustment can exempt a person from the requirements of a particular land use ordinance. Several cases have come before the Board concerning three ordinances. One ordinance states that religious and other organizations cannot build places of worship or meeting halls in residential zones. A second ordinance states that any garage must be less than 25% of the size of a house on the same lot, while a third ordinance restricts a person's right to convert a one-family house to a two-family house.

It is interesting to note how a person can be in favor of an exemption in one case but opposed to exemption in another. For example, one homeowner applied to build a garage 45% of the size of her house but was opposed to a neighbor converting his house from a one-family to a two-family house. This second homeowner was opposed to a church being built in his neighborhood. The woman opposed to his proposal was all for the church construction project.

The pressure on Board of Adjustment members who also live in the community is tremendous. It must sometimes seem to them that any decision is the wrong one. But that is what Boards of Adjustment are for, and we can only hope that this example of America in action will best serve the community and those who live there.

8. Which of the following sentences is the author of the passage most likely to DIS-AGREE with?

    (A) These Boards serve a useful purpose.
    (B) No exemptions should be granted to any zoning ordinance.
    (C) People can be very fickle when it comes to the exemptions they favor.
    (D) Some people may try to influence Board of Adjustment members.
    (E) The garage the woman wanted to build was about twice the allowable size.

9. The author finds people's reactions to exemption requests interesting because

    (A) so many different types of exemptions are applied for.
    (B) a person's reaction is often based on religious principles and beliefs.
    (C) a person can both support and not support requested exemptions.
    (D) people put so much pressure on Board members.
    (E) men usually oppose exemptions sought by women.

10. In which of the following publications would you expect this passage to appear?

    (A) A government textbook
    (B) A local newspaper
    (C) A national newspaper
    (D) A civics textbook
    (E) A newsmagazine

11. We can infer from this passage that the actions of a Board of Adjustment

    (A) oppress religious and community groups.
    (B) favor men over women.
    (C) enforce town ordinances.
    (D) are examples of America in action.
    (E) exempt people from property taxes.

12. Which of the following does the passage convey?

    (A) A person should be consistently for or against Board exemptions.
    (B) The Board of Adjustment should act only when all agree.
    (C) People are interested in their own needs when it comes to zoning.
    (D) Board of Adjustment members should not be from town.
    (E) The Board of Adjustment should not approve any of the requests.

13. The college sororities are "interviewed" by students during rush week. Rush week is a time when students get to know about the different sororities and decide which ones they want to join. Each student can pledge only one sorority. Once students have chosen the three they are most interested in, the intrigue begins. The sororities then choose from among the students who have chosen them.

    Which of the following strategies will help assure a student that she will be chosen for at least one sorority and preferably get into a sorority she likes?

    I   Choose at least one sorority she is sure will choose her
    II   Choose one sorority she wants to get into
    III Choose her three favorite sororities
    IV   Choose three sororities she knows will choose her

    (A) I and II
    (B) I and III
    (C) I only
    (D) III only
    (E) IV only

14. During a Stage 4 alert, workers in an energy plant must wear protective pants, a protective shirt, and a helmet, except that protective coveralls can be worn in place of protective pants and shirt. When there

Practice PPST 1231

is a Stage 5 alert, workers must also wear filter masks in addition to the requirements for the Stage 4 alert.

During a Stage 5 alert, which of the following could be worn?

  I masks, pants, helmet
 II coveralls, helmet, mask
III coveralls, mask

(A) I only
(B) II only
(C) III only
(D) I and II only
(E) I, II, and III

Questions 15 and 16 are based on this passage.

Using percentages to report growth patterns can be deceptive. If there are 100 new users for a cereal currently used by 100 other people, the growth rate is 100%. However, if there are 50,000 new users for a cereal currently used by 5,000,000 people, the growth rate is 1%. It seems obvious that the growth rate of 1% is preferable to the growth rate of 100%. So while percentages do provide a useful way to report growth patterns, we must know the initial number the growth percentage is based on before we make any conclusions.

15. Which of the following statements about growth rates is the author most likely to agree with?

(A) Lower growth rates mean higher actual growth.
(B) Higher growth rates mean higher actual growth.
(C) The growth rate depends on the starting point.
(D) The growth rate does not depend on the starting point.
(E) A lower starting point means a higher growth rate.

16. Which of the following can be inferred from this passage?

(A) Don't believe any advertisements.
(B) Question any percentage growth rate.

(C) Percentages should never be used.
(D) Any growth rate over 50% is invalid.
(E) Percentages are deceptive advertising.

17. (1) The science fiction story started with a description of the characters.
    (2) Some of the descriptions were hard for me to understand.
    (3) The book was about time travel in the 22nd century, an interesting subject.
    (4) The authors believed time travel would be possible by then.

In these four sentences, a person describes a science fiction book. Which of the following choices most accurately characterizes these statements made by the person describing the book?

(A) (2) alone states an opinion
(B) (1) and (4) alone state facts
(C) (3) states both facts and opinion
(D) (1), (3), and (4) state facts only
(E) (4) states an opinion

18. The public schools in Hinman have devoted extra resources to mathematics instruction for years. Their programs always reflect the most current thinking about the way mathematics should be taught, and the schools are always equipped with the most recent teaching aids. These extra resources have created a mathematics program that is now copied by other schools throughout America.

The mathematics program at the Hinman schools is copied by other schools because

(A) their programs always reflect the most current thinking about the way mathematics should be taught.
(B) the schools are always equipped with the most recent teaching aids.
(C) the schools use the NCTM standards.
(D) extra resources were devoted to mathematics instruction.
(E) their successful programs were publicized to other schools.

Questions 19–24 apply to this passage.

Computer graphing programs are capable of graphing almost any equations, including advanced equations from calculus. The student just types in the equation and the graph appears on the computer screen. The graphing program can also show the numerical solution for any entered equation. I like having a computer program that performs the mechanical aspects of these difficult calculations. However, these programs do not teach about graphing or mathematics because the computer does not "explain" what is going on. A person could type in an equation, get an answer, and have not the slightest idea what either meant.

Relying on this mindless kind of graphing and calculation, students will be completely unfamiliar with the meaning of the equations they write or the results they get. They will not be able to understand how to create a graph from an equation or to understand the basis for the more complicated calculations.

It may be true that a strictly mechanical approach is used by some teachers. There certainly is a place for students who already understand equations and graphing to have a computer program that relieves the drudgery. But these computer programs should never and can never replace the teacher. Mathematical competence assumes that understanding precedes rote calculation.

19. What is the main idea of this passage?

   (A) Mechanical calculation is one part of learning about mathematics.
   (B) Teachers should use graphing programs as one part of instruction.
   (C) Graphing programs are not effective for initially teaching mathematics.
   (D) Students who use these programs won't learn mathematics.
   (E) The programs rely too heavily on a student's typing ability.

20. Which of the following questions could be answered from the information in the passage?

   (A) How does the program do integration and differentiation?
   (B) What type of mathematics learning experiences should students have?
   (C) When is it appropriate to use graphing programs?
   (D) Why do schools buy these graphing programs?
   (E) Which graphing program does the author recommend?

21. If the reasoning about learning to use a graphing calculator was applied to all learning, then all learning should emphasize

   (A) competence.
   (B) thoroughness.
   (C) teaching.
   (D) mathematics.
   (E) understanding.

22. What can we infer about the aspect of graphing programs that the author of the passage likes?

   (A) That you just have to type in the equation
   (B) That the difficult mechanical operations are performed
   (C) That the calculations and graphing are done very quickly
   (D) That you don't have to know math to use them
   (E) That they can't replace teachers

23. Which of the following could be used in place of the first sentence of the last paragraph?

   (A) It may be true that some strict teachers use a mechanical approach.
   (B) It may be true that some teachers use only a mechanical approach.

(C) It may be true that a stringently mechanical approach is used by some teachers.

(D) It may be true that inflexible mechanical approaches are used by some teachers.

(E) It may be true that the mechanical approach used by some teachers is too rigorous.

24. Which of the following conclusions is supported by the passage?

(A) Using a graphing program to display the graph of an equation

(B) Relying on mindless graphing and calculation

(C) Strictly mechanical approaches

(D) Using microcomputers to graph equations and find solutions

(E) Being able to just type in equations

25. An analysis of models of potential space vehicles prepared by engineers revealed that the parts of the hull of the vehicles that were strongest were the ones that had the most potential for being weak.

Which of the following statements about hull design is the author most likely to agree with?

(A) The parts of the hull that are potentially strongest should not receive as much attention from engineers as those that are potentially weakest.

(B) The potentially weaker parts of the hull appear stronger in models than the potentially stronger parts of the hull.

(C) Being potentially weaker, these parts of the hull appear relatively stronger in a model.

(D) Potentially weaker parts of the hull have the most potential for being stronger.

(E) The parts of the hull that are potentially weakest receive less attention from engineers than those parts that are potentially stronger.

Questions 26 and 27 are based on this passage.

The growth of the town led to a huge increase in the number of students applying for kindergarten admission. Before this time, students had been admitted to kindergarten even if they were "technically" too young. At first the school administrators considered a testing plan for those applicants too young for regular admission, admitting only those who passed the test. Luckily the administrators submitted a plan that just enforced the official, but previously ignored, birth cut-off date for kindergarten admission. This decision set the stage for fairness throughout the town.

26. What main idea is the author trying to convey?

(A) Testing of young children doesn't work.

(B) All children should be treated equally.

(C) Tests are biased against minority children.

(D) The testing program would be too expensive.

(E) Age predicts a child's performance level.

27. Which of the following is the primary problem with this plan for the schools?

(A) Parents will sue.

(B) Parents will falsify birth certificates to get their children in school.

(C) Next year the schools will have to admit a much larger kindergarten group.

(D) Missing kindergarten because a child is born one day too late doesn't seem fair.

(E) Parents would not be able to dispute the results of an objective testing plan.

28. A person who is not treated with respect cannot be expected to be a good worker.

Which of the following can be concluded from this statement?

(A) A person treated with respect can be expected to be a good worker.

(B) A person who is expected to be a good worker should be treated with respect.

(C) A person who cannot be expected to be a good worker is not treated with respect.

(D) A person not treated with respect can still be expected to be a good worker.

(E) A person who is not a good worker can't expect to be treated with respect.

Questions 29 and 30 are based on these circumstances.

The state highway department has sets of regulations for the number of lanes a highway can have and how these lanes are to be used. A summary of these regulations follows.

- All highways must be five lanes wide and either three or four of these lanes must be set aside for passenger cars only.

- If four lanes are set aside for passenger cars, then one of these lanes must be set aside for cars with three or more passengers, with a second lane of the four passenger lanes also usable by school vehicles such as buses, vans, and cars.

- If three lanes are set aside for passenger cars, then one of these lanes must be set aside for cars with two or more passengers, except that school buses, vans, and cars may also use this lane.

29. Officials in one county submit a plan for a five-lane highway, with three lanes set aside for passenger cars, and school buses able to use the lane set aside for cars with two or more passengers. Based on their regulations, which of the following is most likely to be the state highway department's response to this plan?

(A) Your plan is approved because you have five lanes with three set aside for passenger cars and one set aside

for passenger cars with two or more passengers.

(B) Your plan is approved because you permitted school buses to use the passenger lanes.

(C) Your plan is disapproved because you don't include school vans and school cars among the vehicles that can use the lane for cars with two or more passengers.

(D) Your plan is disapproved because you include school buses in the lane for passenger cars with two or more passengers.

(E) Your plan is disapproved because you set aside only three lanes for passenger cars when it should have been four.

30. County officials send a list of three possible highway plans to the state highway department. Using their regulations, which of the following plans would the state highway department approve?

   I 5 lanes—3 for passenger cars, 1 passenger lane for cars with 3 or more passengers, school buses and vans can also use the passenger lane for 3 or more people

  II 5 lanes—4 for passenger cars, 1 passenger lane for cars with 3 or more passengers, 1 of the 4 passenger lanes can be used by school buses, vans, and cars

 III 5 lanes—3 for passenger cars, 1 passenger lane for cars with 2 or more passengers, school vehicles can also use the passenger lane for 2 or more passengers

(A) I only

(B) II only

(C) III only

(D) I and II only

(E) II and III only

Questions 31–34 are based on this passage.

The choice of educational practices sometimes seems like choosing fashions. Fashion is driven by the whims, tastes, and zeitgeist of the current day. The education system should not be driven by these same forces. But consider, for example, the way mathematics is taught. Three decades ago, teachers were told to use manipulative materials to teach mathematics. In the intervening years, the emphasis was on drill and practice. Now teachers are being told again to use manipulative materials. This cycle is more akin to random acts than to sound professional practice.

31. What does the author most likely mean by the word *zeitgeist* in the second sentence?

    (A) Tenor
    (B) Emotional feeling
    (C) Fabric availability
    (D) Teaching methods
    (E) Intelligence

32. Which of the following sentences contains an opinion?

    (A) "But consider for example . . . ."
    (B) "Three decades ago . . . ."
    (C) "In the intervening years . . . ."
    (D) "Now teachers are being told . . . ."
    (E) "This cycle is more akin . . . ."

33. Which of the following best describes how this passage is organized?

    (A) The author presents the main idea followed by examples.
    (B) A comparison is made between two dissimilar things followed by the author's main idea.
    (C) The author describes chronological events followed by an explanation of those events.
    (D) The author presents a trend and explains why that trend will not continue.
    (E) The author describes effective techniques and then gives examples of those techniques.

34. Which of the following could be substituted for the phrase "random acts" in the last sentence?

    (A) Unsound practice
    (B) A fashion designer's dream
    (C) The movement of hemlines
    (D) A fashion show
    (E) Pressure from mathematics manipulative manufacturers

35. Empty halls and silent walls greeted me. A summer day seemed like a good day for me to take a look at the school in which I would student teach. I tiptoed from door to door looking. Suddenly the custodian appeared behind me and said, "Help you?" "No sir," I said. At that moment, he could have been Aristotle or Plato for all I knew. Things worked out.

Which of the following best describes the main character in the passage?

    (A) Timid and afraid
    (B) Confident and optimistic
    (C) Pessimistic and unsure
    (D) Curious and respectful
    (E) Careful and quiet

Questions 36–38 are based on the following reading.

I remember my childhood vacations at a bungalow colony near a lake. Always barefoot, my friend and I spent endless
Line hours playing and enjoying our fantasies.
(5) We were pirates, rocket pilots, and detectives. Everyday objects were transformed into swords, ray guns, and two-way wrist radios. With a lake at hand, we swam, floated on our crude rafts made of old
(10) lumber, fished, and fell in. The adult world seemed so meaningless while our world seemed so full. Returning years later I saw the colony for what it was— tattered and torn. The lake was shallow
(15) and muddy. But the tree that had been our lookout was still there. And there was the house where the feared master spy hid from the FBI. There was the site

of the launching pad for our imaginary
(20) rocket trips. The posts of the dock we
had sailed from many times were still vis-
ible. But my fantasy play did not depend
on this place. My child-mind would have
been a buccaneer wherever it was.

36. Which of the following choices best characterizes this passage?

(A) An adult describes disappointment at
growing up.
(B) A child describes the adult world
through the child's eyes.
(C) An adult discusses childhood viewed
as a child and as an adult.
(D) An adult discusses the meaning of
fantasy play.
(E) An adult describes a wish to return to
childhood.

37. The sentence "The adult world seemed so
meaningless while our world seemed so
full." on lines (10), (11), and (12) is used
primarily to

(A) emphasize the emptiness of most
adult lives.
(B) provide a transition from describing
childhood to describing adulthood.
(C) show how narcissistic children are.
(D) describe the difficulty this child had
relating to adults.
(E) emphasize the limited world of the
child compared to the more comprehensive world of the adult.

38. Which of the following best characterizes
the last sentence in the passage?

(A) The child would have been rebellious,
no matter what.
(B) Childhood is not a place but a state
of mind.
(C) We conform more as we grow older.
(D) The writer will always feel rebellious.
(E) A part of us all stays in childhood.

Questions 39–40 apply to this passage.

Sometimes parents are more involved in
little league games than their children. I remember seeing a game in which a player's parent
came on the field to argue with the umpire. The
umpire was not that much older than the
player.

Before long, the umpire's mother was on
the field. There the two parents stood, toe to
toe. The players and the other umpires formed
a ring around them and looked on in awe.

Of course, I have never gotten too involved
in my children's sports. I have never yelled at
an umpire at any of my kid's games. I have
never even—well, I didn't mean it.

39. What other "sporting" event is the author
trying to re-create in the second paragraph?

(A) Bullfight
(B) Wrestling match
(C) Boxing match
(D) Football game
(E) Baseball game

40. The author portrays herself as "innocent"
of being too involved in her children's
sports. How would you characterize this
portrayal?

(A) False
(B) A lie
(C) Tongue in cheek
(D) Noble
(E) Self-effacing

Writing Test

Take this test in a realistic, timed setting. You should not take this practice test until you have completed Chapter 3 and the targeted test at the end of that chapter.

The test rules allow exactly 30 minutes for this section.

Keep the time limit in mind as you work. Answer the easier questions first. Be sure you answer all the questions. There is no penalty for guessing. You may write on the test booklet and mark up the questions.

Each question or statement has five answer choices. Exactly one of these choices is correct. Mark your choice on the answer sheet provided for this test.

Your score is based on the spaces you fill in on the answer sheet. Make sure that you mark your answer on the answer sheet in the correct space next to the correct question number.

When you are ready, turn the page and begin.

WRITING

38 ITEMS   30 MINUTES

Usage

> **Directions:** You will read sentences with four parts underlined and lettered. Determine whether one of the underlined parts contains grammatical, word use, or punctuation errors. If so, mark the letter of that part on your answer sheet. If there are no errors, mark E.

1. Disgusted by the trash left behind by
   (A)   (B)
   picnickers, the town council passed a
                     (C)
   law requiring convicted litterers to
            (D)
   spend five hours cleaning up the town

   park. No error.
        (E)

2. The teacher was sure that the child's
                  (A)
   difficult home life effected her
          (B)   (C)
   school work. No error.
        (D)   (E)

3. It took Ron a long time to realize that
       (A)   (B)
   the townspeople were completely
          (C)   (D)
   opposed to his proposal. No error.
                            (E)

4. A newspaper columnist promised to
                  (A)
   print the people who were involved in
            (B)   (C)
   the secret negotiations concerning the

   sports stadium in the next column.
         (D)
   No error.
      (E)

5. The silent halo of a solar eclipse
                (A)   (B)
   could be seen by astronomers across
        (C)
   asia. No error.
   (D)   (E)

6. Also found during the archaeological
      (A)
   dig was a series of animal bone
       (B)   (C)
   fragments, fire signs, and arrow points.
                              (D)
   No error.
      (E)

7. The teacher asked all of her students to
       (A)   (B)
   bring in they're permission slips
             (C)
   to go on the Washington trip. No error.
       (D)   (E)

8. The plumber did not go to the dripping
        (A)   (B)
   water than to the place the water
         (C)
   seemed to be coming from. No error.
        (D)   (E)

9. The driver realized that she

   would either have to go completely out of
          (A)   (B)
   the way or have to wait for the
       (C)
   swollen creek to subside. No error.
       (D)   (E)

10. The <u>tracker</u> was so <u>good that</u> he could
       (A)   (B)
    tell the <u>difference between</u> a hoofprint
                 (C)
    made by a horse with a saddle <u>or</u> a
                                  (D)
    hoofprint made by a horse without a

    saddle. <u>No error.</u>
            (E)

11. The mayor <u>estimated</u> that it <u>would cost</u>
                 (A)   (B)
    $1,200 for each <u>citizen individually</u> to
                         (C)
    repair the storm damage <u>to the town.</u>
                               (D)

    <u>No error.</u>
       (E)

12. Sustaining a <u>month-long</u> winning streak
       (A)   (B)
    in the town baseball A B league, the

    young team <u>pressed on</u> with
                   (C)
    <u>unwavering determination.</u> <u>No error.</u>
              (D)   (E)

13. The fire chief, <u>like the police chief,</u>
                       (A)
    <u>has so much</u> responsibility, that
       (B)
    <u>they often have</u> a personal <u>driver.</u>
          (C)   (D)
    <u>No error.</u>
       (E)

14. A talented chef <u>making customers</u>
                        (A)
    smack their lips at her great

    <u>gustatorial delights,</u> the likes of which
          (B)
    <u>are not available</u> in any
          (C)
    <u>ordinary restaurant.</u> <u>No error.</u>
          (D)   (E)

15. The fate of small towns in America,

    which were <u>popularized</u> in movies
                   (A)
    when it seemed that everyone came

    from a small town <u>and now</u> face
                          (B)
    <u>anonymity</u> as cars on highways speed
       (C)
    by, <u>is perilous.</u> <u>No error.</u>
          (D)   (E)

16. The coach <u>not only</u> <u>works with</u> each
                  (A)   (B)
    pitcher and each catcher, but he

    <u>also has to change</u> <u>him.</u> <u>No error.</u>
          (C)   (D)   (E)

17. When I <u>was a child,</u> a wet washcloth
               (A)
    was the <u>main method</u> of first <u>aid;</u> it
                (B)   (C)
    reduced swelling, eliminated pain,

    and <u>inflammation was</u> reduced. <u>No error.</u>
            (D)   (E)

18. I am going to a <u>World Cup game</u> next
                        (A)
    week, and I <u>would be surprised</u> if
                    (B)
    <u>there is even</u> one empty seat
       (C)
    <u>in the stadium.</u> <u>No error.</u>
          (D)   (E)

19. It is <u>not uncommon</u> for the claims of
             (A)
    land developers to <u>go too</u> far, <u>like</u> the
                           (B)   (C)
    one reported several years ago in which

    <u>the land was</u> on the side of a sheer cliff.
       (D)
    <u>No error.</u>
       (E)

20. During the fall, some fruits are in
      (A)   (B)
    so short supply that the prices triple.
         (C)   (D)
    No error.
       (E)

21. The volleyball team won their
              (A)
    third consecutive scholastic title,
                (B)
    both because of their dedication and
         (C)
    because they are talented. No error.
              (D)   (E)

Sentence Correction

Directions: You will read sentences with some or all of the sentence underlined, followed by five answer choices. The first answer choice repeats the underlined portion and the other four present possible replacements. Select the answer choice that best represents standard English without altering the meaning of the original sentence. Mark that letter on the answer sheet.

22. The quality of the parts received in the most recent shipment was inferior to parts in the previous shipments, but still in accordance with manufacturers' specifications.

    (A) was inferior to parts in the previous shipments, but still in accordance with
    (B) were inferior to the previous shipments' parts but still in accordance with
    (C) was the inferior of the previous shipments' parts but still in accordance with
    (D) was inferior to the previous parts' shipments but still not on par with
    (E) was inferior to the previous parts' shipments and the manufacturers' specifications

23. The painful rabies treatment first developed by Pasteur saved the boy's life.

    (A) The painful rabies treatment first developed by Pasteur
    (B) The painful rabies treatment which was first discovered by Pasteur
    (C) Pasteur developed the painful rabies treatment
    (D) First developed by Pasteur the treatment for painful rabies
    (E) The fact that Pasteur developed a rabies treatment

24. By 10:00 A.M. every morning, the delivery service brought important papers to the house in sealed envelopes.

    (A) the delivery service brought important papers to the house in sealed envelopes
    (B) important papers were brought to the house by the delivery service in sealed envelopes
    (C) sealed envelopes were brought to the house by the delivery service with important papers
    (D) the delivery service brought important papers in sealed envelopes to the house
    (E) the deliver service brought sealed envelopes to the house containing important papers

25. The shadows shortened as the sun begun the ascent into the morning sky.

    (A) begun the
    (B) begin the
    (C) began the
    (D) begun that
    (E) begun an

26. Liz and Ann spent all day climbing the mountain, and <u>she was almost</u> too exhausted for the descent.

    (A) she was almost
    (B) they were almost
    (C) they were
    (D) she almost was
    (E) was

27. The embassy announced that at the present time, they could neither confirm <u>nor deny that the ambassador would return home in the event that</u> hostilities broke out.

    (A) nor deny that the ambassador would return home in the event that
    (B) or deny that the ambassador would return home in the event that
    (C) nor deny that the ambassador would return home if
    (D) nor deny that the ambassador would leave
    (E) nor deny that ambassador will return home in the event that

28. Every person <u>has the ultimate capacity to</u> control his or her own destiny.

    (A) has the ultimate capacity to
    (B) ultimately has the capacity to
    (C) has the capacity ultimately to
    (D) can
    (E) could

29. In all likelihood, her mother's absence would be devastating, <u>were it not</u> for the presence of her sister.

    (A) were it not
    (B) it was not
    (C) it were not
    (D) were they not
    (E) was it not

30. She had listened very carefully to all the candidates, and the Independent candidate was the only <u>one who had not said something that did not make sense.</u>

    (A) one who had not said something that did not make sense
    (B) one who did not make sense when he said something
    (C) one who had only said things that made sense
    (D) one to not say something that made sense
    (E) one who never said anything that made no sense

31. The author knew that the book would be finished <u>only by working every day and getting</u> lots of sleep at night.

    (A) only by working every day and getting
    (B) only working every day and getting
    (C) only by working every day and by getting
    (D) only through work and sleep
    (E) only by daily work and by sleepless nights

32. The teacher was sure that Tom's difficult home life affected <u>his school work.</u>

    (A) his school work
    (B) his school's work
    (C) him school work
    (D) his school works
    (E) him school works

33. Small town sheriffs in America, <u>whom were popularized in movies when it seemed that everyone came from a small town,</u> now face anonymity.

    (A) whom were popularized in movies when it seemed that everyone came from a small town
    (B) who were popularized in movies when it seemed that everyone came from a small town

(C) whom were popularized in movies when it seemed that anyone came from a small town

(D) whom were popularized in movies when they seemed that everyone came from a small town

(E) whom were popularized in movies when it seemed that everyone comes from a small town

34. The professor asked the class to consider the development of the human race. She pointed out that, throughout the ages, human beings has learned to communicate by nonverbal means.

(A) human beings has learned to communicate by nonverbal means

(B) human beings had learned to communicate by nonverbal means

(C) human beings has learn to communicate by nonverbal means

(D) human beings have learn to communicate by nonverbal means

(E) human beings have learned to communicate by nonverbal means

35. There are a number of specialty business stores. Office World, the office supply store, claimed to be the quintessential supplier of office machines in the United States.

(A) claimed to be the quintessential supplier of office machines in the United States

(B) claiming to be the quintessential supplier of office machines in the United States

(C) claimed to be the quardassential supplier of office machines in the United States

(D) claims to be the quintessential supplier of office machines in the United States

(E) has claim to be the quintessential supplier of office machines in the United States

36. The *Hardy Boys* was a book series. As a child he read the *Hardy Boys* series of books and was in awe of the author Franklin Dixon.

(A) As a child he read the *Hardy Boys* series of books and was in awe of the author Franklin Dixon.

(B) As a child he read the *Hardy Boys* series of books, but was in awe of the author Franklin Dixon.

(C) As a child he read the *Hardy Boys* series of books; however he was in awe of the author Franklin Dixon.

(D) As a child he read the *Hardy Boys* series of books but was also in awe of the author Franklin Dixon.

(E) As a child he read the *Hardy Boys* series of books; however he was also in awe of the author Franklin Dixon.

37. Bob is deciding which event to compete in. He is a strong swimmer but he is best known for his diving.

(A) He is a strong swimmer but he is best known for his diving.

(B) He is a strong swimmer; but, he is best known for his diving.

(C) He is a strong swimmer, but he is best known for his diving.

(D) He is a strong swimmer: but he is best known for his diving.

(E) He is a strong swimmer, but, he is best known for his diving.

38. It was almost time for the test. Vincent and Laura said to their friends "I wonder if we're through studying for the PPST"?

(A) their friends "I wonder if we're through studying for the PPST"?

(B) their friends ",I wonder if we're through studying for the PPST"?

(C) their friends, "I wonder if we're through studying for the PPST"?

(D) their friends, "I wonder if we're through studying for the PPST?"

(E) their friends ",I wonder if we're through studying for the PPST?"

Essay

Take this test in a realistic, timed setting. You should not take this practice test until you have completed Chapter 3 and the targeted test at the end of that chapter.

Write an essay on the topic found on the next page. Write on this topic only. An essay written on another topic, no matter how well done, will receive a 0. You have 30 minutes to complete the essay.

Use the space provided to briefly outline your essay and to organize your thoughts before you begin to write. Use this opportunity to demonstrate how well you can write but be sure to cover the topic.

Write your essay on the lined paper provided. Write legibly and do not skip any lines. Your entire essay must fit on these pages.

Once the test is complete, ask an English professor or English teacher to evaluate your essay holistically using the rating scale on page 36.

When you are ready, turn the page and begin.

ESSAY

Directions: You have 30 minutes to complete this essay question. Use the lined pages to write a brief essay based on this topic.

> **To encourage talented people to enter teaching, teachers who score higher on standardized tests should make significantly more money than those teachers who receive lower test scores.**

Describe the extent to which you agree or disagree with this statement. Support your response with specific details, examples, and experiences.

Write a brief outline here.

Mathematics Test

Take this test in a realistic, timed setting. You should not take this practice test until you have completed Chapter 4 and the targeted test at the end of that chapter.

The test rules allow you exactly 60 minutes for this test.

Keep this time limit in mind as you work. Answer the easier items first. Be sure you answer all the items. There is no penalty for guessing. You may write in the test booklet and mark up the items.

Each item has five answer choices. Exactly one of these choices is correct. Mark your choice on the answer sheet provided for the test.

Your score is based on the spaces you fill in on the answer sheet. Make sure you mark your answer in the correct space next to the correct item number.

When you are ready, turn the page and begin.

MATHEMATICS

40 ITEMS   60 MINUTES

Directions: Each item below includes five answer choices. Select the best choice for each item and mark that letter on the answer sheet.

1.

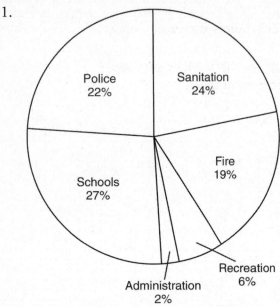

Tax money spent on town services.

A town collects $2,600,000 in taxes. The town needs $624,000 for police. Any needed money will come from sanitation. The percents in the circle graph are recalculated. What percent is left for sanitation?

(A) 22%
(B) 20%
(C) 19%
(D) 18%
(E) 16%

2. Steve pays $520 a month for rent, and his monthly paycheck after taxes is $1,300. Which computation shows the percent of Steve's paycheck that is used to pay rent?

(A) $(1300 \div 520) \cdot 100$
(B) $(520 \div 1300) \cdot 100$
(C) $(5.2 \cdot 1300) \cdot 100$
(D) $(13 \cdot 520) \cdot 100$
(E) $(5.2 \cdot 13) \cdot 100$

3. All of the windows in the house are rectangles. None of the windows in the house are squares.

Which of the following conclusions in the statements above are true?

(A) Some of the windows have four sides of equal length.
(B) None of the windows contain right angles.
(C) None of the windows are parallelograms.
(D) None of the windows have four sides of equal length.
(E) All of the windows contain an acute angle.

4. The area of a square is 4 in². There is a larger square made up of 49 of these squares. What is the length of one side of the larger square?

(A) 7 in
(B) 14 in
(C) 28 in
(D) 56 in
(E) 112 in

5. What is the value of the number in the table below that is expressed in scientific notation?

	A	B	C
1.	53794×10	537.94×10^4	5.3794×10
2.	5379.4×10	53.794×10^2	53794×10^2

(A) 5.37940
(B) 53794
(C) 5379.4
(D) 537.94
(E) 53.794

6. 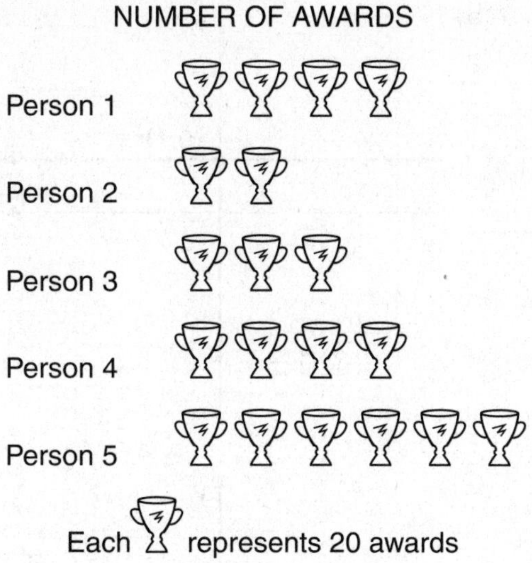   NUMBER OF AWARDS

Person 1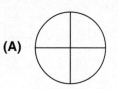

Person 2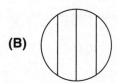

Person 3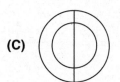

Person 4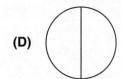

Person 5

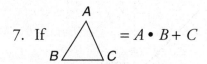
Each 🏆 represents 20 awards

How many more awards did person 5 have than person 3?

(A) 20
(B) 40
(C) 60
(D) 80
(E) 100

7. If

$$\triangle = A \bullet B + C$$

(with A at top, B at bottom-left, C at bottom-right)

then

(triangle with -4 at top, 2 at bottom-left, 11 at bottom-right)

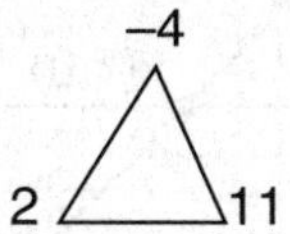

(A) −88
(B) −19
(C) −3
(D) 3
(E) 19

8. The following is a list of the ages of ten different people: 53, 27, 65, 21, 7, 16, 70, 41, 57, and 37.

What is the difference between the mean age and the median age of the group?

(A) 0.4
(B) 4
(C) 39
(D) 39.4
(E) 13

9. A pizza has crust all around the edge. Which of the following figures shows a way to cut the pizza into four equal pieces where only two have crust?

(A) (circle divided into quarters)

(B) (circle divided by two vertical lines into three sections)

(C) (circle with smaller concentric circle, horizontal line through center)

(D) (circle divided by one diagonal line)

(E) (circle with triangle inscribed)

10.

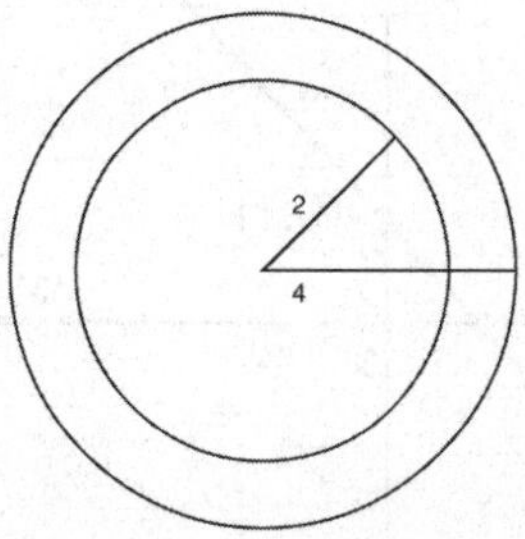

(two concentric circles with radii 2 and 4 marked)

What is the difference between the area of the inner circle and the area of the outer circle?

(A) 2π
(B) 4π
(C) 6π
(D) 12π
(E) 14π

11. Frank has 2 dogs, 5 cats, and 1 bunny. What percent of these animals are cats?

   (A) 5%
   (B) $\frac{5}{8}$%
   (C) 50%
   (D) 58%
   (E) 62.5%

12. $\frac{4}{9}$ is less than which of the following?

   (A) 44%
   (B) 0.45
   (C) 0.4444
   (D) $\frac{4}{10}$
   (E) 44.4%

13. 0.45 is how many times 45,000?

   (A) 0.1
   (B) 0.01
   (C) 0.001
   (D) 0.0001
   (E) 0.00001

14. Which of the following shows a line with *x*- and *y*-intercepts equal to 1?

(A)

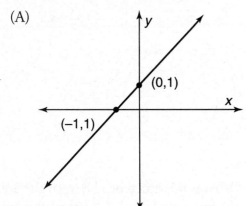

(B)

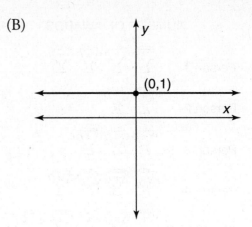

(C)

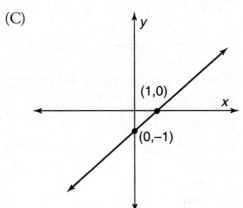

(D)

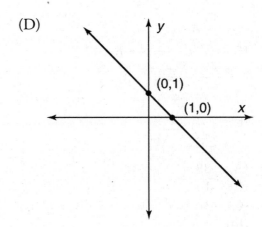

(E)

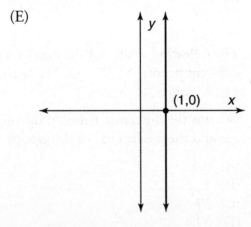

15. All of the following numbers are equal except for:

(A) 4/9
(B) 44/90
(C) 404/909
(D) 444/999
(E) 4044/9099

16.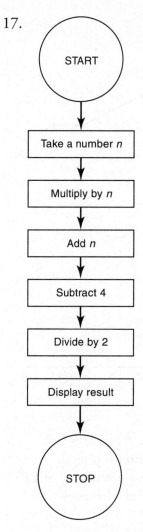

If the lengths of the bases in the trapezoid $(A = \frac{h}{2}(b_1 + b_2))$ above are doubled, the area of the new trapezoid is given by the formula:

(A) $A = \frac{h}{2}(b_1 + b_2)$

(B) $A = 2h(b_1 + b_2)$

(C) $A = \frac{h}{4}(b_1 + b_2)$

(D) $A = h(b_1 + b_2)$

(E) $A = 4h(b_1 + b_2)$

where b_1 and b_2 are the lengths of the original bases.

17.

If $n = 5$, what is the result of the computation outlined in the flow chart?

(A) 12
(B) 13
(C) 14
(D) 15
(E) 16

18.

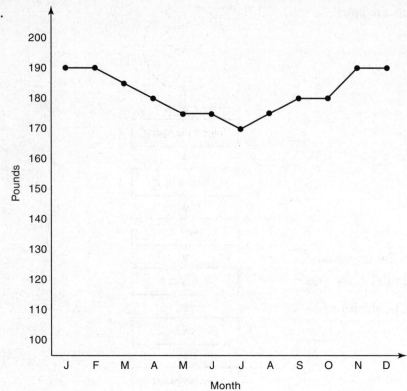

The above line graph displays Jack's weight over a 12-month period. Approximately what percentage of Jack's highest weight is Jack's lowest weight?

(A) 97%
(B) 94%
(C) 91%
(D) 89%
(E) 85%

19. Alice arrived at work at 7:45 A.M. and left work at 7 P.M. If she receives $20 an hour salary and no salary for her 1 hour lunch, how much did Alice earn as salary for the day?

(A) $175
(B) $195
(C) $205
(D) $215
(E) $225

20. Which of the following figures could be used to disprove the following statement: "If a quadrilateral has one pair of congruent sides, then it has two pairs of congruent sides."

    (A)

    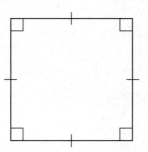

    (B)

    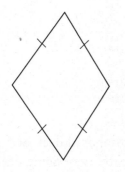

    (C)

    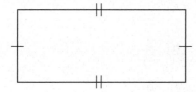

    (D)

    (E)

    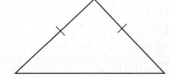

21. The five shapes seen below are made up of identical semi-circles and identical quarter-circles. Which of the five shapes has the greatest perimeter?

    (A)

    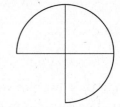

    (B)

    (C)

    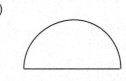

    (D)

    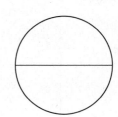

    (E)

    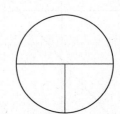

22. Which of the following choices is not equivalent to the others?

    (A) $3^4 \times 9 \times 12$
    (B) $3^3 \times 27 \times 12$
    (C) $3^5 \times 36$
    (D) $3^3 \times 9^3 \times 4$
    (E) $3^5 \times 4 \times 9$

23. Company employees just received their earning report. The earnings of 4 individuals in a company are:
    Person 1: $45,250
    Person 2: $78,375
    Person 3: $52,540
    Person 4: $62,325

    The total earnings of these individuals, in thousands of dollars, is closest to:

    (A) $237 thousand
    (B) $238 thousand
    (C) $239 thousand
    (D) $240 thousand
    (E) $241 thousand

24. Which of the following is true about the graph seen below?

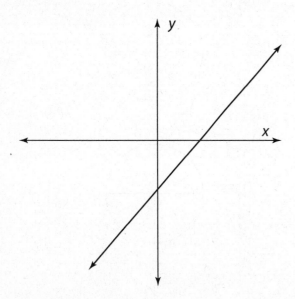

    (A) As x increases, y decreases
    (B) As x decreases, y does not change
    (C) As x decreases, y increases
    (D) As x increases, y increases
    (E) As x decreases, y decreases

25. If x is 65% of 400, then what is the value of x?

    (A) 660
    (B) 540
    (C) 260
    (D) 200
    (E) 140

26. What is the average of $\frac{1}{2}$, $\frac{2}{3}$, and $\frac{5}{12}$?

    (A) $\frac{19}{12}$

    (B) $\frac{19}{24}$

    (C) $\frac{19}{36}$

    (D) $\frac{19}{44}$

    (E) $\frac{19}{52}$

27. In a standard deck of 52 cards, what is the probability of being dealt a king, a queen, or a jack?

    (A) $\frac{1}{3}$

    (B) $\frac{2}{13}$

    (C) $\frac{3}{13}$

    (D) $\frac{4}{13}$

    (E) $\frac{5}{13}$

28. To estimate 2.3×10^5 you could multiply 20 by

    (A) 10
    (B) 100
    (C) 1,000
    (D) 10,000
    (E) 100,000

29. A circle can be a part of any of the following except a

    (A) circle.
    (B) sphere.
    (C) cylinder.
    (D) cone.
    (E) cube.

30. Weather reports require accurate temperature readings. According to the thermometer, what is the temperature?

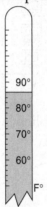

    (A) 80.3°F
    (B) 86°F
    (C) 80.4°F
    (D) 83°F
    (E) 80.6°F

31. If $6x + 2y = 10$, which of the following choices are possible values for x and y?

    (A) $x = 2, y = -1$
    (B) $x = 2, y = 11$
    (C) $x = 3, y = 4$
    (D) $x = 3, y = 14$
    (E) $x = 4, y = -8$

32. Tickets for a baseball game are $8 each, or 4 tickets for $30. What is the lowest cost for 18 tickets?

    (A) $144
    (B) $136
    (C) $132
    (D) $130
    (E) $126

33. If $4A + 6 = 2(B - 1)$, then $B = ?$

    (A) $2A + 4$
    (B) $8A + 13$
    (C) $2A + 2$
    (D) $4A + 7$
    (E) $4A + 5$

34. Which of the following measurements is not equal to the others?

    (A) 230,000 millimeters
    (B) 0.23 kilometers
    (C) 23 meters
    (D) 23,000 centimeters
    (E) 2.3 hectometers

35. Which of the following choices is a multiple of 7 when 4 is added to it?

    (A) 58
    (B) 114
    (C) 168
    (D) 78
    (E) 101

36. Ryan has gone $3\frac{1}{5}$ miles of his 5-mile run. How many more miles has he left to run?

    (A) A little less than 2 miles
    (B) A little more than 2 miles
    (C) A little less than 3 miles
    (D) A little more than 3 miles
    (E) A little less than 4 miles

37. For every 2 hours that Barbara works she earns $17. How much money will she earn if she works 45 hours?

    (A) $391
    (B) $382.50
    (C) $374
    (D) $365.50
    (E) $357

38. The pictograph shows TV sales for each month for all the stores in a chain. About how many times greater is the number of televisions sold in December than the number of televisions sold in January?

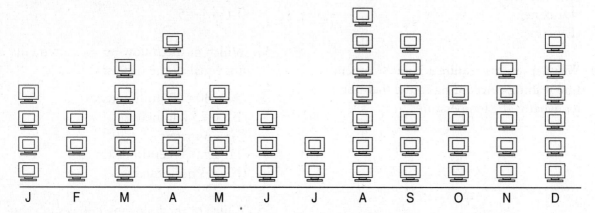

J F M A M J J A S O N D

(A) 1.5
(B) 2
(C) 2.5
(D) 3
(E) 3.5

39.

Principal Amount	Simple Interest Rate
$1–$5,000	5%
$5,001–$10,000	5.25%
$10,001–$15,000	5.5%
$15,001–$20,000	5.75%
$20,001–$25,000	6%
$25,001 and over	6.25%

The table above shows the interest rate a person will earn based on the principal amount invested. Using the formula $I = P \cdot R \cdot T$, how much interest will a person have earned after 7 years if he or she invests a principal amount of $20,000?

(A) $1,150
(B) $8,400
(C) $1,200
(D) $8,050
(E) $9,800

40. Which of the following figures has a volume of 72π?

(A)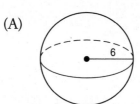

(B)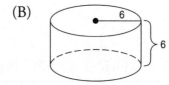

(C)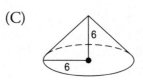

(D)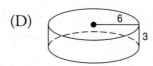

(E)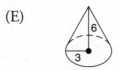

Answer Key
PRACTICE PPST 1

Reading

1. D	5. D	9. C	13. A	17. C	21. E	25. A	29. C	33. B	37. B
2. E	6. C	10. B	14. B	18. D	22. B	26. B	30. B	34. C	38. B
3. C	7. C	11. D	15. C	19. C	23. B	27. C	31. B	35. D	39. C
4. D	8. B	12. C	16. B	20. C	24. B	28. B	32. E	36. C	40. C

Writing

USAGE

1. E	4. B	7. C	10. D	13. C	16. E	19. C
2. C	5. D	8. C	11. C	14. A	17. D	20. C
3. E	6. B	9. E	12. E	15. B	18. B	21. D

SENTENCE CORRECTION

22. A	24. D	26. B	28. D	30. C	32. A	34. E	36. A	38. D
23. A	25. C	27. C	29. A	31. C	33. B	35. D	37. C	

Mathematics

1. A	5. E	9. C	13. E	17. B	21. B	25. C	29. E	33. A	37. B
2. B	6. C	10. D	14. D	18. D	22. D	26. C	30. B	34. C	38. A
3. D	7. D	11. E	15. B	19. C	23. B	27. C	31. A	35. E	39. D
4. B	8. A	12. B	16. D	20. D	24. D	28. D	32. B	36. A	40. C

Test Scoring

The scoring information from these tests is just a rough estimate. Passing raw scores on ETS tests vary widely, and this test will likely not have the same difficulty level of the actual PPST you take. That is why this scoring information is advisory only, as a guide to further study. You should NOT try to predict your scale score from these practice test results.

> Please read the reminders on pages 9–10 before you proceed.

Mark the multiple-choice test. Write your raw score for each test as the percent correct.

PERCENT CORRECT

Reading _____ %   Writing _____ %   Mathematics _____ %

Read your essay and assign a score from 1 to 6. Multiply the score by two to represent the scores of two readers. If you have difficulty scoring your essay, you may want to show it to an English expert for an evaluation.

Essay Score _____ out of 12

> Review the scoring information on pages 10–11 and estimate your scale scores.

ESTIMATED SCALE SCORE

Reading _____   Writing _____   Mathematics _____

> Look at your state's passing scale score on page 9. Write it here.

PASSING SCALE SCORE

Reading _____   Writing _____   Mathematics _____

Compare your estimated scale scores to your passing scale scores as a guide for further study only, and not as a prediction of the scale score you will receive on the actual PPST.

Practice PPST 1—Answers Explained

READING

1. **(D)** The paragraph describes how careful shopping can result in lower prices.

2. **(E)** The author is trying to raise AIDS awareness and not to present any particular fact.

3. **(C)** The passage explains that AIDS is transmitted through blood and other bodily fluids.

4. **(D)** The sentence for this choice is the best conclusion for this passage.

5. **(D)** The retired basketball player mentions youth basketball as one of the reasons why today's players were better athletes. The passage also mentions an increased focus on training. However, the question does not ask for all the factors the retired player mentioned.

6. **(C)** This writer believes that generals should be judged by results. Even if you do not agree, that is the view of this writer.

7. **(C)** The author writes that the question still cannot be answered. The author does not say that the question can never be answered.

8. **(B)** The author never questions or attacks Boards of Adjustment.

9. **(C)** The passage gives an example of a person who both supported and did not support requested exemptions.

10. **(B)** The author is writing about a local issue.

11. **(D)** In the last paragraph the author uses these words to describe Boards of Adjustment.

12. **(C)** The author gives several examples in which people support or don't support exemptions based on their own needs.

13. **(A)** Strategies I and II, together, assure the student that she will be chosen and give her a chance to get into a sorority she wants.

14. **(B)** List II is the only list that meets all the requirements.

15. **(C)** The rate, alone, does not provide enough information. You must also know the starting point.

16. **(B)** You should question any growth rate when only the percentage is given.

17. **(C)** Choice C is correct. A sentence can state both a fact and an opinion. "(2) alone states an opinion" means that it is the only sentence that states an opinion.

18. **(D)** This choice gives the fundamental reason why the schools' programs are copied. The other reasons grow out of the decision to provide extra resources.

19. **(C)** The author objects to using these programs with students who don't know mathematics.

20. **(C)** This is the only question that can be answered from information in the passage. The answer is that it can be used when students already understand equations and graphing.

21. **(E)** The author emphasizes understanding in the second paragraph with a discussion of the "mindless kind of graphing . . ." that can occur with graphing calculators.

22. **(B)** The author mentions liking this aspect in the middle of the first paragraph.

23. **(B)** Choice B replicates the intent of the original sentence.

24. **(B)** The author presents this information in the first sentence of the second paragraph.

25. **(A)** This is the only choice that has a plausible explanation of why potentially weaker spots appear stronger.

26. **(B)** The author's view is that all children should be treated the same.

27. **(C)** Choice C describes the problem. All the students who might have been admitted early this year will be admitted next year along with the other kindergarten students.

28. **(B)** Only this choice is a logical conclusion.

29. **(C)** When there are three lanes for passenger cars, school buses, school vans, and school cars can all use the lane for cars with two or more passengers.

30. **(B)** Only this choice meets all the rules.

31. **(B)** The context tells us that the answer is the tenor (direction, tendency) of the times.

32. **(E)** Of the listed sentences, only "This cycle is more akin . . ." contains an opinion.

33. **(B)** The author compares fashion to education, and then finally gets to the main point of the passage. That is, education practices seem random, like fashion, rather than based on sound educational practices.

34. **(C)** Hemlines move without apparent reason, which is this author's point about educational practices.

35. **(D)** The character visited the school and so is certainly curious. The character's reaction to the custodian shows respectfulness.

36. **(C)** The author discusses childhood from each of the perspectives described in C. Choice D is incorrect because the meaning of fantasy play is never discussed.

37. **(B)** This sentence juxtaposes adulthood and childhood and provides a transition to discussing adulthood.

38. **(B)** The author says that these childhood experiences would have occurred regardless of the location.

39. **(C)** The description of going toe to toe inside a ring reminds us of a boxing match.

40. **(C)** The author is not lying, but the story is obviously not meant to be taken seriously.

WRITING
Usage

1. **(E)** This sentence does not contain an error.

2. **(C)** The word *effected* is incorrect. It should be replaced by the word *affected*.

3. **(E)** This passage also contains no errors. *Townspeople* is an appropriate word.

4. **(B)** You can't print people. The underlined section should be *names of the people*.

5. **(D)** The word *Asia* is capitalized.

6. **(B)** The correct verb is *were*.

7. **(C)** The contraction *they're* (they are) is used incorrectly. *Their* is the correct word.

8. **(C)** The phrase *than to* is incorrectly used here. *But to* is the correct phrase.

9. **(E)** There are no underlined errors in this sentence.

10. **(D)** The conjunction *or* is incorrectly used here. The correct conjunction is *and*.

11. **(C)** There is no reason to use the word *individually*. Each citizen is an individual. The word *individually* should be removed.

12. **(E)** The passage contains no errors in underlined parts.

13. **(C)** The word *they* creates confusion because it could mean that there is one driver for both of them. A better usage is *each often has*.

14. **(A)** *Making* is the wrong verb. *Made* is the correct choice.

15. **(B)** The words *and now* should read *and which now*, in order to clarify just what faces anonymity.

16. **(E)** This sentence contains no underlined errors.

17. **(D)** This part of the sentence does not follow a parallel development. The correct usage is *reduced inflammation*.

18. **(B)** The correct replacement for *would be surprised* is *will be surprised*.

19. **(C)** The word *like* is incorrectly used here. The correct replacement is *such as*.

20. **(C)** The correct replacement for *so short supply* is *such short supply*.

21. **(D)** These words do not continue a parallel development. The correct replacement is *of their talent*.

Sentence Correction

22. **(A)** The underlined portion is appropriate.

23. **(A)** The underlined portion is appropriate.

24. **(D)** The rewording in D clarifies that the papers are in sealed envelopes—not in the house.

25. **(C)** This choice is the best wording from among the five choices available.

26. **(B)** This choice creates an agreement in number between nouns and pronoun.

27. **(C)** This choice replaces the wordy *in the event that* with *if*.

28. **(D)** This wordy expression is replaced by *can*.

29. **(A)** The underlined portion is appropriately worded.

30. **(C)** This choice appropriately replaces the double negative underlined in the original sentence.

31. **(C)** Adding the word *by* creates the desired parallel development in the sentence.

32. **(A)** The sentence is correct. The pronoun *his* agrees with the antecedent *Tom*.

33. **(B)** *Who* correctly shows the subjective case.

34. **(E)** *Have learned* indicates this has occurred and may continue.

35. **(D)** *Office World* is singular and takes the singular verb *claims*.

36. **(A)** The sentence is correct. The conjunction *and* shows that the two clauses are equally important.

37. **(C)** Use a comma before the conjunction that joins these two independent clauses. An independent clause can stand on its own as a sentence.

38. **(D)** Punctuation before a quote goes outside the quotation marks, while punctuation following a quote goes inside the quotation marks.

ESSAY

Compare your essay to the sample essay that follows. You may want to show your essay to an English expert for further evaluation. You will record your essay score on the Test Scoring section for this test on page 258.

This essay would likely receive a score of 5 or 6 out of 6 (515 words).

Paying Teachers Because They Score High Is a Bad Idea

A higher standardized test score does not tell anything about what a person will be like as a teacher. How many of us have known someone who could do very well on tests, but could not interact effectively with others? The same thing is true of people who do well on tests and can't explain what they know to another person. This does not mean that doing well on tests is a bad thing. It does seem to me that doing well on tests does not by itself mean that someone will be a good teacher. Besides that it is very hard to pay teachers on an incentive basis because there are so many differences among the pupils that teachers work with that you could never tell whether students did well because of a teacher or because of some other reason.

I don't agree that teacher's should be paid more to do something that lasts for a year because they scored higher on a test that lasts for hours, and I don't think it is possible to pay teachers by merit in most situations. I am going to write some things about each of these.

Just try to imagine this situation. There are two first grade teachers. One teacher scored much higher on a standardized test. Both teachers have to help their students learn about reading. But the teacher with the higher score for some reason or another can't deal with these young children. They do not have the patience to work with them all day long. It could be that the teacher with the higher score does not know how to teach reading. The teacher with the lower score is just the opposite. That other teacher works well with the children they have the patience to deal with them and they know how to teach reading. I do not think we could find a person anywhere who would not think that this low scoring teacher is the one we would want in the classroom.

The idea of paying teachers by merit is a part of this question. I think paying teachers in that way would be great if there was any way to tell that a teacher was the reason students were doing better or poorer as they learned. But I do not think there is. I can think of classes I was in where we did better because of the students who were in my class. To be honest the teacher did not help that much. But if you pay by merit then the teacher would have been paid more, not because of the teacher, but because of the students. That is not right.

In conclusion, I disagree with the statement because there is not evidence that indicates that teachers with higher standardized scores are better teachers. If some teachers have higher standardized scores, it is probably something about them and not the scores they received. This idea of paying teachers this way is an idea that should not be used in schools.

Rating Scale

6 This essay is extremely well written. It is the equivalent of an A in-class assignment. The essay addresses the question and provides clear supporting arguments, illustrations, or examples. The paragraphs and sentences are well organized and show a variety of language and syntax. The essay may contain some minor errors.

5 This essay is well written. It is the equivalent of a B+ in-class assignment. The essay addresses the question and provides some supporting arguments, illustrations, or examples. The paragraphs and sentences are fairly well organized and show a variety of language and syntax. The essay may contain some minor mechanical or linguistic errors.

4 This essay is fairly well written. It is the equivalent of a B in-class assignment. The essay adequately addresses the question and provides some supporting arguments, illustrations, or examples for some points. The paragraphs and sentences are acceptably organized and show a variety of language and syntax. The essay may contain mechanical or linguistic errors but is free from an identifiable pattern of errors.

3 This essay may demonstrate some writing ability, but it contains obvious errors. It is the equivalent of a C+ in-class assignment. The essay may not clearly address the question and may not give supporting arguments or details. The essay may show problems in diction including inappropriate word choice. The paragraphs and sentences may not be acceptably developed. There will be an identifiable pattern or grouping of errors.

2 This essay shows only the most limited writing ability. It is the equivalent of a C in-class assignment. It contains serious errors and flaws. This essay may not address the question, it may be poorly organized, or it may provide no supporting arguments or detail. It usually shows serious errors in diction, usage, and mechanics.

1 This essay does not demonstrate minimal writing ability. It is the equivalent of a D or F on an in-class assignment. This essay may contain serious and continuing errors, or it may not be coherent.

MATHEMATICS

1. **(A)** Divide to find what percent $624,000 is of $2,600,000. $624,000 \div 2,600,000 = 0.24 = 24\%$. The town needs 24% for police, 2% more than in the pie chart. Take 2% from sanitation, leaving 22% for sanitation.

2. **(B)** To find what percent 520 is of 1300, divide 520 by 1300 to get the decimal representation of percent. Then multiply by 100 to get the answer into percent form.

3. **(D)** A is not true because none of the windows are squares. All of the windows are rectangles, so B, C, and E are not true. Choice D meets both of the requirements.

4. **(B)** The larger square has seven of the smaller squares along each side. The area of the smaller square is 4 in², so each side of the smaller square is 2 in. The length of one side is 2 in $\cdot$ 7 = 14 in.

5. **(E)** The only number in the table that qualifies as a scientific number is (1A). A scientific number is between (1–10). (E) is the value of this number.

6. **(C)** Person 5 had 3 more awards than person 3. Therefore person 5 had $3 \cdot 20 = 60$ more awards than person 3.

7. **(D)** $A \cdot B + C = -4 \cdot 2 + 11 = -8 + 11 = 3$

8. **(A)** The mean is 39.4 while the median is 39. The difference is 0.4 of a year.

9. **(C)** None of the other choices cut into four equal pieces have two pieces containing crust.

10. **(D)** The formula for the area of a circle is πr^2.
    Area of the inner circle $= \pi(2)^2 = 4\pi$
    Area of the outer circle $= \pi(4)^2 = 16\pi$
    $16\pi - 4\pi = 12\pi$

    That is the area for the portion of the outer circle outside the inner circle. (A), (B), and (C) are all incorrect because these choices do not show the correct area.

11. **(E)** There are a total of 8 animals, 5 of which are cats. Therefore the answer is $\frac{5}{8} = 0.625 = 62.5\%$.

12. **(B)** $\frac{4}{9} = 0.444 \ldots$, which is less than 0.45.

13. **(E)** $45{,}000 \cdot 0.00001 = 0.45$

14. **(D)** (0, 1) shows an x-intercept of 1.
    (1, 0) shows a y-intercept of 1.

15. **(B)** The decimal equivalents of each answer choice are:
    A. $0.\overline{4}$
    B. $0.4\overline{8}$
    C. $0.\overline{4}$
    D. $0.\overline{4}$
    E. $0.\overline{4}$
    Answer choices A, C, D, and E are equal.

16. **(D)** The formula for the area of a trapezoid is $A = \frac{h}{2}(b_1 + b_2)$.

    However, in the new trapezoid the length of each base is doubled; therefore, the formula is

    $$A = \frac{h}{2}(2b_1 + 2b_2) =$$

    $$\frac{h}{2} \cdot 2(b_1 + b_2) =$$

    $$h(b_1 + b_2)$$

17. **(B)** Follow the steps.
    $5 \cdot 5 = 25$
    $25 + 5 = 30$
    $30 - 4 = 26$
    $26 \div 2 = 13$

18. **(D)** Jack's lowest weight is 170 pounds and Jack's highest weight is 190 pounds.
    $170 \div 190 \approx 0.89 \approx 89\%$

19. **(C)** It is $11\frac{1}{4}$ hours from 7:45 A.M. to 7:00 P.M. Subtract 1 hour for lunch. That

    leaves $10\frac{1}{4}$ work hours.

    $10\frac{1}{4} \times \$20 = \$205$.

20. **(D)** The trapezoid, choice D, has only one pair of congruent sides.

21. **(B)** Each diameter in choice B is part of the perimeter. When answering this question, consider only the perimeter and not any segments within a figure.

22. **(D)** A. $3^4 \times 9 \times 12 = 3^4 \times 9 \times 4 \times 3 = 3^5 \times 4 \times 9$
    This is choice E.

    B. $3^3 \times 27 \times 12 = 3^3 \times 9 \times 3 \times 4 \times 3 = 3^5 \times 4 \times 9$
    This is choice E.

    C. $3^5 \times 36 = 3^5 \times 4 \times 9$
    This is choice E.

    D. $3^3 \times 9^3 \times 4 = 3^3 \times 3^2 \times 9^2 \times 4 = 3^5 \times 4 \times 9^2 \neq 3^5 \times 4 \times 9$
    This is **not** choice E.

23. **(B)** $45,250 + 78,375 + 52,540 + 62,325 = 238,490 \approx 238,000$

24. **(D)** The *y*-value (vertical axis) moves up as the *x*-value (horizontal axis) moves right.

25. **(C)** $65\% = 0.65$ $\quad$ $(0.65) \cdot 400 = 260$

26. **(C)** $\dfrac{1}{2} = \dfrac{6}{12}, \dfrac{2}{3} = \dfrac{8}{12}, \dfrac{5}{12}$

$$\left(\dfrac{6}{12} + \dfrac{8}{12} + \dfrac{5}{12}\right) \div 3 =$$

$$\dfrac{19}{12} \div 3 =$$

$$\dfrac{19}{12} \cdot \dfrac{1}{3} = \dfrac{19}{36}$$

27. **(C)** In a standard deck of cards there are 12 "face cards"—4 kings, 4 queens, and 4 jacks out of 52 possible cards.

$$P(\text{face card}) = \dfrac{12}{52} = \dfrac{3}{13}$$

28. **(D)** Change 2.3 to 23 and then round to 20. (This involves multiplying by 10. 10^5 means multiply by 100,000. So you need to move the decimal four more places to the right.

29. **(E)** These figures show, a circle within a circle, a sphere, a cylinder, and a cone. A cube does not contain a circle.

30. **(B)** Each mark on the scale represents two degrees.

31. **(A)** $6(2) + 2(-1) = 12 - 2 = 10$

32. **(B)** There are 18 tickets and you can buy 16 of the tickets for $120 ($4 \times \$30$) and the remaining two tickets at $16.
$$\$120 + \$16 = \$136$$

33. **(A)** $4A + 6 = 2(B - 1)$

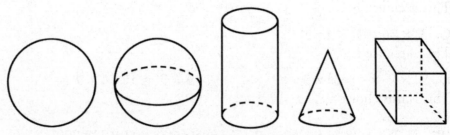

Divide by 2 on both sides: $\quad 2A + 3 = B - 1$
Add 1 to both sides: $\quad\quad\quad 2A + 4 = B$

$B = 2A + 4$

34. **(C)** Use this chart

Kilo	Hecto	Deka	Unit	Deci	Centi	Milli
1,000	100	10	1	0.1	0.01	0.001

Given below is each answer choice in meters.

A. 230 meters
B. 230 meters
C. 23 meters
D. 230 meters
E. 230 meters

Choice C is not equal to the others.

35. **(E)** $101 + 4 = 105 = 7 \cdot 15$

36. **(A)** $5 - 3\frac{1}{5} = 1\frac{4}{5}$, which is a little less than 2 miles.

37. **(B)** If Barbara earns $17 every 2 hours, she earns $\frac{\$17}{2} = \$8.50$ per hour. In 45 hours she earns $\$8.50 \cdot 45 = \$382.50$.

38. **(A)** There are 4 pictures of televisions in January and 6 pictures of televisions in December; $\frac{6}{4} = 1.5$. It does not matter how many televisions each picture represents, the answer will still be the same.

39. **(D)** The interest rate is based on the principal amount, and does not increase. Since the principal invested is $20,000, the interest rate is 5.75%. The time (T) is 7 years.
$I = \$20,000 \cdot .0575 \cdot 7 = \$8,050$

40. **(C)** A. $V = \frac{4}{3}\pi r^3 = \frac{4}{3}\pi(6)^3 = 288\pi$

B. $V = \pi r^2 h = \pi(6)^2(6) = 216\pi$

C. $V = \frac{1}{3}\pi r^2 h = \frac{1}{3}\pi(6)^2(6) = 72\pi$

D. $V = \pi r^2 h = \pi(6)^2(3) = 108\pi$

E. $V = \frac{1}{3}\pi r^2 h = \frac{1}{3}\pi(3)^2(6) = 36\pi$

CHAPTER 7

Practice PPST 2

TEST INFO BOX

Reading	40 items	60 minutes
Writing Multiple Choice	38 items	30 minutes
Writing Essay	1 essay	30 minutes
Mathematics	40 items	60 minutes

Take this test in a realistic, timed setting. You should not take this practice test until you have completed practice PPST 1.

The setting will be most realistic if another person times the test and ensures that the test rules are followed exactly. If another person is acting as test supervisor, he or she should review these instructions with you and say "Start" when you should begin a section and "Stop" when time has expired.

Use the multiple-choice answer sheet on page 273.

Use a pencil to mark the answer sheet. The actual test will be machine scored, so completely darken in the answer space.

Once the test is complete, review the answers and explanations for each item as you correct the test.

Answer Sheet

PRACTICE PPST 2

Reading—60 minutes

1 Ⓐ Ⓑ Ⓒ Ⓓ Ⓔ	11 Ⓐ Ⓑ Ⓒ Ⓓ Ⓔ	21 Ⓐ Ⓑ Ⓒ Ⓓ Ⓔ	31 Ⓐ Ⓑ Ⓒ Ⓓ Ⓔ
2 Ⓐ Ⓑ Ⓒ Ⓓ Ⓔ	12 Ⓐ Ⓑ Ⓒ Ⓓ Ⓔ	22 Ⓐ Ⓑ Ⓒ Ⓓ Ⓔ	32 Ⓐ Ⓑ Ⓒ Ⓓ Ⓔ
3 Ⓐ Ⓑ Ⓒ Ⓓ Ⓔ	13 Ⓐ Ⓑ Ⓒ Ⓓ Ⓔ	23 Ⓐ Ⓑ Ⓒ Ⓓ Ⓔ	33 Ⓐ Ⓑ Ⓒ Ⓓ Ⓔ
4 Ⓐ Ⓑ Ⓒ Ⓓ Ⓔ	14 Ⓐ Ⓑ Ⓒ Ⓓ Ⓔ	24 Ⓐ Ⓑ Ⓒ Ⓓ Ⓔ	34 Ⓐ Ⓑ Ⓒ Ⓓ Ⓔ
5 Ⓐ Ⓑ Ⓒ Ⓓ Ⓔ	15 Ⓐ Ⓑ Ⓒ Ⓓ Ⓔ	25 Ⓐ Ⓑ Ⓒ Ⓓ Ⓔ	35 Ⓐ Ⓑ Ⓒ Ⓓ Ⓔ
6 Ⓐ Ⓑ Ⓒ Ⓓ Ⓔ	16 Ⓐ Ⓑ Ⓒ Ⓓ Ⓔ	26 Ⓐ Ⓑ Ⓒ Ⓓ Ⓔ	36 Ⓐ Ⓑ Ⓒ Ⓓ Ⓔ
7 Ⓐ Ⓑ Ⓒ Ⓓ Ⓔ	17 Ⓐ Ⓑ Ⓒ Ⓓ Ⓔ	27 Ⓐ Ⓑ Ⓒ Ⓓ Ⓔ	37 Ⓐ Ⓑ Ⓒ Ⓓ Ⓔ
8 Ⓐ Ⓑ Ⓒ Ⓓ Ⓔ	18 Ⓐ Ⓑ Ⓒ Ⓓ Ⓔ	28 Ⓐ Ⓑ Ⓒ Ⓓ Ⓔ	38 Ⓐ Ⓑ Ⓒ Ⓓ Ⓔ
9 Ⓐ Ⓑ Ⓒ Ⓓ Ⓔ	19 Ⓐ Ⓑ Ⓒ Ⓓ Ⓔ	29 Ⓐ Ⓑ Ⓒ Ⓓ Ⓔ	39 Ⓐ Ⓑ Ⓒ Ⓓ Ⓔ
10 Ⓐ Ⓑ Ⓒ Ⓓ Ⓔ	20 Ⓐ Ⓑ Ⓒ Ⓓ Ⓔ	30 Ⓐ Ⓑ Ⓒ Ⓓ Ⓔ	40 Ⓐ Ⓑ Ⓒ Ⓓ Ⓔ

Writing—30 minutes

1 Ⓐ Ⓑ Ⓒ Ⓓ Ⓔ	11 Ⓐ Ⓑ Ⓒ Ⓓ Ⓔ	21 Ⓐ Ⓑ Ⓒ Ⓓ Ⓔ	31 Ⓐ Ⓑ Ⓒ Ⓓ Ⓔ
2 Ⓐ Ⓑ Ⓒ Ⓓ Ⓔ	12 Ⓐ Ⓑ Ⓒ Ⓓ Ⓔ	22 Ⓐ Ⓑ Ⓒ Ⓓ Ⓔ	32 Ⓐ Ⓑ Ⓒ Ⓓ Ⓔ
3 Ⓐ Ⓑ Ⓒ Ⓓ Ⓔ	13 Ⓐ Ⓑ Ⓒ Ⓓ Ⓔ	23 Ⓐ Ⓑ Ⓒ Ⓓ Ⓔ	33 Ⓐ Ⓑ Ⓒ Ⓓ Ⓔ
4 Ⓐ Ⓑ Ⓒ Ⓓ Ⓔ	14 Ⓐ Ⓑ Ⓒ Ⓓ Ⓔ	24 Ⓐ Ⓑ Ⓒ Ⓓ Ⓔ	34 Ⓐ Ⓑ Ⓒ Ⓓ Ⓔ
5 Ⓐ Ⓑ Ⓒ Ⓓ Ⓔ	15 Ⓐ Ⓑ Ⓒ Ⓓ Ⓔ	25 Ⓐ Ⓑ Ⓒ Ⓓ Ⓔ	35 Ⓐ Ⓑ Ⓒ Ⓓ Ⓔ
6 Ⓐ Ⓑ Ⓒ Ⓓ Ⓔ	16 Ⓐ Ⓑ Ⓒ Ⓓ Ⓔ	26 Ⓐ Ⓑ Ⓒ Ⓓ Ⓔ	36 Ⓐ Ⓑ Ⓒ Ⓓ Ⓔ
7 Ⓐ Ⓑ Ⓒ Ⓓ Ⓔ	17 Ⓐ Ⓑ Ⓒ Ⓓ Ⓔ	27 Ⓐ Ⓑ Ⓒ Ⓓ Ⓔ	37 Ⓐ Ⓑ Ⓒ Ⓓ Ⓔ
8 Ⓐ Ⓑ Ⓒ Ⓓ Ⓔ	18 Ⓐ Ⓑ Ⓒ Ⓓ Ⓔ	28 Ⓐ Ⓑ Ⓒ Ⓓ Ⓔ	38 Ⓐ Ⓑ Ⓒ Ⓓ Ⓔ
9 Ⓐ Ⓑ Ⓒ Ⓓ Ⓔ	19 Ⓐ Ⓑ Ⓒ Ⓓ Ⓔ	29 Ⓐ Ⓑ Ⓒ Ⓓ Ⓔ	
10 Ⓐ Ⓑ Ⓒ Ⓓ Ⓔ	20 Ⓐ Ⓑ Ⓒ Ⓓ Ⓔ	30 Ⓐ Ⓑ Ⓒ Ⓓ Ⓔ	

Mathematics—60 minutes

1 Ⓐ Ⓑ Ⓒ Ⓓ Ⓔ	11 Ⓐ Ⓑ Ⓒ Ⓓ Ⓔ	21 Ⓐ Ⓑ Ⓒ Ⓓ Ⓔ	31 Ⓐ Ⓑ Ⓒ Ⓓ Ⓔ
2 Ⓐ Ⓑ Ⓒ Ⓓ Ⓔ	12 Ⓐ Ⓑ Ⓒ Ⓓ Ⓔ	22 Ⓐ Ⓑ Ⓒ Ⓓ Ⓔ	32 Ⓐ Ⓑ Ⓒ Ⓓ Ⓔ
3 Ⓐ Ⓑ Ⓒ Ⓓ Ⓔ	13 Ⓐ Ⓑ Ⓒ Ⓓ Ⓔ	23 Ⓐ Ⓑ Ⓒ Ⓓ Ⓔ	33 Ⓐ Ⓑ Ⓒ Ⓓ Ⓔ
4 Ⓐ Ⓑ Ⓒ Ⓓ Ⓔ	14 Ⓐ Ⓑ Ⓒ Ⓓ Ⓔ	24 Ⓐ Ⓑ Ⓒ Ⓓ Ⓔ	34 Ⓐ Ⓑ Ⓒ Ⓓ Ⓔ
5 Ⓐ Ⓑ Ⓒ Ⓓ Ⓔ	15 Ⓐ Ⓑ Ⓒ Ⓓ Ⓔ	25 Ⓐ Ⓑ Ⓒ Ⓓ Ⓔ	35 Ⓐ Ⓑ Ⓒ Ⓓ Ⓔ
6 Ⓐ Ⓑ Ⓒ Ⓓ Ⓔ	16 Ⓐ Ⓑ Ⓒ Ⓓ Ⓔ	26 Ⓐ Ⓑ Ⓒ Ⓓ Ⓔ	36 Ⓐ Ⓑ Ⓒ Ⓓ Ⓔ
7 Ⓐ Ⓑ Ⓒ Ⓓ Ⓔ	17 Ⓐ Ⓑ Ⓒ Ⓓ Ⓔ	27 Ⓐ Ⓑ Ⓒ Ⓓ Ⓔ	37 Ⓐ Ⓑ Ⓒ Ⓓ Ⓔ
8 Ⓐ Ⓑ Ⓒ Ⓓ Ⓔ	18 Ⓐ Ⓑ Ⓒ Ⓓ Ⓔ	28 Ⓐ Ⓑ Ⓒ Ⓓ Ⓔ	38 Ⓐ Ⓑ Ⓒ Ⓓ Ⓔ
9 Ⓐ Ⓑ Ⓒ Ⓓ Ⓔ	19 Ⓐ Ⓑ Ⓒ Ⓓ Ⓔ	29 Ⓐ Ⓑ Ⓒ Ⓓ Ⓔ	39 Ⓐ Ⓑ Ⓒ Ⓓ Ⓔ
10 Ⓐ Ⓑ Ⓒ Ⓓ Ⓔ	20 Ⓐ Ⓑ Ⓒ Ⓓ Ⓔ	30 Ⓐ Ⓑ Ⓒ Ⓓ Ⓔ	40 Ⓐ Ⓑ Ⓒ Ⓓ Ⓔ

Reading Test

You should not take this practice test until you have completed practice PPST 1.

The test rules allow you exactly 60 minutes for this test.

Keep the time limit in mind as you work. Answer the easier questions first. Be sure you answer all the questions. There is no penalty for guessing. You may write on the test booklet and mark up the questions.

Each question or statement on the multiple-choice portions of the test has five answer choices. Exactly one of these choices is correct. Mark your choice on the answer sheet provided for this test.

Your score is based on the spaces you fill in on the answer sheet. Make sure that you mark your answer on the answer sheet in the correct space next to the correct question number.

Once the test is complete, review the answers and explanations for each item as you correct the test.

When you are ready, turn the page and begin.

READING

40 ITEMS   60 MINUTES

Directions: You will read selections followed by one or more questions with five answer choices. Select the best answer choice based on what the selection states or implies and mark that letter on the answer sheet.

1. Cellular phones, once used by the very rich, are now available to almost everyone. With one of these phones, you can call just about anywhere from just about anywhere. Since the use of these phones will increase, we need to find legal and effective ways for law enforcement agencies to monitor calls.

   Which of the following choices is the best summary of this passage?

   (A) Criminals are taking advantage of cellular phones to avoid legal wiretaps.
   (B) The ability to use a cellular phone to call from just about anywhere makes it harder to find people who are using the phones.
   (C) The increase in cellular phone use means that we will have to find legal ways to monitor cellular calls.
   (D) Cellular phones are like regular phones with a very long extension cord.
   (E) Since cellular phones are more available to everyone, they are certainly more available to criminals.

2. The moon takes about 28 days to complete a cycle around the earth. Months, 28 days long, grew out of this cycle. Twelve of these months made up a year. But ancient astronomers realized that it took the earth about 365 days to make one revolution of the sun. Extra days were added to some months and the current calendar was born.

   The passage indicates that the current calendar

   (A) describes the moon's movement around the earth.
   (B) is based on the sun's position.

   (C) is based on the earth's rotation and position of the moon.
   (D) combines features of the moon's cycle and the earth's revolution.
   (E) was based on the number 12.

3. Occasionally, college students will confuse correlation with cause and effect. Correlation just describes the degree of relationship between two factors. For example, there is a positive correlation between poor handwriting and intelligence. However, writing more poorly will not make you more intelligent.

   The author's main reason for writing this passage is to

   (A) explain the difference between correlation and cause and effect.
   (B) encourage improved penmanship.
   (C) explain how college students can improve their intelligence.
   (D) make those with poor penmanship feel more comfortable.
   (E) describe a cause-and-effect relationship.

Questions 4–6 are based on this passage.

It is striking how uninformed today's youth are about Acquired Immune Deficiency Syndrome. Because of their youth and ignorance, many young adults engage in high-risk behavior. Many of these young people do not realize that the disease can be contracted through almost any contact with an infected person's blood and bodily fluids. Some do not realize that symptoms of the disease may not appear for ten years or more. Others do not realize that the danger in sharing needles to inject intravenous drugs comes from the small amounts of another's blood injected during this process. A massive education campaign is needed to fully inform today's youth about AIDS.

4. The main idea of this passage is

    (A) previous education campaigns have failed.
    (B) AIDS develops from the HIV virus.
    (C) the general public is not fully informed about AIDS.
    (D) people should not share intravenous needles.
    (E) young people are not adequately informed about AIDS.

5. Which of the following is the best summary of the statement about what young people don't realize about how AIDS can be contracted?

    (A) The symptoms may not appear for ten years or more.
    (B) AIDS is contracted because of ignorance.
    (C) AIDS is contracted from intravenous needles.
    (D) AIDS is contracted through contact with infected blood or bodily fluids.
    (E) You will not contract AIDS if you know what to avoid.

6. Which of the following best describes how the author views young people and their knowledge of AIDS?

    (A) Stupid
    (B) Unaware
    (C) Dumb
    (D) Unintelligible
    (E) Reluctant

7. When Lyndon Johnson succeeded John F. Kennedy, he was able to gain congressional approval for programs suggested by

Kennedy but never implemented. These programs, called Great Society programs, included low-income housing and project Head Start. To some, this made Johnson a better president.

Based on this statement, Johnson

    (A) was a better president than Kennedy.
    (B) gained approval for programs proposed by Kennedy.
    (C) was a member of a Great Society.
    (D) was president before Kennedy.
    (E) originally lived in low-income housing.

Questions 8–9 are based on this passage.

I think women are discriminated against; however, I think men are discriminated against just as much as women. It's just a different type of discrimination. Consider these two facts: Men die about 6 years earlier than women, and men are the only people who can be drafted into the armed forces. That's discrimination!

8. What is the author's main point in writing this passage?

    (A) Men are discriminated against more than women are.
    (B) Both sexes are discriminated against.
    (C) Women are not discriminated against.
    (D) On average, men die earlier than women.
    (E) Men are not discriminated against.

9. Which of the following could be substituted for the word *drafted* in the next to last sentence?

    (A) Inducted against their will
    (B) Signed up
    (C) Pushed in by society
    (D) Drawn in by peer pressure
    (E) Serve in a foreign country

Questions 10–11 are based on this passage.

Alice in Wonderland, written by Charles Dodgson under the pen name Lewis Carroll, is full of symbolism, so much so that a book titled *Understanding Alice* was written containing the original text with marginal notes explaining the symbolic meanings.

10. By symbolism, the author of the passage above meant that much of *Alice in Wonderland*

    (A) was written in a foreign language.
    (B) contained many mathematical symbols.
    (C) contained no pictures.
    (D) had a figurative meaning.
    (E) was set in a special type.

11. What does the author mean by the phrase "marginal notes" found in the last sentence?

    (A) Explanations of the musical meaning of the text
    (B) Notes that may not have been completely correct
    (C) Notes written next to the main text
    (D) Notes written by Carroll but not included in the original book
    (E) An explanation of the text by Alice Liddell, the real Alice

12. Following a concert, a fan asked a popular singer why the songs sounded so different in person than on the recording. The singer responded, "I didn't record my emotions!"

    Which of the following statements is suggested by this passage?

    (A) The singer was probably not in a good mood during that performance.
    (B) The fan was being intrusive, and the performer was "brushing her off."
    (C) The performance was outdoors where sound quality is different.
    (D) The fan didn't realize the controls available for studio recordings.
    (E) The performance may vary depending on the mood of the performer.

Questions 13–18 are based on this passage.

The War of 1812 is one of the least understood conflicts in American history. However, many events associated
Line with the war are among the best remem-
(5) bered from American History. The war began when the United States invaded British colonies in Canada. The invasion failed, and the United States was quickly put on the defensive. Most Americans
(10) are not aware of how the conflict began. During the war, the *USS Constitution* (Old Ironsides) was active against British ships in the Atlantic. Captain William Perry, sailing on Lake Erie, was famous
(15) for yelling to his shipmates, "Don't give up the ship." Most Americans remember Perry and his famous plea, but not where or in which war he was engaged.

Most notably, British troops sacked
(20) and burned Washington, D.C. during this conflict. Subsequent British attacks on Fort McHenry near Baltimore were repulsed by American forces. It was during one of these battles that Francis Scott
(25) Key wrote the "Star Spangled Banner" while a prisoner on a British ship. The "rockets red glare, bombs bursting in air" referred to ordnance used by the British to attack the fort. Many Americans mis-
(30) takenly believe that the "Star Spangled Banner" was written during or shortly after the Revolutionary War.

13. All the following statements can be implied from the passage EXCEPT:

    (A) The British did not start the war.
    (B) Francis Scott Key was not at Fort McHenry when he wrote the "Star Spangled Banner."
    (C) The rockets referred to in the "Star Spangled Banner" were part of a celebration.
    (D) The British army entered Washington, D.C., during the war.
    (E) The nickname for the *USS Constitution* was Old Ironsides.

14. Which of the following words is the most appropriate replacement for "sacked" in line 19?

    (A) Entered
    (B) Ravished
    (C) Invaded
    (D) Enclosed
    (E) Encapsulated

15. Which of the following statements best summarizes the difference referred to in the passage between Perry's involvement in the War of 1812 and the way many Americans remember his involvement?

    (A) Perry was a drafter of the Constitution and later served on the *Constitution* in the Atlantic, although many Americans don't remember that.
    (B) Perry served in the Great Lakes, but many Americans don't remember that.
    (C) Perry served in Washington, D.C., although many Americans don't remember that.
    (D) Perry served on the *Constitution* at Fort McHenry during the writing of the "Star Spangled Banner," although many Americans do not remember that.
    (E) Perry served on the *Constitution* in the Atlantic, but many Americans don't remember that.

16. What can be inferred about Francis Scott Key from lines 23–26 of the passage?

    (A) He was killed in the battle.
    (B) All his papers were confiscated by the British after the battle.
    (C) He was released by or escaped from the British after the battle.
    (D) He returned to Britain where he settled down.
    (E) He was a British spy.

17. Based on the passage, which of the following words best describes the United States' role in the War of 1812?

    (A) Colonizer
    (B) Neutral
    (C) Winner
    (D) Loser
    (E) Aggressor

18. What main point is the author making in this passage?

    (A) The Americans fought the British in the War of 1812.
    (B) The Revolutionary War continued into the 1800s.
    (C) The British renewed the Revolutionary War during the 1800s.
    (D) Many Americans are unaware of events associated with the War of 1812.
    (E) Americans should remember the treachery of the army that invaded Washington during this war.

Questions 19–24 are based on this passage.

Computer-based word processing programs have spelling checkers and even a thesaurus to find synonyms and antonyms for highlighted words. To use the thesaurus, the student just types in the word, and a series of synonyms and antonyms appears on the computer screen. The program can also show recommended spellings for misspelled words. I like having a computer program that performs these mechanical aspects of writing. However, these programs do not teach about spelling or word meanings. A person could type in a word, get a synonym and have not the slightest idea what either meant.

Relying on this mindless way of checking spelling and finding synonyms, students will be completely unfamiliar with the meanings of the words they use. In fact, one of the most common misuses is to include a word that is spelled correctly but used incorrectly in the sentence.

It may be true that a strictly mechanical approach to spelling is used by some teachers. There certainly is a place for students who already understand word meanings to use a computer program that relieves the drudgery of checking spelling and finding synonyms. But these computer programs should never and can never replace the teacher. Understanding words—their uses and meanings—should precede this more mechanistic approach.

19. What is the main idea of this passage?

    (A) Mechanical spell checking is one part of learning about spelling.
    (B) Programs are not effective for initially teaching about spelling and synonyms.
    (C) Teachers should use word processing programs as one part of instruction.
    (D) Students who use these programs won't learn about spelling.
    (E) The programs rely too heavily on a student's typing ability.

20. Which of the following information is found in the passage?

    I. The type of computer that runs the word processor
    II. The two main outputs of spell checking and thesaurus programs
    III. An explanation of how to use the word-processing program to teach about spelling and synonyms

    (A) I only
    (B) II only
    (C) I and II only
    (D) II and III only
    (E) I, II, and III

21. Which aspect of spell checking and thesaurus programs does the author like?

    (A) That you just have to type in the word
    (B) That the synonyms and alternative spellings are done very quickly
    (C) That the difficult mechanical aspects are performed

    (D) That you don't have to know how to spell to use them
    (E) That they can't replace teachers

22. Which of the following questions could be answered from the information in the passage?

    (A) When is it appropriate to use spell checking and thesaurus programs?
    (B) How does the program come up with recommended spellings?
    (C) What type of spelling learning experiences should students have?
    (D) Why do schools buy these word processing programs?
    (E) Which word program does the author recommend?

23. Which of the following statements could be used in place of the first sentence of the last paragraph?

    (A) It may be true that some strict teachers use a mechanical approach.
    (B) It may be true that a stringently mechanical approach is used by some teachers.
    (C) It may be true that inflexible mechanical approaches are used by some teachers.
    (D) It may be true that the mechanical approach used by some teachers is too rigorous.
    (E) It may be true that some teachers use only a mechanical approach.

24. According to this passage, what could be the result of a student's unfamiliarity with the meanings of words or synonyms?

    (A) Using a program to display the alternative spellings
    (B) Relying on mindless ways of checking spelling and finding synonyms
    (C) Strictly mechanical approaches
    (D) Using microcomputers to find synonyms for highlighted words
    (E) Being able to just type in a word

Questions 25–28 are based on this passage.

As a child he read the *Hardy Boys* series of books and was in awe of the author, Franklin Dixon. As an adult, he read a book entitled the *Ghost of the Hardy Boys*, which revealed that there was no Franklin Dixon and that ghost writers had authored the books. The authors were apparently working for a large publishing syndicate.

25. Which of the following is the likely intent of the author of this passage?

    (A) To describe a book-publishing practice
    (B) To contrast fiction and fact
    (C) To contrast childhood and adulthood
    (D) To correct the record
    (E) To dissuade children from reading the Hardy Boys books

26. Which of the following best describes the author's attitude toward Franklin Dixon?

    (A) Awe
    (B) Childlike
    (C) Syndicated
    (D) Disappointment
    (E) Satisfaction

27. What does the word *Ghost* in the title of the second mentioned book refer to?

    (A) A person who has died or was dead at the time the book was published
    (B) A person who writes books without credit
    (C) A person who influences the way a book is written
    (D) The mystical images of the mind that affect the way any author writes
    (E) A person who edits a book after the author has submitted it for publication

28. Which of the following would NOT be an acceptable replacement for the word *awe* in the first sentence?

    (A) Wonder
    (B) Admiration
    (C) Esteem
    (D) Aplomb
    (E) Respect

Questions 29–32 are based on this passage.

The Iroquois nation consisted of five main tribes—Cayuga, Mohawk, Oneida, Onondaga, and Seneca. Called the Five Nations or the League of Five Nations, these tribes occupied much of New York State. Since the tribes were arranged from east to west, the region they occupied was called the long house of the Iroquois.

The Iroquois economy was based mainly on agriculture. The main crop was corn, but they also grew pumpkins, beans, and fruit. The Iroquois used wampum (hollow beads) for money, and records were woven into wampum belts.

The Iroquoian Nation had a remarkable democratic structure, spoke a common Algonquin language, and were adept at fighting. These factors had made the Iroquois a dominant power by the early American colonial period. In the period just before the Revolutionary War, Iroquoian conquest had overcome most other Indian tribes in the northeastern United States as far west as the Mississippi River.

During the Revolutionary War, most Iroquoian tribes sided with the British. At the end of the Revolutionary War the tribes scattered, with some migrating to Canada. Only remnants of the Seneca and Onondaga tribes remained on their tribal lands.

29. Which of these statements best explains why the Iroquois were so successful at conquest?

    (A) The Iroquois had the support of the British.
    (B) The Iroquois had a cohesive society and were good fighters.

(C) All the other tribes in the area were too weak.

(D) There were five tribes, more than the other Indian nations.

(E) The Iroquois had developed a defensive structure called the long house.

30. Which of the following best describes the geographic location of the five Iroquoian tribes?

(A) The northeastern United States as far west as the Mississippi River
(B) Southern Canada
(C) Cayuga
(D) New York State
(E) The League of Nations

31. Which of the following best describes why the area occupied by the Iroquois was called the long house of the Iroquois?

(A) The tribes were arranged as though they occupied different sections of a long house.
(B) The Iroquois lived in structures called long houses.
(C) The close political ties among tribes made it seem that they were all living in one house.
(D) The Iroquois had expanded their original tribal lands through conquest.
(E) It took weeks to walk the trail connecting all the tribes.

32. According to the passage, which of the following best describes the economic basis for the Iroquoian economy?

(A) Wampum
(B) Corn
(C) Agriculture
(D) Conquest
(E) Warfare

Questions 33–38 are based on this passage.

Europeans had started to devote significant resources to medicine when Louis Pasteur was born December 7, 1822. By the time he died in the fall of 1895, he had made enormous contributions to science and founded microbiology. At 32, he was named professor and dean at a French university dedicated to supporting the production of alcoholic beverages. Pasteur immediately began work on yeast and fermentation. He found that he could kill harmful bacteria in the initial brewing process by subjecting the liquid to high temperatures. This finding was extended to milk in the process called pasteurization. This work led him to the conclusion that human disease could be caused by germs. In Pasteur's time, there was a widely held belief that germs were spontaneously generated. Pasteur conducted experiments that proved germs were always introduced and never appeared spontaneously. This result was questioned by other scientists for over a decade. He proved his theory of vaccination and his theory of disease during his work with anthrax, a fatal animal disease. He vaccinated some sheep with weakened anthrax germs and left other sheep unvaccinated. Then he injected all the sheep with a potentially fatal dose of anthrax bacteria. The unvaccinated sheep died while the vaccinated sheep lived. He developed vaccines for many diseases and is best known for his vaccine for rabies. According to some accounts, the rabies vaccine was first tried on a human when a young boy, badly bitten by a rabid dog, arrived at Pasteur's laboratory. The treatment of the boy was successful.

33. What is topic of this passage?

(A) Microbiology
(B) Pasteur's scientific discoveries
(C) Germs and disease
(D) Science in France
(E) Louis Pasteur

34. What does the process of pasteurization involve?

    (A) Inoculating
    (B) Experimenting
    (C) Hydrating
    (D) Heating
    (E) Fermenting

35. Which of the following statements could most reasonably be inferred from this passage?

    (A) The myth of spontaneous generation was dispelled immediately following Pasteur's experiments on the subject.
    (B) The pasteurization of milk can aid in the treatment of anthrax.
    (C) Pasteur's discoveries were mainly luck.
    (D) Even scientists don't think scientifically all the time.
    (E) Injecting sheep with fatal doses of anthrax is one way of vaccinating them.

36. Which of the following statements can be implied from this passage?

    (A) That germs do not develop spontaneously was already a widely accepted premise when Pasteur began his scientific work.
    (B) Scientists in European countries had made significant progress on the link between germs and disease when Pasteur was born.
    (C) Europe was ready for scientific research on germs when Pasteur conducted his experiments.
    (D) Most of Pasteur's work was the replication of other work done by French scientists.
    (E) The theory that germs could cause human disease was not yet accepted at the time of Pasteur's death.

37. Which of the following choices best characterizes the reason for Pasteur's early work?

    (A) To cure humans
    (B) To cure animals
    (C) To help the French economy
    (D) To study germs
    (E) To be a professor

38. According to this passage, the rabies vaccine

    (A) was developed after Pasteur had watched a young boy bitten by a rabid dog.
    (B) was developed from the blood of a rabid dog, which had bitten a young boy.
    (C) was developed from the blood of a young boy bitten by a rabid dog.
    (D) was developed in addition to the vaccines for other diseases.
    (E) was developed in his laboratory where a young boy had died of the disease.

Questions 39–40 are based on this passage.

I believe that there is extraterrestrial life—probably in some other galaxy. It is particularly human to believe that our solar system is the only one that can support intelligent life. But our solar system is only an infinitesimal dot in the infinity of the cosmos and it is just not believable that there is not life out there—somewhere.

39. What is the author of this passage proposing?

    (A) That there is other life in the universe
    (B) That there is no life on earth
    (C) That humans live on other planets
    (D) That the sun is a very small star
    (E) That we should explore other galaxies

40. The words *infinitesimal* and *infinite* are best characterized by which pair of words below?

    (A) Small and large
    (B) Very small and very large
    (C) Very small and limitless
    (D) Large and limitless
    (E) Small and very large

Writing Test

Take this test in a realistic, timed setting. You should not take this practice test until you have completed practice PPST 1.

The test rules allow exactly 30 minutes for this section.

Keep the time limit in mind as you work. Answer the easier questions first. Be sure you answer all the questions. There is no penalty for guessing. You may write on the test booklet and mark up the questions.

Each question or statement has five answer choices. Exactly one of these choices is correct. Mark your choice on the answer sheet provided for this test.

Your score is based on the spaces you fill in on the answer sheet. Make sure that you mark your answer on the answer sheet in the correct space next to the correct question number.

When you are ready, turn the page and begin.

WRITING

38 ITEMS   30 MINUTES

Usage

Directions: You will read sentences with four parts underlined and lettered. Determine whether one of the underlined parts contains grammatical, word use, or punctuation errors. If so, mark the letter of that part on your answer sheet. If there are no errors, mark E.

1. A professional golfer told the <u>new golfer</u>
                                          (A)
    that <u>professional instruction</u> or more
                 (B)
    practice <u>improve</u> most golfers' <u>scores</u>.
                 (C)   (D)
    <u>No error</u>.
     (E)

2. It was <u>difficult for</u> the farmer
               (A)
    <u>to comprehend</u> the unhappiness he
         (B)
    <u>encountered among</u> so many of the rich
          (C)
    <u>produce buyers</u> in the city. <u>No error</u>.
          (D)   (E)

3. No goal is <u>more noble</u>—no feat more
                    (A)
    <u>revealing</u>—<u>as the</u> exploration <u>of space</u>.
       (B)   (C)   (D)
    <u>No error</u>.
     (E)

4. The soccer player's <u>slight</u> strain from the
                           (A)
    <u>shot</u> on goal led to a <u>pulled</u> muscle,
     (B)   (C)
    <u>resulted</u> in the player's removal from the
     (D)
    game. <u>No error</u>.
            (E)

5. The <u>young college graduate</u> had
              (A)
    no family to help her but

    <u>she was fortunate</u> to get a job with a
         (B)
    <u>promising school district superintendent</u>
                      (C)
    and <u>eventually became a superintendent</u>
                      (D)
    herself. <u>No error</u>.
               (E)

6. He <u>was concerned</u> about crossing the
           (A)
    bridge, <u>but the</u> officer said <u>that</u> it was
              (B)   (C)
    <u>all right</u> to cross. <u>No error</u>.
       (D)   (E)

7. As the students <u>prepared to take</u> the
                          (A)
    test, they <u>came to realize</u> that it was not
                    (B)
    only what they knew <u>and also</u> how well
                              (C)
    they <u>knew how to</u> take tests. <u>No error</u>.
              (D)   (E)

8. As <u>many</u> as a ton of bananas may have
         (A)
    <u>spoiled</u> when the <u>ship</u> was <u>stuck</u> in the
       (B)   (C)   (D)
    Panama Canal. <u>No error</u>.
                     (E)

9. Employment agencies <u>often place</u>
                              (A)
   newspaper advertisements <u>when no</u>
                                  (B)
   jobs <u>exist</u> to get the names of <u>potential</u>
        (C)   (D)
   employees on file. <u>No error.</u>
                          (E)

10. Visitors <u>to New York can</u> expect
                 (A)
    <u>to encounter people,</u> noise, and
         (B)
    <u>finding themselves in traffic</u> just
                  (C)
    <u>about any day of the</u> week. <u>No error.</u>
           (D)   (E)

11. It <u>was obvious</u> to Kim that neither
          (A)
    her family <u>or her friends</u> could
                    (B)
    <u>understand why</u> the <u>study of science</u> was
         (C)   (D)
    so important to her. <u>No error.</u>
                              (E)

12. While <u>past safaris</u> had entered the jungle
               (A)
    to hunt <u>elephants with rifles,</u> this safari
                 (B)
    had only a <u>single armed</u> guard to protect
                     (C)
    <u>the tourists as</u> they took photographs.
            (D)
    <u>No errors.</u>
         (E)

13. <u>Buddhism is</u> an interesting <u>religion</u>
         (A)   (B)
    because Confucius <u>was born</u> in India,
                           (C)
    but the religion never <u>gained lasting</u>
                                 (D)
    popularity there. <u>No error.</u>
                           (E)

14. John Dewey's <u>progressive</u> philosophy
                      (A)
    <u>influenced</u> thousands of teachers;
         (B)
    however, Dewey was often <u>displeased</u>
                                   (C)
    with <u>there</u> teaching methods. <u>No error.</u>
             (D)   (E)

15. <u>While only</u> in the school for
         (A)
    <u>a few weeks,</u> the gym teacher
         (B)
    was starting to <u>felt comfortable</u> with
            (C)   (D)
    the principal. <u>No error.</u>
                        (E)

16. The <u>carnival,</u> which <u>featured</u> a wild
            (A)   (B)
    animal act was due to <u>arrive</u> in town
            (C)   (D)
    next week. <u>No error.</u>
                    (E)

17. <u>While</u> the bus <u>driver</u> <u>waited,</u> the motor
        (A)   (B)   (C)
    runs and uses <u>expensive</u> gasoline.
                       (D)
    <u>No error.</u>
        (E)

18. <u>Having needed</u> to eat <u>and earn</u> money,
         (A)   (B)
    the college <u>graduate decided</u> it was
                     (C)
    <u>time to</u> look for a job. <u>No error.</u>
        (D)   (E)

19. The salesman <u>spent the day</u> calling
                      (A)
    contacts <u>with which</u> he had
                 (B)
    <u>previously had</u> <u>business dealings.</u>
         (C)   (D)
    <u>No error.</u>
        (E)

20. Thomas, the only player to go
            (A)
    undefeated through the preliminary round,
        (B)
    giving him the highest position for the
      (C)   (D)
    tournament final. No error.
                (E)

21. Because his father was a wonderful
               (A)
    student, Jim's teachers expected him
               (B)
    to be a good student just as his sister
      (C)
    Beth did. No error.
      (D)   (E)

Sentence Correction

Directions: You will read sentences with some or all of the sentence underlined, followed by five answer choices. The first answer choice repeats the underlined portion and the other four present possible replacements. Select the answer choice that best represents standard English without altering the meaning of the original sentence. Mark that letter on the answer sheet.

22. The dean was famous for delivering grand sounding but otherwise unintelligible speeches.

    (A) but otherwise unintelligible speeches.
    (B) but in every other way speeches that could not be intelligible.
    (C) but speeches which were not that intelligent.
    (D) but otherwise speeches that could be understood.
    (E) but speeches that could be unintelligible.

23. The hiker grew tired greater as the day wore on.

    (A) The hiker grew tired greater
    (B) The hiker grew tired more
    (C) The hiker grew greater tired
    (D) The hiker's tired grew greater
    (E) The hiker grew more tired

24. The man knew that to solve the problem now can be easier than putting it off for another day.

    (A) to solve the problem now can be easier
    (B) to solve the problem now is easier
    (C) to solve the problem now can be less difficult

    (D) solving the problem now can be easier
    (E) to try to solve the problem now

25. Lee's mother and father insists that he call if he is going to be out after 8:00 P.M.

    (A) mother and father insists that
    (B) mother and father insist that
    (C) mother and father insists
    (D) mother and father that insist
    (E) mother and father that insists

26. The weather forecaster said that people living near the shore should be prepared in the event that the storm headed for land.

    (A) in the event that
    (B) if the event happened and
    (C) the event
    (D) if
    (E) and

27. After years of observation, the soccer coach concluded that women soccer players were more aggressive than men who played soccer.

    (A) men who played soccer.
    (B) men soccer players.
    (C) soccer playing men.
    (D) those men who played soccer.
    (E) men.

28. The stockbroker advised her client to sell the stock before it <u>could no longer be popular</u>.

    (A) could no longer be popular.
    (B) could be popular no longer.
    (C) may be popular no longer.
    (D) could become unpopular.
    (E) was no longer popular.

29. Bringing in an outside consultant usually means that it will take too long for the consultant to understand what's going on, <u>the functioning of the office will be impaired</u> and, because a new person has been introduced into the company, it will create dissension.

    (A) the functioning of the office will be impaired
    (B) the impairment of office functioning will follow
    (C) caused impairment in office functioning
    (D) office functioning impairment will occur
    (E) it will impair the functioning of the office

30. The primary election was very <u>important because winning could give the candidate a much more</u> clearer mandate.

    (A) important because winning could give the candidate a much more
    (B) important because winning there could give the candidate a much more
    (C) important because a win there could give the candidate a
    (D) important because winning could give the candidate a
    (E) important because a loss there would be devastating

31. She had become a doctor with the noble purpose of saving lives; however, <u>the process of applying for medical benefits and the responsibilities for managing the office had become her primary and over-riding concern.</u>

    (A) the process of applying for medical benefits and the responsibilities for managing the office had become her primary and overriding concern.
    (B) applying for medical benefits and managing the office had become her main concerns.
    (C) applying for medical benefits, and the responsibilities for managing the office had become her primary and overriding concern.
    (D) applying for medical benefits and office work had become her main concern.
    (E) she soon found out that being a doctor was not noble.

32. Among the most popular television programs are those that critics classify <u>is soap operas</u>.

    (A) is soap operas.
    (B) are soap operas.
    (C) as soap operas.
    (D) in soap operas.
    (E) with soap operas.

33. If a person <u>has the ability in music</u>, then he should try to develop this ability by taking music lessons.

    (A) has the ability in music
    (B) has musical ability
    (C) can play an instrument
    (D) is a talented musician
    (E) is interested in music

34. The players on the national team were supposed by some of their countrymen to have almost superhuman ability.

    (A) The players on the national team were supposed by some of their countrymen to have almost superhuman ability.
    (B) The players on the national team had superhuman ability, according to some of their countrymen.
    (C) The players in the national team were better at the sport than most of their countryman.
    (D) Suppose the players on the national team were not good enough, thought some of their countrymen.
    (E) Some of their countrymen thought that the players on the national team had almost superhuman ability.

35. Mr. Littler had managed to stay popular with the students, even though any serious breach of discipline inevitably brought them to his office.

    (A) inevitably brought
    (B) brought inevitably
    (C) was inevitable
    (D) considerably brought
    (E) inevitably bring

36. No matter how much she tried, she could never convince her father that he should stop smoking cigarettes.

    (A) that he should stop
    (B) he should stop
    (C) should stop
    (D) to stop
    (E) about stopping

37. The main error of superhighway driving is to forget what the speedometer reads.

    (A) of superhighway driving is to forget
    (B) driving is to forget on superhighways
    (C) is speeding on superhighways
    (D) people make when they drive on superhighways is to forget
    (E) is forgetting on superhighways to drive

38. People who set fires are frequently captured, and it is common at the scene of the crime.

    (A) and it is common
    (B) and common
    (C) in common at the
    (D) and
    (E) commonly

Essay

Take this test in a realistic, timed setting. You should not take this practice test until you have completed practice PPST 1.

Write an essay on the topic found on the next page. Write on this topic only. An essay written on another topic, no matter how well done, will receive a 0. You have 30 minutes to complete the essay.

Use the space provided to briefly outline your essay and to organize your thoughts before you begin to write. Use this opportunity to demonstrate how well you can write but be sure to cover the topic.

Write your essay on the lined paper provided. Write legibly and do not skip any lines. Your entire essay must fit on these pages.

Once the test is complete, ask an English professor or English teacher to evaluate your essay holistically using the rating scale on page 36.

When you are ready, turn the page and begin.

ESSAY

A college student who received a poor grade in a class should be able to have any record of the class and the grade removed from his or her transcript.

Describe the extent to which you agree or disagree with this statement. Support your response with specific details, examples, and experiences.

Write a brief outline here.

Mathematics Test

Take this test in a realistic, timed setting. You should not take this practice test until you have completed practice PPST 1.

The test rules allow you exactly 60 minutes for this section.

Keep the time limit in mind as you work. Answer the easier items first. Be sure you answer all the items. There is no penalty for guessing. You may write on the test booklet and mark up the items.

Each item has five answer choices. Exactly one of these choices is correct. Mark your choice on the answer sheet provided for this test.

Your score is based on the spaces you fill in on the answer sheet. Make sure that you mark your answer in the correct space next to the correct item number.

When you are ready, turn the page and begin.

Practice PPST 2

MATHEMATICS

40 ITEMS   60 MINUTES

Directions: Each item below includes five answer choices. Select the best choice for each item and mark that letter on the answer sheet.

1. A representative of the magazine advertising department is responsible for 9 to 10 full-page ads, 12 to 14 half-page ads, and 15 to 20 quarter-page ads per issue. The minimum and maximum numbers of ads that each representative is responsible for are

    (A) 9 and 20
    (B) 9 and 15
    (C) 15 and 20
    (D) 36 and 44
    (E) 10 and 20

2. 7.17 is between

    (A) 7.0 and 7.2
    (B) 7.02 and 7.10
    (C) 7.5 and 7.9
    (D) 7.00 and 7.04
    (E) 7.012 and 7.102

3. Which of the following expresses the relationship between x and y shown in the table?

x	y
0	1
3	7
6	13
7	15
9	19

    (A) $y = 3x - 2$
    (B) $y = 2x + 1$
    (C) $y = x + 3$
    (D) $y = 2x - 2$
    (E) $y = 2x + 3$

4. It took Liz 12 hours to travel by train from New York to North Carolina at an average speed of 55 miles per hour. On the return trip from North Carolina to New York, Liz traveled by bus and averaged 45 miles per hour. How much longer was her return trip?

    (A) $2\frac{2}{3}$

    (B) $3\frac{2}{3}$

    (C) $4\frac{2}{3}$

    (D) 5

    (E) $6\frac{2}{3}$

5. In the figure above, what percent of the regions are shaded?

    (A) $66\frac{2}{3}\%$

    (B) 40%
    (C) 25%
    (D) 60%

    (E) $33\frac{1}{3}\%$

6. $5 \times 10^5 \bigcirc 0.05 \times 10^7$. Which symbol makes the sentence true?

    (A) >
    (B) <
    (C) =
    (D) ≥
    (E) ≤

7. Which of the following could be the length of a couch?

   (A) 75 cm
   (B) 4 meters
   (C) 150 mm
   (D) 1.2 decimeters
   (E) 0.5 kilometers

8. *C* is 5 more than half of *B*. Which of the following expressions states this relationship?

   (A) $C + 5 = B/2$
   (B) $C = \frac{1}{2}B + 5$
   (C) $C + 5 = 2B$
   (D) $C + 5 > B/2$
   (E) $C + 5 < B/2$

9. If your commission for this month is 15% of $500, which of the following commissions is more than yours?

   (A) 20% of $380
   (B) 10% of $500
   (C) 1% of $1000
   (D) 10% of $750
   (E) 25% of $280

10. Which of these figures has a perimeter measure different from the others?

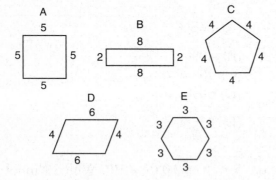

Time	8 A.M.	9 A.M.	10 A.M.	11 A.M.	12 NOON
Temp	50°	55°	60°	60°	70°
Time	1 P.M.	2 P.M.	3 P.M.	4 P.M.	
Temp	75°	80°	70°	65°	
Time	5 P.M.	6 P.M.	7 P.M.	8 P.M.	
Temp	55°	50°	50°	45°	

11. The above table shows the temperature tracked for a 12-hour period of time. Which graph best illustrates this information?

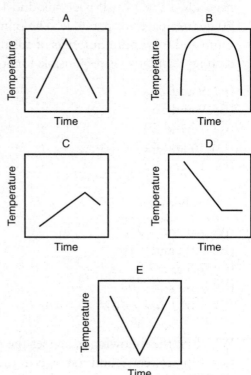

12. A rectangular garden measures 23 feet by 63 feet. What is the greatest number of nonoverlapping 5-foot square plots that can be ruled off in this garden?

   (A) 48
   (B) 57
   (C) 58
   (D) 289
   (E) 290

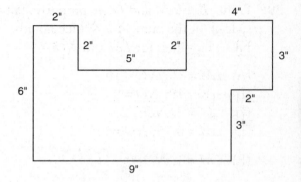

Miles Traveled Each Day
on a Family Camping Trip

13. Which is closest to the average mileage traveled per day on the trip?

(A) 125 miles
(B) 200 miles
(C) 175 miles
(D) 140 miles
(E) 100 miles

14. $\dfrac{1}{100} + \dfrac{1}{10,000} =$

(A) 0.101
(B) 0.0101
(C) 1.01
(D) 1.10
(E) 0.011

15. A junior high school has a teacher-student ratio of 1 to 15. If there are 43 teachers, how many students are there?

(A) 645
(B) 430
(C) 215
(D) 630
(E) 600

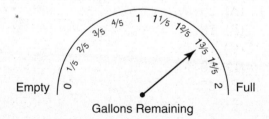

16. The gauge shows the amount of gas in the tank after mowing the lawn. If the tank was fall at the start of mowing, which of the following is the best estimate of how many "mows" are left?

(A) 2
(B) 3
(C) 4
(D) 5
(E) 6

17. A floor plan is drawn with a scale of 5 feet per inch. If the diagram represents the floor plan, what is the actual perimeter of the house?

(A) 38 inches
(B) 38 feet
(C) 200 feet
(D) $7\dfrac{2}{5}$ feet
(E) 190 feet

18. Mary must make tablecloths for 12 banquet tables. She needs a piece of cloth 5 ft. by 8 ft. for each tablecloth. Each cloth must be made from the same bolt and cannot be sewn. Of the five bolts listed here, which one must be eliminated due to insufficient material?

(A) 25 yd. remaining on an 8-ft. wide bolt
(B) 33 yd. remaining on a 6-ft. wide bolt
(C) 25 yd. remaining on a 5-ft. wide bolt
(D) 20 yd. remaining on an 8-ft. wide bolt
(E) 36 yd. remaining on a 7-ft. wide bolt

19. Blaire bought a pair of shoes at 25 percent off the regular price of $40.00. She had a coupon, which saved her an additional 15 percent off the sale price. What price did she pay for the shoes?

    (A) $24.00
    (B) $15.00
    (C) $25.50
    (D) $11.25
    (E) $27.50

20. Points *L, M, N,* and *O* are proportionally spaced on the same line. Which could NOT be values for *LM* and *NO*?

    (A) *LM* = 15; *NO* = 10
    (B) *LM* = 12; *NO* = 9
    (C) *LM* = 3; *NO* = 2
    (D) *LM* = 0.75; *NO* = 0.5
    (E) *LM* = 1; $NO = \frac{2}{3}$

21. Store A has DVDs in packs of 3 for $15.60. Store B sells DVDs for $6.00 each. How much is saved (if any) on each DVD if you buy six DVDs from Store A instead of 6 DVDs from Store B?

    (A) $3.40
    (B) $.80
    (C) $1.80
    (D) $2.40
    (E) There is no saving.

22. Two different whole numbers are multiplied. Which of the following could not result?

    (A) 0
    (B) 1
    (C) 7
    (D) 19
    (E) 319

23. Which of the following does not have the same value as the others?

    (A) (0.9 + 0.2) × 3.2
    (B) (0.9 × 3.2) + (0.2 × 3.2)
    (C) 0.9 + (0.2 × 3.2)
    (D) 3.2 × (0.2 + 0.9)
    (E) 3.2 × (1.1)

24. In the figure, if the first cube represents a weight of 100 grams, which of the other cubes most likely represents 25 grams?

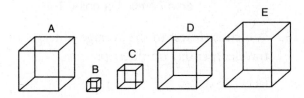

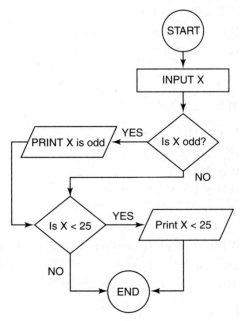

25. One of these numbers was put through the program represented by the flow chart, and nothing was printed. Which number was it?

    (A) 25
    (B) 18
    (C) 13
    (D) 38
    (E) 27

26. A calculator displays a multiple-digit whole number ending in 0. All the following statements must be true about the number EXCEPT:

    (A) it is an even number.
    (B) it is a multiple of 5.
    (C) it is a power of 10.
    (D) it is a multiple of 10.
    (E) it is the sum of 2 odd numbers.

27. Some values of *Y* are more than 50. Which of the following could not be true?

    (A) 60 is not a value of *Y*.
    (B) 45 is not a value of *Y*.
    (C) There are *Y* values more than 50.
    (D) All values of *Y* are 50 or less.
    (E) Some values of *Y* are more than 50.

28. A pedometer shows distance in meters. A distance of 0.5 kilometers would have a numerical display that is

    (A) 100 times as great.
    (B) twice as great.
    (C) half as great.
    (D) 1000 times as great.
    (E) $\frac{1}{10}$ times as great.

29. Which of the following shows the least to greatest ordering of the fractions?

    (A) $\frac{12}{13}, \frac{99}{100}, \frac{25}{24}, \frac{17}{16}, \frac{5}{4}$
    (B) $\frac{99}{100}, \frac{25}{24}, \frac{17}{16}, \frac{5}{4}, \frac{12}{13}$
    (C) $\frac{25}{24}, \frac{12}{13}, \frac{99}{100}, \frac{5}{4}, \frac{17}{16}$
    (D) $\frac{17}{16}, \frac{5}{4}, \frac{25}{24}, \frac{12}{13}, \frac{99}{100}$
    (E) $\frac{5}{4}, \frac{12}{13}, \frac{17}{16}, \frac{99}{100}, \frac{25}{24}$

30. Two dice are rolled. What is the probability that the sum of the numbers is even?

    (A) $\frac{1}{2}$
    (B) $\frac{16}{36}$

(C) $\frac{3}{4}$

(D) $\frac{1}{12}$

(E) $\frac{5}{6}$

31. If the product of *P* and 6 is *R*, then the product of *P* and 3 is

    (A) 2*R*
    (B) *R*/2
    (C) $\frac{1}{2}P$
    (D) 2*P*
    (E) *P*/6

32. The multiplication and division buttons on a calculator are reversed. A person presses ÷ 5 = and the calculator displays 625. What answer should have been displayed?

    (A) 125
    (B) 625
    (C) 25
    (D) 50
    (E) 250

33. If *V, l, w,* and *h* are positive numbers and $V = l \times w \times h$, then *l* =

    (A) $\frac{1}{3}whv$
    (B) $\frac{v}{hw}$
    (C) $\frac{lw}{v}$
    (D) *vlw*
    (E) $w(v + h)$

34. If 0.00005 divided by *X* = 0.005, then *X* =

    (A) 0.1
    (B) 0.01
    (C) 0.001
    (D) 0.0001
    (E) 0.00001

35. The product of two numbers is 900. One number is tripled. In order for the product to remain the same, the other number must be

    (A) multiplied by 3.

    (B) divided by $\frac{1}{3}$.

    (C) multiplied by $\frac{1}{3}$.

    (D) subtracted from 900.

    (E) quadrupled.

36. Which of the following could be the face of the cross section of a cylinder?

(A)

(B)

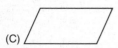
(C)

(D)

(E)

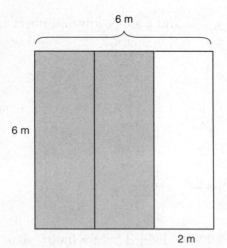

37. What is the area of the shaded portion of the figure?

    (A) 12 square meters

    (B) 22 square meters

    (C) 20 square meters

    (D) 36 square meters

    (E) 24 square meters

38. Which is the best estimate of the answer for $124 \times \frac{49}{24}$?

    (A) 200
    (B) 250
    (C) 325
    (D) 500
    (E) 10

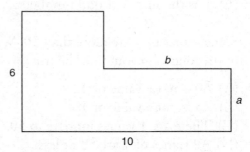

39. Which of the following dimensions would be needed to find the area of the figure?

    (A) *a* only
    (B) *b* only
    (C) neither *a* nor *b*
    (D) both *a* and *b*
    (E) either *a* or *b*

40. Deena finished the school run in 52.8 seconds. Lisa's time was 1.3 seconds faster. What was Lisa's time?

    (A) 51.5 seconds
    (B) 54.1 seconds
    (C) 53.11 seconds
    (D) 65.8 seconds
    (E) 52.93 seconds

Practice PPST 2

Answer Key
PRACTICE PPST 2

Reading

1. C	5. D	9. A	13. C	17. E	21. C	25. D	29. B	33. B	37. C
2. D	6. B	10. D	14. B	18. D	22. A	26. D	30. D	34. D	38. D
3. A	7. B	11. C	15. B	19. B	23. E	27. B	31. A	35. D	39. A
4. E	8. B	12. E	16. C	20. B	24. B	28. D	32. C	36. C	40. C

Writing

USAGE

1. C	4. D	7. C	10. C	13. E	16. C	19. B
2. E	5. C	8. A	11. B	14. D	17. C	20. C
3. C	6. E	9. E	12. B	15. D	18. A	21. D

SENTENCE CORRECTION

22. A	24. D	26. D	28. E	30. D	32. C	34. E	36. D	38. E
23. E	25. B	27. B	29. E	31. B	33. B	35. A	37. D	

Mathematics

1. D	5. B	9. A	13. D	17. E	21. B	25. D	29. A	33. B	37. E
2. A	6. C	10. E	14. B	18. C	22. B	26. C	30. A	34. B	38. B
3. B	7. B	11. A	15. A	19. C	23. C	27. D	31. B	35. C	39. D
4. A	8. B	12. A	16. B	20. B	24. C	28. D	32. C	36. E	40. A

Test Scoring

The scoring information from these tests is just a rough estimate. Passing raw scores on ETS tests vary widely, and this test will likely not have the same difficulty level of the actual PPST you take. That is why this scoring information is advisory only, as a guide to further study. You should NOT try to predict your scale score from these practice test results.

> Please read the reminders on pages 9–10 before you proceed.

Mark the multiple-choice test. Write your raw score for each test as the percent correct.

PERCENT CORRECT

Reading _____ %   Writing _____ %   Mathematics _____ %

Read your essay and assign a score from 1 to 6. Multiply the score by two to represent the scores of two readers. If you have difficulty scoring your essay, you may want to show it to an English expert for an evaluation.

Essay Score _____ out of 12

> Review the scoring information on pages 10–11 and estimate your scale scores.

ESTIMATED SCALE SCORE

Reading _____ .   Writing _____   Mathematics _____

> Look at your state's passing scale score on page 9. Write it here.

PASSING SCALE SCORE

Reading _____   Writing _____   Mathematics _____

Compare your estimated scale scores to your passing scale scores as a guide for further study only, and not as a prediction of the scale score you will receive on the actual PPST.

Practice PPST 2—Answers Explained

READING

1. **(C)** This choice paraphrases the last sentence of the passage.

2. **(D)** The passage identifies both the moon's cycle and the earth's revolution as factors contributing to the development of the current calendar.

3. **(A)** The author explains the difference with the description and an example.

4. **(E)** The passage is about youth and constantly refers to what they do not know about AIDS.

5. **(D)** This choice paraphrases the third sentence in the paragraph.

6. **(B)** The passage uses many synonyms of this word to describe young people's knowledge of AIDS.

7. **(B)** This choice paraphrases the first sentence in the passage.

8. **(B)** The author says, and then gives an example to show, that men are discriminated against just as much as women.

9. **(A)** Drafted, in the sense used here, means to be inducted into the armed forces against one's will.

10. **(D)** *Alice in Wonderland*, a fanciful story about a young girl's adventures underground, has underlying figurative meanings.

11. **(C)** The content reveals that marginal means the area of a page to the left and right of the text.

12. **(E)** Music is more than notes and varies with the mood of the performer.

13. **(C)** The passage states that rockets refer to ordnance or weapons used by the British.

14. **(B)** *Ravished* is the best choice and describes what happens when a town is sacked.

15. **(B)** The last sentence of the first paragraph says that most Americans remember Perry, but not where he served.

16. **(C)** Francis Scott Key must have been able to distribute his "Star Spangled Banner" in America, so he must have been released by or escaped from the British.

17. **(E)** The second sentence in the paragraph identifies the United States as the aggressor.

18. **(D)** The author signals this main point in the first sentence of the passage.

19. **(B)** The next to the last sentence in the first paragraph indicates that these programs do not teach about spelling or word meanings.

20. **(B)** The type of computer used and teaching methods are not mentioned in the passage.

21. **(C)** The fourth sentence in the first paragraph explains that the author likes having a program to perform the mechanical aspects.

22. **(A)** This question can be answered from information in the passage's last paragraph.

23. **(E)** This choice paraphrases the first sentence in the last paragraph.

24. **(B)** This information is found in the first sentence of the first paragraph.

25. **(D)** The author wants to share what he or she learned about the Hardy Boys books.

26. **(D)** The author is more disappointed than anything else upon learning that a favorite childhood author did not really exist.

27. **(B)** A ghost writer is someone who writes books but does not receive credit.

28. **(D)** Every other choice is an acceptable replacement for the word *awe*.

29. **(B)** The second sentence in the third paragraph supports this choice.

30. **(D)** This information is contained in the first sentence of the first paragraph.

31. **(A)** This choice is supported by the last sentence in the first paragraph.

32. **(C)** The first sentence of the second paragraph provides this information.

33. **(B)** This paragraph is about Pasteur's scientific discoveries and not about Pasteur the person.

34. **(D)** This answer can be found in lines 10–13 of the passage.

35. **(D)** The passage contains examples of scientists who opposed Pasteur's theories even though Pasteur had proven his theories scientifically.

36. **(C)** The first sentence indicates that Europeans had already started to devote resources to medicine when Pasteur was born, and theories about germs existed when Pasteur began his work.

37. **(C)** The passage mentions that his early work was at a university dedicated to supporting an important product of the French economy.

38. **(D)** The third from last sentence in the passage mentions that Pasteur developed vaccines for many diseases.

39. **(A)** This choice paraphrases the first sentence in the paragraph.

40. **(C)** *Infinitesimal* means very small, and *infinite* means without limit.

WRITING
Usage

1. **(C)** This singular verb should end in *s*.

2. **(E)** This sentence contains no errors.

3. **(C)** The phrase *as the* should be replaced by the word *than*.

4. **(D)** *Resulted* should be replaced by *resulting*.

5. **(C)** It is not possible to tell whether the school district or the superintendent is promising.

6. **(E)** This sentence contains no errors.

7. **(C)** Replace *and also* with *but also*.

8. **(A)** Replace *many* with *much*.

9. **(E)** This sentence contains no errors.

10. **(C)** Remove *finding themselves in* to maintain the parallel development of this sentence.

11. **(B)** Replace *or* with *nor*.

12. **(B)** This phrase makes it seem that elephants are armed with rifles.

13. **(E)** This sentence contains no errors.

14. **(D)** Replace *there* with *their*.

15. **(D)** Replace *felt* with *feel*.

16. **(C)** A comma is missing.

17. **(C)** Replace *waited* with *waits.*

18. **(A)** Replace *having needed* with *needing.*

19. **(B)** Replace *which* with *whom.*

20. **(C)** Replace *giving him* with *earned* or *had.*

21. **(D)** Replace *did* with *was.*

Sentence Correction

22. **(A)** The underlined portion is acceptable as written.

23. **(E)** Use this replacement for the awkward wording in the original sentence.

24. **(D)** Use this replacement for the awkward wording in the original sentence.

25. **(B)** The plural verb does not end in *s.*

26. **(D)** Use the word *if* in place of the wordy underlined phrase.

27. **(B)** This wording is clearer and more understandable than the original wording in the sentence.

28. **(E)** The correct verb is *was,* rather than *could . . . be.*

29. **(E)** Use this replacement to maintain the parallel structure of the sentence.

30. **(D)** The words *much more* in the original sentence are not needed. Choice C is not correct because it unnecessarily changes the sentence.

31. **(B)** Use this more direct wording to replace the underlined portion of the sentence.

32. **(C)** Replace *is* with *as.*

33. **(B)** Use this more direct wording to replace the underlined portion of the sentence.

34. **(E)** Use this more direct wording to replace the underlined portion of the sentence.

35. **(A)** The underlined portion of the sentence is acceptable as written.

36. **(D)** *To stop* is more effective and compact than the original underlined wording.

37. **(D)** While this choice is longer than the underlined wording, it is much easier to understand.

38. **(E)** Use *commonly* to replace the awkward and wordy *and it is common.*

ESSAY

Compare your essay to the sample essay that follows. You may want to show your essay to an English expert for further evaluation. You will record your essay score on the Test Scoring section for this test on page 298.

This essay would likely receive 5 or 6 out of 6 points (510 words).

I think that the idea of removing any record of a poor grade in a class and any record of the class from a transcript is one of the worst ideas I've ever heard of. A transcript is a record of work in college and that record should not be tampered with. I am going to explain why and try to explain why people might think it is a good idea for them and why that does not make it right.

A class and a grade on a final transcript is a record of what has happened in a college classroom. It is a reflection of what happens between a professor and a student. If a students got a poor grade there is certainly a good reason for it. Not only would this practice strike at the very basis of academic it would encourage students to pay less attention to their studies, knoing that they could just have any grade they wanted to have removed. Besides that there are many ways besides their performance in class that a student can stop a grade from appearing on their final record. The first is to withdraw. Every college has withdrawal policies that allow a students to leave a class and have no grade recorded. Often students can withdraw very late from a class, even after they know what their grade will be. The second thins is grade appeal. Every college has a grade appeal process. In what I see at the college I attend if a student really did not deserve a grade the grade will be overturned on appeal. Most colleges also have hardship provisions. That means say you were in a hospital, or something else tragic happeed in your life, a college committee can decide not to record your grade on a transcript. But once the grade is there after all the things to protect students then it belongs there.

There will be some people who write in favor of this statement because they apply it to themselves. They say "wow" it would be great if I could just go through my transcript and remove every grade and course I did not like. Of course that is what they are going to write. But it is so serving of themselves that we just can't pay attention to them. It would be giving the wrong people a say over what is happening in our college where there are already enough questions about the quality of what goes on there. Why not just take the tuition money and let the students write their own grades.

To summarize my position I disagree with the statement about a college student being able to have any grade and class removed from their transcript. There are already many, many safeguards for students to stop the grade from appearing or to challenge a grade if it is incorrect or was because of some hardship. Things are bad enough as they are without removing this one last tiny bit of honesty in colleges and universities throughout the country.

MATHEMATICS

1. **(D)** Add the three smaller numbers and then the three larger numbers to find this answer.

2. **(A)** 7.17 is always between 7.0 and 7.2.

3. **(B)** Multiply x by 2 and then add 1 to find y.

4. **(A)** Multiply 12 times 55 = 660 to find the total length of the trip. Divide 660 by 45 = $14\frac{2}{3}$, . . . to find the number of hours for the return trip. Subtract $14\frac{2}{3} - 12 = 2\frac{2}{3}$.

5. **(B)** The shaded parts total $\frac{2}{5} + \frac{5}{9} + \frac{1}{4} = \frac{72}{180} + \frac{100}{180} + \frac{45}{180} = \frac{217}{180}$. There are three circles. Multiply by $\frac{1}{3}\left(\frac{1}{3} \times \frac{217}{180}\right) = \frac{217}{540}$ = about 40%.

6. **(C)** $5 \times 10^5 = 500{,}000$
$0.05 \times 10^7 = 500{,}000$
The values are equivalent.

7. **(B)** Four meters, or about 12 feet, is the only plausible answer.

8. **(B)** This equation correctly expresses the relationship.

9. **(A)** $0.15 \times 500 = 75$; $0.20 \times 380 = 76$.

10. **(E)** All the other figures have a perimeter of 20 except this hexagon, which has a perimeter of 18.

11. **(A)** This graph best represents the steady movement up and then down of the temperatures.

12. **(A)** $5\overline{)23}$ = 4 R 3; $5\overline{)63}$ = 12 R 3; $4 \times 12 = 48$.

13. **(D)** $(125 + 200 + 150 + 225 + 75 + 150 + 50) \div 7$ = the average (139.3) miles per day. 140 is closest.

14. **(B)** This is the correct decimal representation for the sum of the fractions.

15. **(A)** Write the proportion $\frac{1}{15} = \frac{43}{x}$, so $x = 645$.

16. **(B)** The lawnmower tank total capacity equals 2g. The amount left in the tank is $1\frac{3}{5}$g. $2 - 1\frac{3}{5} = \frac{2}{5}$g. The amount used for 1 mowing. $1\frac{3}{5} \div \frac{2}{5} = 4$. This is the number of "mows" still possible.

17. **(E)** Add the perimeters to find the total of 38 inches; $5 \times 38 = 190$.

18. **(C)** Choice C yields a piece 75 feet by 5 feet. Mary needs a piece 96 feet by 5 feet.

19. **(C)** $0.25 \times \$40 = \$10$; $\$40 - \$10 = \$30$; $0.15 \times \$30 = \$4.50$; $\$30 - \$4.50 = \$25.50$.

20. **(B)** The ratio of *LM* to *NO* is 3:2. Choice B does not reflect this ratio.

21. **(B)** Three DVDs cost $15.60 at Store A and $18.00 at Store B. The saving for all three DVDs is $2.40. The saving on one DVD is $0.80.

22. **(B)** The product of two whole numbers is 1 only if both whole numbers are 1.

23. **(C)** The value of each of the other choices is 3.52.

24. **(C)** This choice is closest to one-quarter of the first cube.

25. **(D)** The flow chart prints numbers that are odd or less than 25.

26. **(C)** Powers of 10 are 1, 10, 100, 1000. The calculator could be displaying 20, which is not a power of 10.

27. **(D)** If some of the values of *Y* are more than 50, then all of the values of *Y* could not be less than 50.

28. **(D)** The display would show 500, which is 1000 times (0.5).

29. **(A)** The fractions that have a numerator that is smaller than the denominator are smallest $\left(\dfrac{12}{13} \ \& \ \dfrac{99}{180}\right)$. Use cross products to compare. $\dfrac{12}{13}$ is smallest. Only answer (A) shows this.

30. **(A)** There are 36 possible outcomes. Half of these outcomes are even and half are odd.

31. **(B)** $6 \cdot P = R$. Divide both sides by 2 to get $3 \cdot P = R/2$.

32. **(C)** Every time the $=$ key is pressed, the calculator multiplies: $125 \times 5 = 625$, which correlates to $125 \div 5 = 25$, the correct answer.

33. **(B)** $V = l \times w \times h$. Divide both sides by $w \times h$ to get $V/w \times h = 1$.

34. **(B)** Dividing by 0.01 is the same as multiplying by 100.

35. **(C)** Multiplying by $\dfrac{1}{3}$ is the same as dividing by 3.

36. **(E)** Imagine a cylinder with a height equal to its diameter. The vertical cross section of this cylinder is a square.

37. **(E)** The area of the figure is 36 square meters. Two-thirds of the figure is shaded, so $\frac{2}{3} \times 36 = 24$.

38. **(B)** Use 125×2 to estimate. The answer is about 250.

39. **(D)** Both dimensions are needed to find the area of the right-hand rectangle in the figure.

40. **(A)** Faster times are represented by smaller numbers. Subtract $52.8 - 1.3$ to find Lisa's time.

Practice Computer-Based PPST

TEST INFO BOX

Reading	46 items	75 minutes
Writing Multiple Choice	44 items	38 minutes
Writing Essay	1 essay	30 minutes
Mathematics	46 items	75 minutes

Take this test in a realistic timed setting. You should not take this practice test until you have completed PPST 2.

The setting will be most realistic if another person times the test and ensures that the test rules are followed. If another person is acting as test supervisor, he or she should review these instructions with you and say "Start" when you should begin and "Stop" when time has expired.

You use your pencil on this test as you will use a mouse and a cursor on the actual Computer-Based PPST. Answer the items on the test page.

Use a word processor to type the essay. Turn off the spell-check and grammar-check features.

Once the test is complete, review the answers and explanations for each item as you correct the test.

Reading Test

You should not take this test until you have completed both PPST Practice Reading Tests.

The test rules allow you 75 minutes for this test. Use a pencil to mark your answers in the test page. On the actual Computer-Based PPST you will click on the screen to make your choices. Keep the time limit in mind as you work. Be sure to answer all the items. There is no penalty for guessing.

Once the test is complete, review the answers and explanations for each item.

When you are ready, turn the page and begin.

Reading

46 ITEMS   75 MINUTES

There was very little oxygen in the Earth's atmosphere about 3.5 billion years ago. We know that molecules (much smaller than a cell) can develop spontaneously in this type of environment. This is how life probably began on Earth about 3.4 billion years ago.

Line

(5)   Eventually these molecules linked together to form complex groupings of molecules. These earliest organisms must have been able to ingest and live on nonorganic compounds. Over a period of time these organisms adapted and began using the sun's energy. The organisms began to use photosynthesis, which released oxygen into the oceans and the atmos-
(10) phere. The stage was set for more advanced life forms.

The first cells were prokaryotes (bacteria), which created energy (respired) without oxygen (anaerobic). Next these cells developed into blue-green algae prokaryotes, which were aerobic (create energy with oxygen) and used photosynthesis. The advanced eukaryotes were developed from these primitive cells.

(15)   Algae developed about 750 million years ago. Even this simple cell contained an enormous amount of DNA and hereditary information. It took about 2.7 billion years to develop life to this primitive form. This very slow process moved somewhat faster in the millennia that followed as animal and plant forms slowly emerged.

(20)   Animals developed into vertebrate (backbone) and invertebrate (no backbone) species. Mammals became the dominant vertebrate species and insects became the dominant invertebrate species. As animals developed, they adapted to their environment. The best adapted survived. This process is called natural selection. Entire species have vanished from Earth.

(25)   Mammals and dinosaurs coexisted for more than 100 million years. During that time, dinosaurs were the dominant species. When dinosaurs became extinct 65 million years ago, mammals survived. Freed of dinosaurian dominance, mammals evolved into the dominant creatures they are today.

1. Which of the following statements is the best description of the main idea of the second paragraph (lines 5–10)?

    ⬭ Molecules can only ingest nonorganic compounds.

    ⬭ Evolution is based on adaptation.

    ⬭ Photosynthesis allowed organisms to exist without the need of sunlight.

    ⬭ Oxygen is more important to life than the sun's energy.

    ⬭ Molecules will eventually become complex groupings.

2. According to the information in the passage,

    ◯ the prokaryote cells developed with the help of the sun's energy.

    ◯ the Earth was formed about 3.5 billion years ago.

    ◯ the early development of animals depended on resistance to bacteria.

    ◯ the extinction of dinosaurs led to the development of mammals.

    ◯ other reptiles survived the dinosaurs; so entire species have not vanished from the Earth.

3. Which of the following occurred between ingestion of inorganic components and anerobic respiration?

    ◯ Eukaroytes

    ◯ Respiration with oxygen

    ◯ Oxygen release

    ◯ Development of molecules

    ◯ 700 million years ago

4. This passage suggests

    ◯ that bacteria cause disease in animals.

    ◯ that mammals were the more intelligent species.

    ◯ how life evolved on Earth.

    ◯ that mammals and dinosaurs are natural enemies.

    ◯ that the environment did not affect evolution.

5. Which of the following is the best way to describe the organization of this passage?

    ◯ The passage begins with general ideas and moves to more specific ideas.

    ◯ The passage follows a general chronological plan.

    ◯ The passage offers a summary and then gives specific examples of parts of that summary.

    ◯ The passage describes general processes and then gives specific examples of each process.

    ◯ The passage follows a progression based on geographical and biological relationships.

Before the Vietnam War, that country was called French Indochina. During WW II the United States supported Ho Chi Minh in Vietnam as he attacked Japan. After the war, the United States supported the French over *Line* Ho Chi Minh as France sought to regain control of its former colony.

(5)   Fighting broke out between the French and Ho Chi Minh with support from Mao Tse-tung, the leader of mainland China. Even with substantial material aid from the United States, France could not defeat Vietnam. In 1950 the French were defeated at Dien Bien Phu.

Subsequent negotiations in Geneva divided Vietnam into North and *(10)* South with Ho Chi Minh in control of the North. Ngo Dinh Diem was installed by the United States as a leader in the south. Diem never gained popular support in the south.

When Kennedy came to office, he approved a CIA coup to overthrow Diem. When Johnson took office he was not interested in compromise. In *(15)* 1964 Johnson started a massive buildup of forces in Vietnam until the number ultimately reached over 500,000. The Gulf of Tonkin Resolution, passed by Congress, gave Johnson discretion in pursuing the war.

Living and fighting conditions were terrible. Although American forces had many victories, neither that nor the massive bombing of North Vietnam led *(20)* to victory. In 1968, the Vietcong launched the Tet Offensive. While ground gained in the offensive was ultimately recaptured, the offensive shook the confidence of military leaders.

At home, there were deep divisions. War protests sprung up all over the United States. Half a million people protested in New York during 1967 while *(25)* the tension between hawks and doves increased throughout the country.

6. In this passage the author expresses a bias against

   ◯ the Eisenhower administration.
   ◯ the French people.
   ◯ the military.
   ◯ hawks.
   ◯ Henry Kissinger.

7. The passage implies which of the following?

   ◯ The Vietnam War was a glorious war.
   ◯ The Vietnam War cost more than the Great Society.
   ◯ Kennedy laid the foundation for the war.
   ◯ The United States paid a great price for this war.
   ◯ The people of the United States gave united support for the war effort.

8. Select the word or phrase that has the same meaning as "popular" (line 12).

   ◯ Widespread
   ◯ Complete
   ◯ Well liked
   ◯ Major
   ◯ Famous

9. What was a direct result of the negotiations mentioned in the reading?

   ◯ The Vietnam War
   ◯ Dien Bien Phu
   ◯ South Vietnam
   ◯ Gulf of Tonkin Resolution
   ◯ The Tet Offensive

10. With which of these statements is the author of this passage most likely to agree?

   ◯ Loss of life is the unfortunate reality of defending freedom.
   ◯ The CIA played an important role in the war.
   ◯ Congress opposed the Vietnam War.
   ◯ The $175 billion spent on the war could have been used for domestic programs.
   ◯ America's support of the French in Indochina was not a factor in the war.

We use language, including gestures and sounds, to communicate. Humans first used gestures, but it was spoken language that opened the vistas for human communication. Language consists of two things. First we *Line* have the thoughts that language conveys and then the physical sounds, writ-
(5) ing, and structure of the language itself.

Human speech organs (mouth, tongue, lips, etc.) were not developed to make sounds but they uniquely determined the sounds and words humans could produce. Human speech gradually came to be loosely bound together by unique rules for grammar.

(10) Many believe that humans developed their unique ability to speak with the development of a specialized area of the brain called Broca's area. If this is so, human speech and language probably developed in the past 100,000 years.

11. What is the main idea of this passage?

   ◯ Language consists of thoughts and physical sounds.
   ◯ Human communication includes gestures.
   ◯ We use language to communicate.
   ◯ Human speech and language slowly developed through the years.
   ◯ Broca's area of the brain controls speech.

12. In this passage, the author is primarily concerned with

   ◯ comparing and contrasting.
   ◯ presenting a point of view.
   ◯ describing a time sequence.
   ◯ refuting an argument.
   ◯ defining vocabulary words.

13. Applying the reasoning about human speech in this passage to clothing, we can say that clothes will change when the fundamental form of which of the following changes?

   ◯ People
   ◯ Fashion
   ◯ Weather
   ◯ Color
   ◯ Beauty

14. Which of the following words, if substituted for the word "unique" in line 9, would MOST change the meaning of the sentence?

   ◯ Exclusive
   ◯ Distinct
   ◯ Particular
   ◯ Sole
   ◯ Common

Information can be retrieved from books, magazines, and other print sources by simply picking up the reading materials and turning and flipping through the pages. The book, newspaper, or periodical remains one of the
Line most efficient ways to access print information. Print materials are also found
(5) in libraries or other storage locations on microfilm and microfiche.

Other information can be retrieved on or through the computer or an electronic book reader. Written materials can be entered on a computer, usually with a word processor. This information can be accessed directly through the computer's hard disk. Special features of most word processors and other util-
(10) ities permit the user to search electronically for words and phrases. Sound, graphics, and animation may also be stored on a computer's hard disk. These sounds and images may be accessed using specialized computer programs.

15. The author's purpose for writing this passage was to

   ◯ persuade.
   ◯ narrate.
   ◯ inform.
   ◯ entertain.
   ◯ list.

16. Which of the following means the same as "storage locations" in line 5?

   ◯ Hard disks
   ◯ Repositories
   ◯ Microfiche
   ◯ Annexes
   ◯ Video disks

Are you ready? It's computer time. That's right. Everyone will need to be able to use a computer to just survive. If you can't use a computer, watch out—you may find yourself on the unemployment line. In less than 20 years
Line computers have gone from being slow, wimpy, and unavailable to fast, pow-
(5) erful, and affordable. You can buy a computer for your home that is more powerful than computers that filled buildings. Computers enable you to communicate all over the world, to see animation, hear sounds, and recognize speech—all in addition to word processing and number crunching. Face it—you live in a world in which computer competence is required.

17. What is the topic of this passage?

○ Computers and survival in the 21st century.
○ Computer animation in the next decade.
○ Computers past and present.
○ Who needs a computer?
○ Information can be stored in computers.

18. According to the information in the passage,

○ home computers are more powerful than any computer in buildings.
○ home computers are less powerful than computers that used to fill whole buildings.
○ if you don't know how to use a home computer, you will be unemployed.
○ home computers are now fast and affordable.
○ home computers will be adding word processing and number crunching.

19. Which of the following assumptions was made by the author of this passage?

○ The reader knows how a computer works.
○ The reader has a computer.
○ The reader is not computer literate.
○ The reader knows about the Internet.
○ Some computers are not slow.

Eliza, a runaway slave, made her desperate retreat across the river just in the dusk of twilight. The gray mist of evening, rising slowly from the river, enveloped her as she disappeared up the bank, and the swollen current and
Line floundering masses of ice presented a hopeless barrier between her and her
(5) pursuer. Haley, the pursuer, therefore slowly and discontentedly returned to the little tavern.

He was startled by the loud and dissonant voice of a man who was apparently dismounting at the door. He hurried to the window.

"By the land! if this yer an't the nearest, now, to what I've heard folks call
(10) Providence," said Haley. "I do b'lieve that ar's Tom Loker."

Haley hastened out. Standing by the bar, in the corner of the room, was a brawny, muscular man, full six feet in height and broad in proportion. In the head and face every organ and lineament expressive of brutal and unhesitating violence was in a state of the highest possible development. Indeed, *(15)* could our readers fancy a bull-dog come into man's estate, and walking about in a hat and coat, they would have no unapt idea of the general style and effect of his physique. He was accompanied by a traveling companion, in many respects an exact contrast to himself. The large man poured out a big tumbler half full of raw spirits, and gulped it down without a word. The *(20)* little man stood tiptoe, and putting his head first to one side and then to the other, and snuffing considerately in the directions of the various bottles, ordered at last a mint julep, in a thin and quivering voice, and with an air of great circumspection.

20. Which of following events occurs between the brawny man standing at the bar and when the last mint julip was ordered?

   ◯ Haley hastens out.
   ◯ The little man stood tiptoe.
   ◯ Gray mist rises.
   ◯ Tom Loker is recognized.
   ◯ Ice presents a barrier between the slave and her pursuer.

21. We can infer from the passage that

   ◯ the runaway slave drowned in the river.
   ◯ Haley will eventually catch the runaway slave.
   ◯ Haley and Loker will start to pursue the runaway slave again.
   ◯ the mist prevented Haley from pursuing the runaway slave.
   ◯ the tavern was far from the river.

22. The author most likely mentions "desperate retreat" to

   ◯ show that the slave was wrong to run away.
   ◯ emphasize the urgency she felt.
   ◯ focus on the terrible conditions at the river.
   ◯ show the danger that her pursuer felt.
   ◯ point out that Eliza may have had a child with her.

23. Which of the following is a true statement about Tom Loker?

   ◯ He stood by the bar in the corner of the room.
   ◯ Haley saw him through the tavern window.
   ◯ He met Haley outside the tavern.
   ◯ He was an ex-slave.
   ◯ His real name was Marks.

About two hundred yards from the tree a small brook crossed the road and ran into a marshy and thickly wooded glen, known by the name of Wiley's swamp. On that side of the road where the brook entered the wood,
Line a group of oaks and chestnuts, matted thick with wild grapevines, threw a
(5) cavernous gloom over it. To pass this bridge was the severest trial. It was at this identical spot that the unfortunate André was captured, and under the covert of those chestnuts and vines were the sturdy yeomen concealed who surprised him.

As he approached the stream his heart began to thump; he summoned up,
(10) however, all his resolution, gave his horse half a score of kicks in the ribs, and attempted to dash briskly across the bridge; but instead of starting forward, the perverse old animal made a lateral movement and ran broadside against the fence. Ichabod, whose fears increased with the delay, jerked the reins on the other side, and kicked lustily with the contrary foot; it was all in vain;
(15) his steed started, it is true, but it was only to plunge to the opposite side of the road into a thicket of brambles and alder bushes. The schoolmaster now bestowed both whip and heel upon the starveling ribs of old Gunpowder, who dashed forward, snuffling and snorting, but came to a stand just by the bridge . . . .

24. What is the author's attitude toward Ichabod?

○ Bitter
○ Disgusted
○ Amused
○ Angry
○ Outraged

25. Which of the following is a synonym for the word "steed" in line 15?

○ Saddle
○ Shadow
○ Pursuer
○ Nag
○ Mud

26. Which of the following is not associated with a description of Ichabod's horse?

○ Perverse
○ Jerked the reins
○ Into a thicket
○ Lateral movement
○ Starveling ribs

Early, advanced civilizations developed in the Indus Valley. The inhabitants were called Dravidians. Around 2500 B.C. a series of floods and foreign invasions appears to have all but destroyed these civilizations. Between *Line* 2500 B.C. and 1500 B.C. the Dravidians were forced into southern India by (5) a nomadic band with Greek and Persian roots.

The conquerors brought a less sophisticated civilization to India. It was this latter group that formed the Indian civilization. The result was Dravidians serving as slaves.

After a time, the society developed around religious, nonsecular concerns. (10) The Mahabarata became a verbal tradition around 1000 B.C. It describes a war hero, Krishna. The Mahabarata's most significant impact was the frequent descriptions of correct conduct and belief. The Mahabarata also describes how the soul remains immortal through transmigration—the successive occupation of the soul of many bodies.

27. We can infer from this passage that

⬭ the Dravidians were slaves about 1000 A.D.
⬭ the verbal tradition mentioned in the passage survived until about 2500 B.C.
⬭ many Dravidians were slaves about 1500 B.C.
⬭ Krishna was an early Dravidian deity.
⬭ floods led to the establishment of the Mahabarata.

Confederate Major General W. H. C. Whiting was recuperating in a prisoner-of-war camp in New York. He said, "This is the worst place for us to lose, with the possible exception of Richmond." Whiting died unexpectedly of his wounds in the prison camp.

28. What is the most likely location of the "worst place" referred to in this passage?

⬭ New York State
⬭ New York City
⬭ Richmond
⬭ the Carolinas
⬭ Canada

County highway officials have to submit all road construction plans to the state highway department for approval. The state highway department must approve all plans, but officials are most attentive to plans for new con-*Line* struction, and less concerned about plans for work on existing roads. A state (5) highway inspector visits every site for a limited access highway. The department also uses a computer simulation analysis to determine the traffic flow impact of these roads. The state highway department may require a county to identify a similar road configuration elsewhere in the state to fully determine traffic flow characteristics. The department is also very cautious about (10) roads that may be used by school buses. The state highway department has found that there are more accidents on narrow, rural roads and they have taken planning steps to ensure that roads of this type are not built.

29. The author is most likely to recommend which of the following as an effective step to reduce accidents?

- ◯ Build wide roads.
- ◯ Use computer simulation analysis.
- ◯ Require detailed construction plans.
- ◯ Determine traffic flow characteristics.
- ◯ Visit every site for a limited access highway.

30. Which of the following words could be used in place of "simulation" in line 6?

- ◯ Investigation
- ◯ Replication
- ◯ Determination
- ◯ Authentication
- ◯ Fabrication

    Lyndon Johnson was born in a farmhouse in central Texas in 1908. He grew up in poverty and had to work his way through college. He was elected to the United States House of Representatives in 1937, and served in the *Line* U.S. Navy during World War II. Following 12 years in the House of (5) Representatives, he was elected to the United States Senate, where he became the youngest person chosen by any party to be its Senate leader.

31. According to this passage, Lyndon Johnson

- ◯ lived in a farmhouse while he went to college.
- ◯ was the youngest person elected to the United States Senate.
- ◯ joined the Navy while a U.S. Representative.
- ◯ served in the Senate for 12 years.
- ◯ was born in the 1930s.

    Archaeological techniques can be relatively simple, or very complex. One method of archaeology uses magnetic imaging to locate sites that may yield useful archaeological artifacts. Topsoil magnetic mapping is used to identify *Line* patterns in the landscape and to identify these resonance patterns that indi- (5) cate where archaeological site work is indicated. The movement of topsoil into ditches and other features often leads to the development of pockets of material that may later be transformed into the topsoil by agricultural activity. It may be that the resulting patterns from agricultural activity will lead to the discovery of even smaller prehistoric ditches and other features. The (10) presence of prehistoric features is reflected in the lower magnetic readings, particularly when compared to the higher background readings. These magnetic surveys can be combined with the results from other surveys to determine the efficacy of further archaeological investigations.

Other techniques may just rely on the examination of existing relics for
(15) sustained patterns or relationships. Frequently, advanced numeric methods are
useful for a full analysis of these patterns. In other cases, informed observation
alone may reveal striking cultural information. But still, the success of these
informed observations may presuppose a knowledge of mathematics or physics.

32. The author of this passage would most likely recommend which of the follow-
    ing to archaeologists?

    ◯ Look for areas with high background readings.
    ◯ Conduct work in deep forests.
    ◯ Find the most recently ploughed fields.
    ◯ Do your work right after a heavy rainfall.
    ◯ Find an area that has been completely uninhabited.

33. Which of the following words could be used in place of the word "efficacy"
    on the last line of the first paragraph?

    ◯ Limits
    ◯ Placement
    ◯ Effectiveness
    ◯ Results
    ◯ Relationship

34. According to this passage, the resulting patterns from agricultural activity

    ◯ may later be transformed into topsoil.
    ◯ offer a great deal of assistance to archaeologists.
    ◯ require a knowledge of mathematics or physics.
    ◯ may lead to the discovery of prehistoric ditches.
    ◯ can be simple or complex.

I grew up in Kearny, New Jersey, now known as Soccer Town USA. I played football in high school, and barely knew that the soccer team existed. However, a look
back at my high school yearbook revealed that the soccer team won the state cham-
pionship and we had a .500 season. So much for awareness.

35. The author most likely wrote the above passage to

    ◯ describe a situation.
    ◯ reflect on past events.
    ◯ present a point of view.
    ◯ express irony.
    ◯ narrate a story.

Most of the Internet ad company's ads were banner ads. A banner ad comes up when a particular Internet page appears. The average representative sells 9 to 10 "A" banner ads each day. They base their advertising rates
Line on the number of times the ad appears in a month. For example, an "A" ban-
(5) ner ad costs $85 per thousand appearances up to 100,000 appearances, and $75 per thousand for each thousand over 100,000 appearances. The smallest banner ad is about half the price of the largest banner ad, and the average representative sells about 15 to 20 of these ads each day.

The agency offers other types of Internet ads as well. One type is where
(10) the advertiser pays a fee each time the online user pushes a "button" that takes the user to the advertiser's home page. The average representative sells 6 to 10 of these ads each day, while the average representative sells 12 to 14 middle size banner ads. This advertising agency can also arrange for an ad to appear when a particular search term is entered. These ads are the most
(15) expensive, and the average representative sells 2 to 4 of these ads each day.

36. How many different types of Internet ads are discussed in this passage?

◯ One
◯ Two
◯ Three
◯ Four
◯ Five

37. We can conclude from this passage that the total maximum and minimum of banner ads that the average representative sells each day is

◯ 30 and 15
◯ 30 and 24
◯ 44 and 36
◯ 54 and 42
◯ 58 and 44

During the Civil War, blockade runners had to pass through either the New Inlet or the Old Inlet to enter the Cape Fear River and travel north to Wilmington, North Carolina. Whichever inlet blockade runners took, they
Line passed by Fort Fisher. Blockade runners were just about immune from
(5) Union attack once they came under the fort's protection. Other fortifications protected the Cape Fear River. Fort Holmes was on Smith Island, which was west across the New Inlet from Fort Fisher. Fort Caswell was west across the Old Inlet from Fort Holmes, and Fort Johnson was across the Cape Fear River from Fort Fisher.

38. A blockade runner approached Wilmington with goods from Nova Scotia. The blockade runner passed through the New Inlet, so we can infer from the passage that Fort Fisher is

  ◯ west of Fort Caswell.
  ◯ generally to the north.
  ◯ generally to the east.
  ◯ generally to the south.
  ◯ north of Wilmington.

The two DNA strands are held together by weak bonds between the bases on each strand, forming base pairs (bp). Genome size is usually stated as the total number of base pairs; the human genome contains roughly 3 billion
Line bp. Strict base-pairing rules are adhered to; adenine will pair only with
(5) thymine (an A-T pair) and cytosine with guanine (a C-G pair). Each daughter cell receives one old and one new DNA strand. The cells' adherence to these base-pairing rules ensures that the new strand is an exact copy of the old one. This minimizes the incidence of errors (mutations) that may greatly affect the resulting organism or its offspring.

39. What is the guaranteed outcome of base pairing rules?

  ◯ Adenine will pair only with thymine.
  ◯ New strands exactly replicate old strands.
  ◯ Genome size is usually stated as the total number of base pairs.
  ◯ The human genome contains roughly 3 billion bp.
  ◯ A C-G pair will be produced.

School officials were trying to decide how students arrived at school each morning. This information was important because those at the school had to decide how many bike stands to have and how much space to set aside for parents to drop off their children at school.

40. Which factor should school officials be most aware of as they determine how students get to school each morning?

  ◯ The weather
  ◯ The number of existing bike stands
  ◯ The number of students in the school
  ◯ The size of the school driveway
  ◯ The parents

The Iroquois were present in upstate New York about 500 years before the Europeans arrived. According to Iroquois oral history, this Indian nation was once a single tribe subject to the rule of the Adirondack Indians. This
Line tribe was located in the valley of the St. Lawrence River, but they left and
(5) moved south to be free from Adirondack control. According to reports from French explorers, there were still Iroquoian villages around the St. Lawrence between Quebec and Montreal in the early 1500s. But when these explorers returned around 1600, these villages had disappeared.

41. The author most likely wrote the passage above to

○ describe a situation.

○ reflect on past events.

○ present a point of view.

○ express concern.

○ tell a story.

42. According to the passage, the Iroquois

○ ruled the Adirondacks.

○ were located along the Hudson River.

○ traded with the French.

○ were an Indian nation.

○ disappeared around 1600.

The space vehicle verification program is designed to show that the vehicle meets all design and performance specifications. The verification program also seeks to ensure that all hazards and sources of failure have been *Line* either eliminated or reduced to acceptable levels. The specific spacecraft (5) verification is based on a series of carefully monitored testing protocols. The verification tests are conducted under the strictest controls including temperature and stress levels. Full-scale hull models are used to verify the drawn specifications.

43. Which of the following words could be used in place of the word "verification" in line 5?

○ elimination

○ corroboration

○ allocation

○ renovation

○ contamination

Population experts estimate that there may be 300 million inhabitants in South America. About 7% of the inhabitants speak native languages, and pockets of native civilizations can still be found in the countryside. Most South Americans with European origins trace their roots to Portugal, Spain, and Italy.

44. When the passage refers to native languages, it most likely means the languages

○ spoken by those born in South America.

○ of those residents of South America who are native to Portugal, Spain, and Italy.

○ of those living in the pockets of civilization in the countryside.

○ of those born in South America with European origins who are not from Portugal, Spain, or Italy.

○ of those natives of Europe who came to South America.

Music consists of pitch, the actual frequency or sound of a note, and duration. A tone has a specific pitch and duration. Different tones occurring simultaneously are called chords. A melody is the tones that produce the dis-
Line tinctive "sound" of the music. Harmony is chords with duration. Pitches
(5) separated by specific intervals are called a scale. Most music is based on the diatonic scale found on the piano white keys (C, D, E, F, G, A, B). The chromatic scale includes the seven notes of the diatonic scale with the five sharps and flats corresponding to the white and black keys on the piano.

45. According to the passage, the chromatic scale

○ corresponds to the white keys on the piano.
○ consists of the flats and sharps not contained in the diatonic scale.
○ is contained in the diatonic scale.
○ can be played only on the piano.
○ includes notes corresponding to the first seven letters in the alphabet.

The Black Plague—bubonic plague—was pandemic in Europe during a 200-year period in the middle of the twentieth century. The plague was a severe infection caused by bacteria that was untreatable until antibiotics
Line were available. At its height, the plague killed two million people a year.
(5) AIDS has already claimed over ten million lives, and AIDS in Africa is at the same pandemic levels as the Black Plague in the Middle Ages. In some African nations more than 10 percent of the population, already infected with AIDS, will die from the disease. These deaths will create millions of orphans and will shatter the social fabric of the continent.

46. According to the passage, AIDS

○ is most likely to kill defenseless orphans.
○ is caused by a bacteria not treatable by antibiotics.
○ will likely last for at least 200 years.
○ is epidemic in entire countries.
○ will eventually claim 10 million lives.

Writing Test

You should not take this test until you have completed both Practice PPST Writing Tests.

Each item of the multiple-choice section consists of a sentence with four underlined parts. Look for the underlined part that is inappropriate in well-written English. If you find one, circle that portion. If there are no errors, circle No error. A sentence will not have more than one error.

On the actual Computer-Based PPST you will click on the underlined portion of your choice.

The test rules allow you 38 minutes for the multiple-choice test and 30 minutes for the essay. Keep the time limit in mind as you work. Be sure to answer all the items. There is no penalty for guessing.

Once the test is complete, review the answers and explanations.

When you are ready, turn the page and begin.

MULTIPLE CHOICE 38 MINUTES

Directions: You will read sentences with four parts underlined. Determine whether one of the underlined parts contains grammatical, word use, or punctuation errors. If so, circle that part. If there are no errors, circle <u>No error</u>.

24 usage items   Suggested time: 20 MINUTES

1. Most people <u>would</u> <u>enjoying</u> four <u>weeks</u> vacation <u>last year</u>. <u>No error</u>.

2. The tugboat <u>strains against</u> the <u>ship, revved</u> up its engines, <u>and was able</u> to <u>maneuver</u> the ship into the middle of the channel. <u>No error</u>.

3. A newspaper columnist <u>promised</u> <u>to print</u> the story about the <u>secret negotiations</u> concerning the sports stadium in <u>their</u> next column. <u>No error</u>.

4. The flower shop is <u>pleasant</u> and <u>possess</u> an <u>aroma that</u> <u>welcomes</u> its customers. <u>No error</u>.

5. The <u>incredible</u> <u>intense</u> seminar held all <u>the participants</u> in a <u>hypnotic</u> trance. <u>No error</u>.

6. Many students <u>prefer to gain</u> <u>life experience</u> outside <u>college. Such as the Peace Corps</u>. <u>No error</u>.

7. <u>Weather</u> conditions have <u>a controlling</u> <u>affect</u> on our air <u>traffic</u>. <u>No error</u>.

8. Europeans <u>had started</u> to <u>devote significant</u> resources to <u>medicine, when</u> Louis Pasteur <u>was born</u> December 7, 1822. <u>No error</u>.

9. Because of their <u>immaturity</u> and <u>ignorance. Many</u> young people <u>engage</u> in <u>high-risk</u> behavior. <u>No error</u>.

10. <u>These same questions</u> was <u>asked</u> by <u>other lawyers</u> for decades after the trial ended. <u>No error</u>.

11. It may be <u>true that</u> a strictly mechanical approach is used by some <u>teachers, however,</u> there is <u>certainly</u> a way for <u>their students</u> to develop more difficult concepts. <u>No error.</u>

12. Computer graphing programs are <u>capable</u> of graphing almost any equations <u>including</u> advanced equations from <u>calculus the</u> student just types in the equation and the <u>graph appears</u> on the screen. <u>No error.</u>

13. The <u>Board of Adjustment</u> can <u>exempt</u> a person from the requirements of a <u>particular</u> land-use <u>ordnance</u>. <u>No error.</u>

14. <u>Succulent</u> crab, <u>plentiful</u> shrimp, and meaty lobster are the <u>mainly</u> dishes advertised by the <u>Lobster Hut</u>. <u>No error.</u>

15. Charles Monroe III and his family <u>enjoys</u> yachting, <u>swimming, and</u> polo, <u>when</u> <u>on holiday,</u> <u>delighting</u> in the South of France. <u>No error.</u>

16. The teacher asked all <u>her students</u> to bring in <u>his</u> permission slips <u>to go on</u> the <u>Washington trip</u>. <u>No error.</u>

17. The <u>shower dripped</u> for an hour <u>after each</u> person <u>bathed</u> until finally a repairman <u>had been call</u> to fix it. <u>No error.</u>

18. They will not <u>be able to</u> understand how to <u>create</u> a sculpture from ice or to <u>understands</u> the <u>basis</u> for the more complicated sculptures. <u>No error.</u>

19. Erik <u>walks</u> three miles every <u>day and he</u> <u>rubbed</u> the dirt off his sneakers as he <u>went</u>. <u>No error.</u>

20. I <u>have talked</u> to my daughter about <u>telling</u> the <u>truth countless</u> times over the <u>past</u> few weeks. <u>No error.</u>

21. A <u>masive</u> <u>education campaign</u> <u>is needed</u> to fully inform <u>today's youth</u> about AIDS. <u>No error.</u>

22. The <u>dairy farm</u> is maintained by the support of 60 new <u>cows in</u> addition <u>there</u> are 35 original <u>cows who</u> still supply some milk. <u>No error.</u>

23. <u>I am going</u> to visit <u>my</u> aunt so <u>I</u> left a message for <u>whoever</u> may need to locate me. <u>No error.</u>

24. The <u>retired</u> baseball player haggled <u>unexpectedly</u> with the <u>younger child</u> over who played <u>good</u>. <u>No error.</u>

SENTENCE CORRECTION

Directions: You will read sentences with some or all of the sentence underlined, followed by five answer choices. The first answer choice repeats the underlined portion and the other four present possible replacements. Select the answer choice that best represents standard English without altering the meaning of the original sentence. Shade the oval for that answer.

20 sentence correction items   Suggested time: 18 MINUTES

25. The class president was a good, <u>but undistinguished, student</u>.

⬭ but undistinguished, student
⬭ but in every way a student that could not be distinguished
⬭ but a student who could not be distinguished
⬭ but not distinguishable from the rest of the students
⬭ but distinguished

26. <u>The height of the tree grew slower</u> over the years.

⬭ The height of the tree grew slower
⬭ The tree grew slower
⬭ The tree height slower grew
⬭ The tree's height grew slower
⬭ The tree height grew slower

27. <u>To climb the mountain now will be better</u> than waiting until it gets colder.

⬭ To climb the mountain now will be better
⬭ To climb the mountain is better
⬭ Climbing the mountain now can be better
⬭ Climbing the mountain now is better
⬭ To try to climb the mountain now will be better

28. <u>The three largest trees stands at</u> the entrance to the forest.

⬭ The three largest trees stands at
⬭ The three largest tree's stands at
⬭ The three largest trees stand at
⬭ The largest three trees stand's at
⬭ The three largest tree stands at

29. The train engineer blew the whistle <u>in the eventuality that</u> a road crossing appeared.

  ◯ in the eventuality that
  ◯ if the event of a
  ◯ when the eventuality
  ◯ when
  ◯ and

30. The study concluded that good test scores resulted from subject matter competence and <u>the way a person took the test.</u>

  ◯ the way a person took the test
  ◯ test-taking strategies
  ◯ the approach a person took to the test
  ◯ testing strategies
  ◯ the way a test taker takes the test

31. The road to the ocean washed away and <u>could no longer be in use.</u>

  ◯ could no longer be in use
  ◯ could be in use no longer
  ◯ may be in use no longer
  ◯ could become unused
  ◯ was no longer in use

32. The coach was pleased with the team's progress; <u>the players were confident;</u> the fans were happy, and it was true that the students were pleased.

  ◯ the players were confident
  ◯ the player were confident
  ◯ it was true the players were confident
  ◯ the player's were confident
  ◯ it was true the player's were confident

33. It was clear from the news reports that the plant <u>represented an exclusive, distinctive, unique approach to the problem.</u>

  ◯ represented an exclusive, distinctive, unique approach to the problem
  ◯ represented a exclusive, distinctive, unique approach to the problem
  ◯ represented an approach to the problem
  ◯ represents an exclusive, distinctive, unique approach to the problem
  ◯ represented a unique approach to the problem

34. When he became a teacher he had no idea that the <u>effort on volumes of</u> <u>paperwork and the work required for playground duty and bus duty would</u> <u>become his main responsibility</u>.

- ◯ effort on volumes of paperwork and the work required for playground duty and bus duty would become his main responsibility
- ◯ efforts on volumes of paperwork and the work required for playground duty and bus duty would become his main responsibility
- ◯ paperwork and non-teaching duties would become his main responsibility
- ◯ work required for volumes of paperwork and the work required for playground duty and bus duty would become his main responsibility
- ◯ effort on volumes of paperwork and the effort required for playground duty and bus duty would become his main responsibility

35. Season tickets to the college basketball games <u>is difficult to get</u> at this time of year.

- ◯ is difficult to get
- ◯ is difficult to come by
- ◯ are difficult to get
- ◯ was difficult to get
- ◯ is not difficult to get

36. A teacher must arrange for a substitute <u>if she is going to be absent</u>.

- ◯ if she is going to be absent
- ◯ if she's going to be absent
- ◯ if they are going to be absent
- ◯ if he or she is going to be absent
- ◯ if she is going to absent herself

37. The student in the woodworking <u>class made a real tall bookshelf</u>.

- ◯ class made a real tall bookshelf.
- ◯ class made a really tall bookshelf
- ◯ class made a very real tall bookshelf
- ◯ class made a really high bookshelf
- ◯ class made a real high bookshelf

38. The bus <u>ran smoothly, but the</u> driver was always concerned about a breakdown.

- ◯ ran smoothly, but the
- ◯ ran smooth, but the
- ◯ runs smooth, but the
- ◯ run smoothly, but the
- ◯ run smooth, but the

39. The contractor wanted to finish the job, but first he had to convince the zoning board to approve a permit <u>so that work could start</u>.

   ◯ so that work could start
   ◯ so that work could begin
   ◯ to start work
   ◯ for starting work
   ◯ so that the actual work could begin

40. <u>Ronaldo, the clown with the big nose</u> made his entrance into the big top.

   ◯ Ronaldo, the clown with the big nose
   ◯ Ronaldo the clown, with the big nose,
   ◯ Ronaldo, the clown with the big nose,
   ◯ Ronaldo, the clown with the big, nose
   ◯ Ronaldo the clown with the big nose

41. Tomorrow I am going on <u>vacation today I have</u> a lot of work to do.

   ◯ vacation today I have
   ◯ vacation, today I have
   ◯ vacation but today I have
   ◯ vacation and today I have
   ◯ vacation; today I have

42. There is absolutely no way to be sure that the dog <u>will come when it's owner calls</u>.

   ◯ will come when it's owner calls
   ◯ will come when his owner calls
   ◯ will come when their owner calls
   ◯ will come when its owner calls
   ◯ will come when her owner calls

43. The clockmaker <u>was particularly expert at designing</u> musical chimes.

   ◯ was particularly expert at designing
   ◯ was particular expert at designing
   ◯ was particular expertise at designing
   ◯ had particularly expert at designing
   ◯ had a particularly expert at designing

44. The thoroughbred <u>horse run very fast</u> around the track.

   ◯ horse run very fast
   ◯ horse runs very fast
   ◯ horse running very fast
   ◯ horse are running very fast
   ◯ horse do run very fast

Essay

Take this test in a realistic, timed setting.

Write an essay on the topic found on the next page. Write on this topic only. An essay on another topic, no matter how well done, will receive a 0. You have 30 minutes to complete the essay. Keep the time limit in mind as you work.

Use the space provided to briefly outline your essay and to organize your thoughts before you begin to write. Use this opportunity to demonstrate how well you can write but be sure to cover the topic.

Type your essay on a word processor. Do not use the spell checker or the grammar checker.

Once the test is complete, ask an English professor or English teacher to evaluate your essay holistically using the rating scale on page 265.

When you are ready, turn the page and begin.

ESSAY

A college should offer an entire degree program over the Internet, without students ever coming to the campus.

Describe the extent to which you agree or disagree with this statement. Support your response with specific details, examples, and experiences.

Write a brief outline here.

Mathematics Test

You should not take this practice test until you have completed both Practice PPST Mathematics Tests.

The test rules allow you exactly 75 minutes for this test.

Use a pencil to fill in the oval next to the correct answer. On the actual test, you will use a mouse and a keyboard.

Once the test is complete, review the answers and explanations.

When you are ready, turn the page and begin.

MATHEMATICS

46 ITEMS   75 MINUTES

1. The bar graph below shows the number of birds sold in a pet store over a 12-month period. What percent of the birds were sold in June and July?

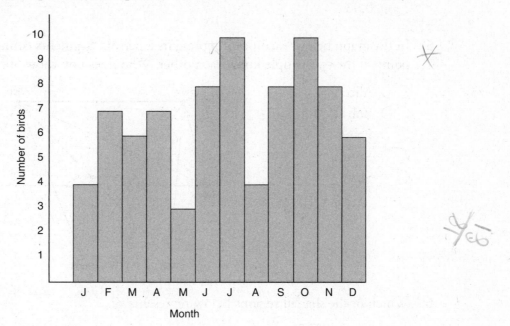

- ⬭ 22%
- ⬭ 8%
- ⬭ 11%
- ⬭ 17%
- ⬭ 30%

2. The radius and height are needed to calculate the volume of which of the following figures?

- ⬭ Circle
- ⬭ Cone
- ⬭ Sphere
- ⬭ Cube
- ⬭ Pyramid

3. Jane has three brothers, two of whom are twins. The sum of the ages of the brothers is 25, and the brother who is not a twin is 9 years old. How old is each of the twins?

- ⬭ 6 years old
- ⬭ 7 years old
- ⬭ 8 years old
- ⬭ 9 years old
- ⬭ 10 years old

4. Which of the following equals 3 out of 5?

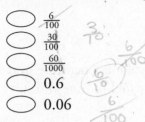

$\frac{6}{100}$

$\frac{30}{100}$

$\frac{60}{1000}$

0.6

0.06

5. In the graph below, each point represents a person. Segments connect to points if the two people know each other. Who does not know Steve?

Alice

Bob

Frank

Ronni

Scott

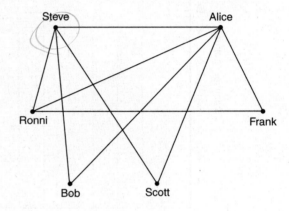

6. Which of the shaded regions below represents ⅔?

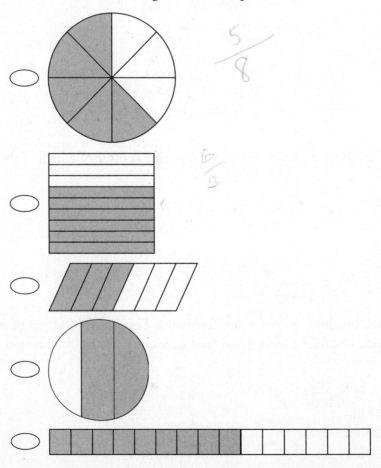

7. The high temperature on a certain day was 86°, and the low was 54°. What is the average temperature for this day.

   ◯ 32°
   ◯ 70°
   ◯ 72°
   ◯ 74°
   ◯ 86°

8. Chad takes home $1,500 a month. He pays $550 a month in rent, $300 a month for food, $50 a month for phone bills, and $100 a month for utility bills. After Chad pays these bills, he evenly divides the remaining money between savings and miscellaneous expenses. How much money will Chad save after one year?

   ◯ $250
   ◯ $500
   ◯ $750
   ◯ $3000
   ◯ $6000

9. Greg is 19 years old and will be twice as old as Todd next year. What is the sum of Greg and Todd's ages at this time?

   ◯ 54
   ◯ 36
   ◯ 28
   ◯ 18
   ◯ 9

10. The original price of a pair of pants was $30, but they are now on sale for $21. The sale price is what percent of the original price?

   ◯ 3%
   ◯ 7%
   ◯ 21%
   ◯ 30%
   ◯ 70%

$$\frac{21}{30} = \frac{x}{100}$$

$$\frac{21}{30} \quad \frac{x}{100}$$

$$21(100) = 30x$$

$$2100 = 30x$$

$$\frac{2100}{30} = 70 = x$$

11. Use the figure below. Which combination of statements is true?

I. ∠*EBD* and ∠*DBC* are complementary angles ＝ 9 0
II. ∠*EBD* and ∠*DBC* are supplementary angles ＝ 180
III. m∠*EBD* + m∠*DBC* = 90°

⬭ Just I
⬭ I and II
⬭ II and III
⬭ I and III
⬭ I, II, and III

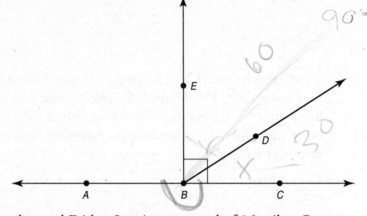

12. On Monday, Wednesday, and Friday, Joanie ran a total of 26 miles. On Wednesday, Joanie ran 3 more miles than she did on Monday, and on Friday, she ran 2 more miles than she ran on Wednesday. How many miles did Joanie run on Friday?

⬭ 5
⬭ 6
⬭ 11
⬭ 18
⬭ 26

13. The pictograph below represents the number of points that Irene scored in 5 different games. Each basketball represents two points. What percent of the points Irene scored in all five games were scored in the second game?

⬭ 6%
⬭ 18.75%
⬭ 37.5%
⬭ 40%
⬭ 60%

GAME 1	🏀🏀🏀🏀🏀🏀🏀
GAME 2	🏀🏀🏀🏀🏀🏀
GAME 3	🏀🏀🏀
GAME 4	🏀🏀🏀🏀🏀🏀🏀🏀
GAME 5	🏀🏀🏀🏀🏀🏀🏀🏀🏀

14. In a cookie jar there are 3 chocolate chip cookies, 5 oatmeal cookies, 4 sugar cookies, and 2 gingerbread cookies. If a person pulls out a cookie without looking, what is the probability of not choosing a gingerbread cookie?

⬭ $\frac{1}{7}$
⬭ $\frac{1}{6}$
⬭ $\frac{3}{14}$
⬭ $\frac{9}{14}$
⬭ $\frac{6}{7}$

15. Jack works 8 hours a day. If Jack has already worked 270 minutes, what percent of work time does Jack have remaining?

- ⬭ 41.65%
- ⬭ 43.75%
- ⬭ 49.30%
- ⬭ 56.25%
- ⬭ 62.5%

16. Which of the following is not equal to the others?

- ⬭ $\sqrt{16}$
- ⬭ 2^2
- ⬭ $2 + 2$
- ⬭ 4×1
- ⬭ 1^4

17. A car traveling at a constant speed went 197.4 miles in 3 hours. At this speed, what is the total distance traveled in 6 hours?

- ⬭ 65.8 miles
- ⬭ 197.4 miles
- ⬭ 394.8 miles
- ⬭ 592.2 miles
- ⬭ 1184.4 miles

$$\frac{3 \text{ hrs}}{197.4 \text{ m}} = \frac{6 \text{ hrs}}{x \text{ m}}$$

18. Company A, company B, and company C are the top three cellphone providers in a certain area of the country with a total of 65,000 subscribers. The ratio of subscribers of A to B to C is 2:5:6. What is the total number of subscriptions between company A and company C?

- ⬭ 55,000
- ⬭ 40,000
- ⬭ 35,000
- ⬭ 30,000
- ⬭ 25,000

$$\frac{8}{13} = \frac{x}{65000} \quad 6x$$

19. Which of the following represents the nth term of the sequence 2, 5, 10, 17, 26, 37, . . .

- ⬭ $2n^2$
- ⬭ $2n - 1$
- ⬭ $n^2 - 1$
- ⬭ $n^2 + 1$
- ⬭ $2n + 1$

20. The graph below shows the distribution of grades on a test. What percent of the students received at least a B?

    ○ 20%
    ○ 30%
    ○ 40%
    ○ 50%
    ○ 60%

21. Which of the measurements represents the shortest distance?

    ○ 1,500 centimeters
    ○ 15,000 centimeters
    ○ 150 meters
    ○ 1.5 kilometers
    ○ 150,000 millimeters

22. John paid $360 to get his car fixed. The table below is an itemized list of the charges, including taxes. How much did John have to pay for the hourly labor charge?

    ○ $62
    ○ $40
    ○ $58
    ○ $136
    ○ $124

    SERVICE CHARGES

Oil	$20
Brakes	$80
2 tires	$60 per tire
4 spark plugs	$4 per spark plug
2 hours labor	
No tax	

23. Ken hit more home runs than Joe, but fewer home runs than Sam. Mark hit more home runs than Ken. Which combination of statements is true?

    I. Mark hit the most home runs.
    II. Sam hit more home runs than Ken.
    III. Joe hit the least home runs.

    ○ I only
    ○ I and II
    ○ I and III
    ○ II and III
    ○ I, II, and III

24. Which of these fractions is greatest?

    ◯ 30/38
    ◯ 51/57
    ◯ 73/74
    ◯ 96/99
    ◯ 102/111

25. Ron has a $300 a month car payment, and Ron's monthly paycheck after taxes is $2,400. On a circle graph representing Ron's expenses, what would be the size of the central angle representing his car payments?

    ◯ 25°
    ◯ 180°
    ◯ 90°
    ◯ 45°
    ◯ 150°

26. Which of the following is 10% of a trillion?

    ◯ 500,000
    ◯ 50,000,000
    ◯ 500,000,000
    ◯ 50,000,000,000
    ◯ 500,000,000,000

27. Which of the letters could be rotated less than 360 degrees and look like the original letter?

    ◯ A
    ◯ K
    ◯ S
    ◯ T
    ◯ W

28. Some of the triangles are isosceles triangles.
    None of the triangles are equilateral triangles.

    Which of the following conclusions is true?

    ◯ Some of the triangles have three sides of equal length.
    ◯ None of the triangles contains a right angle.
    ◯ All of the triangles have three sides of equal length.
    ◯ None of the triangles have two sides of equal length.
    ◯ Some of the triangles have two sides of equal length.

29. The area of a rectangle is 12 cm². Each side of a square is the larger side of a rectangle. Which of the following could be the perimeter of the square?

    ○ 12 cm
    ○ 36 cm
    ○ 48 cm
    ○ 60 cm
    ○ 72 cm

30. Each of the following is equal to 23.794 EXCEPT

    ○ 2379.4×10^{-2}
    ○ 237.94×10^{-1}
    ○ 2.3794×10^{0}
    ○ 2.3794×10^{1}
    ○ $.23794 \times 10^{2}$

31. This is a list of the ten highest school basketball scores.

    153, 127, 165, 121, 113, 116, 170, 141, 157, and 137. What must be the 11th highest score, if when it is averaged with these scores the mean drops 5 points?

    ○ 100
    ○ 90
    ○ 85
    ○ 80
    ○ 75

32. The numbers 1 through 9 are each written on a slip of paper. What fraction of the slips has a prime number?

    ○ $\frac{1}{6}$
    ○ $\frac{4}{5}$
    ○ $\frac{4}{9}$
    ○ $\frac{5}{9}$
    ○ $\frac{9}{4}$

33. Each of the following is equivalent to 10% of 780 EXCEPT?

    ○ 780×10^{-1}
    ○ 78.0×10^{0}
    ○ 7.80×10^{1}
    ○ 780×10^{-2}
    ○ 0.780×10^{2}

34. A number is three less than the product of two and five.
Which of these equations could you use to find the number?

  ◯ $n - 3 = 5 \times 2$
  ◯ $n = (5 \times 2) - 3$
  ◯ $n = 5 \times (2 - 3)$
  ◯ $n - (5 \times 2) = 3$
  ◯ $n - (5 - 3) = 2$

35. What is the product of the largest and smallest values shown below?
$$\left\{ \frac{3}{7}, \frac{5}{8}, \frac{7}{9}, \frac{2}{5} \right\}$$

  ◯ $\frac{15}{56}$
  ◯ $\frac{6}{35}$
  ◯ $\frac{14}{45}$
  ◯ $\frac{1}{4}$
  ◯ $\frac{1}{3}$

36. Liz left her office in New York City at 8:30 A.M. She arrived back $3\frac{1}{2}$ hours later, which is when she called her client in Los Angeles, California. What time was that in Los Angeles?

  ◯ 7:00 A.M.
  ◯ 8:30 A.M.
  ◯ 9:00 A.M.
  ◯ 11:00 A.M.
  ◯ Noon

37. Each of the following is equivalent to 55% of 400 EXCEPT

  ◯ $400 \times \frac{11}{20}$
  ◯ $440 \div 2$
  ◯ $.22 \times 10^3$
  ◯ 4×55
  ◯ 400×55

38. Sixty blue marbles and 40 red marbles are in a jar. How many red marbles must be removed from the jar so that the probability of choosing a blue marble from the jar is $\frac{3}{4}$?

  ◯ 5
  ◯ 10
  ◯ 15
  ◯ 20
  ◯ 25

39. A restaurant operates on a budget of $85 in income for every $60 in expenses. The restaurant weekly budget for expenses is $15,954. Which of the following amounts would meet the amount of income the restaurant would need?

○ $11,261.65
○ $22,601.50
○ $20,601.00
○ $13,361.50
○ $18,601.50

40. A camping tent went on sale from $80 to $60. A camping chair that originally cost $20 was discounted by the same percentage. What is the new price of the camping chair?

○ $25
○ $20
○ $15
○ $10
○ $5

41. Cutting through a cylinder could produce each of these shapes, EXCEPT

○

○

○

○

○

42. Which of the following is always true?

○ a − (b − c) = (a − b) − c
○ (a ÷ b) ÷ c = a ÷ (b ÷ c)
○ (a × b) × c = a × (b × c)
○ (a + b) × c = a + (b × c)
○ a − (b ÷ c) = (a − b) ÷ c

43. Concert tickets are on sale for $16 each, or 4 tickets for $60. What is the lowest cost for 26 tickets?

   ⬭ $276
   ⬭ $360
   ⬭ $392
   ⬭ $416
   ⬭ $420

44. Let P be a prime number greater than 3. How many distinct prime factors does $16 \cdot P$ have?

   ⬭ 1
   ⬭ 2
   ⬭ 3
   ⬭ 4
   ⬭ 5

45. List the following numbers from least to greatest.

$$0.571, \tfrac{4}{7}, 0.5715, \tfrac{13}{23}, 0.57153$$
$$\text{(A)} \quad \text{(B)} \quad \text{(C)} \quad \text{(D)} \quad \text{(E)}$$

   ⬭ A, B, C, D, E
   ⬭ C, B, D, E, A
   ⬭ E, D, A, B, C
   ⬭ D, A, B, C, E
   ⬭ B, A, D, E, C

46. Ryan ran $3\frac{1}{5}$ miles yesterday and $6\frac{1}{4}$ miles today. How many more miles has he left to run 16 miles?

   ⬭ a little less than six and three-quarter miles
   ⬭ a little more than seven miles
   ⬭ a little less than seven and one-quarter miles
   ⬭ a little more than six miles
   ⬭ a little less than seven and a quarter miles

Answers Explained

READING

1. Which of the following statements is the best description of the main idea of the second paragraph (lines 5–10)?

   ● Molecules can only ingest nonorganic compounds.
   ○ Evolution is based on adaptation.
   ○ Photosynthesis allowed organisms to exist without the need of sunlight.
   ○ Oxygen is more important to life than the sun's energy.
   ○ Molecules will eventually become complex groupings.

   This is the main idea of the paragraph.

2. According to the information in the passage,

   ● the prokaryote cells developed with the help of the sun's energy.
   ○ the Earth was formed about 3.5 billion years ago.
   ○ the early development of animals depended on resistance to bacteria.
   ○ the extinction of dinosaurs led to the development of mammals.
   ○ other reptiles survived the dinosaurs; so entire species have not vanished from the Earth.

   The second paragraph mentions that the early organisms developed and began using the sun's energy.

3. Which of the following occurred between ingestion of inorganic compounds and anerobic respiration?

   ○ Eukaroytes
   ○ Respiration with oxygen
   ● Oxygen release
   ○ Development of molecules
   ○ 700 million years ago

   The release of oxygen is mentioned on line 9.

4. This passage suggests

   ○ that bacteria cause disease in animals.
   ○ that mammals were the more intelligent species.
   ● how life evolved on Earth.
   ○ that mammals and dinosaurs are natural enemies.
   ○ that the environment did not affect evolution.

   The overall theme of the passage is how life evolved on earth.

5. Which of the following is the best way to describe the organization of this passage?

   ◯ The passage begins with general ideas and moves to more specific ideas.

   ⬤ The passage follows a general chronological plan.

   ◯ The passage offers a summary and then gives specific examples of parts of that summary.

   ◯ The passage describes general processes and then gives specific examples of each process.

   ◯ The passage follows a progression based on geographical and biological relationships.

The passage begins near the start of life on Earth, and takes the reader along a developmental timeline. The progression is not based on geographical or biological relationships.

6. In this passage the author expresses a bias against

   ◯ the Eisenhower administration

   ◯ the French people

   ◯ the military

   ⬤ hawks

   ◯ Henry Kissinger

The passage implies that hawks were responsible for the war casualties and costs.

7. The passage implies which of the following?

   ◯ The Vietnam War was a glorious war.

   ◯ The Vietnam War cost more than the Great Society.

   ◯ Kennedy laid the foundation for the war.

   ⬤ The United States paid a great price for this war.

   ◯ The people of the United States gave united support for the war effort.

The final sentences in the passage reassert this point.

8. Select the word or phrase that has the same meaning as "popular" (line 12).

   ⬤ Widespread

   ◯ Complete

   ◯ Well liked

   ◯ Major

   ◯ Famous

In this context, "popular" means "widespread."

9. What was the direct result of the negotiations mentioned in the reading?

   ⬭ The Vietnam War
   ⬭ Dien Bien Phu
   ⬛ South Vietnam
   ⬭ Gulf of Tonkin Resolution
   ⬭ The Tet Offensive

   The third paragraph mentions that negotiations led to the establishment of South Vietnam.

10. With which of these statements is the author of this passage most likely to agree?

    ⬭ Loss of life is the unfortunate reality of defending freedom.
    ⬭ The CIA played an important role in the war.
    ⬭ Congress opposed the Vietnam War.
    ⬛ The $175 billion spent on the war could have been used for domestic programs.
    ⬭ America's support of the French in Indochina was not a factor in the war.

    The author shows strong opposition to the Vietnam War, and would most likely agree with this statement about how the money spent on the war could have been better used. It may seem logical, but there is nothing in the passage to suggest that the CIA had an important role in the war.

11. What is the main idea of this passage?

    ⬭ Language consists of thoughts and physical sounds.
    ⬭ Human communication includes gestures.
    ⬭ We use language to communicate.
    ⬛ Human speech and language slowly developed through the years.
    ⬭ Broca's area of the brain controls speech.

    The author is primarily concerned with describing the way language developed over time.

12. In this passage, the author is primarily concerned with

    ⬭ comparing and contrasting.
    ⬭ presenting a point of view.
    ⬛ describing a time sequence.
    ⬭ refuting an argument.
    ⬭ defining vocabulary words.

    The author is primarily concerned with describing the way language developed over time.

13. Applying the reasoning about human speech in this passage to clothing, we can say that clothes will change when the fundamental form of which of the following changes?

⬤ People
◯ Fashion
◯ Weather
◯ Color
◯ Beauty

The passage makes the point that our speech was determined by the form and the shape of our speech organs. That idea applied to clothing means that clothes will change when the shape or form of humans change. The other choices are certainly relevant, even more relevant than the marked choice. But these other choices are not supported by the reasoning in the passage.

14. Which of the following words, if substituted for the word "unique" in line 9, would MOST change the meaning of the sentence?

◯ Exclusive
◯ Distinct
◯ Particular
◯ Sole
⬤ Common

The other choices are synonymous with unique.

15. The author's purpose for writing this passage was to

◯ persuade.
◯ narrate.
⬤ inform.
◯ entertain.
◯ list.

There is a lot of information for the author to present.

16. Which of the following means the same as "storage locations" in line 5?

◯ Hard disks
⬤ Repositories
◯ Microfiche
◯ Annexes
◯ Video discs

Repositories are storage locations.

17. What is the topic of this passage?

    ● Computers and survival in the 21st century.
    ○ Computer animation in the next decade.
    ○ Computers past and present.
    ○ Who needs a computer?
    ○ Information can be stored in computers.

    The fourth sentence conveys the topic.

18. According to the information in the passage,

    ● home computers are more powerful than any computer in buildings.
    ○ home computers are less powerful than computers that used to fill whole buildings.
    ○ if you don't know how to use a home computer you will be unemployed.
    ○ home computers are now fast and affordable.
    ○ home computers will be adding word processing and number crunching.

    Lines 5–6 make this point.

19. Which of the following assumptions was made by the author of this passage?

    ○ The reader knows how a computer works.
    ○ The reader has a computer.
    ● The reader is not computer literate.
    ○ The reader knows about the Internet.
    ○ Some computers are not slow.

    This passage is very simple, very fundamental. We are left wondering why such a simple passage would appear today. The only explanation is that the author of the passage assumes the reader is not computer literate.

20. Which of the following events occurs between the brawny man standing at the bar and when the last mint julep was ordered?

    ○ Haley hastens out.
    ● The little man stood tiptoe.
    ○ Gray mist rises.
    ○ Tom Loker is recognized.
    ○ Ice presents a barrier between the slave and her pursuer.

    The phrase "the little man stood tiptoe" is on lines 19–20.

21. We can infer from the passage that

   ○ the runaway slave drowned in the river.
   ○ Haley will eventually catch the runaway slave.
   ○ Haley and Loker will start to pursue the runaway slave again.
   ● the mist prevented Haley from pursuing the runaway slave.
   ○ the tavern was far from the river.

The passage does not state it directly, but we can infer that it is the mist, and not the river, that blocked Haley's pursuit. There is nothing in the passage to indicate that the pursuers will continue to look for the runaway slave.

22. The author most likely mentions "desperate retreat" to

   ○ show that the slave was wrong to run away.
   ● emphasize the urgency she felt.
   ○ focus on the terrible conditions at the river.
   ○ show the danger that her pursuer felt.
   ○ point out that Eliza may have had a child with her.

The runaway slave has an urgent need to escape from her pursuers, which is emphasized by the words "desperate retreat." Be careful of the emotional appeal in the last choice. There is nothing in the passage to suggest that Eliza has a child with her.

23. Which of the following is a true statement about Tom Loker?

   ○ He stood by the bar in the corner of the room.
   ● Haley saw him through the tavern window.
   ○ He met Haley outside the tavern.
   ○ He was an ex-slave.
   ○ His real name was Marks.

Lines 7–10 support this answer.

24. What is the author's attitude toward Ichabod?

   ○ Bitter
   ○ Disgusted
   ● Amused
   ○ Angry
   ○ Outraged

The author is certainly more amused than the attitude reflected in the other choices. There is nothing to indicate bitterness, disgust, anger, or outrage. There might have been other choices that would draw your attention, but "amused" is the correct choice from among the choices listed. A correct answer will always be the best choice from among the answers listed.

25. Which of the following is a synonym for the word "steed" in line 15?

    ○ Saddle
    ○ Shadow
    ○ Pursuer
    ● Nag
    ○ Mud

    A nag is a horse.

26. Which of the following is not associated with a description of Ichabod's horse?

    ● Perverse
    ○ Jerked the reins
    ○ Into a thicket
    ○ Lateral movement
    ○ Starveling ribs

    "Jerked the reins" is on line 13; "into a thicket" is on line 16; "lateral movement" is on line 12; "starveling ribs" is on line 17.

27. We can infer from this passage that

    ○ the Dravidians were slaves about 1000 A.D.
    ○ the verbal tradition mentioned in the passage survived until about 2500 B.C.
    ● many Dravidians were slaves about 1500 B.C.
    ○ Krishna was an early Dravidian deity.
    ○ floods led to the establishment of the Mahabarata.

    Lines 3–5 indicate that conquerors forced the Dravidians into southern India by 1500 B.C. This resulted in the Dravidians being treated as slaves. From among the choices given, it is most reasonable to infer that many Dravidians were slaves about 1500 B.C. The word "many" in this answer choice makes it easier to select.

28. What is the most likely location of the "worst place" referred to in this passage?

    ○ New York State
    ○ New York City
    ○ Richmond
    ● the Carolinas
    ○ Canada

    The Carolinas is the only other Southern location (in addition to Richmond) that is offered in the answer.

29. The author is most likely to recommend which of the following as an effective step to reduce accidents?

   ⬤ Build wide roads.
   ◯ computer simulation analysis.
   ◯ Require detailed construction plans.
   ◯ Determine traffic flow characteristics.
   ◯ Visit every site for a limited access highway.

   The last sentence of the passage identifies this approach as a known solution.

30. Which of the following words could be used in place of "simulation" in line 6?

   ◯ Investigation
   ⬤ Replication
   ◯ Determination
   ◯ Authentication
   ◯ Fabrication

   Replication is synonymous with simulation.

31. According to this passage, Lyndon Johnson

   ◯ lived in a farmhouse while he went to college.
   ◯ was the youngest person elected to the United States Senate.
   ⬤ joined the Navy while a U.S. Representative.
   ◯ served in the Senate for 12 years.
   ◯ was born in the 1930s.

   The third sentence indicates that he entered the Navy while he was in the House of Representatives.

32. The author of this passage would most likely recommend which of the following to archaeologists?

   ⬤ Look for areas with high background readings.
   ◯ Conduct work in deep forests.
   ◯ Find the most recently ploughed fields.
   ◯ Do your work right after a heavy rainfall.
   ◯ Find an area that has been completely uninhabited.

   In lines 9–11 the author discusses how prehistoric features are best identified when higher background radiation is present. The author does not directly make this statement in the passage; however, it is the statement he is most likely to agree with.

Answers Explained

33. Which of the following words could be used in place of the word "efficacy" in the next to last line of the first paragraph?

    ○ Limits
    ○ Placement
    ● Effectiveness
    ○ Results
    ○ Relationship

    Effectiveness is synonymous with efficacy.

34. According to this passage, the resulting patterns from agricultural activity

    ○ may later be transformed into topsoil.
    ○ offer a great deal of assistance to archaeologists.
    ○ require a knowledge of mathematics or physics.
    ● may lead to the discovery of prehistoric ditches.
    ○ can be simple or complex.

    This answer is found in lines 8–9.

35. The author most likely wrote the above passage to

    ○ describe a situation.
    ○ reflect on past events.
    ○ present a point of view.
    ● express irony.
    ○ narrate a story.

    How ironic—the writer did not even know about the soccer team in Soccer Town USA.

36. How many different types of Internet ads are discussed in this passage?

    ○ One
    ○ Two
    ● Three
    ○ Four
    ○ Five

    Three types of ads are discussed: banner, button, and search term.

37. We can conclude from this passage that the total maximum and minimum of banner ads that the average representative sells each day is

⬭ 30 and 15
⬭ 30 and 24
⬛ 44 and 36
⬭ 54 and 42
⬭ 58 and 44

The first paragraph tells us the average representative sells <u>9 to 10</u> "A" banner ads each day and <u>15 to 20</u> of the smallest banner ads each day. The second paragraph tells us the average representative sells <u>12 to 14</u> middle-size banner ads each day.

Add $10 + 20 + 14 = 44$ for the maximum number.
Add $9 + 15 + 12 = 36$ for the minimum number.

38. A blockade runner approached Wilmington with goods from Nova Scotia. The blockade runner passed through the New Inlet, so we can infer from the passage that Fort Fisher is

⬭ east of Fort Caswell.
⬭ generally to the north.
⬛ generally to the east.
⬭ generally to the south.
⬭ north of Wilmington.

"Fort Holmes was on Smith Island, which was west across the New Inlet from Fort Fisher." That means that Fort Fisher was on the east side of the New Inlet.

39. What is the guaranteed outcome of base pairing rules?

⬭ Adenine will pair only with thymine.
⬛ New strands exactly replicate old strands.
⬭ Genome size is usually stated as the total number of base pairs.
⬭ The human genome contains roughly 3 billion bp.
⬭ A C-G pair will be produced.

The correct choice means the same as the next-to-last sentence in the paragraph. The first choice is a base-pairing rule, not a guaranteed outcome of the rules. The third and fourth choices are taken directly from the passage but are not related to this item. The last choice is one outcome, not a guaranteed outcome.

40. Which factor should school officials be most aware of as they determine how students get to school each morning?

    ⬤ The weather
    ◯ The number of existing bike stands
    ◯ The number of students in the school
    ◯ The size of the school driveway
    ◯ The parents

School officials will have to observe students as they arrive at school. The factor most likely to have an impact on arrival methods is the weather.

41. The author most likely wrote the passage above to

    ◯ describe a situation.
    ◯ reflect on past events.
    ◯ present a point of view.
    ◯ express concern.
    ⬤ tell a story.

The author most likely wrote the passage to tell a story of about a portion of Iroquois history.

42. According to the passage, the Iroquois

    ◯ ruled the Adirondacks.
    ◯ were located along the Hudson River.
    ◯ traded with the French.
    ⬤ were an Indian nation.
    ◯ disappeared around 1600.

The second sentence refers to the Iroquois as "this Indian nation."

43. Which of the following words could be used in place of the word "verification" in lines 4–5?

    ◯ elimination
    ⬤ corroboration
    ◯ allocation
    ◯ renovation
    ◯ contamination

"Verification" and "corroboration" both mean to check that something is correct.

44. When the passage refers to native languages, it most likely means the languages

 ○ spoken by those born in South America.
 ○ of those residents of South America who are native to Portugal, Spain, and Italy.
 ● of those living in the pockets of civilization in the countryside.
 ○ of those born in South America with European origins who are not from Portugal, Spain, or Italy.
 ○ of those natives of Europe who came to South America.

The passage indicates that pockets of native civilizations are in the countryside.

45. According to the passage, the chromatic scale

 ○ corresponds to the white keys on the piano.
 ○ consists of the flats and sharps not contained in the diatonic scale.
 ○ is contained in the diatonic scale.
 ○ can be played only on the piano.
 ● includes notes corresponding to the first seven letters in the alphabet.

The chromatic scale includes the diatonic scale, which includes the notes corresponding to the first seven letters in the alphabet.

46. According the passage, AIDS

 ○ is most likely to kill defenseless orphans.
 ○ is caused by a bacteria not treatable by antibiotics.
 ○ will likely last for at least 200 years.
 ● is epidemic in entire countries.
 ○ will eventually claim 10 million lives.

The word "pandemic" means epidemic in entire countries.

WRITING MULTIPLE CHOICE

1. Most people would enjoying four weeks vacation last year. No error.

 would enjoy   *have enjoyed*

 Use the correct verb tense.

2. The tugboat strains against the ship, revved up its engines, and was able to maneuver the ship into the middle of the channel. No error.

 strained against

 The past tense *strained* agrees with the other verbs.

3. A newspaper columnist <u>promised</u> <u>to print</u> the story about the <u>secret</u> <u>negotiations</u> concerning the sports stadium in their next column. <u>No error</u>.

his or her

These pronouns agree with the antecedent *columnist*.

4. The flower shop is <u>pleasant</u> and possess an <u>aroma that welcomes</u> its customers. <u>No error</u>

possesses

***Flower shop* is singular and takes the singular verb *possesses*.**

5. The incredible intense seminar held all <u>the participants</u> in a <u>hypnotic</u> trance. <u>No error</u>.

incredibly

Use the adverb *incredibly* to modify the adjective *intense*.

6. Many students <u>prefer to</u> gain <u>life</u> experience outside college. Such as the Peace Corps. <u>No error</u>.

college such

***Such as the Peace Corps* is not a sentence.**

7. <u>Weather</u> conditions have a <u>controlling</u> affect on our air <u>traffic</u>. <u>No error</u>.

effect

The correct word is *effect*.

8. Europeans <u>had started</u> to <u>devote significant</u> resources to medicine, when Louis Pasteur <u>was born</u> December 7, 1822. <u>No error</u>.

medicine when

When the main clause is followed by a dependent clause, no comma is necessary.

9. Because of their <u>immaturity</u> and ignorance. Many young people <u>engage</u> in <u>high-risk</u> behavior. <u>No error</u>.

ignorance many

***Because of their immaturity and ignorance* is not a sentence.**

10. <u>These same questions</u> was <u>asked</u> by <u>other lawyers</u> for decades <u>after the</u> trial ended. <u>No error.</u>

    This same question

    This change agrees with the singular verb *was.*   .

11. It may be <u>true that</u> a strictly mechanical approach is used by some <u>teachers, however,</u> there <u>is certainly</u> a way for <u>their students</u> to develop more difficult concepts. <u>No error.</u>

    teachers; however,

    Set off the independent clause with a semicolon.

12. Computer graphing programs are <u>capable</u> of graphing almost any equations <u>including</u> advanced equations from <u>calculus the</u> student just types in the equation and the <u>graph appears</u> on the screen. <u>No error.</u>

    calculus. The

    Correct the run-on sentence.

13. The <u>Board of Adjustment</u> can <u>exempt</u> a person from the requirements of a <u>particular</u> land-use <u>ordnance.</u> <u>No error.</u>

    ordinance

    Use the correct word.

14. <u>Succulent</u> crab, <u>plentiful</u> shrimp, and meaty lobster are the <u>mainly</u> dishes advertised by the <u>Lobster Hut.</u> <u>No error.</u>

    main

    Use the adjective *main.*

15. Charles Monroe III and his family <u>enjoys</u> yachting, <u>swimming, and</u> polo, <u>when on holiday,</u> <u>delighting</u> in the South of France. <u>No error.</u>

    enjoy

    The subject is plural and takes the plural verb *enjoy.*

16. The teacher asked all her <u>students</u> to bring in <u>his</u> permission slips <u>to go on</u> the <u>Washington trip</u>. <u>No error</u>.

    their

    The substitution is *their*, which agrees with the antecedent.

17. The <u>shower dripped</u> for an hour <u>after each</u> person <u>bathed</u> until finally a repairman <u>had been call</u> to fix it. <u>No error</u>.

    had been called

    The past tense *called* is correct.

18. They will not <u>be able to</u> understand how to <u>create</u> a sculpture from ice or to <u>understands</u> the <u>basis</u> for the more complicated sculptures. <u>No error</u>.

    understand

    The plural subject *They* takes the plural verb *understand.*

19. Erik <u>walks</u> three miles every <u>day and he</u> <u>rubbed</u> the dirt off his sneakers as he <u>went</u>. <u>No error</u>.

    walked

    Use the past tense to agree with the other verbs.

20. I <u>have talked</u> to my daughter about <u>telling</u> the <u>truth countless</u> times over the <u>past</u> few weeks. <u>No error</u>.

    No error.

    The verbs are correct.

21. A <u>masive</u> <u>education campaign</u> <u>is needed</u> to fully inform <u>today's youth</u> about AIDS. <u>No error</u>.

    massive

    Use the correct spelling.

22. The <u>dairy farm</u> is maintained by the support of 60 new <u>cows in</u> addition <u>there</u> are 35 original <u>cows who</u> still supply some milk. <u>No error</u>.

    cows. In

    Correct the run-on sentence.

23. I <u>am going</u> to visit <u>my</u> aunt so I left a message for <u>whoever</u> may need to locate me. <u>No error</u>.

    No error.

    All the pronouns are correct.

24. The <u>retired</u> baseball player haggled <u>unexpectedly</u> with the <u>younger child</u> over who played <u>good</u>. <u>No error</u>.

    well

    Use the adverb *well* to modify the verb *played*.

25. The class president was a good, but <u>undistinguished, student</u>.

    - ⬤ but undistinguished, student
    - ◯ but in every way a student that could not be distinguished
    - ◯ but a student who could not be distinguished
    - ◯ but not distinguishable from the rest of the students
    - ◯ but distinguished

    The underlined portion is correct.

26. <u>The height of the tree grew slower</u> over the years.

    - ◯ The height of the tree grew slower
    - ⬤ The tree grew slower
    - ◯ The tree height slower grew
    - ◯ The tree's height grew slower
    - ◯ The tree height grew slower

    Use this less wordy replacement for the original wording.

27. <u>To climb the mountain now will be better</u> than waiting until it gets colder.

    - ◯ To climb the mountain now will be better
    - ◯ To climb the mountain is better
    - ◯ Climbing the mountain now can be better
    - ⬤ Climbing the mountain now is better
    - ◯ To try to climb the mountain now will be better

    This replacement is less awkward than the original underlined portion of the sentence.

28. <u>The three largest trees stands at</u> the entrance to the forest.

    ○ The three largest trees stands at
    ○ The three largest tree's stands at
    ● The three largest trees stand at
    ○ The largest three trees stand's at
    ○ The three largest tree stand at

    The plural verb does not end in "s."

29. The train engineer blew the whistle <u>in the eventuality that</u> a road crossing appeared.

    ○ in the eventuality that
    ○ if the event of a
    ○ when the eventuality
    ● when
    ○ and

    Replace the wordy underlined passage with the single word "when."

30. The study concluded that good test scores resulted from subject matter competence and <u>the way a person took the test</u>.

    ○ the way a person took the test
    ● test-taking strategies
    ○ the approach a person took to the test
    ○ testing strategies
    ○ the way a test taker takes the test

    This wording is clearer and creates a parallel sentence structure.

31. The road to the ocean washed away and <u>could no longer be in use</u>.

    ○ could no longer be in use.
    ○ could be in use no longer.
    ○ may be in use no longer.
    ○ could become unused.
    ● was no longer in use.

    The correct verb is "was," not "could . . . be."

32. The coach was pleased with the team's progress; <u>the players were confident</u>; the fans were happy; and it was true that the students were pleased.

   - ⬤ the players were confident
   - ◯ the player were confident
   - ◯ it was true the players were confident
   - ◯ the player's were confident
   - ◯ it was true the player's were confident.

   This part of the sentence is correct. It maintains the parallel structure of the sentence.

33. It was clear from the news reports that the plant <u>represented an exclusive, distinctive, unique approach to the problem</u>.

   - ◯ represented an exclusive, distinctive, unique approach to the problem
   - ◯ represented a exclusive, distinctive, unique approach to the problem
   - ◯ represented an approach to the problem
   - ◯ represents an exclusive, distinctive, unique approach to the problem
   - ⬤ represented a unique approach to the problem

   This choice excludes the wordiness ("exclusive, distinctive") found in the original sentence.

34. When he became a teacher he had no idea that the <u>effort on volumes of paperwork and the work required for playground duty and bus duty would become his main responsibility</u>.

   - ◯ effort on volumes of paperwork and the work required for playground duty and bus duty would become his main responsibility
   - ◯ efforts on volumes of paperwork and the work required for playground duty and bus duty would become his main responsibility
   - ⬤ paperwork and non-teaching duties would become his main responsibility
   - ◯ work required for volumes of paperwork and the work required for playground duty and bus duty would become his main responsibility
   - ◯ effort on volumes of paperwork and the effort required for playground duty and bus duty would become his main responsibility

   Use this clear and direct wording to replace the lengthy wording in the original sentence.

35. Season tickets to the college basketball games <u>is difficult to get</u> at this time of year.

   ◯ is difficult to get
   ◯ is difficult to come by
   ⬤ are difficult to get
   ◯ was difficult to get
   ◯ is not difficult to get

   The subject is plural. Use the plural verb "are" in place of the singular verb "is."

36. A teacher must arrange for a substitute <u>if she is going to be absent</u>.

   ◯ if she is going to be absent
   ◯ if she's going to be absent
   ◯ if they are going to be absent
   ⬤ if he or she is going to be absent
   ◯ if she is going to absent herself

   This choice corrects the gender nonagreement found in the original sentence.

37. The student in the woodworking <u>class made a real tall bookshelf</u>.

   ◯ class made a real tall bookshelf
   ⬤ class made a really tall bookshelf
   ◯ class made a very real tall bookshelf
   ◯ class made a really high bookshelf
   ◯ class made a real high bookshelf

   This choice replaces the adjective "real" with the correct adverb "really."

38. The bus <u>ran smoothly, but the</u> driver was always concerned about a breakdown.

   ⬤ ran smoothly, but the
   ◯ ran smooth, but the
   ◯ runs smooth, but the
   ◯ run smoothly, but the
   ◯ run smooth, but the

   The original sentence is correct.

39. The contractor wanted to finish the job, but first he had to convince the zoning board to approve a permit <u>so that work could start</u>.

   ◯ so that work could start
   ◯ so that work could begin
   ⬤ to start work
   ◯ for starting work
   ◯ so that the actual work could begin

   The shorter, more direct wording of this choice is superior to the original sentence.

40. <u>Ronaldo, the clown with the big nose</u> made his entrance into the big top.

    ○ Ronaldo, the clown with the big nose
    ○ Ronaldo the clown, with the big nose,
    ● Ronaldo, the clown with the big nose,
    ○ Ronaldo, the clown with the big, nose
    ○ Ronaldo the clown with the big nose

    This choice correctly uses commas to set off the phrase.

41. Tomorrow I am going on <u>vacation today I have</u> a lot of work to do.

    ○ vacation today I have
    ○ vacation, today I have
    ○ vacation but today I have
    ○ vacation and today I have
    ● vacation; today I have

    This choice correctly uses a semicolon to separate two independent clauses.

42. There is absolutely no way to be sure that the dog <u>will come when it's owner calls</u>.

    ○ will come when it's owner calls
    ○ will come when his owner calls
    ○ will come when their owner calls
    ● will come when its owner calls
    ○ will come when her owner calls

    Use the possessive form "its."

43. The clockmaker <u>was particularly expert at designing</u> musical chimes.

    ● was particularly expert at designing
    ○ was particular expert at designing
    ○ was particular expertise at designing
    ○ had particularly expert at designing
    ○ had a particularly expert at designing

    The original sentence is correct.

44. The thoroughbred <u>horse run very fast</u> around the track.

    ○ horse run very fast
    ● horse runs very fast
    ○ horse running very fast
    ○ horse are running very fast
    ○ horse do run very fast

    This choice makes correct use of the singular verb.

ESSAY

Compare your essay to the sample essay that follows. You may want to show your essay to an English expert for further evaluation. You will record your essay score on the Test Scoring section for this test on page 383.

This essay would likely earn a score of 5 or 6 out of 6 (506 words).

An Internet Degree Worked for Me

My position on this statement is yes, I do think that a college should be able offer an entire degree program over the Internet. I agree that students do not have to come to the campus. But there have to be limits on how the college offers its programs. I have to disclose something first. I attended a college where the entire degree was offered over the Internet so I have a lot of specific experiences.

You do not have to live in the middle of nowhere to understand why an Internet degree program is so useful. I just think of myself. There I was working long hours day and nights to get through college, which was about 45 minutes away. That is not terrible but the campus classes were all offered when I was working. There was no way that I could have finished without an Internet only program. It is also true that I was able work on classes by my own schedule, and I saved about eight hours a week in time to commute and walk on campus to a class, but I save a lot of money in gas, tolls and wear and tear on my old car. That is an awful big advantage to a poor struggling college student. The classes were good and may even a little more was asked than I heard about the same classes on campus. I was able to write back and forth to the instructor and other students and it seemed that maybe I was more in touch than the people on the campus.

As good as the degree program was for me there are real problems that a college should take care of with an Internet Program. The first thing is that it's hrad to tell if the students is the person doing the work. It was like once we took a test on the Internet all at the same time but I knew some way or other that for some of the students another person was taking the test. That is the same for most of the assignments too. I am pretty sure there were students who finished the program and never did any of the work themselves. There is always some cheating and copying, but I am pretty sure it is much, much more with Internet programs than on campus programs. That is a real problem.

Of course do not meet a lot of actual people when you are working on your computer. It is probably true that none of the students live near you. That is a definite drawback. There was always the feeling of being removed and I may not have felt that way if the campus was more further away than it was.

To conclude, I think Internet programs are great for students and one got me through college. But I think that colleges have to be careful to find a way to be sure that students are doing their own work.

Practice Computer-Based PPST **371**

MATHEMATICS

1. ● 22%
   ◯ 8%
   ◯ 11%
   ◯ 17%
   ◯ 30%

   Total sold = 4 + 7 + 6 + 7 + 3 + 8 + 10 + 4 + 8 + 10 + 8 + 6 = 81
   June/July Total = 18
   $18 \div 81 = 22\%$

2. ◯ Circle
   ● Cone
   ◯ Sphere
   ◯ Cube
   ◯ Cylinder

   The formula for the area of a circle is πr^2.
   The formula for volume of a cone is $V = \frac{1}{3}\pi r^2 h$.
   The formula for volume of a sphere is $V = \frac{3}{4}\pi r^3$.
   The formula for volume of a cube is $V = s^3$.
   The formula for volume of a cylinder is $V = \pi r^2 h$.

3. ◯ 6 years old
   ◯ 7 years old
   ● 8 years old
   ◯ 9 years old
   ◯ 10 years old

   Use t for the age of each twin.
   Then:
   $2t + 9 = 25$
   $2t = 16$
   $t = 8$
   The twins are each 8 years old.

4. ◯ $\frac{6}{100}$
   ◯ $\frac{30}{100}$
   ◯ $\frac{60}{1000}$
   ● 0.6
   ◯ 0.06

5. ◯ Alice
   ◯ Bob
   ⬤ Frank
   ◯ Ronni
   ◯ Scott

There is no segment connecting Steve and Frank.

6.

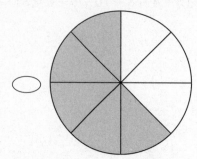

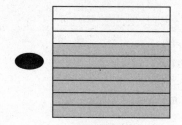

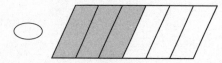

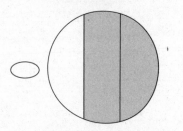

$\frac{6}{9} = \frac{2}{3}$

7. ◯ 32°
   ⬤ 70°
   ◯ 72°
   ◯ 74°
   ◯ 86°

Estimate the average. 86° + 54° = 140°. 140° ÷ 2 = 70°.

8.   ⬭ $250
     ⬭ $500
     ⬭ $750
     ⬛ $3000
     ⬭ $6000

$1,500 − ($550 + $300 + $50 + $100) = $500 remaining each month.
$500 ÷ 2 = $250 saved each month.
$250 × 12 = $3,000 saved in a year.

9.   ⬭ 54
     ⬭ 36
     ⬛ 28
     ⬭ 18
     ⬭ 9

Greg is 19 years old and he will be twice as old as Todd next year, which means that Todd is 9 years old.

The sum of their ages is $19 + 9 = 28.$ $19 + 1 = 2(x + 1)$
                                                $20 = 2x + 2$
                                                $18 = 2x;\ x = 9$

10. ⬭ 3%
     ⬭ 7%
     ⬭ 21%
     ⬭ 30%
     ⬛ 70%

Divide the sale price by the original price.
$\frac{\$21}{\$30} = 0.70$

$0.70 = 70\%$

11. ⬭ Just I
     ⬭ I and II
     ⬭ II and III
     ⬛ I and III
     ⬭ I, II, and III

From the figure we can see that $\angle EBD$ and $\angle DBC$ are complementary angles.

Therefore $\angle EBD$ and $\angle DBC$ are not supplementary angles.

$m\angle EBD + m\angle DBC = 90°$ because the angles are complementary.

12.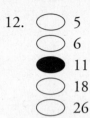

   ○ 5
   ○ 6
   ● 11
   ○ 18
   ○ 26

Let *m* represent the number of miles that Joanie ran on Monday.

Then $m + (3 + m) + (5 + m) = 26$.
$3m + 8 = 26$
$3m = 18$
$m = 6$

The miles run on Friday = $m + 5$.

Joanie ran 6 miles on Monday, so she ran 11 miles on Friday.

13.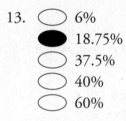

   ○ 6%
   ● 18.75%
   ○ 37.5%
   ○ 40%
   ○ 60%

Count the numbers of balls found in the Game 2 row and divide by the total number of balls in the pictograph. (You don't need to consider what each ball represents.)

We get $\frac{6}{32} = 0.1875$.

$0.1875 = 18.75\%$ of the points were scored in Game 2.

14.

   ○ $\frac{1}{7}$
   ○ $\frac{1}{6}$
   ○ $\frac{3}{14}$
   ○ $\frac{9}{14}$
   ● $\frac{6}{7}$

There are 14 cookies in the cookie jar, of which $14 - 2 = 12$ are not gingerbread cookies.

The probability of not picking a gingerbread cookie is $\frac{12}{14} = \frac{6}{7}$.

15. ○ 41.65%
    ● 43.75%
    ○ 48.30%
    ○ 56.25%
    ○ 62.5%

8 hours is 8 • 60 minutes = 480 minutes.
If Jack already worked 270 minutes, he has 480 − 270 = 210 minutes of work left.
Divide the work time remaining by the total work time. $\frac{210}{480} = 0.4375$.
0.4375 = 43.75% of work remaining.

16. ○ $\sqrt{16}$
    ○ 2^2
    ○ 2 + 2
    ○ 4 × 1
    ● 1^4

$\sqrt{(16)} = 4$ $2^2 = 4$ 2 + 2 = 4   4 × 0 = 4 $1^4 = 1$
1^4 is not equal to the others.

17. ○ 65.8 miles
    ○ 197.4 miles
    ● 394.8 miles
    ○ 592.2 miles
    ○ 1184.4 miles

Divide to find the speed per hour: $\frac{197.4}{3} = 65.8$ miles per hour.

Multiply to find the total distance: 65.8 × 6 = 394.8 miles

18. ○ 55,000
    ● 40,000
    ○ 35,000
    ○ 30,000
    ○ 25,000

Using the ratio 2:5:6, there are a total of 13 parts representing a total of 65,000 subscribers. 8 of the 13 parts represent the number of subscribers for companies A and C. Set up a proportion and solve.

$\frac{8}{13} = \frac{x}{65,000} \rightarrow = (8)(65,000) = 13x \rightarrow 520,000 = 13x = 40,000 = x$

So companies A and C have a total of 40,000 subscribers.

19. ○ $2n^2$
    ○ $2n - 1$
    ○ $n^2 - 1$
    ● $n^2 + 1$
    ○ $2n + 1$

To find a term, square the number of the term and add 1. The nth term is $n^2 + 1$.

20. ○ 20%
    ○ 30%
    ○ 40%
    ○ 50%
    ● 60%

12 of the 20 students earned at least a B. $\frac{12}{20} = \frac{60}{100} = 60\%$

21. ● 1,500 centimeters
    ○ 15,000 centimeters
    ○ 150 meters
    ○ 1.5 kilometers
    ○ 150,000 millimeters

1,500 centimeters = 15 meters. This is the shortest distance.
15,000 centimeters = 150 meters
150,000 millimeters = 150 meters
1.5 kilometers equals 1,500 meters

22. ● $62
    ○ $40
    ○ $58
    ○ $136
    ○ $124

$20 + $80 + (2 \times $60) + (4 \times $4) + 2x = $360
$20 + $80 + $120 + $16 + 2x = $360
$236 + 2x = $360
2x = $124
x = $62 per hour labor charge

23.
  ○ I only
  ○ I and II
  ○ I and III
  ● II and III
  ○ I, II, and III

M—Number of Mark's home runs
K—Number of Ken's home runs
J—Number of Joe's home runs
S—Number of Sam's home runs

Create inequalities. J < K < S
                    K < M

We can't tell if Mark or Sam hit the most home runs.
We can conclude that Sam hit more home runs than Ken.
We can conclude that Joe hit the fewest home runs.

24.
  ○ $\frac{30}{38}$
  ○ $\frac{51}{57}$
  ● $\frac{73}{74}$
  ○ $\frac{96}{99}$
  ○ $\frac{102}{111}$

Quite frequently, when the numerator and denominator of a fraction differ
by one, that fraction is largest.

25.
  ○ 25°
  ○ 180°
  ○ 90°
  ● 45°
  ○ 150°

$300 \div 2400 = .125 = 12.5\%$
Divide the car payment by the monthly salary and multiply by 100 to find
the percent used for car payments. A circle has 360° so 12.5% of 360° = 45°.

26.
  ○ 500,000
  ○ 50,000,000
  ○ 500,000,000
  ● 50,000,000,000
  ○ 500,000,000,000

A trillion is a 1 followed by 12 zeros. Half of a trillion is 500,000,000,000.
Divide by 10 to find 10% of a half-trillion and get 50,000,000,000.

27. ○ A
    ○ K
    ● S
    ○ T
    ○ W

Turn the paper a half turn (180 degrees) to find that only S looks the same.

28. ○ Some of the triangles have three sides of equal length.
    ○ None of the triangles contains a right angle.
    ○ All of the triangles have three sides of equal length.
    ○ None of the triangles have two sides of equal length.
    ● Some of the triangles have two sides of equal length.

First choice—NO because of statement 2
Second choice—NO Nothing in the statements indicates this
Third choice —NO because of statement 2
Fourth choice—NO because of statement 1
Fifth choice—YES Supported by both statements

29. ○ 12 cm
    ○ 36 cm
    ● 48 cm
    ○ 60 cm
    ○ 72 cm

The square is 12 cm on a side, and the perimeter is 48 cm.

30. ○ $2379.4 \times 10^{-2} - 10^{-2}$ moves the decimal point 2 places left.
    ○ $237.94 \times 10^{-1} - 10^{-1}$ moves the decimal point 1 place left.
    ● $2.3794 \times 10^{0} - 10^{0}$ equals 1. The decimal point does not move.
    ○ $2.3794 \times 10^{1} - 10^{1}$ moves the decimal point 1 place right.
    ○ $0.23794 \times 10^{2} - 10^{2}$ moves the decimal point 2 places right.

All the answers are 23.794 except $2.3794 \times 10^{0} = 2.3794$.

31. ○ 100
    ○ 90
    ● 85
    ○ 80
    ○ 75

Add the scores, and then divide the sum of 1400 by the number of scores (10) to find the mean, which is 140. $140 - 5 = 135 \times 11 = 1485 - 1400 = 85$.

32.
- ○ $\frac{1}{6}$
- ○ $\frac{4}{5}$
- ● $\frac{4}{9}$
- ○ $\frac{5}{9}$
- ○ $\frac{9}{4}$

The numerator shows how many prime numbers (4) and the denominator shows the total number of slips (9).

33.
- ○ $780 \times 10^{-1} = 78.0$
- ○ $78.0 \times 10^{0} = 78.0$
- ○ $7.80 \times 10^{1} = 78.0$
- ● $780 \times 10^{-2} = 7.80.$ This is not equal.
- ○ $.780 \times 10^{2} = 78.0$

$10\% \times 780 = 78.0$

34.
- ○ $n - 3 = 5 \times 2$
- ● $n = (5 \times 2) - 3$
- ○ $n = 5 \times (2 - 3)$
- ○ $n - (5 \times 2) = 3$
- ○ $n - (5 - 3) = 2$

First multiply 5 and 2, then subtract 3.

35.
- ○ $\frac{15}{56}$
- ○ $\frac{6}{35}$
- ● $\frac{14}{45}$
- ○ $\frac{1}{4}$
- ○ $\frac{1}{3}$

Use cross products. The smallest fraction is $\frac{2}{5}$ and the largest is $\frac{7}{9}$. Their product is $\frac{14}{45}$.

36.
- ○ 7:00 A.M.
- ○ 8:30 A.M.
- ● 9:00 A.M.
- ○ 11:00 A.M.
- ○ Noon

Liz arrived back in her office at noon New York time. That's 9:00 A.M. Los Angeles time.

37. ⬭ $400 \times \frac{11}{20} = 220$
    ⬭ $440 \div 2 = 220$
    ⬭ $.22 \times 10^3 = 220$
    ⬭ $4 \times 55 = 220$
    ⬛ $400 \times 55 = 22000$

    This is not equivalent. 55% of 400 = 220.

38. ⬭ 5
    ⬭ 10
    ⬭ 15
    ⬛ 20
    ⬭ 25

    P (Blue) $= \frac{60}{80} = \frac{6}{8} = \frac{3}{4}$. If 20 red marbles are removed, then there are 60 blue marbles and 20 red marbles left.

39. ⬭ $11,261.65
    ⬛ $22,601.50
    ⬭ $20,601.00
    ⬭ $13,361.50
    ⬭ $18,601.50

    Set up an expense-to-income ratio.

    $\frac{E}{I} = \frac{60}{85} = \frac{15.945}{x}$. Solve using cross products.

    $(85)(15954) = 60x$; $x = 22,601.50$

40. ⬭ $25
    ⬭ $20
    ⬛ $15
    ⬭ $10
    ⬭ $5

    Discount $= \frac{20}{80} = \frac{1}{4} = 25\%$ off.

    25% of $20 = $5 off.
    $20 − $5 = $15.

41.

The first choice could result from a horizontal cut.
The second choice could result from a vertical cut where diameter and height are equal.
The third choice is impossible.
The fourth choice could result from a vertical cut.
The fifth choice could result from a diagonal cut.

42. ◯ $a - (b - c) = (a - b) - c$
◯ $(a \div b) \div c = a \div (b \div c)$
⬤ $(a \times b) \times c = a \times (b \times c)$
◯ $(a + b) \times c = a + (b \times c)$
◯ $a - (b \div c) = (a - b) \div c$

The correct choice shows the associative property of multiplication.

43. ◯ $276
◯ $360
⬤ $392
◯ $416
◯ $420

Six sets of 4 tickets (24 tickets) costs $360.
Two single tickets cost $32, for a total of $392.

44. ◯ 1
⬤ 2
◯ 3
◯ 4
◯ 5

Plug any prime number greater than 3 in for P. Let P = 5. $16 = 16 \cdot 5 = (2)^4 \cdot 5$.
There are two distinct prime factors, 2 and 5.
It does not matter which prime number we pick, because 16 has just one distinct prime factor.

45. ◯ A, B, C, D, E
    ◯ C, B, D, E, A
    ◯ E, D, A, B, C
    ⬤ D, A, B, C, E
    ◯ B, A, D, E, C

(A) (B)   (C)   (D)   (E)

$0.571, \frac{4}{7}, 0.5715, \frac{13}{23}, 0.57153$

↓   ↓

0.57142   0.56521

Change B and D to decimals.
Compare decimals place by place until you see the correct order.

46. ⬤ A little less than six and three-quarter miles
    ◯ A little more than seven miles
    ◯ A little less than seven and one-quarter miles
    ◯ A little more than six miles
    ◯ A little less than seven and a quarter miles

$3\frac{1}{5} + 6\frac{1}{4}$ is a little less than $9\frac{1}{2}$. That leaves a little more than $6\frac{1}{2}$ miles left to go.

That's just like having a little less than $6\frac{3}{4}$ miles left to go.

Test Scoring

The scoring information from these tests is just a rough estimate. Passing raw scores on ETS tests vary widely, and this test will likely not have the same difficulty level of the actual PPST you take. That is why this scoring information is advisory only, as a guide to further study. You should NOT try to predict your scale score from these practice test results.

> Please read the reminders on pages 9–10 before you proceed.

Mark the multiple-choice test. Write your raw score for each test as the percent correct.

PERCENT CORRECT

Reading _____%   Writing _____%   Mathematics _____%

Read your essay and assign a score from 1 to 6. Multiply the score by two to represent the scores of two readers. If you have difficulty scoring your essay, you may want to show it to an English expert for an evaluation.

Essay Score _____ out of 12

> Review the scoring information on pages 10–11 and estimate your scale scores.

ESTIMATED SCALE SCORE

Reading _____   Writing _____   Mathematics _____

> Look at your passing scale score on page 9. Write it here.

PASSING SCALE SCORE

Reading _____   Writing _____   Mathematics _____

Compare your estimated scale scores to your passing scale scores as a guide for further study only, and not as a prediction of the scale score you will receive on the actual PPST.

Index